This book is dedicated to children —

Our future knowledge workers, who will use the Internet to grow,
learn, collaborate, and pursue great dreams.

All royalties from this book will be donated to **e-Learning for Kids** (www.e-learningforkids.org),
a non-profit foundation for children that provides schools in need with Internet-based learning solutions.

Contents

An e-Learning Launch:
A Study In Change Management

The early days of e-learning were product-driven, and the dialogue about e-learning took place primarily among vendors who were heavily funded by investment capital. Competing vendors touted the benefits of their infrastructure technology, but little attention was paid to the issues surrounding implementation or to the usage of e-learning by the end users. Often it was only after the introduction of e-learning within an organization that a company came to grips with the fact that e-learning is really a change management process. Included in a change management strategy must be a detailed analysis and action plan to obtain buy-in, ensure the implementation, secure alignment with a real and pressing business need, determine measurement and marketing issues, and put into place a tracking system to update management. A successful e-learning launch requires close consideration of all these processes that support an effective organizational transition.

Now the main challenges that are addressed in *The e-Learning Fieldbook* include answers to the following questions:

> *If we build it, will they come?*
> *If they come, will they learn?*
> *If they learn, will it matter to the business?*

These questions are interlinked in the chapters and case studies that follow. The book presents a commonality of experience and shared perceptions about how to successfully launch an e-learning program. Several themes taken from the book can be summarized as follows:

- **e-Learning should be regarded as a change initiative that has the potential to impact business results.**

  While many of the case studies point to the need to use e-learning to train a distributed audience at a reduced cost, the successful initiatives identify the need to reduce the time-to-competency in launching new products and services. At STMicroelectronics, this meant launching an e-learning version of its Fundamentals of Semiconductor Technology to increase the speed with which its workforce improved their skills and competencies. The goal was not simply to obtain a return on investment from reduced travel costs, but to significantly change the speed-to-competency and thereby impact the business.

- **e-Learning is a developmental journey that results in a new way of learning.**

  Successful blended learning programs redefine learning as work-based activities engaging people in communities of practice. For example, the Unilever Leaders into Action Program, a five-month leadership development journey, was delivered as a blended model, balancing online work with face-to-face classroom sessions and coaching. Learning took place when Unilever managers worked on authentic problems that were relevant to their business. Importantly, the journey was both individual and team-based and supported by a robust virtual learning community of online coaches. Learning was more than what happened online, or even onsite. It was about learning from others in the workplace and understanding how to contribute as an active member of an online learning community.

- **Successful e-learning initiatives devote time and resources to developing robust learning support services.**

If content was king in the 1990s, the new mantra is *learning support services* are deal breakers. The greatest impact on e-learning retention is the creation of appropriate learning support services, which start with a 24-hour Help Desk but go beyond that to include:

- ✓ A library of e-learning courses
- ✓ Online coaching and mentoring
- ✓ Online advisors
- ✓ An e-bookstore
- ✓ Discussion forums
- ✓ Online assessments
- ✓ Online pre- and post-tests
- ✓ Access to local and national career planning information and credentialing

As Sir John Daniel former Chancellor of Open University, the UK's largest university, said, *"The one thing I have learned over the years in watching the growth of Open University is the importance of online student services. Students use the Internet more to engage in administrative transactions, make course selections, read digitized books, and communicate with faculty and peers than to study course material online."* Although support is frequently seen as crucial to the learning experience, the degree and effectiveness of what is offered has been haphazard in how these services are provided in most organizations.

- **Successful e-learning programs come with a new language, a set of different expectations, and a new group of vendors.**

The case studies detailed in this Fieldbook illustrate that successful e-learning entails a host of teaching and learning practices that are convenient for the learner but are far more labor intensive for the faculty and training staff. Creating courses, maintaining chat rooms, developing a Web-based community, administering online assessments and responding to e-mails from e-learners around the clock require far more time and energy than the development and maintenance of traditional training programs. What has become clear is the need to develop an array of outsource partners, who can assist an organization in supporting an online learning community.

- **The target audience for e-learning is moving to customers and even to end users.**

Numerous e-learning programs that have met with success have targeted customers, sales channel partners, and end users. This has been far more frequent with companies involved in product launches where training a distributed sales force or sales partners can significantly improve productivity and business results. But perhaps the real opportunity is to use e-learning for end-user training by extending product knowledge directly to consumers. Training is not yet viewed by marketing and sales executives as integral to their success, but in the hands of a creative Chief Learning Officer (CLO), end-user training can reap bottom-line results.

- **Measurement and marketing plans are crucial for proving results to top management.**

In all the case studies represented in this Fieldbook, there were processes and plans in place to track the results of an investment in e-learning. Importantly, this was with results specific to achieving strategic business goals, rather than large ROI percentage increases.

- **New skills are needed for a digital age.**

As you read through the book and accompanying case studies, it is important to note just how significantly the job of a Chief Learning Officer has evolved to create and sustain an e-learning initiative. This small group of first generation Chief Learning Officers has shown the type of new skills required in the digital age. These skills can be thought of as:

> **Entrepreneur**—Being a visionary and champion for the creation of a new learning culture within the organization. This means that CLOs must see themselves as builders of a new competency—e-learning strategy, design, and implementation. They must be excited by the opportunity to grow a business and build a new network of vendors. These new vendors extend beyond the traditional training vendors to include traditional universities that have a demonstrated competency in distance learning, for-profit universities, publishers, technology infrastructure firms, online community building firms, learner support service firms, and online assessment firms. This spirit of *newness, adventure, and risk taking* is key to starting a new e-learning function within an organization.

> **Change Manager**—Aligning diverse groups around a common learning vision and preparing the organization for change. To a large degree, a Chief Learning Officer must see the big picture of what the CEO is trying to accomplish by investing in learning and then be able to translate this big picture with a razor focus into a set of action steps and deliverable results. Of course, these results must correspond to the projects and processes that will give an organization its competitive edge. For example, the driving impetus to establish an e-learning program at Liberty Group, a South African insurance firm, was the necessity to have all sales people accredited in line with the insurance industry's new legal requirements. What's more, this accreditation had to be delivered within a six-month time period to a geographically dispersed audience. The results exceeded the goal, and the accreditations continue on a monthly basis.

> **Business Manager**—Providing fiscal management to a function that has been traditionally a back-office cost center. According to Michael Bleyhl, Director of e-Learning at Invensys, a technology and manufacturing firm, *"At Invensys, we decided to bundle e-learning into our customer's service agreement so we had a competitive edge in the marketplace."* The result was the creation of a value-added enhancement to a service agreement. This type of business-driven thinking is critical to transitioning a training function from a cost center to a profit and loss center.

Learning Technologist—Understanding how to integrate the mix of technologies needed for successful blended learning programs. Most of the media and tools illustrated in the book are a combination of several types of self-paced e-learning and live e-learning, so a Chief Learning Officer must understand when and how to integrate these into an e-learning platform. This means that the Chief Learning Officer has to be sufficiently informed about technologies to evaluate what works, to judge when to adapt a technology to local needs, and to address demanding integration and implementation issues.

Advocate for the e-Learner—Finally, the Chief Learning Officer must decide to be an advocate for the individual e-learner. This means building a support system to assist the e-learner in communicating with faculty and peers, having access to online advisory services, online tutoring, e-libraries, e-bookstores, customized digitized books, and workbooks. E-learners should not have to feel they are learning alone at their computer. Rather, to retain their motivation and interest in learning online, they must feel part of a community that understands and serves their learning goals.

The experiences and the insights of all the organizations included here will provide you with the tools and networking community you need to further your e-learning implementation plans.

I hope you enjoy this book as much as I have. I look forward to connecting with the readers around the globe.

Jeanne Meister, Author and Consultant
Jeannemeister212@aol.com
New York City

Acknowledgements

The e-Learning Fieldbook is the result of a passionate collaboration from a dedicated team of learning professionals, whose individual and collective knowledge, ideas, contributions, and outstanding work in the field of learning, I would like to acknowledge.

The path to create this book was long and arduous, as those of you who have traveled this journey before already know. Many aspects must come together, including: concept development, crafting the research structure and questions, identifying case organizations, scheduling interviews, conducting literature reviews, writing cases and chapters, style, lay-out and design of visuals and cover, review, editing, and finally creating a camera-ready version to send to the printer. In addition, over all of this is the project management that drives the deadlines and the final accomplishment.

All these tasks mentioned have been accomplished primarily during the personal time of learning professionals, who became known in our virtual collaboration as *The e-Learning Fieldbook Team.* Without the effort of this team, this book would not have existed. My sincere thanks and enormous appreciation goes to all of the members of this team including: Teresa Calkins, Katie Coates, Karen Dominick, David Dun, Gregg Fair, Mary Faris, Chrissie Gale, Tamara Ganc, Leslie Gibson, Catlyn Gregory, Alicia Hanna, Candy Haynes, Steve Hendrick, Jennifer Holenstein, Bill Knapp, Doug Liberati, Nancy Nonne, Michelle Ratcliffe, Bernadine Reynolds, Jordan Reynolds, Eileen Rogers, Sunil Sapre, Kathleen Scholz, Susan Schultz, Tammy Sharpless, Gary Siebert, Michael Warner, and Amy Wisely.

Several friends from *The e-Learning Fieldbook Team* made such significant contributions to this book that I want to acknowledge them personally. In alphabetical order, very special thanks to:

Katie Coates, the Deloitte Consulting Learning Director of Learning Design. It was Katie who volunteered to become the overall project manager for this book. She took care that we met the extremely challenging deadlines, and pulled us through this entire project. I want to thank Katie for giving generously of her free time, but more for her outstanding contributions to this book, particularly in the great thinking on designing blended e-learning. Your passion for learning shines through, in all the work that you've done. Thanks also to Marshall for letting you work so many weekends on this project.

David Dun, the Deloitte Consulting Learning Director in Europe. Having served on four continents, David's insights on global cultures and motivation of people's acceptance of e-learning were highly valuable to the development of the concepts in this book. You are my best example of a Digital Immigrant, who has lost his 'analog' accent completely. e-Learning must have been invented for people like you!

Gregg Fair, the master behind the 'look and feel'. Gregg made a significant contribution to the design of a number of great visuals for the book and also ensured that the entire book was delivered camera-ready. Your patience as new changes surfaced, even after final deadlines, was enormously appreciated. Thanks for making it possible to attain the 'pre-flight' tests in time.

Tamara Ganc, the lead visual designer for this book. Tamara has an amazing ability to visualize the ideas from the left side of my brain, and to make my drawings on the whiteboard come alive in dynamic and creative ways that I had only imagined. I can only question what this book would have looked like without your creative genius and design ideas.

Alicia Hanna, who did an amazing job in scheduling all the interviews. Within a very short time frame, so many case organizations were engaged in interviews due to her friendly and persistent manner in getting on everybody's calendar. Your charming Southern accent made a huge difference in getting people on-board.

Candy Haynes, the Deloitte Consulting Learning Associate Chief Learning Officer. Candy was a great help in thinking through the original concept of this book. With her son sitting patiently on her lap, she contributed knowledge on e-learning technology, working with vendors, and gaining stakeholder support. Special thanks for helping me to keep pushing for innovation in learning, and for the strong support in the execution of our learning vision. Your special humor and camaraderie at moments of work-overload have encouraged me tremendously.

Nancy Nonne, for editing the entire manuscript. You have done such a fantastic job in a thorough review of each case and chapter, catching all errors and inconsistencies, and ensuring that the flow was right. Your eye for detail and final touch has made the book so much better.

Michelle Ratcliffe, for contributing to the research questions and generating the first example case. You helped everybody tremendously by asking good and tough questions. Thanks for all your work on the case studies; this has helped so much to develop a high quality book. It was fantastic having you on the team. Forgive my impatience and the constant push for getting things done faster.

Eileen Rogers, special thanks for your enthusiasm for learning, your untiring writing and research, and for making all the content edits to this entire Fieldbook. Significantly valuable was also your knowledge of global business and insights on the cultural differences in the adoption of e-learning. Your contribution to the book has been enormous. I have such a great time with you in exploring new ideas and solutions. Thanks for the passion we share for people development and learning.

Kathy Scholz, the Deloitte Consulting Learning Director of Learning Technology Infrastructure. I have deep appreciation for your extremely valuable work and experience in the measurement of e-learning shared in this book. This is such a great significance for learning professionals, as it is one of the most difficult tasks to accomplish effectively. You are the best in getting agreed-to deliverables in on time. I have learned so much from you.

The e-Learning Fieldbook would not exist without all the pioneering and innovative e-learning fieldwork that has been done by all the organizations featured in this book. I want to thank all of the professionals from the case organizations for taking the time for the interviews, providing their insights, and sharing their successes, challenges, and lessons learned.

Organization	Contributing Professionals
3Com	W.G. O'Brien, Director of Education
American Skandia	R.L. Ray, Senior Vice President, Director of Training
Anglo Platinum	J. Openshaw, Manager, HRD IT Systems
Austrade	D. Kerrins, Manager Learning and Development; G. Pettigrove, Manager IT Training

Babson College	Dr. T. Moore, Vice President of Corporate Programs, Babson School of Executive Education, Babson College
Black & Decker Corporation	M.H. DeFeo, Vice President, Training, Recruiting and Sales Services; J.B. Davis, Director e-Learning, Black & Decker University
BMW of North America, LLC	V. Macdonald, Training Manager
Cingular Wireless	R. Lauber, Executive Director of Learning Services; B. Cotton, Manager of Employee Development
Defense Acquisition University	Dr. J.B. Ainsley, Deputy Executive Director, Curricula Development and Support Center
Deloitte Consulting	K. Coates, Director of Learning Design; M. Ratcliffe, Senior Manager Learning
Deloitte Touche Tohmatsu	M.G. Shields, Global Director of Knowledge Management & e-Learning, Management Solutions; A. Hill, CEO, Smartfirm Inc.
The Home Depot	C.V. Gardner, Director, e-Learning Center; A.S. Liaguno, e-Learning Designer
INSEAD OnLine	J.W. Sommers-Kelly, Director, Company Specific Programs and INSEAD OnLine
Invensys Foxboro	M. Bleyhl, Director e-Learning, Global Learning
JPMorgan Chase	C. Dobson; H.J. Catlaw; P. Jones
Liberty Group	J. Naidoo, Head of Technical Training, Sales Development and Accreditation
McDonald's Corporation	J. Jordan, e-Learning Program Manager, Worldwide Training, Learning & Development
Oracle Corporation	C.J. Pirie, Vice President, Oracle University
The Iams Company	S.P. George, Training Manager, e-Learning
Prudential Financial	S.S. LeVan, Director, Learning
STMicroelectronics	S. Vigne, ST University e-Learning Program Manager; A. Bucher, ST University Communications Manager
The Hartford	D. Finnegan, AVP, Corporate Education
Unilever	R. Edwards, Head of e-Learning; D. Coleman, Learning Specialist, International Management Training
Wachovia Corporation	S.A. Sutker, Vice President, Learning Strategy Group
Wyndham International, Inc.	D.M. Brossart, Director, Brand Communications; M.R. Eggers, Manager, OnLine Learning; T. Greene, Manager, Distribution Technology; S. Schuller, Director, Training & Communications; H. Valenti, Director, Distribution Technology Training

Special thanks also are due to the people who have reviewed and critiqued the book including:

- Daphne Batka, Global Head Learning Infrastructure, Deutsche Bank
- Sushant Buttan, Chief Executive Officer, Maximize Learning
- Tony Gleeson, Global Director e-Learning, Deloitte Touche Tomatsu
- Andy Hill, Chief Executive Officer, Smartfirm Inc.
- Jeff Schwartz, Partner, Global Human Capital Practice, Deloitte Consulting

Thanks also to:

- Cushing Anderson, Program Director for IDC's Learning Services Research, for sharing important data and research with me and for our intriguing discussions on the future of e-learning.
- Sushant Buttan, and the excellent professionals at Maximize Learning for developing *The e-Learning Fieldbook* Web site—at no cost, to support the *e-Learning for Kids Foundation*.
- Jeanne Meister, for sharing your industry experience and providing names from your learning network, and special thanks for writing the forward to this book.
- Richard Narramore, Senior Editor, McGraw-Hill for his trust in the concept and development of this Fieldbook, and his unshakable confidence that the deadline would be met. Thanks also for your valuable advice on the manuscript, and the support in making this unique book very special in content and style.

Finally, my family deserves the most appreciation. My six-year old son Yannick is a source of constant inspiration, watching him play and discover while engaging in e-learning. But he deserves special thanks for sharing his bedroom as a study with me. It was a source of comfort in long nights of work to see him sleeping next to my desk as I was reading, writing, thinking, and drawing new visuals for the Fieldbook.

Most important to my life and work is my wife Judith, who is the real leader and driving force behind all of my achievements. She has my deepest love and gratitude for firing my imagination, sharpening my thinking on concepts, and inspiring my thinking with art, photography, piano music, and delicious dinners.

Developing this book was a fantastic and fun learning experience. I feel very privileged to know and to have received the on-going support of all the people mentioned in the creation of *The e-Learning Fieldbook*. Thank you.

Nick van Dam
Chadds Ford/Philadelphia, May, 2003

Preface

e-Learning is no longer a new phenomenon, but it has not ceased to be a hot topic.

Now that the first wave of e-learning implementations has been completed, companies are starting to uncover the reality of what works and what doesn't work in the brave new world of e-learning. *The e-Learning Fieldbook* moves the dialogue about e-learning from theory into applications of this new methodology to real-time business challenges. It is the first e-learning *business* book that presents the lessons learned by leading companies as they have implemented e-learning strategies. The book is based on extensive case studies of best practices in e-learning and blended e-learning implementation from 25 name brand companies representing a variety of industries, global geographies, and organizational sizes, including: The Home Depot, JPMorgan Chase, Unilever, Wachovia Corporation, Deloitte Consulting, McDonald's Corporation, INSEAD OnLine, BMW of North America, Prudential Financial, Oracle Corporation, and STMicroelectronics, among others.

This book is for everyone—business leaders, human resource development professionals, trainers and teachers, consultants, and students. *The e-Learning Fieldbook* explains what it takes to make an e-learning implementation succeed. The book also describes the critical issues and concerns confronting professionals in the e-learning environment, and gives insights into the most common challenges organizations have in aligning e-learning with business goals, designing e-learning and blended learning programs, and deploying e-learning solutions.

By reading this Fieldbook, you will be able to:

- Learn from other organizations and avoid costly delays and pitfalls in your own e-learning initiatives
- Understand the reality versus the hype in e-learning implementation
- Explore the concepts, techniques, and approaches that are really working

What is the impact of e-Learning for the learner and classroom training?

I strongly believe that e-learning will put employees in charge of their own learning and growth. No longer will their access to learning programs depend upon management approval to attend a typically limited number of classroom learning events. The availability of e-learning programs will empower people to take practically as much e-learning as they want and need, and help them prepare for their next job.

Although, the uptake of e-learning keeps growing fast, it will be hard for many to leave behind the 1,000 year-old classroom model and tradition of learning. Human beings are social creatures, and this has not changed since the oldest university was established in Bologna, Italy. I strongly believe that face-to-face classroom events will continue to play an important role in learning, especially in areas such as:

- Team building
- Personal coaching
- Networking
- Culture building

As will be discussed in this book, e-learning enables an entirely different approach to the learning continuum. Now learning extends well beyond the classroom in a *blended learning* deployment model, powered by the virtual capabilities of e-learning. The importance of face-to-face classroom learning will be integral to this extended learning environment; however, it will be just one feature of a rich and varied approach to the learner's continued growth and development.

I hope that you will gain many insights from this Fieldbook, and that you will be able to leverage the provided examples and concepts to make knowledgeable, creative, and professional decisions in your e-learning strategy.

Nick van Dam
nickvandam@elearningfieldbook.com

How This Book Is Organized

The e-Learning Fieldbook is designed to provide the critical information and expertise you need to build and deploy a vibrant, dynamic learning strategy that effectively utilizes e-learning technology, content, and services.

The experiences of the organizations who contributed case studies to this Fieldbook verify that the question is not *whether* to use e-learning as a component of an overall strategic learning portfolio. The fact that e-learning is a critical aspect of a total learning continuum is established beyond doubt. The question has become *how* best to ensure that the e-learning employed is targeted, cost-effective, engaging, easy to access, and complete.

Thus, this Fieldbook is organized into two resources that convey this information as you venture into deeper and broader e-learning initiatives:

- **The e-Learning Fieldbook, and its companion on the Web, www.elearningfieldbook.com**

  I. The e-Learning Fieldbook:

  - **Part One:** Lessons from the First Wave of e-Learning-What's Working and What's Not Working

    What You Will Find in Part One:

    Part One of this book focuses on current trends, lessons learned, and valuable insights into many key aspects of an e-learning strategy. This part serves as a conceptual and applied *how-to* handbook, where you will find many topics of interest whether you are an experienced e-learning professional or just beginning the journey.

    The following table summarizes the content for each chapter in Part One to help you find the topics of most interest to you.

| Part One: Lessons From the First Wave of e-Learning-What's Working and What's Not Working |||
Chapter	Title of the Chapter	Main Themes
1	Does e-Learning Have a Credibility Problem?	• The First Wave of e-Learning • The State of e-Learning Today • The Second Wave of e-Learning
2	Does e-Learning Make Business Sense?	• How Can You Align e-Learning with Business Goals? • What Is the Business Impact of e-Learning? • Developing a Winning e-Learning Strategy
3	What Gains the Commitment of People That Matter?	• Gaining Top Management Support • Gaining Information Technology Support • Gaining the Support of the Training Department
4	How Do You Design Blended Learning Programs?	• What Have We Learned So Far? • Designing Blended Learning Solutions • Other Design Considerations • What is Next For Blended Learning?

5	What Makes e-Learning Technology Work?	• What are the Elements of an e-Learning Architecture? • What e-Learning Technology Architecture Implementation Options Exist? • What are the Challenges in Implementing an e-Learning Architecture? • What Support and Maintenance Infrastructure is Required for e-Learning Technologies?
6	How Do You Measure e-Learning Initiatives and Results?	• Why Track e-Learning? • What Can Be Tracked in e-Learning? • Laying the Foundation for Tracking and Reporting • Designing and Building Reports
7	What Does It Take to Work Successfully With Vendors?	• Why Do I Need Vendors? • How Do I Select the Right Vendor For My Specific Learning Solution? • How Do I Know I'm Not Paying Too Much? • How Do I Establish Successful Vendor Partnerships?
8	What Motivates People to Engage in e-Learning?	• e-Learning Enablers • e-Learning Drivers • e-Learning Motivators
9	How Do You Launch e-Learning to a Global Workforce?	• Key Drivers for Cross-Cultural Adoption of e-Learning • e-Learning Culture Prints • Crafting a Multicultural e-Learning Strategy

- **Part Two:** How Organizations are Aligning e-Learning with Business Goals—25 e-Learning Case Studies from Leading Organizations

What You Will Find in Part Two:

Part Two includes twenty-five case studies from organizations that are successfully implementing e-learning solutions. Each case study is presented in a way that helps the reader apply the lessons learned to their own organization. The cases describe not only successes, but also the difficulties encountered in the journey—the pitfalls, surprises, discoveries, and warning signals—and the contributing organizations share these experiences so that others can make use of them to blaze new trails of their own.

Case Chapter Structure and Design

Each case study includes the following descriptive information:

- Introduction
- How was the program aligned with the business?
- How was the program designed?
- How was the program deployed?
- What was the business impact of the program?
- Summary
- Lessons learned

You will find additional useful information in each case study, including:

Company Facts and Figures

Why e-Learning?

Key Business Drivers

Media and Tools

Marketing Approach

Learner Perspectives

Lessons Learned

Check It Out Online!
www.elearningfieldbook.com

II. The e-Learning Fieldbook on the Web (www.elearningfieldbook.com):

- To encourage the extension of your own learning continuum in a virtual world, *The e-Learning Fieldbook* companion Web site includes:

    - Examples of e-learning programs featured in this book

    - A number of visuals from this book

    - Useful resources, such as checklists, job aids, whitepapers, and samples

    - Links to additional information

The e-Learning Fieldbook Web site is envisioned as an ongoing dynamic exchange, and it is our hope that you will communicate with the author and *The e-Learning Fieldbook Team* to contribute your experiences, insights, challenges, and tips for others.

The e-Learning Fieldbook

Part I:

Lessons of the first wave
of e-learning…
what's working and
what's not working

CHAPTER

1

Does e-Learning Have a Credibility Problem?

The main themes for this chapter are:

- *The First Wave of e-Learning*
- *The State of e-Learning Today*
- *The Second Wave of e-Learning*

Introduction:
Does e-Learning Have a Credibility Problem?

The First Wave of e-Learning

In 1995, a few learning professionals with a passion for technology in learning were listening to a multimedia-based presentation led by Brandon Hall, who heads one of today's leading e-learning research companies. The participants had worked on CD-ROM-based training in the United States and Europe and were interested in knowing more about the latest technologies and applications.

Brandon Hall presented his latest CD-ROM library and shuffled one CD-ROM after another into his computer. Everybody was excited with the level of instructional design and different applications. This alone characterized the status of technology-based learning in that year; no word was said about the use of the Internet for future technology-based learning. In 1996, the American Society for Training and Development (ASTD) devoted only one workshop during their annual seminar to Internet-based training.

However, 1996 was really the launch of a deeper and broader interest in the application of e-learning to training and development requirements. In fact, the first article on *Internet-Based Training* appeared in Training Magazine in 1997, the same year that Elliott Masie founded the TechLearn Conference. A new industry was born! New e-learning vendors, backed up by an infusion of venture capital and the dream of a successful initial public offering (IPO), sprung up everywhere offering solutions, such as learning management systems, authoring tools, portals, academic degree programs, and testing and assessment tools.

The height of the e-learning visibility hype was in 2000 when John Chambers, the Chairman of Cisco Systems, Inc., declared that *"e-learning is the next killer app."* At seminars, sales demonstrations, and in magazines, everybody could learn about the new paradigm: e-learning!

At that time, exuberant predictions of e-learning impact and anticipated results were expressed, including:

- All classroom training will be replaced by e-learning.
- It is very easy and cheap to design and develop e-learning courseware.
- e-Learning technologies are easy to use and integrate.
- e-Learning technology infrastructure is easy to implement.
- Employees from almost all cultures like e-learning.
- e-Learning is mostly about how to use technology.
- Significant costs savings can be made by adoption of e-learning.
- The e-learning market will at least quadruple annually.

Many organizations quickly jumped on the e-learning bandwagon and purchased and/or developed their first generation of e-learning technologies and courseware. The e-learning market grew from a few million dollars in 1995, to US$3.4 billion worldwide in 2000 (IDC 2003). These were amazing results for such a new industry, but the data did not support the over-hyped expectations projected earlier for the industry.

The stock market fell sharply in 2000, followed by a crash of stock prices in 2001, and the decline continued in 2002. The economy slowed down, venture capital disappeared, and many e-learning vendors had to close their door because of shortfalls in planned revenue and/or lack of profitability and future growth probabilities. The consolidation in the e-learning industry had started. A time flow depicted in Chief Learning Officer (CLO) magazine, and shown in Figure 1-1, illustrates this progression through the stages of early excitement, inflated expectations, and gradual disappointment into the *trough of disillusionment* that was experienced in 2002.

The last event in the time flow is the merger in the e-learning industry between SmartForce and SkillSoft in 2002. This merger created the largest global e-learning vendor in the industry, and it is viewed by CLO magazine as the beginning of the trend toward Enlightenment and Productivity. It is the premise of this Fieldbook that this view of the future is accurate, and that the experiences and contributions of the 25 case study organizations verify this upward lift.

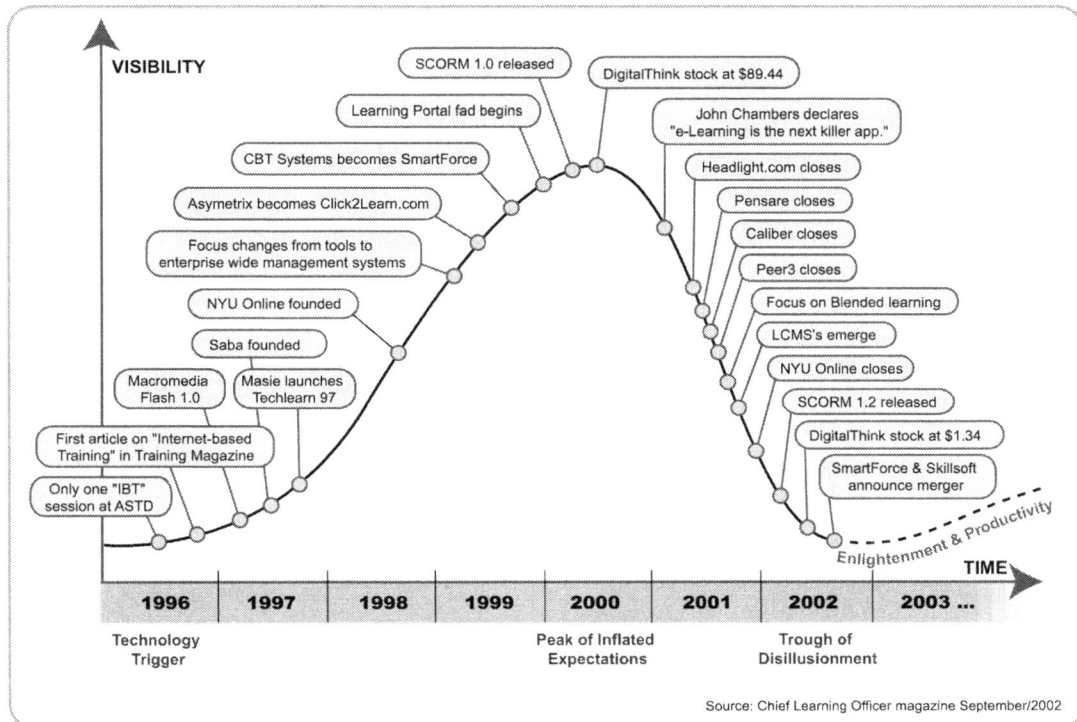

Figure 1-1: e-Learning Visibility Hype 1996 to 2002

What did we learn during the intervening years about the application of e-learning to training and development initiatives in enterprises around the world that is now allowing us to move into this period of productivity?

During the first wave of e-learning, research was undertaken and published by institutions such as The Masie Center, ASTD, Brandon-Hall, and market researchers including IDC, Gartner, Forrester, and Eduventures. This research and a significant number of case studies have provided us with valuable insights and intelligence from these experiences in developing and deploying e-learning. It is the hope of the author of this Fieldbook, that the dedication and hard work of the e-learning pioneers recounted in the company cases will add to this body of knowledge on when, how, and why to employ e-learning to best advantage.

The State of e-Learning Today

What is the state of e-learning today? Organizations face a number issues and challenges, including:

- There are only a few organizations that have moved practically their entire classroom-based curriculum to the Internet.

- e-Learning start-rates vary broadly within these organizations, and completion rates can be low.

- The quality of e-learning programs has been very spotty, and some courseware could actually be categorized as unsatisfactory at best, as experienced in *online page-turners* and in the *Las Vegas style* e-learning programs enhanced by a lot of *bells and whistles.*

- High-quality, well-designed e-learning courseware actually requires a significant investment of both time and money in assessment, scoping, design, development, and deployment.

- The adoption of e-learning is very different by country, among different industries, and even within companies, where there are differences by business unit, department, and function.

- e-Learning technology integration appeared to be complex at first, and has actually proven even more difficult than imagined, becoming a disappointing experience for a number of organizations.

- Connectivity and speed issues have been ongoing challenges for many organizations due to a lack of high bandwidth.

- A number of e-learning technology implementations have been very time consuming and also required cultural changes, initially underestimated by many.

- Many organizations have not been able to develop solid e-learning business cases for senior executive leadership and thus received insufficient funding for e-learning initiatives.

- e-Learning is not that much about *technology* but more about *Learning, using technology.*

- Cost-savings and return on investment (ROI) are not a given for all e-learning initiatives.

- Buyers have been confused in the market by the diverse results and experiences in e-learning implementations, resulting in a tendency toward risk-aversion.

- The lack of set standards in e-learning is also causing uncertainty, in addition to the fact that no existing standard is easy to implement.

If one would compare the e-learning expectations cited earlier with the described state of e-learning today, it is easy to jump into the conclusion that e-learning has not lived up to its promises.

This context and the results of these early years, leads to the question:

Does e-learning have a credibility problem?

Undoubtedly, the launch of questionable e-learning courseware combined with some less successful e-learning implementations has bruised the image of e-learning to some extent. However, ultimately, e-learning has proved first and foremost to be very credible as a new opportunity and approach to learning for people and enterprises globally.

Many believe that there is no doubt about the importance of applying e-learning when and where it adds value. Most major organizations around the world, including the organizations who contributed case studies for this Fieldbook, find that they will continue application of e-learning, albeit in a more measured and knowledgeable way. In addition, the pioneering experiences we have observed since 1996 will contribute significantly to their future success.

Lessons from Experience

Organizations have valuable lessons to share from their e-learning experiences. For example:

- The value proposition for e-learning has not gone away. Enterprises operate in a very complex and increasingly competitive global environment and are challenged to create shareholder value. e-Learning has successfully proven to have a significant business impact, as you will find in Chapter 2 of this Fieldbook.

- A large number of organizations have successfully implemented e-learning initiatives, which were well aligned with specific business goals and have had an impact on business and solid ROI. Most organizations have plans to expand their initiatives beyond their initial pilot programs in specific departments, business units, and countries. This definitely applies to all 25 case organizations that are featured here.

- Experience has been gained in designing e-learning programs resulting in new design models and methodologies that have emerged as best practices, making the e-learning, experience more engaging, powerful, and valuable (see Chapter 4).

> **e-Learning Value Proposition for McDonald's Corporation***
>
> ✓ Provide consistent and convenient training to all employees globally
>
> ✓ Provide a cost-efficient method of training
>
> ✓ Increase efficiency in training
>
> ✓ Track employee training paths
>
> ✓ Efficiently update training curriculum
>
> *See Chapter 14: Educating a Global Workforce

- Technology integration challenges have been largely overcome (see Chapter 5). New evolving e-learning technologies and better e-learning functionality will be a significant market driver.

- Many employees globally are eager to develop new knowledge and skills, and there are best practices to support multicultural adoption of e-learning (see Chapter 9).

- Globally, wireless Internet access and high bandwidth connections will grow significantly. In addition, there will be more technology solutions that provide people with the opportunity to take e-learning courseware using visuals, sound, and video features in low bandwidth connection mode.

Furthermore, if e-learning really had been proven to add no value to training and development, the worldwide corporate e-learning market would not have continued to grow as it has (see Figure 1-2).

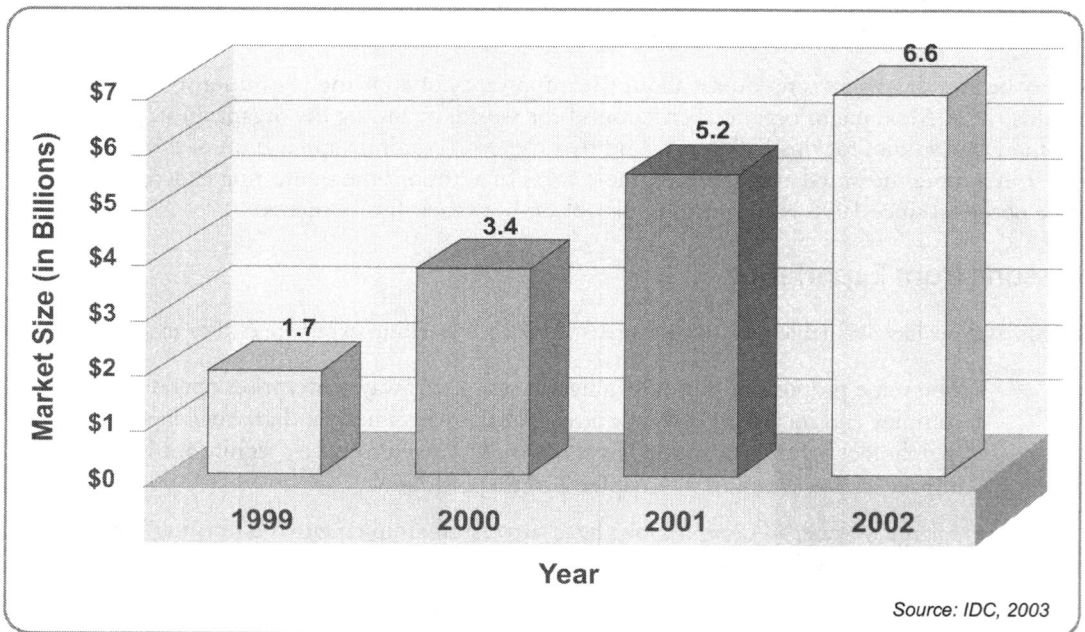

Figure 2: Worldwide Corporate e-Learning Market Growth: 1999 to 2002

The Second Wave of e-Learning

The future of e-learning can be looked at from the perspectives included in this Fieldbook:

- Aligning e-learning with the Business
- e-Learning Solutions
- Deployment of e-learning

Trends in Aligning e-Learning with the Business

A host of opportunities to leverage e-learning for high business impact have been discovered as the early e-learning pioneers have explored various applications of this new learning delivery methodology. Business goals that can be achieved through e-learning include, but are not limited to:

- Expeditious time-to-market of new products and services (Chapter 10)
- Rapid implementation of new information systems and business processes (Chapter 11)
- Complete compliance with legal and regulatory mandates (Chapter 12)
- Efficient on-boarding of new hires in the organization (Chapter 13)
- Integration of a global workforce and creation of a strong business culture (Chapter 14)
- Enhanced leadership and generation of new business development (Chapter 15)
- Improved sales by developing a knowledgeable and effective sales force (Chapter 16)
- Effective retention of customers and suppliers through training in products and services (Chapter 17)

Obviously, to attract senior executive support and to contribute real value to the organization, the main objective of e-learning must be to create or enhance the shareholder value—the company's growth in profitability and value in the marketplace—by linking the e-learning initiative to the business drivers and by proposing a value proposition for future investments in e-learning (see Chapter 2).

> **Impact of an e-Learning Program at JPMorgan Chase***
>
> ✓ An opportunity to build key relationships within the company and build their credibility as a learning organization
>
> ✓ A sharp jump in the number of people requesting and participating in online learning
>
> ✓ Increased accuracy and amount of key information being shared with customers
>
> ✓ Customer satisfaction has increased from 75 to 80 percent in some areas
>
> *See Chapter 16: Training the Sales Force of the Future

Trends in e-Learning Solutions

In the first wave, e-learning focused on courseware designed to transfer knowledge, called *online education*, and to develop skills, called *online training*. These are still important components of the total e-learning vision for the future (see Figure 1-3).

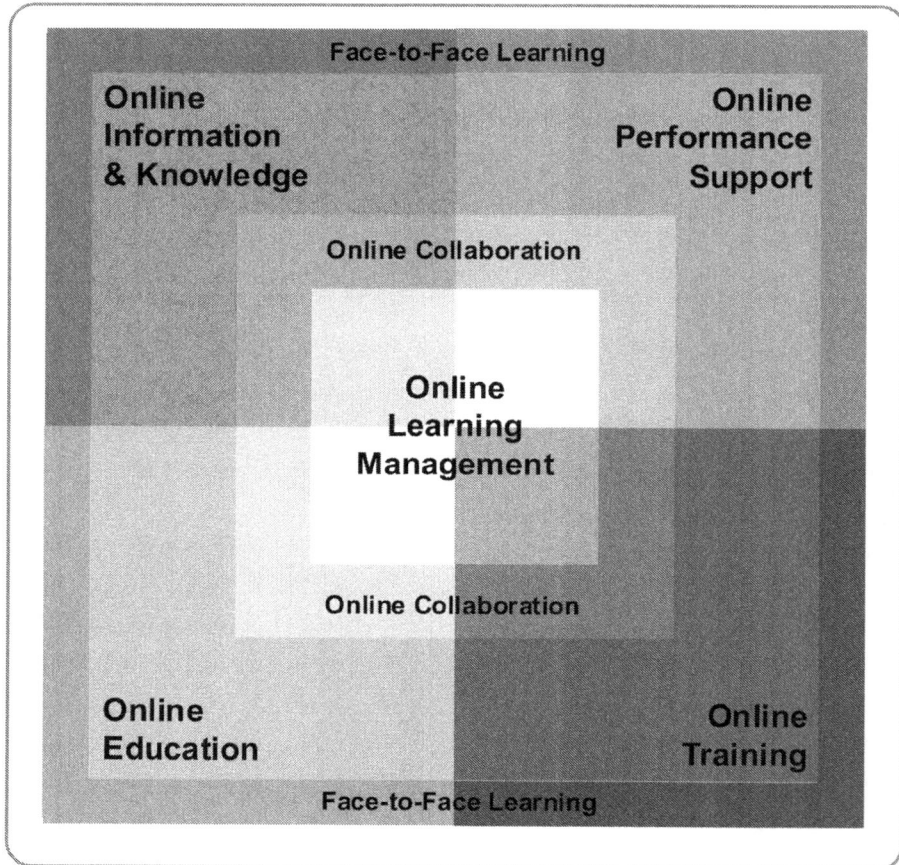

Figure 1-3: Integrated e-Learning Solutions

Organizations now recognize the importance of additional online learning solutions, including:

- *Online performance support solutions:* Enabling workers to improve performance on-the-job, through job-aids, online coaching, embedded systems, and wizards

- *Online information and knowledge:* Improving access to documents and research that inform the employee's work

- *Online collaboration:* Leveraging the shared capabilities of resources through learning communities, supported by a number of tools, such as e-mail, instant messenger, chat, threaded discussions, electronic whiteboards, application and document sharing, Web meetings, and file transfer

At the heart of future online learning solutions will be *online learning management*. This refers to the online guidance, facilitation, and management of all the learner's experiences. It creates the overall learning experience and supports the learning process, including: registration, tracking, assignments, assessments, coaching, mentoring, and reporting.

Face-to-face learning refers to the physical classroom training experience where two or more people participate in a workshop, a course, or seminar in one location at the same time.

From this vantage point, the learning professionals who are preparing the learning roadmap will consider the full range of options and capabilities and apply with accuracy the e-learning technologies, tools, and methodologies that create a dynamic and effective learning solution.

Integrating e-Learning Solutions

What are some trends for integrating e-learning solutions today?

- Learning programs, which are currently deployed through a variety of media, such as PowerPoint presentations, electronic documents, books, CD-ROM, audio tapes, and video tapes, will be converted into e-learning solutions.

- Face-to-face training (classroom-based training) will be redesigned and become part of larger blended learning programs.

- More online courseware will be available for various industries, applications, and functions. Companies will look for best-in-class vendor courseware. Some course titles will be commoditized, which will have a positive impact on pricing. However, most e-learning courseware required by enterprises is not available to the public market, as it is very specific to an individual organization, product, service, or culture. Therefore, the demand for customized courseware design and development will grow significantly.

- Customized content development requires much more than people skilled with authoring tools. Specifically, for the design and development of the more sophisticated e-learning courseware, it is critical to have people with a strong background and solid experience in instructional design. Due to the lack of professionals with these skills, headcount limitations and cost control efforts, a significant portion of customized e-learning design will be outsourced to vendors who have made e-learning design their core competency.

- With the rollout of e-learning in different cultures, there will be a growing need for localization of content as well, where the look and feel of the content and learning experience is matched more closely to the culture of the learner.

- Finally, the younger generations who have grown up in the digital age, will demand more engaging, interesting, and fun learning experiences that are consistent with the way they collaborate, work, and learn. Game- and simulation-based learning is definitely a strong trend in the future.

Trends in Deployment of e-Learning

There are a number of trends in the deployment of e-learning. For example:

- Organizations have become more knowledgeable about, and smarter in, identifying and selecting the best vendors for their e-learning technology infrastructure, courseware, services, and implementations.

- Newer and better e-learning technologies will become available to the market and e-learning will be deployed on more devices, such as personal digital assistants and tablet PCs. Wireless high-speed Internet will be available in many places and geographies through Wireless Fidelity (WIFI) technologies, making it easier to for people to take e-learning any place.

> **Marketing e-Learning at Cingular Wireless***
>
> ✔ Provide e-learning resource guides for managers
>
> ✔ Use live e-learning conferences
>
> ✔ Send e-learning e-mail announcements
>
> ✔ Contribute articles to company online newsletter
>
> ✔ Offer on-site demonstrations
>
> *See Chapter 13: Educating New Hires

- IDC forecasts that vendor revenue from live e-learning should exceed US$5 billion in 2006, compared to US$500 million in 2001. Live e-learning is very popular because of its strong value proposition, the value of live and interactive instruction, speed of development, ease of distribution for large audiences and opportunities to reuse knowledge through recordings of live online sessions.

- More emphasis will be placed on making the e-learning event part of the overall workflow. For example, online performance support, and online coaching, and mentoring, and learning will be more integrated with evolving business processes.

- The usage, start and drop-out rates will continue to be a challenge for most organizations. Employees are very busy and an e-learning program can become just another to-do on top of an already oversubscribed schedule. To deploy a successful e-learning strategy, it is important to put e-learning enablers in place including a strong marketing approach, a change management strategy including a time-to-learn policy, and a connection to performance management. You will find more information about these in Chapter 8.

- Outsourcing has proven to be a good solution for content development, application maintenance and administration, and systems integration.

Future Growth of e-Learning

The business alignment, content, and deployment trends will continue to support a significant growth in e-learning globally as shown in Figure 1-4.

Additionally, Gartner is very positive about the e-learning market and expects that the e-learning market will be as high as US$35 billion in 2005 (Gartner 2002). As times goes by, we will become even smarter about e-learning.

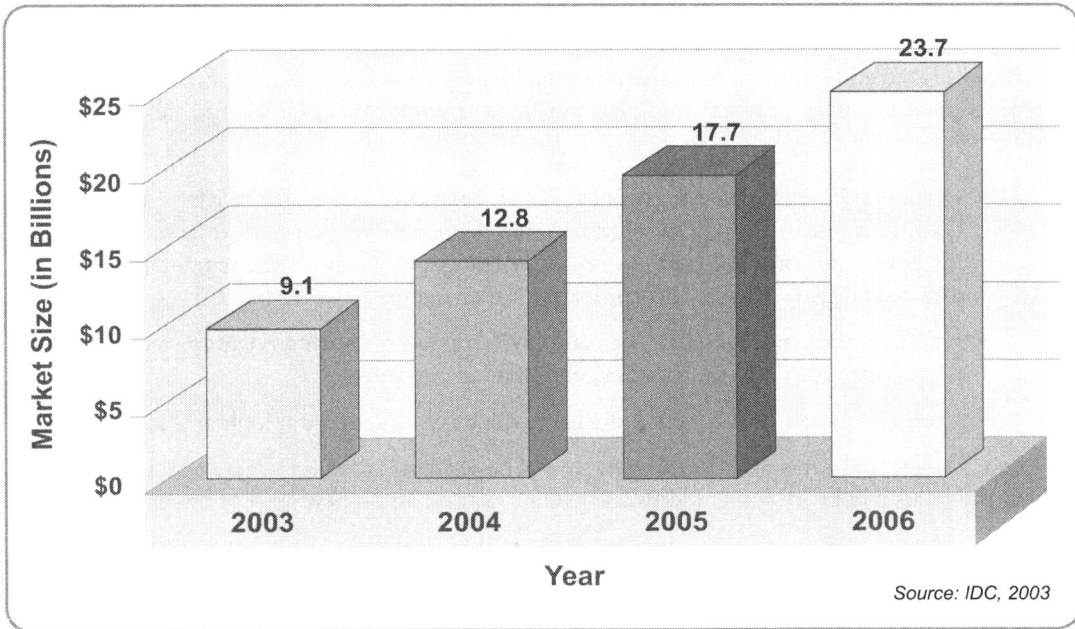

Figure 1-4: Worldwide Corporate e-Learning Market Forecast: 2003 to 2006

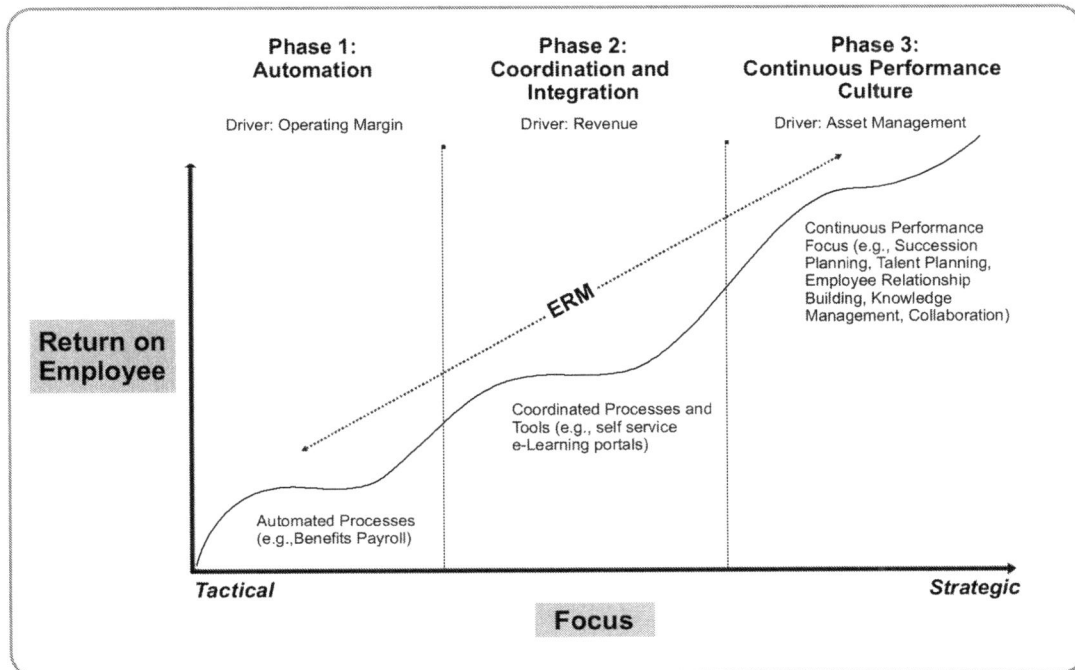

Figure 1-5: Employee Relationship Management

e-Learning is increasingly a key building block in emerging employee performance and work place solutions. By leveraging common business processes (for example, production enabled by Enterprise Resource Planning or sales managed enabled by Customer Relationship Management), companies are developing strategies and programs for employee and enterprise portals, which combine:

- Employee Performance (often called ERM, Employee Relationship Management or B2E, Business to Employee solutions) that focuses on worker performance by integrating corporate communications, e-mail, learning, knowledge management and collaboration, and performance and competency management (see Figure 1-5)

- E-HR, such as online, self-service employee human resource services for recruitment, payroll, benefits, and time and expense management

- Common portal infrastructure, security, standards, log on, and look and feel

While companies move toward e-learning as part of larger employee performance and portal initiatives, the focus will be on integration issues, maintenance, and a new level of benefits.

As the knowledge, experience and applications of e-learning increases there will be significant contributions in more languages and from many cultures. The dissemination to the community of learning professionals through books, articles, research, e-learning professional organizations, conferences, seminars, courses, workshops, experience in enterprises, vendors and knowledge sharing will grow as the visionary explorers continue to apply new concepts to the capabilities provided by e-learning.

There are many lessons to be learned from the first wave of e-learning, and you will find nuggets of experience contributed by major organizations in the various chapters of this Fieldbook. In the next chapter you will learn whether e-learning makes business sense for your organization.

CHAPTER

2

Does e-Learning Make Business Sense?

The main themes for this chapter are:

- *How Can You Align e-Learning with Business Goals?*
- *What Is the Business Impact of e-Learning?*
- *Developing a Winning e-Learning Strategy*

Does e-Learning Make Business Sense?

Our global business environment is characterized by a fluid exchange of money, technology, processes, people, ideas, information, and knowledge. This rate of change compounds daily, if not hourly, driving some of the challenges that confront enterprises around the world, including:

✓ *A high-velocity business environment*

- Slow growth in the global economy and increased competition
- Demand to move rapidly up the learning, change, and technology curves

✓ *Globalization and decentralization*

- Orchestrating disparate operations toward a common purpose
- Increasing requirements that employees work outside their cultural comfort zones when collaborating with teams in other firms and other countries

✓ *Mergers and acquisitions*

- Acceleration of mergers and acquisitions to win market share, increase access to additional financial resources, and expand geographic/global presence, among other reasons

✓ *Legal and regulatory mandates*

- Professional certification requirements have long been established in industries such as finance, healthcare, and accounting, and legal and regulatory requirements have increased in other segments as well.

✓ *Limited pool of talented people*

- A shift in the industrial nations toward a strong services economy moves knowledge front and center in meeting customer needs, at the same time as baby boomers are beginning to retire, leaving a huge talent vacuum in companies and industries

Virtually every company has seen part of their business transformed by new technologies and processes, launch of new products and services, and penetration of new market areas, among other trends in the global economy. This requires a change in the skills and roles of employees, and therefore engenders an increased need for training and education, in other words—***Learning!***

Training and performance improvement programs represent a significant expenditure. This expenditure in most organizations ranges from 1.3 to 13 percent of total payroll costs (Galvin 2001). Though learning needs have increased significantly in organizations over the last few years, only a small number of organizations have increased their budgets. For most organizations budgets have been flat, at best, or have been cut. But more importantly, there are organizations that have been able to allocate money to invest in e-learning initiatives, while others have experienced less success in acquiring, or reallocating existing budgets, for e-learning.

The lack of e-learning initiative funding has been due primarily to insufficient visible alignment with specific business goals and no real proven impact on the business, in other words the programs may have been just *nice to have* or were simply too expensive compared to the potential benefits and measured results. The 25 cases presented in Chapters 10 through 17, will provide company specific perspectives gained from e-learning experiences, including:

- Aligning e-learning initiatives with business goals
- Ensuring the business impact of learning initiatives

This chapter discusses whether e-learning makes business sense for your organization and offers assistance on how to create a vision, strategy, and business case for your initiative.

How Can You Align e-Learning with Business Goals?

First, let's look at some aspects that shape the business value proposition for e-learning, including: reach, cost-effectiveness, business drivers, and diverse learner requirements.

Unlimited Reach to Individual Learners

Self-paced e-learning can be taken *any time* and is therefore a just-in-time approach for development of important knowledge and skills. e-Learning can be taken at *any place*—in the office, at home or other locations, which eliminates the travel needs and costs. Skills acquisition and knowledge development will take place at *any pace* and *any path*, as the learning experience is solely driven by the participant, and therefore very personalized. *Anyone* in the organization can engage in e-learning and participate and share experience and knowledge in e-learning collaboration sessions.

The potential cost savings depend on a combination of a number of factors which need to be assessed on a program-by-program basis, including the cost of travel, hotel, facilities, administration, instructors, course materials production and shipping, and audio visual.

Cost Effectiveness

The overall development and deployment costs of e-learning have proven to be between 30 to 70 percent less expensive than classroom training (Deloitte Consulting Research 2001).

Support of Critical Business Drivers

e-Learning has been proven capable of supporting the realization of important business goals, such as shown in Figure 2-1. Many of the chapters and organizational case studies of e-learning focus on various aspects and applications of e-learning to achieving these goals.

Varied Applications for Diverse Learner Needs

e-Learning initiatives have been applied to meet learning needs on a wide variety of topics to reach varied audiences of professions and employees, including global employees, new hires, executives, and the sales force. These programs have also been utilized to reach and extend value outside the organization to prospective employees, customers, suppliers and partners.

BUSINESS CHALLENGES	BUSINESS GOALS	BUSINESS IMPACT	STAKEHOLDERS IMPACT
• A high velocity business environment • Globalization and decentralization • Mergers and acquisitions • Legal and regulatory mandates • Limited pool of talented people	• Improved customer services • Faster launch of products/services • Compliance with legal and regulatory mandates • Speedy deployment of new information systems and processes • Increased customer service and customer retention • Enhancement of employee productivity • Development of a strong organizational culture • Serving the extended enterprise (customers, suppliers, partners, distributors) • Geographic and/or industry expansion • Retooling employees for new roles • Attract and retain the best people • Develop a capacity for ongoing innovation	**Increase:** • **Revenue** • **Profitability** • **Growth** • **Sustainability**	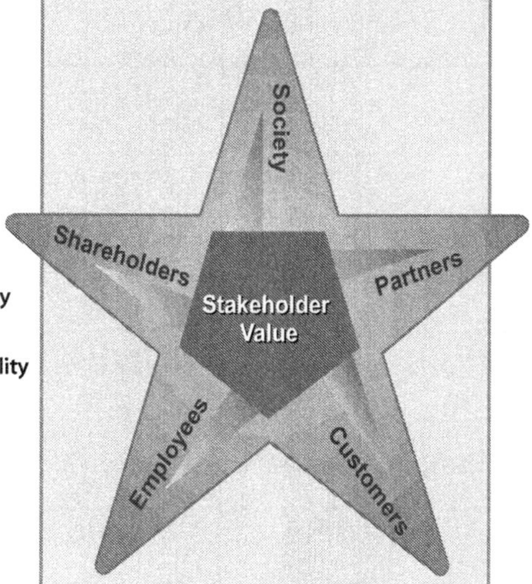 Society Shareholders Partners Stakeholder Value Employees Customers

Figure 2-1: Business Challenges and Goals

What Is The Business Impact of e-Learning?

Even if e-learning initiatives are well-aligned with the business goals, there is no guarantee that they will have a real business impact unless this is explicitly considered during the initial considerations when developing an e-learning solution. Business impact shows up as revenue, earnings, growth, and sustainability, and can appear as hard and/or soft benefits.

✓ *Hard Benefits:* Benefits are easy to quantify in dollars, such as a reduction in expenditures for:

- Travel
- Classroom instructor
- Facility and equipment
- Training administration and course logistics
- Course documentation
- Training function
- Course development and maintenance

And there can be improved bottom-line results, through increased:

- Productivity because of reduced time away from the job
- Sales volume because of reduced time away from the job

- Revenue from customers who are take e-learning, or who enjoy and purchase more products due to e-learning available to them from the company

✓ *Soft Benefits:* These benefits are more difficult to quantify in dollars, for example:

- Faster time-to-market than competitors with new products and services, with a related impact on revenue and market share

- Increased sales volume

- Strengthened brand identification

- Just-in-time training for global workforce

- Reduced costs because of improved risk and project management

- Improved employee morale and reduced turnover rates

- Enhanced usage of implemented technologies and processes

- Improved level of customer service, satisfaction, and retention

- Better teamwork

- Better educated employees, customers, and suppliers

- Expanded access to learning and development of new skills

- Leverage of pre-meeting time through virtual learning and collaboration

---

Business Drivers for e-Learning in Fieldbook Case Organizations

✓ Help sales and marketing workforce quickly acquire common knowledge of semiconductor technology, processes, and company solutions (STMicroelectronics)

✓ Provide critical methodology skills for all practitioners in a globally consistent matter (Deloitte & Touche Tohmatsu)

✓ Increase customer value by providing quality service and information (The Prudential)

✓ Reduce cost of training by decreasing the number of total instructor hours, while maintaining coverage on the sales floor (The Home Depot)

✓ Provide excellent customer service in an increasingly complex financial services market (American Skandia)

✓ Maximize and leverage meeting results by developing knowledge of corporate participants prior to the face-to-face event (INSEAD OnLine)

✓ Give veterinarian more time for field calls (The Iams Company)

However, our new digital world demands different measures and produces different results. Companies have found that the application of successful e-learning is not necessarily driven solely by cost savings, but by the business impact of the dollars spent, as is illustrated Figure 2-2.

This example shows that for the same dollar investment, the number of employees benefiting from the training is 10 times higher, and everyone globally has immediate access to a large and varied learning library that can be utilized at any time and from any place.

Both hard and soft benefits gained through e-learning initiatives improve stakeholder value. Research has provided evidence that companies who invest relatively more in training and learning than their competitors enjoy higher share valuations. Although it is difficult to prove a direct correlation between these two factors, there is definitely a link between the support of a learning culture and share value. In addition, as demonstrated by the case organizations in this Fieldbook, e-learning has been accepted by these leading companies as an integral component of a viable learning strategy.

The Importance of Return On Investment (ROI) in Securing Funding for e-Learning Investments

In most organizations, e-learning has moved beyond the pilot or infancy phase, and significant investments are needed to build and strengthen the e-learning infrastructure, courseware, and other e-learning solutions.

Increasingly, the decision-makers for e-learning are members of the C-Suite, the CEO, CIO, CFO, CMO, and CTO. As a result, these executives will be engaged in assessing the investments, benefits and business impact of e-learning. This places an increased emphasis on accurately and explicitly measuring the impact before and after the e-learning investments are made.

The effects of learning can be measured at different levels. The best known learning evaluation framework comes from the work of Donald Kirkpatrick and Jack J. Phillips. They describe five levels of evaluation important to all learning investments. Jack J. Phillips' Level 5 Evaluation, Return On Investment (ROI) will be discussed in this chapter. The entire framework and the other levels of evaluation are described in detail in Chapter 6.

Business Impact of an e-Learning Program at The Iams Company*

✓ Reduced the learning duration for each learner from 8 hours to 2.5 hours

✓ Increased learner retention and/or exceeded the knowledge gained from the current program

✓ Eliminated travel

✓ Reduced the number of days the sales force was out of the field

✓ Gained additional time for training in advanced topics

✓ Improved the bottom line through related efficiencies

*See Chapter 16, The Iams Company

Learning Investment Options: Classroom Versus e-Learning

- Assume an overall learning budget of a company is US$2 million

- Average duration of a typical classroom course is three days

- Average cost of a three-day classroom course, including facilities, travel, and trainers is $2,000 per participant

Option A: Classroom Environment	Option B: e-Learning
• The total number of people that can be trained in three-day program: 1,000 people • The total number of training days: 3,000	• Purchase of hosted solution of e-learning Library • Number of courses: 2,500, with an average duration of 2 hours • Content Areas: Business Skills, Leadership, IT Skills, and Soft-Skills • Estimated number of employees that can be trained under this contract:10,000 (globally)

Figure 2-2: Business Impact of an e-Learning Solution

An e-learning ROI can be calculated by dividing the net program benefits by the e-learning program costs. (See Figure 2-3) When an estimated ROI evaluation for learning has been established, it can be compared with other investment options.

Although, there is significant value in applying ROI calculations, it is found that in most companies it is not applied to learning investments. The most important reasons for lack of ROI calculations in human resource development initiatives include:

- Lack of experience with ROI calculations, with a related lack of skills and/or insufficient staff to conduct ROI

- Lack of ROI standards or methodology for learning

- A business case that includes hard dollar savings alone, combined with the expected soft benefits, has been sufficient so far to gain executive buy-in and investment approvals

- Difficulty in assigning dollars to soft-business benefits

- Assumption that estimating ROI is time-consuming and expensive

- Executives have not requested a ROI because is has been a traditional aspect of the investment/budget process for education and learning.

Shareholder Value and Learning

✓ Among publicly traded firms, those in the top half (who spend proportionally more on training) have a total stockholder return 86 percent higher than firms in the bottom half.

✓ A firm's employee investment in education and learning is an important predictor of its stock price in the following year. The investment is at least as important a predictor as traditional values, such as R&D expenditures

✓ Sales per-employee in firms that invest an above average amount in education and learning are 58 percent higher than firms that make lower investments.

Source: From e-Learning to Enterprise Learning, Deloitte Consulting Research 2001

One of the earliest methods for evaluating training investments and was the costs benefits analysis process. Benefits-Cost Analysis compares the benefits of a program to its costs through a Benefits-Cost Ratio (BCR).

To calculate BCR:

$$BCR = \frac{Business\ Benefits}{Solution\ of\ Program\ Costs}$$

To calculate ROI:

$$ROI\ (\%) = \frac{Net^*\ Business\ Benefits\ (Hard\ and\ Soft)}{Solution\ or\ Program\ Costs} \times 100$$

Example:

To derive Net Business Benefits

Business Benefits $400,000
Solution Costs $100,000
Net Business Benefits = $400,000 - $100,000 = $300,000
BCR= ($400,000/$100.000) = 4/1.
This means that for each dollar invested in the program, four dollars were returned in benefits

To calculate Return On Investment (ROI):

ROI = ($300,000 Net Business Benefits / $100,000 Costs) x 100 = 300%
This means that for each dollar invested in the program, there is a 300% ROI

*Net= Business Benefits minus Solutions or Program Costs

Figure 2-3: Calculating ROI for e-Learning Investments

The most important benefits of using ROI are that this approach[1]:

- Demonstrates the contribution of selected programs

- Earns the respect of senior management

- Gains the confidence of clients

- Improves learning and the performance improvement process

- Develops a results-based approach

- Alters or eliminates ineffective programs

> "The fears and misconceptions may often act as barriers, but they do not have to inhibit ROI application and implementation. The ROI methodology will require additional time, costs, and new skills to bring change to the design, development, and implementation of solutions. But when the payoff is considered, the benefits exceed the investment, usually by large amounts."
>
> Patricia Philips, The Bottom Line on ROI, 2002

Rapidly, the competitive and cost-focused business environment is demanding increased accountability from all learning functions, requiring them to address both the *business impact* and the *ROI* of learning in their organization. Organizations that want to change from the *expense/cost mindset* to an *investment mindset* must make the effort to quantify the soft-business benefits and measure and explain the ROI for important e-learning initiatives.

Developing a Winning e-Learning Strategy

The first step toward the creation of a winning e-learning strategy is to identify and align with the key business goals and drivers that will enable the organization to succeed, then develop a new vision and strategy for e-learning aligned with the business goals.

Strategic e-learning goals may include a reference to:

- Enhance learning capabilities and solutions globally

- Provide more learning for employees at lower costs

- Decrease time-to-market of new skills

- Build world-class e-learning capabilities and solutions

The second step is to develop a business case focused on a request for an investment in selected critical and beneficial e-learning initiatives, for example:

- Implementation of a learning management system

- Purchase of specific e-learning content and solutions

- Design and development of e-learning programs

- Launch of live e-learning capabilities

The third step is the development of the business case. To do this effectively, it is important to understand the current learning capabilities and how much is being spent on learning within the enterprise. Unfortunately, many organizations still lack the requisite information systems or do

---

[1] Philips, P. P., The Bottom Line on ROI, Atlanta: CEP Press, 2002.

not have the processes in place to track and report on all training and related expenses within the organization. However, a new e-learning strategy can not be effectively developed and promoted without understanding the status quo. Therefore, it is recommended that the first step be an assessment and estimation of total spending on learning.

In addition, most organizations cannot increase their learning budget to implement an e-learning infrastructure. Up-front investments in e-learning need to be compensated by a reduction in operational learning costs. This implies that classroom training and related travel expenses must be reduced. But it has proven to be difficult for companies where classroom learning delivery dollars are managed and controlled at decentralized levels within the organization. These three initial steps are depicted in Figure 2-4.

After approval of the business case, e-learning initiatives need to be prioritized and an implementation plan must be developed, including timing, resources required, vendor/partner selection, investment levels, marketing and change management plans, and risk management.

At this stage it is very important to show the business impact and ROI for specific initiatives. The achievement of all strategic goals may take a few years, and it would be overwhelming and risky to start with all initiatives at once. It is highly recommended to select a limited number of initiatives and try to make progress and achieve tangible successes (quick hits). There needs to be an ongoing dialog and feedback to the business leaders to evaluate projects, validate priorities, and retain funding.

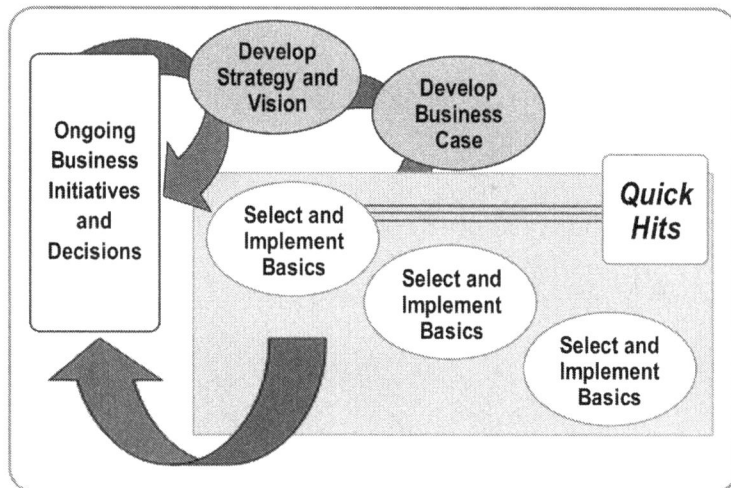

Figure 2-4: Blitz and Stabilize: e-Learning Alignment with Business Drivers

Identify those aspects of your strategy that will immediately prove the value of the e-learning investment to important senior executives in your organization. A solid business case and proven ROI for e-learning initiatives makes executives feel comfortable and will help you to get their support and championship for further implementation and investment.

In the next chapter, we will review strategies and tactics to engage the support of important stakeholders for the e-learning business case.

Lessons Learned

✓ Enterprises have an increased need to enhance learning.

✓ It is critical to align e-learning initiatives with business needs.

✓ The value proposition for e-learning is very strong.

✓ The business benefits of e-learning include both hard dollar and soft dollar benefits.

✓ Most companies approach e-learning from a cost savings perspective, and this does have an important impact bottom line.

✓ However, sooner or later, all learning functions will face increasing accountability and have to address business impact and ROI.

✓ It is important to develop a new vision and strategic objectives for learning.

✓ Using a Blitz and Stabilize implementation approach offers quick 'wins' and demonstrated impact on the business drivers, enabling e-learning to build the business case.

CHAPTER

3

What Gains the Commitment of People That Matter?

The main themes for this chapter are:

- *Gaining Top Management Support*
- *Gaining Information Technology Support*
- *Gaining the Support of the Training Department*

What Gains the Commitment of People That Matter?

Many major e-learning vendors and industry leaders would have us view the advent of e-learning as the panacea of the future for progressive, savvy, and insightful companies, quick enough to take advantage of it. However, the truth is that many organizations, in their zeal to become leaders in this exciting field, frequently find themselves confronted with an unanticipated level of resistance to these new initiatives and an inability to overcome this resistance from one of several different sources:

- Management and leadership
- The Information Technology (IT) department
- The training department itself

This resistance stems from many factors:

- Prohibitively high up-front investment levels, compounded by a poor ability to quantify and clearly articulate the justification for those expenditures in terms of: their overall return to the business; longer-term impact on the learning population; and overall success criteria in terms of measuring the success or failure of the initiative.

- Resistance to the integration of two traditionally separate areas-technology and training. Many training department managers are quick to point to insufficient bandwidth and technology robustness as the cause of failure of their e-learning training initiatives. On the other hand, an equal number of IT managers will happily reciprocate with distrust and skepticism about proposed e-learning products and solutions.

- Massive change management challenges at all three levels in the organization are not supported with adequate planning and implementation efforts to foster adoption of the changes. This discourages management, IT, and the training department from undertaking the radical change efforts needed in how learning is delivered to, and received by, end users in the organization.

- While there have been some highly-touted and admired corporate pioneers and leaders in e-learning initiative, such as Motorola and Dell Universities, among others, there is still a significant amount of concern about an organization's ability to develop a cohesive *roadmap* for achieving that success. The inherent risk involved in embarking in a series of initiatives with high levels of expenditure, and relatively unclear demonstrable success factors, is itself a cause of resistance to beginning on the e-learning path.

While resistance to large-scale e-learning initiatives does provide a significant challenge, it is not an insurmountable one for most organizations. The importance of sustaining, enhancing, and leveraging human intellectual capital to achieve organizational success has become widely recognized. Younger generations are experiencing a total learning environment in their formative years, supported twenty-four hours a day, seven days a week by digital learning opportunities, and are demanding a similar commitment to intensive learning and professional development from their employers. Also, a leaner, more constrained economy is driving organizations to search for mechanisms to retool their existing workforce, at an increasingly more competitive rate, and on a larger, global scale. All of these challenges, opportunities, and constraints can be addressed by e-learning capabilities.

Gaining Top Management Support

Key to gaining top management support for e-learning initiatives and projects is to integrate the evaluation and prioritization of those initiatives as an integral part of the organization's standard investment planning process. Many organizations who have been successful in gaining top management support have implemented rigorous evaluation processes to link their portfolio of potential investments to longer-term strategic and financial goals.

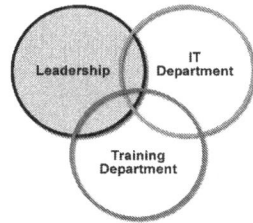

Important questions to ask during this evaluation process are posed in Figure 3-1, and the development of the answers revolving around the most important question, *"Are we allocating funds and resources to best meet our strategic and financial goals?"*, supports the business case for e-learning discussed in Chapter 2.

Historically, traditional learning projects and proposed investments have been handled below the radar screen in the annual investment planning cycle, and may actually have been budgeted in a decentralized mode to departmental or regional tactical budgets. However, the future appears to be more promising.

The challenge for learning departments is to elevate the visibility of e-learning as it relates to the strategic charter of the organization. This requires mapping standard criteria for learning initiatives to those which will relate more closely to

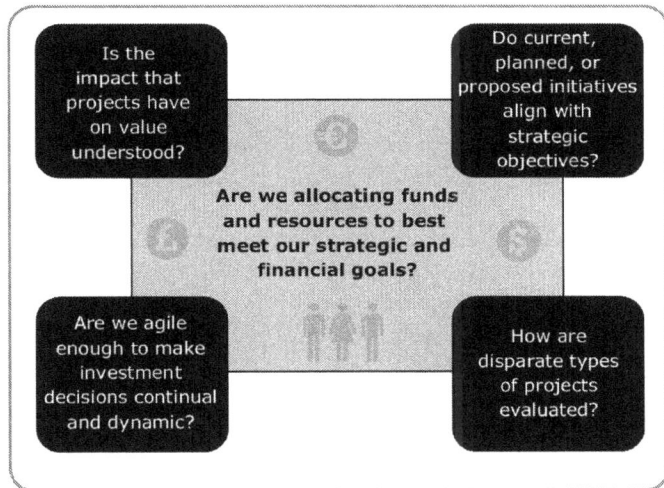

Figure 3-1: Strategy Formulation

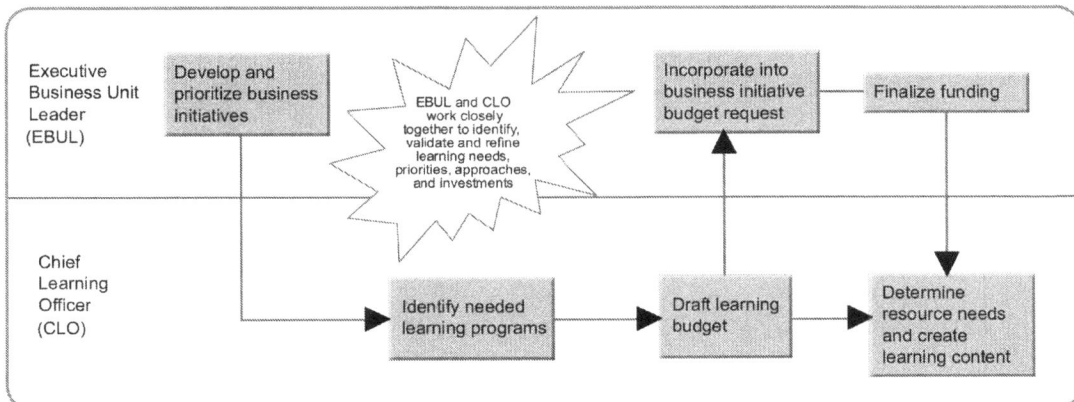

Figure 3-2: e-Learning Investment Decision-Making Process

e-learning and providing top management with a better understanding as to how e-learning initiatives can support firm strategy. By integrating the e-learning initiatives with specific strategic and financial goals, and aligning the benefits of those projects with high priority strategic agendas, the learning organization can elevate e-learning projects to a strategic level of evaluation, and ensure that they are regarded as a highly relevant part of the planning process.

Figure 3-2 illustrates the steps to gaining management support, where the business initiatives identified by the executives, drive the selection of learning programs. To promote the strategic viability of each e-learning project and initiative with management, the learning team needs to revisit the questions in each of the circles in Figure 3-1, with e-learning in focus.

> "Growing market traction on the part of large technology firms such as IBM Global Services, Oracle, and SAP, professional services firms like IBM Global Services, Accenture, Deloitte Consulting, and KPMG, and publishers including Thomson, Pearson, Wiley & Sons, is providing e-learning with more visibility among senior management of large enterprises."
>
> IDC 2003

Do the Company Executives Understand the Impact the Projects Have on Value?

Learning, and in particular e-learning, projects may not tie as clearly to value in the minds of top executives as other corporate initiatives, such as those that link closely to increased revenues, decreased costs, and reduced turnover. The concept of value is one that differs for every organization, but clearly e-learning initiatives must demonstrate a supportable return on investment (ROI) from a quantitative perspective. The investment outlay required for each e-learning initiative must at least satisfy the minimum level of ROI required for implementation of any investment project, regardless of its nature, from an organizational perspective.

Value, for most e-learning initiatives, can be categorized in three different areas as seen in Figure 3-3.

The value of each of the components in the categories in Figure 3-3 is highly dependent on the scope and aggressiveness of the specific initiative; however, in every case, both qualitative and quantitative value, needs to be included in the ROI analysis and value equation. *Reduced expenses* alone are obviously the most easily understood and quantifiable. In addition, reduced expenses clearly will result in a definitive impact on the

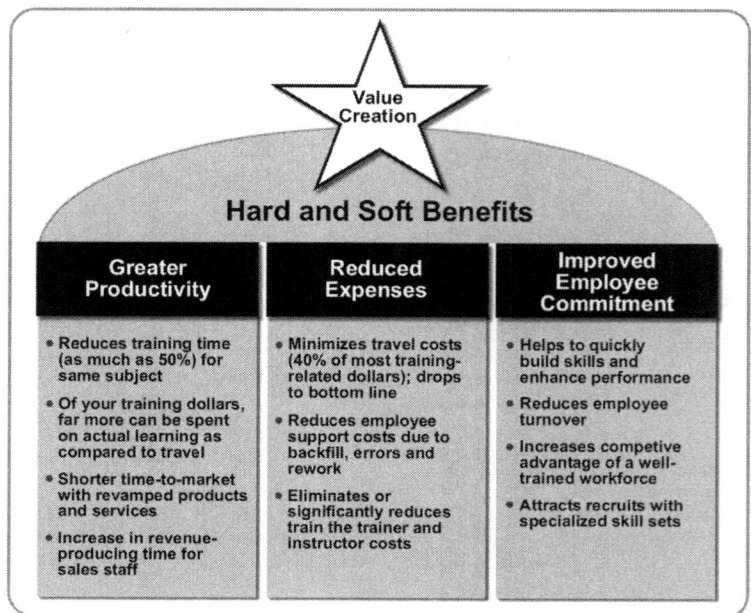

Value Creation

Hard and Soft Benefits

Greater Productivity	Reduced Expenses	Improved Employee Commitment
• Reduces training time (as much as 50%) for same subject	• Minimizes travel costs (40% of most training-related dollars); drops to bottom line	• Helps to quickly build skills and enhance performance
• Of your training dollars, far more can be spent on actual learning as compared to travel	• Reduces employee support costs due to backfill, errors and rework	• Reduces employee turnover
• Shorter time-to-market with revamped products and services	• Eliminates or significantly reduces train the trainer and instructor costs	• Increases competive advantage of a well-trained workforce
• Increase in revenue-producing time for sales staff		• Attracts recruits with specialized skill sets

Figure 3-3: Measurement Categories for e-Learning Initiatives

bottom line. However, it is also possible and imperative to quantify the productivity and employee commitment gained through e-learning initiatives to gain management and leadership support.

In this total valuation of the contribution of e-learning, it is equally important to assess each initiative's impact on the *top line*. Jay Cross of the Internet Time Group provides his view of the top line as follows, *"What's on the top line? Sales. Revenues. Out-surviving the competition. Increasing market share. Building brand. Staying in the game and holding on long enough to score. Reinventing the business (Jay Cross 2001)."* With the renewed focus on the investment considerations for learning, this is a prime time for e-learning proponents to directly tie their initiatives to this new thinking.

How Can Disparate Types of Projects be Evaluated?

What constitutes success for an e-learning project? The answer may be different for each e-learning initiative; but it is critical to be clear at the outset how your definition of success criteria will be employed, in addition to the measurements that will be used to evaluate the level of success and communicate it to management.

Typical evaluation criteria for e-learning may include:

- Percent of employees taking at least one e-learning course within the first year of roll-out
- Total e-learning hours taken within the first year of rollout
- Percent of classroom hours replaced with e-learning hours
- Learner satisfaction with content (based on quantitative evaluation scores)
- Learner performance post-e-learning experience (based on job evaluation scores and performance reviews)
- Repeat e-learners
- Increased levels of compliance with industry standards, such as Capability Maturity Model (CMM), IS09000
- Speed to retooling in specific high priority technology areas
- Reduced employee turnover
- Improved recruiting rates and candidate feedback
- Technical issues associated with e-learning launch

There are many other potential evaluation criteria that could be used to assess any given e-learning initiative. Regardless of the criteria, the important thing is to:

- Identify the criteria as part of the investment planning process
- Identify the metrics to be used to measure performance against those criteria
- Ensure buy-in of those measures as evaluation criteria for the success of the e-learning initiative

See Chapter 6 of this Fieldbook for more specific information on how to measure e-learning initiatives and results.

Many major content and technology e-learning providers are highly aware of the need to provide demonstrable success, and now provide product features and services specifically geared to assist learning organizations in their compilation and reporting of required effectiveness measures.

This includes such features such as:

- Pre-assessment and post-assessment comparison metrics
- Multiple evaluation criteria, such as usability, accessibility, and relevance, for collecting user feedback
- Highly flexible reporting mechanisms

All contribute significantly to the effective evaluation of initiative or project success factors.

While e-learning evaluation criteria may be radically different from those used to measure the effectiveness of other types of projects, once they have been reviewed and approved by top management, they can and will provide a barometer for the success of e-learning projects against others competing for parallel funding and resources.

Do Current, Planned, or Proposed Initiatives Align with Strategic Objectives?

Most significant business unit strategic initiatives and campaigns have an enormous impact, in some way, shape or form, on one of the organization's most important assets—its human capital. Chief Learning Officers (CLOs) and human resource development professionals have recognized this impact, and have been able to demonstrate that learning, and in particular e-learning, is a strategic enabler to achieving goals such as aggressive growth, expanding client readiness, providing internal and external certification, and giving credibility and visibility to practitioner toolsets and capabilities as they embark on new and mission-critical endeavors. Larry Scott, Deloitte Consulting, Global Director, Strategy & Operations Practice, has said that *"Learning has not only enabled us to build mission critical skills and knowledge, but also to foster significant changes in practice direction. We launched an important initiative to develop the best strategy learning available today, fostering a common culture, approach, and skill set to support the development of a world-class practice."*

While e-learning initiatives evaluated on their own merits sometimes filter into high priority development queues, those that are integrally linked to high priority strategic initiatives, and viewed as essential for the success of those initiatives, have a much greater potential of surviving investment reprioritization and restructuring efforts. In addition, if done well, there is the potential to reap major benefits by riding on the coat-tails of successful projects, ultimately making true believers out of key organizational stakeholders.

Making e-learning initiatives visible on the strategic organizational radar screen is not an insignificant task. Key activities, which may help in this process include: a strategy, high visibility projects, communication, and celebration of success.

> *"Consider your business culture when implementing e-learning. It can be tough to move learners to e-learning, particularly among sales and marketing personnel who are people-oriented. Start small and provide a lot of chances to be exposed to the system."**
>
> ** See Chapter 17: 3Com*

✓ *Select a strategy that will make everyone successful.*
Especially in the initial launch of the organization's e-learning strategy, it is critical that the CLO and their team adopt a win/win strategy to ensure the success of initial projects, while constructing the underlying e-learning culture and infrastructure. A win/win strategy includes such components as the right vendors, the right projects, the right team, and the right motivation for embarking on this course. A cohesive strategy for making an e-learning culture successful in your own unique organization is absolutely critical to its success in the long run.

✓ *Select a high visibility, strategic pilot initiative for your launch into e-learning.*
Characteristics of the pilot project should include:

- A relatively short duration program

- A high probability of success

- Support for the work of e-learning-proficient stakeholders (if possible)

- A finite and well-selected audience

- Focus on discrete and well-defined goals and success measures

The successful implementation of the pilot project can provide a launching pad from which to publicize the achievement of critical milestones. It can also be used to bring additional stakeholders on board when it has been demonstrated that e-learning can be a strategic enabler of other broader and more extensive strategic initiatives.

> "One lesson learned is to start smaller and do a pilot. Doing something to roll out to the entire 90,000 people on the first shot is a bad idea. I think you need to start with smaller groups; get some successes; and use those success stories to sell it to everybody else. That has worked really well for us."*
>
> Scott Sutker
> *See Chapter 12: Wachovia Corporation

✓ *Communicate, communicate, communicate*
E-learning requires a huge mindset adjustment at all levels of the organization, but particularly at the executive and management levels. By properly inculcating this new learning culture at the executive level, and enabling top executives to become self-appointed champions for the e-learning initiative, you significantly increase your chances of success for all of your e-learning initiatives. When communication, acceptance, and endorsement start at the CEO level, most business unit groups and end users, are quick to follow. E-enable your management team. Sell them not only on the concept, but let them experience the reality; and let them become the champions of this continually evolving technology.

✓ *Celebrate and publicize initial successes*
Success, at any level, is something that everyone wants to be part of, and take credit for. Once the initial pilot project is complete and measurable success shown, success needs to be communicated at all levels of the organization. Ideally, communication of success should trickle top-down, from the CEO level down to other major business unit stakeholders, and then on to their constituents, generating enthusiasm for the concept and the results, and hopefully evoking additional requests for subsequent projects. The learning team, associated strategic business unit teams, and ultimately the end users impacted by initial projects, should all share in the organization's ability to transform the learning strategy to include e-learning as a critical component.

Are We Agile Enough to Make Investment Decisions Continual and Dynamic?

Organizational agility continues to be a priority for most forward thinking, progressive organizations, particularly in terms of their ability to quickly respond to economic, market, technological and sociopolitical changes and trends. This emphasis on agility and compressed response time, impacts e-learning initiatives in two separate and distinct ways. First, e-learning can ultimately provide unprecedented support for this climate of change; and second, the ability to accomplish this is very dependent on the flexibility of the resources in the learning organization itself!

✓ A well executed e-learning strategy can provide unparalleled benefits in extending the global reach, retooling and refitting capabilities, and achieving rapid time-to-market required by fast-breaking, changing organizational priorities and strategies.

- Historically, to incorporate a major shift in firm strategy or priority into traditional learning content, and communicating this change to a global population would be an extremely slow, costly, and disjointed effort. One of the major advantages of an e-learning-based strategy is the benefit to the organization of being able to rapidly modify a centralized repository of content, and to distribute that knowledge to a widely dispersed audience using a range of existing e-learning technologies.

✓ The efficacy of the e-learning strategy in supporting the organization's strategic repurposing and repositioning activities is, however, highly dependent on the agility and flexibility of the learning team itself.

- To fully take advantage of the benefits of e-learning content and technologies, the learning organization itself must fully understand the role and vision of e-learning in the overall strategy of the organization, and should be cognizant of the various learning approaches, investment requirements, and alternative design techniques available to respond to the organization's evolving needs. As the organization begins to understand the depth and breadth of e-learning opportunities and technologies available, it will be the role and responsibility of the learning organization to properly match organizational requirements to the array of products and services available to meet those needs, taking into consideration costs, shelf life, and implementation time for each specific initiative.

Gaining Information Technology (IT) Support

It is virtually impossible to implement a successful e-learning strategy without the support, cooperation, and even enthusiasm of the Information Technology department. Without a robust and well-tested technology backbone to support e-learning content and learning management systems, e-learning initiatives would surely fail. An organization can have the most progressive e-learning strategy, the highest quality e-learning design and development strategy, and the most advanced content, but without an effective deployment mechanism, and an effective technology architecture on which to build the various e-learning components, users and management alike will never reap the benefits of the full e-learning solution.

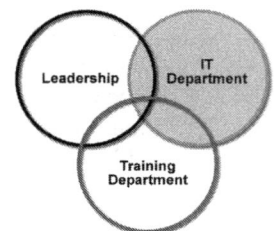

The organizations most successful in rolling out major e-learning initiatives are those in which the CLO, the Chief Information Officer (CIO), and/or the Chief Technology Officer (CTO) have fostered a true partnership between their organizations, and leveraged the strengths of each to build a truly integrated e-learning initiative.

Making the IT partnership work requires an extensive amount of collaboration and cooperation on the part of all functional groups. It is important to:

> *"Build alliances with internal information technology groups. E-learning is a learning initiative, and thus, should be managed by learning professionals. However, as a technology-enabled learning solution, e-learning also requires the involvement of technical resources to be successful.**
>
> **See Chapter 14: McDonald's Corporation*

- ***Have clearly define roles and responsibilities***
  Over the course of any given e-learning project, all groups will fulfill various roles and responsibilities. These roles and responsibilities should be clearly identified and defined from the outset of the project, and agreed upon by these functions prior to project inception. For example, functional requirements are the purview of the Learning team; technical requirements may be better specified by the IT team. Both sets of requirements, however, should be reviewed and approved by all teams, such that they create an integrated whole. If vendor negotiation/integration is within the scope of the e-learning project, the team needs to identify who will negotiate with the vendor; what the ongoing vendor integration/ communication responsibilities will be, and who will assume those responsibilities. Clear identification of roles and responsibilities will help to mitigate confusion in the development process and will avoid any level of assignment of fault if deliverables and milestones are not achieved in adherence with project plan requirements.

- ***Establish a mutual level of respect***
  Over the course of a typical e-learning project, there will be an ebb and flow in team activities, leadership, and decision-making required by each of the teams—Learning and Information Technology. At any given point in the project, based on the scope and the nature of the activities and tasks underway, one group or the other may have a more appropriate skill set or range of capabilities to take the lead and to push that phase through. It is critical to the overall success of the project that the two groups have a high level of mutual respect and that each seamlessly defers to the other at the appropriate time, without turf battles to establish jurisdiction.

- ***Establish clear standards***
  Standards and compliance requirements will be an important facet of any e-learning project. The need to establish standards and guidelines is, of course, highly dependent on the scope of the specific project. Some examples might include: AICC/SCORM standards required for content acquisition; minimum configuration required for content acquisition; standard user configuration to which vendor capabilities must comply; and testing standards/levels of compliance for sign-off on any given project phase. (See Chapters 4 and 6 for more information on AICC and SCORM.)

- ***Dedicate specific IT resources to learning projects***
  Prioritization of information technology resources for learning projects can sometimes be a barrier to success. Typically, many IT departments are overwhelmed with the port-

folio of development needs and priorities in their queue. The priority of learning projects may not be clearly understood by IT resources. The learning curve for the IT resources randomly assigned to learning projects can be very steep, wasting valuable time, thereby unnecessarily extending project timelines and milestone dates. An individual, or cadre of individuals, from IT dedicated to the learning function initiatives is a huge advantage for those organizations progressive enough to dedicate these resources. As additional e-learning initiatives are added to the development stream, IT professionals can quickly grasp the impact of those additional projects on their current architecture; interpret those requirements into an IT framework; and can continue to work with the learning team to ensure that there are no roadblocks in building the e-learning infrastructure in a rational and progressive approach. Once the relationships between learning-dedicated IT resources and the learning team have been built, teamwork and partnership become much easier to achieve.

> *"The role of the training director has shifted to include skills of an IT director. Training directors now must be knowledgeable about implementing learning technology within their organization."**
>
> ** See Chapter 12: BMW*

- ***Ensure regular communication at all levels***
  In addition to informal team communications, a formal communication policy and related schedule should be established. Project status calls and meetings should be conducted between the two teams on a regular basis, preferably weekly or biweekly for high priority projects. Identification of issues and resolution dates for those issues should be an integral part of each session. Those issues which cannot be resolved by the working teams should be elevated to a CIO/CLO level, with communications at that level to take place on an as-needed basis, but preferably at least on a monthly basis.

Gaining the Support of the Training Department

The support of the Training Group would seem to be a given, as most e-learning initiatives certainly are sponsored by and evolve from the Chief Learning Officer and their staff. In truth, however, there may be a significant amount of both overt, and covert, resistance to progression down the e-learning path. This resistance may stem from a number of different factors:

- Deep-seated experience with, and belief in, a classroom training orientation

- A professional skill-set focus on training administration and logistics for classroom training

- Resistance to change in organizational structure and reassignment on the part of existing training professionals

- Fear of technology and resistance to traversing a new and highly challenging learning curve

- Perception of lack of value-add from e-learning initiatives (similar to the management discussion above)

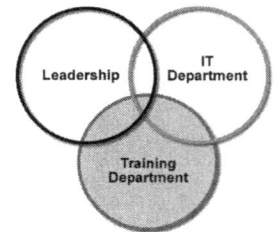

- Feelings of ownership and association with existing non e-learning programs

All of the above can culminate in a substantial fear of job-redundancy, and a lack of empowerment in the organization

Assuming that the rest of the department will be energized on the same wave of enthusiasm, e-learning proponents sometimes overlook activities and information that can help more reserved constituents feel more comfortable with e-learning initiatives, such as:

- Launching the e-learning initiative within the training and development department with an exciting demonstration of the potential of e-learning experiences and the new technologies your organization can utilize

- Providing access to a curriculum of e-learning design and development tutorials and modules for those training department staff not experienced in these skills

- Piloting a mini-version of the e-learning initiative within the training department, from the concept through to the marketing and communication associated with it, and solicitation of feedback from the group prior to full-scale rollout

- Investing the time to map existing training department capabilities and skills to the new skill set required by proposed e-learning initiatives; for example, expert classroom instructors typically make excellent live e-learning facilitators, with minimal additional training in the requisite technologies

Whatever the source, a lack of support on the part of the training organization can severely impact the success of any e-learning initiative. These individuals are the ones who need to be the most ardent supporters, and not cautious observers. In their enthusiasm to promote e-learning initiatives to the rest of the organization and top management, e-learning advocates and visionaries sometimes neglect the due diligence, marketing, and change management strategies that are needed within the training organization prior to any external rollout to ensure solid backing and support.

Perhaps the best, and most effective approach to solidifying training department support, is to maintain a focus in the overall Learning strategy on the importance of the blended learning model (see Chapter 4). E-learning initiatives alone are rarely 100 percent effective, without at least a backbone framework of classroom and live e-learning components. While the trend in the industry is certainly a substantial shift to a wealth of capabilities in e-learning, there will most certainly always be a need for more traditional approaches, and it is important to accommodate those skills in the training department strategy to be fully successful.

In the next chapter, we will look at the application of the blended model for learning design, which deliberately applies the best delivery mechanism of learning to the goals and objectives to be achieved.

Lessons Learned

✓ Align major e-learning initiatives with organizational strategy and business goals.

✓ Be creative in demonstrating value of e-learning initiatives; Evaluate the impact on the "Top Line", as well as the "Bottom Line."

✓ Reinforce the role of the Chief Learning Officer in the corporate investment planning process.

✓ Identify demonstrable success factors for your e-learning initiatives and be sure you have a well-supported measure for each factor.

✓ Ensure you have the right resources and tools to reach your goals; Do not over commit!

✓ Consider a high-visibility, highly strategic pilot initiative for your launch into the e-learning arena.

✓ Build a strategic partnership with IT and leverage the skills of both groups to make your e-learning technology choices a success.

✓ Communicate, communicate, communicate-at all levels in the organization; Celebrate successes and communicate them at all levels.

✓ Emphasize the importance of the training department in the rollout of the overall learning strategy, and clearly define the role of e-learning in that overall strategy.

CHAPTER

4

How Do You Design Blended Learning Programs?

The main themes for this chapter are:

- *What Have We Learned So Far?*
- *Designing Blended Learning Solutions*
- *Other Design Considerations*
- *What Is Next For Blended Learning?*

How Do You Design Blended Learning Programs?

The instructional designer today has a myriad of instructional methods, strategies, media, and deployment mechanisms available to create the ultimate learning experience. So many options in fact, that the choice can become overwhelming. Is the learning goal best supported by a classroom course or a series of self-paced e-learning modules? A case study, or a full blown simulation? A video clip, or graphics with text? A workshop, or a live e-learning session? Or what about a combination of self-paced e-learning modules, a classroom course, and a follow up live e-learning session?

Many organizations have successfully defined, designed, developed, and deployed such blended learning solutions. This blended approach supports the learning over time and designates or matches selected content to the mechanism that best supports the specific learning objective. This Chapter focuses on the design of these blended learning solutions and the practical lessons learned from organizations that are delivering blended learning programs to their employees.

What Have We Learned So Far?

In the world of e-learning, content is king. You will find that statement in most every book or article on the topic of e-learning. Expenditures for e-learning content far exceed the investments in technology and services. In the first wave of e-learning, most content consisted of quick, inexpensive, low-level, online learning design which produced e-reading page-turners-documents that were read online, with limited or no interaction and no dynamic exchanges. Learning materials were simply converted to online learning with little consideration of the difference between reading a book or manual, or viewing a PowerPoint presentation in a classroom with an instructor, and the self-paced, technology-supported opportunity posed by the e-learning capabilities available at that time.

An illustration of this is found in one global organization's early efforts in the design and delivery of an e-learning program were focused on the enterprise-wide launch of a complex curriculum. This initiative had an aggressive strategy and implementation timeline. A small team of subject matter experts and new e-learning designers and developers were asked to design, develop, review, test, and deploy over sixty hours of e-learning content in less than six months. Needless to say, not enough time and resources were dedicated to instructional design and the outcome was a very text-based, page-turner style learning program, comparable to the first generation of computer-based training (CBT) with the green screens. Every employee in the organization was mandated to take this e-learning program and completion was required to receive a high performance rating and a related increase in compensation. Thus, there was a 100 percent completion rate for the program. However, a number of the learners in this organization were disappointed in the experience, and hesitant afterwards to engage in future e-learning courses even though they have vastly improved in quality and approach.

> ### The Hartford's Advice on Designing e-Learning*
>
> "Develop high-quality, interactive programs to help overcome resistance with learners who may remember the "bad old days" of computer-based training. Use media judiciously and verify that all media is educationally appropriate and necessary."
>
> * See Chapter 12: The Hartford

A different extreme was seen in the design and development of Las Vegas style e-learning, including clever images, splashy, trendy graphics, and an animated .gif on each screen. The expensive development using the latest and greatest technology was the major selling point. Quality content that improved performance and changed behavior was secondary. Learners in the first wave who engaged in these types of e-learning programs have also been sorely disillusioned.

Lessons learned include the following:

- Content of an e-learning initiative must be valuable to the learner.
- Poorly designed e-learning content will discourage learners and make them resistant to taking future e-learning programs.
- Technological glitz cannot substitute for content.
- Underestimating the time and resources required to define, design, develop, and deploy high quality e-learning programs can negatively impact outcomes.

In the current wave of e-learning design, the focus is on both quality content and quality learning experiences. Learning leaders, consumers, and learners are demanding it. They require content that satisfies the business needs and learning objectives, that it is relevant and applicable, and that it also is engaging and fun.

Much has happened recently to improve the quality of the e-learning experience. To support standards of excellence in e-learning, the American Society for Training and Development (ASTD) has recently launched the ASTD Certification Institute, a certification program for e-learning courseware. Courses submitted are evaluated against a set of rigorous standards developed by the ASTD Certification Commission. To learn more, visit www.astd.org. Additionally, instructional designers have more experience and a better professional network to access for ideas and resources. Better tools and technologies are available to support the design and development of e-learning. Internet capabilities are more widely applied to support learning program deliveries. The technology infrastructure, including connection speed, is improving. In combination, all of these have contributed to a focus on blended learning models for e-learning.

Designing Blended Learning at Oracle Corporation*

"The original design process for converting the classroom materials to a blended format consisted of sitting down with a 'virtual cardboard box' of content from the classroom and reworking the materials. The team needed to decide what information, concepts, and skills must be covered in this limited face-to-face time. The result is that during a first week of training, students meet with instructors and their peers, learn basic concepts, and get started with basic skills, such as installing the software. The design team for the program was made up of one instructional designer and two instructors. We wanted to capture the instructor experience because the instructional components were of more interest to them than the content."

See Chapter 17: Oracle Corporation

Designing Blended Learning Solutions

Blended learning is the mix of learning strategies, methods, media, and delivery mechanisms which supports the learning objectives and maximizes the efficiency of the learning experience. Using all of the potential learning media over the continuum of time, place, and interactions, is more powerful than a single classroom event in truly impacting the learner and supporting their progress in achieving mastery of the content.

Given that the human aspects of learning have not changed, the e-enablement of learning offers an extension of the learning experience, allowing the learner to guide their own learning experiences to areas of need and interest, while giving them the length of time and frequency of application needed to develop the unconscious competence required for mastery of a concept or skill.

When incorporating e-learning elements into learning solutions, instructional designers have found that the best online learning incorporates the key attributes of the human dimensions of learning wherever possible by engaging the human senses, creating communities of learning, providing online coaching, and supporting a sense of the learning culture, and learning as a lifelong pursuit of excellence through every interaction.

The magic is in the BLEND. E-learning design excellence requires a deliberate, explicit choice of the right method for the level of learning desired. Success depends upon choosing the right mix of methods and media to create an effective and engaging learning experience.

Figure 4-1 offers a framework for designing blended learning. The first column states the purpose or goal for the learning. The remaining columns include sample delivery methods for meeting the goal. These delivery methods are categorized into three types:

- **Face-to-face:** When the instructor and participants are together in the same place at the same time.

- **Self-paced e-learning:** This is typically asynchronous learning, or collaboration where the learner is using technology but is not connected to other learners or instructors at the same time.

- **Live e-learning:** Using technology, the instructor and participants are together at the same time but are in different locations. This is also called synchronous learning.

Once the instructional designer has conducted audience and task/job analysis and has determined the high level objectives for the learning, they can start to explore the variety of delivery methods available. For example, in some organizations, the learning environment is focused primarily on using technology effectively to deliver high quality learning experiences. The classroom opportunities are limited by costs in both expense and time, so the current approach is to maximize the available face-to-face time for those learning experiences that benefit most from immediate interaction, such as:

- In-depth skill building

- Supporting application of the knowledge

- Practicing desired behaviors through role play with feedback

- Peer networking, action-planning, collaboration, and celebration

LEARNING GOALS	LEARNING DELIVERY METHODS		
	Face-to-Face	**Self-paced e-learning**	**Live e-learning**
Acquire Knowledge	• Classroom Presentations	• Self-Study Guides • Self-Paced e-Learning Modules • White Papers and Documentation • Recorded Live e-Learning Sessions	• Live e-Learning Classes
Practice	• Workshops with Application Practice • On-the-Job Training • Coaching and Mentoring	• Simulations • Games • Online Case Studies • Interactive e-Learning Modules	• Live e-Learning Classes with Application Exercises • Online Coaching and Mentoring
Assess Knowledge and Skill Acquisition	• Behavior Observation • Feedback on Activities/ Exercises • Paper-Based Tests	• Online Assessments	• Online Feedback and Assessments During Live e-Learning Classes
Collaborate	• Classroom Events Incorporating Networking, Action Planning and Discussion	• E-Mail • Bulletin Boards • Listservs • Online Communities of Practice	• Live e-Learning Sessions • Chats/Instant Messaging
Support and Reinforce	• Coaching and Mentoring	• Online Help and Expert Systems • Job Aids and Decision Support Tools • Online Knowledge Management Systems	• Online Coaching and Mentoring

Figure 4-1: Framework for Designing Blended Learning

The following are examples of blended learning solutions which include both the learning objectives and some recommended delivery methods.

The example in Figure 4-2 is commonly referred to as digital bookends, wrapping the classroom experience with online pre- and post-work.

A course that illustrates this approach is drawn from Deloitte Consulting's New Manager Program, which a senior consultant attends when they are promoted to manager. The objectives for this program are for the learner to participate in team-building exercises, to develop team leadership skills, to engage in performance coaching and counseling role plays with feedback, and to have the opportunity to network with senior Firm partners and leadership. The New Manager program is designed with digital bookends that include online pre-work for knowledge acquisition and post-work learning for performance support, while the face-to-face program emphasizes skill development and activities that promote Firm culture building, networking, sharing of project experiences, and celebration of the promotion.

Phases	Delivery Method	Learning Goal	Learning Approach
PHASE 1 ↓	Self-paced e-learning 	• Acquire knowledge and assess knowledge	• Read articles • Take self-paced e-learning modules • Take online self-assessments
PHASE 2 ↓	Face-to-face 	• Practice and collaboration	• Participate in role plays with feedback and group discussions
PHASE 3	Self-paced e-learning 	• Support performance	• Download job aids and decision support tools • Read additional reference material • Participate in discussion boards

Figure 4-2: Digital Bookend Blended Learning

The second example of a blended model provides a different approach for new manager or leadership development (see Figure 4-3). If a newly promoted manager needs to create a budget for the first time, he or she can take a self-study guide that outlines the company's requirements, expectations, and best practices for creating a budget. In Phase 2, the new manager is required to complete interactive learning modules, simulations, and games on various management and leadership topics, such as coaching, mentoring, and leading teams.

After each module or simulation, there is an online self-assessment to measure the knowledge and skills acquisition. In Phase 3, the learner is eligible to participate in live e-learning chats with experts and peers to discuss various leadership issues. Leveraging live e-learning technology is an excellent platform for expert discussions and presentations. Finally, the learner attends the classroom portion of the experience to participate in case studies, role plays, and group discussions. This approach is similar to the one used by IBM Corporation for their Basic Blue New Manager learning program.

The blended model shown in Figure 4-4 can be used for sales training. In Phase 1, the learner takes self-paced e-learning modules to learn about the company's products and services. A pre- and post-assessment is given to measure the learner's knowledge. One approach is to require the successful completion of the e-learning modules prior to moving to Phase 2. In Phase 2, the learner goes into the field with their sales manager or a more senior sales representative to observe and also to practice basic sales presentation skills. After completing Phase 2, the learner progresses to the classroom portion of the learning experience.

Phases	Delivery Method	Learning Goal	Learning Approach
PHASE 1	Self-paced e-learning	• Support performance	• Read self-study guides • Watch videos • Take self-paced e-learning module
PHASE 2	Self-paced e-learning	• Self-paced practice and assess knowledge and skills	• Take interactive self-paced e-learning modules, simulations, and games • Take online assessments
PHASE 3	Live e-learning	• Collaborate	• Participate in live e-learning chats with both experts and peers
PHASE 4	Face-to-face	• Practice	• Attend classroom session with participation in role plays, case studies, group discussions, peer-to-peer exchanges, and feedback

Figure 4-3: Another Blended Model Approach

In the classroom, the learner participates in hands-on application exercises using the products, role-play sales activities, and group discussions. After successfully completing an assessment, which is be either paper-based or online, the learner returns to the field to begin practicing new skills, under the guidance of their sales manager. After two weeks in the field and successful completion of a final exam, the learner is offered a full time sales position. This type of program effectively blends self-paced e-learning, practical field experience, classroom training, and manager feedback. The Black and Decker case in Chapter 13 uses a similar approach.

The blended model depicted in Figure 4-5 begins with a Web-enabled orientation to the learning program. During this time, the participants learn about each other, the goals for the program, engage in self-assessments and complete daily assignments, posting findings on the Web for threaded discussion and commentary by peers and coaches. In Phase 2, the cadre is brought together in a classroom to confirm learnings, engage in case studies, debrief self-assessments, and identify and launch a team project.

Phases	Delivery Method	Learning Goal	Learning Approach
PHASE 1	Self-paced e-learning	• Acquire knowledge and assess knowledge acquisition	• Take pre-test • Take self-paced e-learning modules • Take post test
PHASE 2	Face-to-face	• Practice	• On-the-job, apprenticeship training
PHASE 3	Face-to-face	• Practice, collaboration, and assess knowledge and skills	• Attend classroom session and participate in group discussions and hands-on application exercises • Take test
PHASE 4	Face-to-face	• Practice	• On-the-job training: perform tasks and receive one-on-one feedback and coaching from supervisor or mentor
PHASE 5	Self-paced e-learning	• Assess knowledge and skills acquisition	• Take online final exam

Figure 4-4: Blended Model Example for Sales Training

Black & Decker Corporation's Blended New Hire Program*

The original classroom course was 80 percent instruction using PowerPoint presentations, going over facts, figures, and market information. The remaining 20 percent was actually spent using the tools. The new course expertly blends e-learning, practical field experience, classroom training, and manager feedback, which all combined helps to quickly develop effective sales people. As a result, 80 percent of time is spent discussing and using the tools to build real life applications.

See Chapter 13: Black & Decker Corporation

Phases	Delivery Method	Learning Goal	Learning Approach
PHASE 1	Live & self-paced e-learning Online collaboration	• Acquire knowledge and network with peers and coaches	• Attend live e-learning session, post biography on a Web site, complete assignments in the field, post results, complete self-assessments
PHASE 2	Face-to-face Online collaboration	• Acquire knowledge and practice skills	• Case studies • Dialogue and discussion • Coaching and networking • Team project launch
PHASE 3	Live e-learning Online collaboration	• Apply knowledge and skills	• Participate in live e-learning sessions with experts
PHASE 4	Live e-learning Online collaboration	• Practice and collaborate	• Participate in a project with a virtual team
PHASE 5	Face-to-face Online collaboration	• Acquire and assess knowledge and collaborate	• Present team project and learn from expert feedback

Figure 4-5: Blended Model with Web-Enabled Orientation

In a virtual mode during Phase 3 and 4, the participants continue to learn via live e-learning sessions with subject matter experts. In addition, the participants work individually with coaches and together as virtual teams on the assigned project, applying the knowledge gained to business-focused challenges. Finally, in Phase 5, the participants present their project outcomes to a panel of company leaders for feedback and possible funding to move forward.

The Unilever Leaders into Action, found in Chapter 17, best exemplifies this approach.

Developing Leadership Competencies for an Aggressive Global Business Strategy*

To impact and basically change a leader's perspective and embedded way of doing things required a learning experience that extended over time and one which required skilled application of the learning to their work. It was determined that a continuum of leadership development was needed, a journey that combined individual growth and team-based business projects.

*See Chapter 15: Unilever

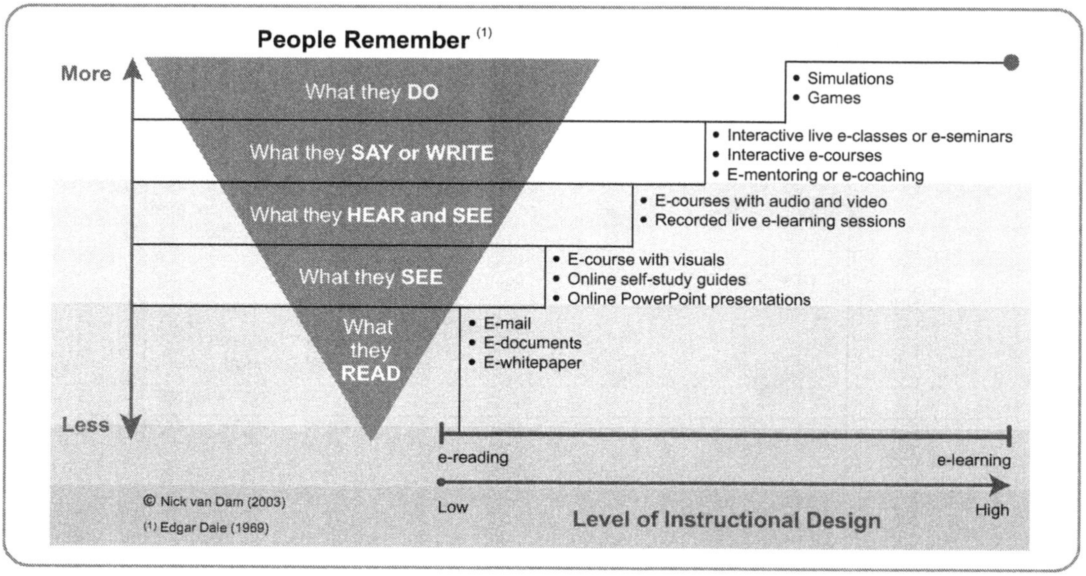

People Remember [1]

More — What they **DO**
- Simulations
- Games

What they **SAY or WRITE**
- Interactive live e-classes or e-seminars
- Interactive e-courses
- E-mentoring or e-coaching

What they **HEAR and SEE**
- E-courses with audio and video
- Recorded live e-learning sessions

What they **SEE**
- E-course with visuals
- Online self-study guides
- Online PowerPoint presentations

What they **READ**
- E-mail
- E-documents
- E-whitepaper

Less

© Nick van Dam (2003)
[1] Edgar Dale (1969)

e-reading   e-learning

Low   **Level of Instructional Design**   High

Figure 4-6: Online Learning Continuum

Other Design Considerations

In addition to the impact that content and desired delivery method have on design decisions, the instructional designer must also consider the:

- Level of learning desired

- Costs related to design, development, and deployment

- Time-to-market requirement

- Technological capabilities available to support the delivery

The level of learning desired drives many of the design decisions. The Online Learning Continuum in Figure 4-6 indicates some possible applications of e-learning methods that best support achieving different levels of learning.

As the instructional designer makes decisions about instructional methods and delivery mechanisms, it is also necessary to consider the amount of effort involved in developing the learning solution. As you move along the continuum from e-reading to e-learning, it is important to note that the degree of investment in instructional design may increase the further up you move. An online business simulation is a powerful learning tool. However, it is one of the most expensive to develop in terms of design capability, time, and resources.

The time, cost, and resources involved in defining, designing, developing, and deploying learning programs, particularly blended solutions, is an important consideration. In most of the literature development ratios can range from 80 to 200 hours of development for one hour of low level interactivity e-learning to 300 to 500 hours of development for one hour of high level interactivity e-learning. But do these estimates really include all of the instructional design and development activities?

Figure 4-7 is a typical instructional design model with sample tasks, resources, and an estimate of the percentages of time required to complete the tasks in each phase.

The maintenance cycle is not included in this model, as the level of effort varies depending on the evaluation feedback that is gathered. It may be necessary to go through the entire instructional design process again to make the requested updates.

Many of the organizations interviewed for this book do not track actual design and development times, and many claimed to have seriously underestimated the effort. To get a true estimate, make sure you consider the cost of time involved in the following:

- Project management
- Instructional design (including needs assessment, analysis, storyboarding)
- Subject matter expert input and reviews
- Development and authoring
- Quality review and user testing
- Revision time
- Deployment time (for example, entry into the learning management system and testing time)

PROCESS	TASK	ROLES	ESTIMATED TIME
Analysis	• Needs Assessment • Audience Analysis • Content Analysis • Course Outline	• Project Manager • Instructional Designer(s) • Subject Matter Experts	20-40%
Design	• Design interactions • Create storyboards • Develop assessments	• Project Manager • Instructional Designer(s) • Writers • Subject Matter Experts	20-40%
Development	• Author content in development tools • Conduct quality reviews • Conduct user testing	• Project Manager • Programmers • Graphic Artists • Writers • Editors	20-40%
Implementation	• Deploy content in LMS • Communicate availability of learning	• Project Manager • LMS Systems Administrator • Communications Specialists	10-20%
Evaluation	• Gather feedback	• Project Manager • Instructional Designers • SMEs	10-20%

Figure 4-7: Instructional Design Model for e-Learning Development and Deployment

Other questions that impact design include:

- What is the shelf life of the content?

- Do I want to invest significant time, money, and resources in developing a sophisticated e-learning simulation for something that will expire as soon as, or shortly after, it is developed?

- How stable is the content?

- If developing an interactive e-learning module for a particular subject area, where the content continually changes, how will it be brought to completion?

- How will the learning program be maintained?

Careful consideration and decision-making on design questions can often be restricted by a requirement for rapid deployment of the learning solution. Thus, an equally important issue is the 80/20 rule of balancing the need for quality, feature-rich content with time-to-market speed. Many times 80 percent of the learning is achieved and sufficient for the purpose, whereas achieving 100 percent of the learning objectives will require delays and extraordinary, and perhaps unnecessary, expense. Sometimes the art of instructional design plays a more important role in this type of decision-making.

> **INSEAD OnLine's Experience in e-Learning Design***
>
> Building content into quality, interactive, online e-learning takes a lot of time and is expensive, thus custom e-learning solutions require innovative blended models leveraging existing e-learning content.
>
> *See Chapter 15: INSEAD*

Another important issue that impacts the instructional design of a learning solution is how the learning will be deployed. Blended learning solutions may have special technical requirements in how the components are organized and sequenced in the learning management system (LMS).

Consider the following questions as early as possible in the design and development process:

- Is the learning solution one course or a program containing several courses? What is the best design for the overall navigation in a blended solution?

- How will the user access the learning program? If a learning management system is in place, how does the learner launch the course or program from the LMS? How will the learner track their progress through the learning program?

- What management tracking and reporting is required? Will the user be tracked as they order the course? Complete an assessment? Spend time in the course? This may require additional programming and testing to be completed during the development phase so that the courseware is AICC or SCORM compliant and interoperates with the learning management system.

- Will the content be available only online? What are the connection speeds for the intended audience? Will there be a requirement for CD-ROM distribution? Does the content need to be downloadable?

What is Next For Blended Learning?

The approaches to delivering learning are diverse and varied. However, for the best companies, it is no longer a question of whether to engage in e-learning as a method to deliver learning, but when to use e-learning. Typically, when the learning must be fast-paced, enterprise-wide and focused on strategic business objectives, e-learning is an integral component of the blended model.

A quick look into the future of Blended Model learning indicates that:

- There will be an increased use of internal subject matter experts, both in the development of content and in the delivery of the learning program.

- With experience, organizations are learning where the hidden costs of e-learning are found and are more able to include these explicitly in their budget projections.

- Increasingly, there will be a strategic contribution required from the learning, in the application of knowledge gained to real-time business problems.

- Blending design and delivery options maximizes the learning and allows an extended learning continuum, rather than a limited and individual event focus.

- As blended models become more popular, the learning management system will give way as the one and only end-to-end solution to a more effective holistic solution that includes HR management, learning and content management, and extends both internally and externally to suppliers and customers.

Companies need to take a hard look at their overall learning curriculum and approach, and deliberately use all the appropriate facets of the blended model to create a total learning environment. Many of the cases in this book provide best practices and ideas for designing blended learning solutions.

The ultimate goal is to meet learner expectations and requirements by converting classroom content to e-learning only where this conversion adds real value, by redesigning classroom experiences for high impact when face-to-face interactions are essential, and by ensuring that the online learning experience offered is dynamic, engaging, and fun.

In the next chapter, we will explore the technology that provides the platform for e-learning.

Lessons Learned

✓ A blended learning model often enables you to make maximum use of all resources while providing the most benefit to learners.

✓ The needs and context of the target audience must be well understood.

✓ Instructional design is key.

✓ Lecture-type material is best covered in self-paced or live e-learning sessions, not wasting valuable face-to-face time. This approach also maximizes the contribution of the subject matter experts.

✓ Blended solutions do not need to be a 50/50 split between classroom and e-learning. In some cases, it can be 20/80.

✓ A focus on quality deliverables promotes a positive first experience and prevents resistance to future e-learning programs.

✓ Don't underestimate the time and resources required to define, design, develop, deploy, and maintain effective e-learning and blended programs.

✓ Consider early in the design process the deployment strategy for your learning solution, as the deployment will have design and development implications.

CHAPTER

5

What Makes e-Learning Technology Work?

The main themes for this chapter are:

- *What are the Elements of an e-Learning Architecture?*
- *What e-Learning Technology Architecture Implementation Options Exist?*
- *What are the Challenges in Implementing an e-Learning Architecture?*
- *What Support and Maintenance Infrastructure is Required for e-Learning Technologies?*

What Makes e-Learning Technology Work?

Even the most creative and advanced e-learning strategy will ultimately fail, if it is not supported by a robust, well-architected technology strategy for the organization. IDC states that in 2003, Fortune 500 companies would lose US$31.5 billion due to inefficiencies resulting from substandard performance *and the inability to locate knowledge resources.* The ability to easily access rich, multimedia content at anytime, from anywhere, is of the utmost importance in today's knowledge-based economy.

Whether the organization chooses to build the technology backbone required for its e-learning strategy, or to outsource the required capabilities to an outside vendor, it is critical to understand the requirements of the enterprise, and to equally understand the capabilities that exist in the marketplace. Figure 5-1 provides an excellent example of the *marriage* that must be made between demand-the drivers that drive a particular strategy, and supply-the ever-evolving array of technology capabilities that must be provided to support that demand.

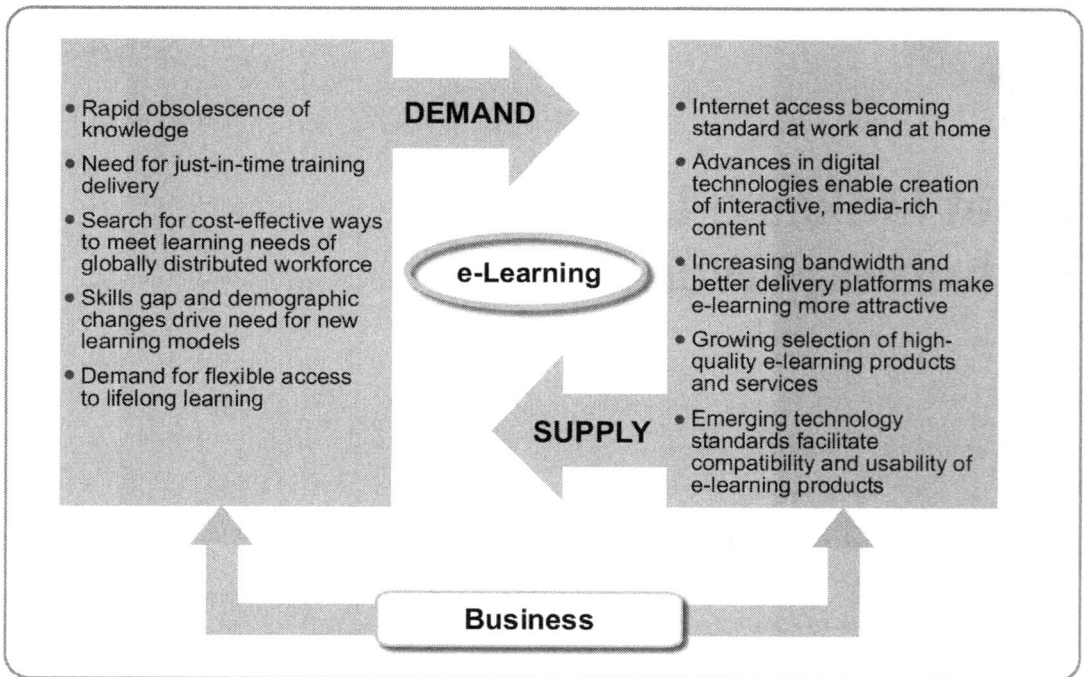

DEMAND

- Rapid obsolescence of knowledge
- Need for just-in-time training delivery
- Search for cost-effective ways to meet learning needs of globally distributed workforce
- Skills gap and demographic changes drive need for new learning models
- Demand for flexible access to lifelong learning

e-Learning

SUPPLY

- Internet access becoming standard at work and at home
- Advances in digital technologies enable creation of interactive, media-rich content
- Increasing bandwidth and better delivery platforms make e-learning more attractive
- Growing selection of high-quality e-learning products and services
- Emerging technology standards facilitate compatibility and usability of e-learning products

Business

Figure 5-1: e-Learning Drivers

The term *technology* typically refers to the integration of software, hardware, and connectivity components to facilitate the exchange of communications, learning, and knowledge in the organization. To build an integrated technology architecture that will optimally support your e-learning strategy, the technical functionality requirements associated with the processes and content included in the e-learning strategy must be evaluated and mapped to current offerings in the marketplace.

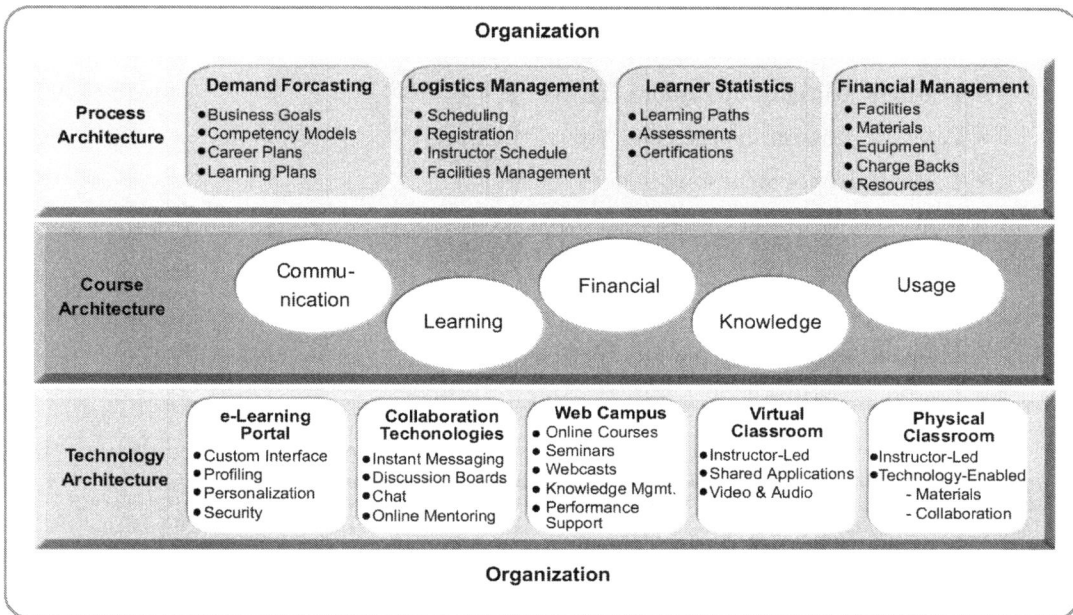

Figure 5-2: Learning Strategy Framework

Many of the enterprise gains from e-learning derive from the cost efficiencies gained through common processes, content, and organizational approaches which are facilitated by the technology architecture. One of the key opportunities in the next wave of e-learning will come from re-engineering learning processes within organizations to realize the benefits from investments in e-learning technologies.

When shaping the architecture for the e-learning technology framework, one also needs to take into consideration the architectural constraints of the overall enterprise technology strategy, which will help to drive the *build-versus-buy* decision in the technology area.

Most progressive e-learning strategies require an *open*, or non-proprietary, architecture, which allows additional process, content, and technology components to be easily added from multiple vendors with overall ease of integration. In addition, the overall framework should include standards for integrating existing elements, such as previously developed content, enterprise applications such as financial or human resource systems, and self-paced and live e-learning components, as well as emerging tools and new content.

What Are the Elements of an e-Learning Architecture?

There is currently a wide range of technology-based products and content-based solutions available in the e-learning market. As the e-learning industry continues to evolve, so too will this portfolio of products and services. However, there are a few generally accepted categories of products which will be addressed in this chapter.

We refer to an integrated view of e-learning architecture as an organization's e-learning *landscape* (see Figure5-3). The key components include:

- Learning management systems (LMS)
- Learning content management systems (LCMS)
- Content development tools
- Collaborative learning tools
- Live e-learning (synchronous) tools
- Assessment tools
- Human Resource Information Systems (HRIS)
- Learning portals

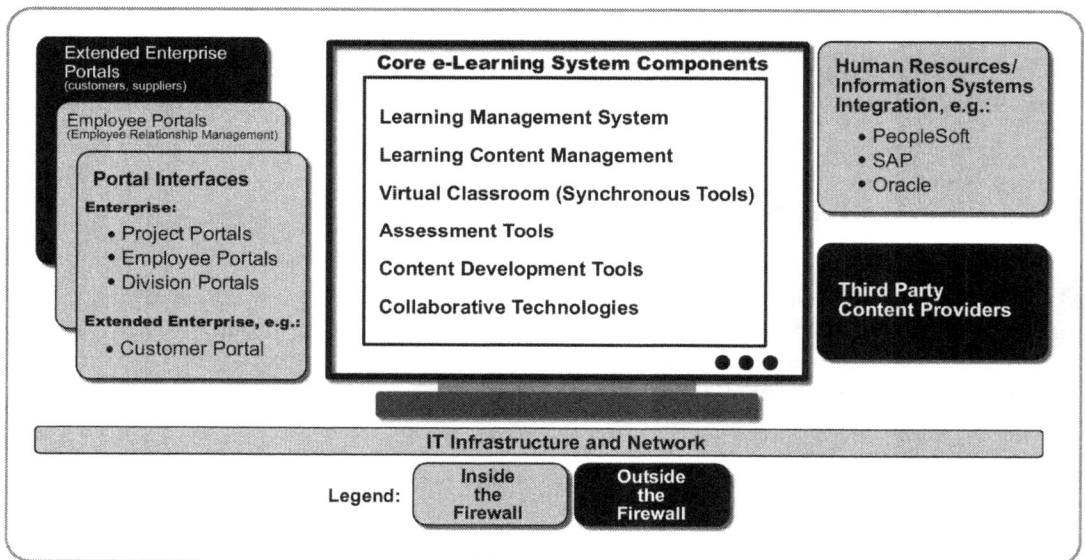

Figure 5-3: Core and Integrated Components of the e-Learning Landscape

Learning Management System (LMS)

Learning management systems provide end users with a single point of access to disparate learning objects and components (see Figure 5-4).

The learning management system is designed to support the management of learner performance by tracking progress and performance across all types of learning activities. It also has functionality for management, administration, and measurement of learning. Typical functions and processes supported by an LMS include:

- Managing courses and course registration
- Tracking student registration, access, and progress
- Managing course information

Figure 5-4: Content Accessed Via the Learning Management System

- Course scheduling and administration including instructors and physical facilities
- Reporting

From a technical perspective, the LMS is the software that links together and integrates all the other software components that make up the technical solution, integrating also with existing Enterprise Resource Planning (ERP) applications, such as financials and human resources. The LMS provides two fundamental capabilities:

- *Learner self-management*, access, and administration of self-paced e-learning, virtual classroom, and classroom-based learning and support

- *Training administration,* including training records and curriculum management; course publishing, tracking, and reporting; and competency management

An LMS ideally provides functionality to manage events ranging from classroom-based instruction, to offline media such as CD-ROM, and online e-learning. Most, however, have a clear area of focus and capabilities in a subset of these areas. For example, an LMS initially developed for management of classroom training will include more functionality around the management of physical training assets, including classrooms, course materials, instructors, and other types of inventory. An LMS initially developed for administration and assignment of e-learning components will include less, or sometimes no functionality, for managing physical facilities, but will provide a much more extensive array of services for tracking access to content and launching content, and will accommodate Web-based, network-based, or CD-ROM-based content. A key factor in determining the right LMS for the enterprise is the portfolio of content platforms that must be supported by the technology architecture.

While Saba, THINQ, Click2learn, Docent, and Vuepoint are perhaps the most prominent *best-of-breed* LMS providers, other successful entrants into this technology space include Anlon, Integrity eLearning, IntraLearn, Avaltus Jupiter Suite, KnowledgePlanet, Knowledge Solutions (UK), Pathlore, and WBT Systems.

Today a major decision is whether to integrate *best-of-breed* e-learning packages, or to utilize the emerging learning applications and solutions which are part of enterprise and infrastructure application suites. Over the past two years, the leading enterprise software companies, including SAP, PeopleSoft, Oracle Corporation, Siebel, and Sun Microsystems have introduced significant applications covering a range of learning management and content management capabilities. For companies with an enterprise software platform, especially in the human resources (HR), portal, and infrastructure areas, serious consideration should be given to these learning applications.

These solutions are designed to integrate with the HR, information systems (IS), and finance systems, as well as with the core underlying technology infrastructure. Since 2000, the leading enterprise software companies have accelerated their investments in these offerings including acquisitions of smaller e-learning technology players. This consolidation and the role of enterprise software companies in the learning technology market will continue and become more critical for larger companies as integration, maintenance, and support increase in importance.

A key consideration in selecting an LMS provider may also be the organization's ability to deliver the LMS using an *application service provider* (ASP), which uses secure networks to provide LMS capabilities to small and mid-size firms. Some firms choose an ASP-based LMS solution rather than investing in their own infrastructure, frequently for reasons of cost. Among the many e-learning companies to develop ASP offerings and host LMS and content are Generation 21 Learning Systems, Saba Software, Inc., and THINQ Learning Solutions, Inc. An ASP solution may provide a welcome alternative to organizations whose existing technology infrastructure and bandwidth cannot support the technical requirements of a more traditionally hosted LMS.

Learning Content Management Systems (LCMS)

Most well-crafted, blended learning programs with e-learning components typically consist of a set of sequentially assembled smaller learning objects, such as those shown in Figure 5-3. Organizations with an interest in creating well-designed blended learning programs would be well advised to explore the capabilities of learning content management systems. The LCMS provides authors with the ability to locate existing learning objects, create new learning objects, and assemble them into standards-compliant e-learning courseware.

According to Stephen Downes, faculty member of the University of Alberta, the LCMS typically contains four essential features: an authoring application; a collection of learning objects (called a *repository*); a means of sending the completed course to a delivery system (called a *delivery interface*); and administration tools.

The advent of the LCMS is much more recent than that of the LMS, but is gaining significant press and attention for those organizations attempting to build a common and centralized repository of learning content that can be shared and accessed by both the designers and learners. The ability to decompose traditional learning objects/programs into *tagged* metadata categories, and to reuse that content for multiple audiences and subject areas, is very compelling for sophisticated e-learning providers.

The LCMS stores online learning content in a central learning object repository as objects, which are managed primarily in the form of XML. These objects are often delivered on the basis of a learner profile, thus enabling highly personalized, *just-for-me* learning. These learning objects are provided to the learner in a composite format on a just-in-time basis to address a specific learning need, and permit reusability across various learning interventions, ranging from online to offline, and from self-paced to collaborative learning.

Learning Portals

A Learning Portal is not a specific product, but rather a concept to consider in the content access strategy, as it provides a coherent access point to a wide array of learning information and services. Typically, these portals are used to organize information on a specific topic or area of interest, and may include significant variety in their content. It is critical for learners to be able to easily locate content and/or have content presented to them. Typically a learning portal will include course catalogs, course registration, assessment and feedback mechanisms, instructional support, and learner forums, such as communities, bulletin boards, and chat.

Many organizations have set up their own internal learning portals for employees and customers, using the LMS as a base. These are termed *business-to-employee* (B2E) portals. These portals enable the organization of the plethora of information available on the Internet and on company intranets. Similar to the LCMS, most sophisticated portals include the capability to profile the intended audience, and to push information and content to the user population based on their personal and organizational interests, thus providing more strategic mapping of learning content to the appropriate audiences.

Learning portal technologies are also frequently embedded in LMS and LCMS product offerings. Using those products, "hierarchies" of portals may be developed at different levels to provide a more extensive structure for the dissemination of knowledge and learning content.

The next wave of learning portals will focus on the integration of learning as part of larger employee performance and employee relationship management (ERM) solutions. Learning is part of a large suite of content and services which need to be integrated to increase employee performance, as was described at the conclusion of Chapter 1.

Collaborative Learning Tools

Collaborative learning tools are technologies which support learning through the exchange and sharing of information and knowledge among learners. These tools support the principles of collaborative e-based learning though real-time document sharing and editing, discussion forums, brainstorming and idea generation, multimedia documents and group productivity. Various studies show that learners who work in collaborative groups appear more satisfied with their learning. As Curtis Bonk, faculty member at the University of Wisconsin, points out: *"Communication and conversation are among the keys to learning."*

Paul Stacey, business developer for the eLearning Innovation Centre (eLINC) at Simon Fraser University, sees *peer-to-peer* learning within an extended online learning community as the "killer app" of e-learning, enabling *"peers to explore, discuss, and access experiences with others who share a common interest or background. The resulting learning goes far deeper than anything we ever experienced in a classroom or lecture hall."*

Bonk argues that collaborative learning tools will play a significant role in the expansion of e-learning, and are thus a critical part of design of the learning technology infrastructure. The most common examples include e-mail, instant messaging, whiteboards, bulletin boards, breakout rooms, online surveys, online file transfer capability, chat lines, online presentation tools and mentoring capabilities.

While many vendors are scrambling to enter this highly popular field, WebEx, Centra, and PlaceWare are currently some of the most significant providers of collaboration software products. In addition to these companies, who concentrate primarily on these e-learning software technologies, many of the major e-learning content providers and LMS providers (best-of-breed and enterprise software companies) are also known to offer many of these types of software products and capabilities as integrated complements to their courseware offerings.

Human Resource Information Systems (HRIS)

Many Human Resource Information Systems, such as SAP, PeopleSoft, and Oracle, are implemented to support not only the storage of personnel information and the management of benefits and payroll activities, but also to support competency and performance profile functionality.

These systems are often the primary source used to populate active directories which facilitate integrated access to all other downstream systems, such as a LMS. By linking the LMS and the HRIS systems, the ability to target learning to a learning customer is greatly enhanced. The ability to profile each learning customer's learning goals and needs, and to push learning out to them is a powerful aid in providing just-in-time learning to the employee base.

This capability, however, comes at a significant cost. To effectively map the HRIS to the downstream learning systems, most organizations must undertake fairly extensive capability and competency mapping initiatives to identify key competency and capability requirements by role and level unique to their own organizations. While many HRIS providers can provide a standard *deck* as part of their products/services, to use those decks effectively, substantial resources will be required to map those capabilities to organizational strategies and business priorities; and then to map the resulting set of capabilities to knowledge and learning offerings available to the end user.

Live e-Learning Tools

Today, learners of all ages, from preschool through university and beyond in the corporate environment, are participants in learning programs that are delivered over computer networks.

Live e-learning, also frequently termed synchronous, marries the beauty and benefits of classroom learning with the sophisticated technologies available through Internet technologies. Live instructors have the ability to engage groups of students in multiple geographic locations and time zones simultaneously, while eliminating the cost of travel and accommodations for the learner. These virtual classrooms are increasingly replacing physical classroom training, as more and more vendors provide increasingly advanced features and functions to enhance the attractiveness of the overall learner experience. Students have the ability to raise their *virtual* hands, ask questions, chat, and share their own documents and deliverables, often never leaving the comfort of their home office or learning studio.

Most live e-learning technology providers have developed products that include capabilities to:

- Manage group discussions
- Facilitate small group breakouts
- Share applications
- Conduct pre-, ad-hoc, and post-assessments
- Explore intranet and Internet Web sites
- Provide handouts
- Conduct private and public chats
- Prepare and edit recordings of the session for those unable to attend live sessions
- Offer voice over IP
- Provide one- or two-way video

Most live e-learning products are designed to run over a standard Web browser and make use of its Java capabilities for various functions, with the majority designed to operate on either of the two dominant browser platforms.

Examples of major live e-learning providers include: Centra, Interwise, PlaceWare, Lotus, Mentergy, and WebEx. Each of these providers provides a very different set of capabilities, and selection of the appropriate live e-learning vendor is highly dependent on the specific functionalities important to the organization's e-learning strategy.

Content Authoring Tools

Programs that help to prepare content for multimedia delivery are called authoring tools. There are several authoring tools designed specifically for e-learning. These tools enable non-programmers to create a learning program by linking together objects such as animations, audio, and graphics, by defining the objects' interrelationships and by sequencing them in an appropriate order. A rich set of features also offers programmers the ability to quickly develop engaging interactivity. Course designers who use authoring tools can produce attractive and useful learning content.

The most prevalent vendors in this area include Macromedia (Authorware and Flash) and Click2Learn.

Other general purpose content authoring software of interest to e-learning designers includes: HTML packages (Dreamweaver and Frontpage); animation tools (Flash and Shockwave); 2D and 3D illustration packages (Adobe Illustrator and Photoshop, and 3D Max); and video tools (RealPlayer, Windows Media Player, and Quicktime).

Again, the critical success factor in evaluating various options in the content authoring tools arena is to review the content strategy of the organization, and to then map that strategy to the tool portfolio and functions available in the industry, as well as to the embedded capabilities that may already be available through existing vendor content or technology relationships.

Assessment Tools

e-Learning assessment tools help to analyze learner capabilities, progress and knowledge, and can ensure a uniform learning standard across the modern global organization.

According to Academy Internet (see Figure 5-5), assessment tools provide functionality to support:

- Pre-course assessment: Testing what is known before the learning experience
- Post-course assessment: Testing what has been learned during the learning experience

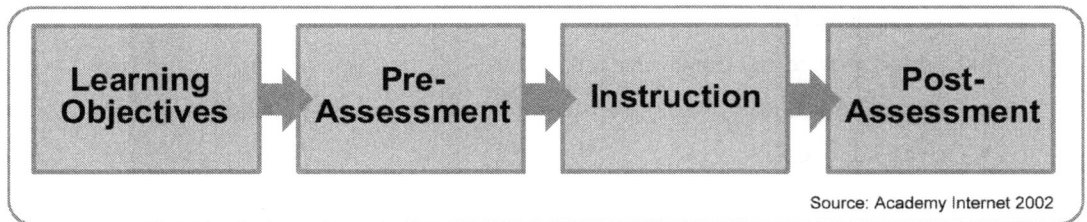

Source: Academy Internet 2002

Figure 5-5: e-Learning Assessment Model

Academy Internet cites that pre-assessment testing results can be used *"to model an adaptive learning path"* for a specific learning customer by using an LCMS to aid in identifying and compiling learning content applicable only to that learner.

Assessment capabilities and tools are important; however, there are a number of assessment tools available through LMS, LCMS, or authoring tool portfolios, which are designed to work with those tools to track the progress and course completions of the learner. The critical decision point for most organizations is to evaluate the robustness of the assessment tools, which are already embedded in their existing technology products/vendors/options, and to evaluate any additional assessment functionality that is not already included in that product suite. For example:

- Can the tool handle the insertion of graphics?
- Does it have the ability to compose different types of questions (multiple choice, free text, true/false) pulling from a bank of questions?
- Is it able to give weight to the questions?

An example of an assessment provider is Question*mark* Perception.

An emerging trend in the industry is that top LMS/LCMS providers are delivering complete solutions that include: learning management, learning content management, live e-learning, competency management, authoring tools, assessment, and reporting and tracking capabilities. (Examples are: Docent, Saba and Vuepoint.)

What e-Learning Technology Architecture Implementation Options Exist?

While the process and content requirements associated with the enterprise learning strategy should definitely drive the development of the optimal technology architecture, there are many other factors that should drive the selection of the optimal implementation strategy for that architecture (see Figure 5-2). Once functional requirements and content composition have been finalized, prioritized technological components and capabilities should be identified and mapped against content and process strategy.

There are a number of different options for supporting various technology infrastructure components:

- Internally hosted solution
- Externally hosted solution or Application Service Provider (ASP) model
- Combination of internal and external hosted solutions

Internally Hosted Solution

Figure 5-6 depicts an internally hosted model. By interfacing with the HR system employee information is given for single sign-on to systems, as well as data on geographies and job roles. The LMS houses the content and provides a single access point for end users. It also tracks and records their learning progress.

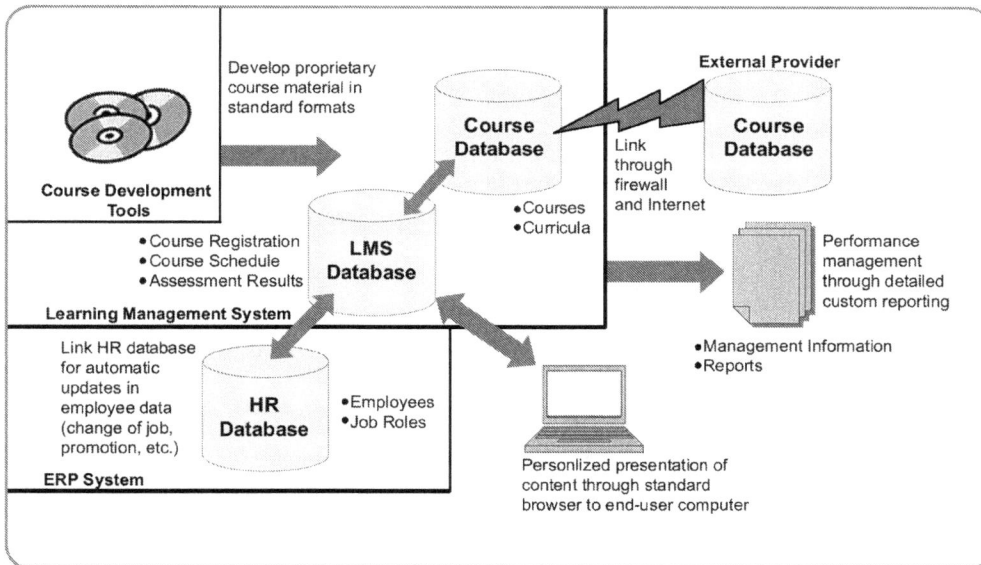

Figure 5-6: e-Learning Technology Infrastructure Solution for an Internally Hosted Model

Benefits of the internally hosted e-learning model include:

- Direct control over timelines for upgrades and changes to the system
- Ensured confidentiality of information and security of content
- Single point of contact with vendors
- Global changes to the provider's site do not impact your system or users
- Consistent quality assurance procedures for all system components
- Avoids lengthy *build* processes and longer response time to problems
- Avoids reliance on vendor performance, which may be inconsistent and/or subject to vendor financial/environmental issues, particularly for shorter term contracts

Some benefits of outsourcing versus a totally internally hosted solution include:

- Outsourcing to a vendor allows the company to concentrate on core business activities and frees up resources to respond faster to other market opportunities.

- Outsourcing to a vendor can be beneficial when qualified resources are not available in-house or internal staff is unable to meet deadlines.

- Outsourcing to a vendor can ensure access to new skills and the latest technologies without having to go through an extensive and expensive hiring or retooling process.

- Many vendors have significant best practices and experiences in these areas, from which most organizations would benefit.

- A better ROI is possible by shortening the overall project lifecycle.

Externally Hosted Solutions (ASP Model)

If you do not currently have an extensive learning infrastructure in place, you may want to consider a vendor-hosted solution that provides immediate access to an online technology platform and/or learning content repository. You may choose to outsource individual functions and features to an external provider; or you may choose to outsource the entire architecture.

Application Service Providers (ASPs) are becoming more popular if you need to offer significant e-learning capabilities in a relatively short time-frame. These are third-party entities that manage and distribute software-based services and solutions to customers across a wide-area network from a central data center.

Benefits of an externally hosted solution include:

- Faster implementation timelines, as most vendors have prescribed, well-tested infrastructure capabilities

- Less reliance on internal resources to implement and support the final solution; outsourcing allows the enterprise to increase their development capacity and offer newer products and services without increasing the in-house staff

- Outsourced solutions may actually provide a higher level of control over operating costs. Most typical vendor agreements clearly spell out expenses, removing the guesswork when it comes to expenses.

- Internal learning teams can benefit significantly from working with experienced vendor team; through this learning process, internal resources will gain proficiency, and may be capable of absorbing additional roles and responsibilities over time

However, there are also challenges posed by this approach, including:

- Changes to the global external site may impact your internal technology environment.
- If the vendor technology is down, you are down.
- The vendor drives the timelines for changes.
- You must rely on the vendor's support structure.
- The vendor may not grow in a direction compatible with your business.

Combination of Internally and Externally Hosted Solution

Perhaps the optimal, and most acceptable, solution for most organizations is to adopt a blended approach to technology implementation. With a blended solution, part of the technology infrastructure (specific functions) will be hosted internally and others will be provided externally. A few examples of this strategy might include:

- LMS and content externally created and hosted, but HRIS functionality internally hosted
- Content internally developed and created, but hosted on external vendor servers
- Some content internally developed, other provided by vendors, some hosted on internal servers, and other hosted externally

There are a myriad of possibilities here. In reality, the crux of the challenge here is to identify those functions and capabilities that you have the capability of doing well, and to outsource those that you do not. One example of such a strategy is shown in Figure 5-7.

The benefits of this blended solution include:

- It allows access to a wide variety of courseware.
- The vendor tracks progress for you.
- Automatic progress and catalog feeds can be established.
- Integration is not necessary, which reduces development and support time.

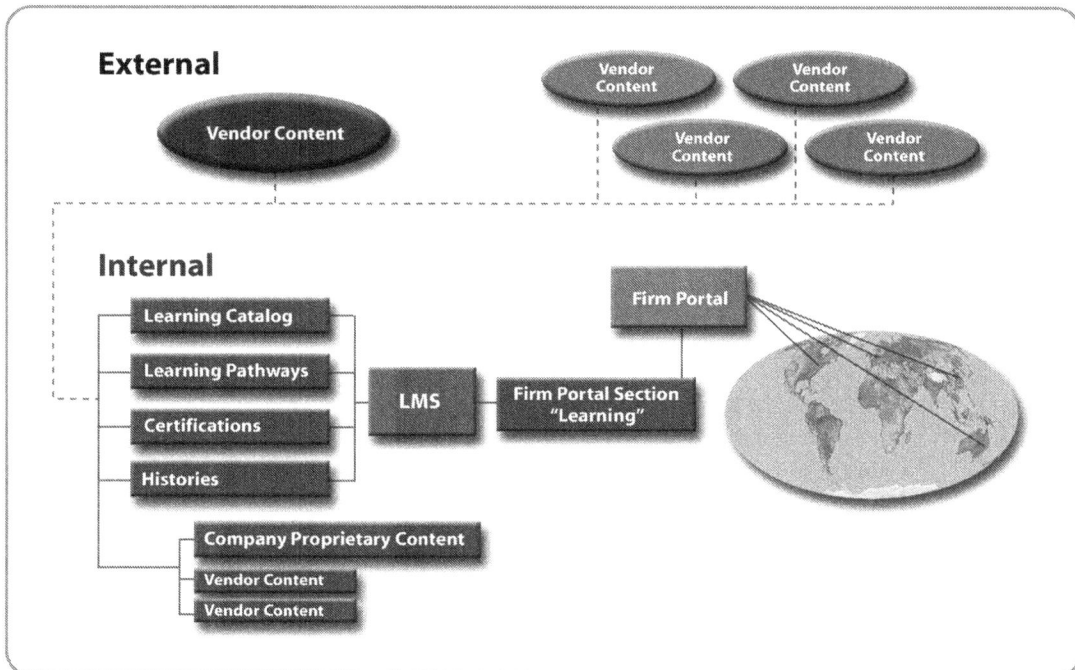

Figure 5-7: Combination of Internally- and Externally-Hosted Infrastructure Components

However, there are challenges, such as:

- Sufficient staff time must be dedicated to managing the vendors.

- Any integration with feeds must be monitored for failure as well as maintained.

- You are reliant on the vendor, and the work is according to their timeline.

What Are the Challenges in Implementing an e-Learning Architecture?

Integration of Systems

If your company does not have a technology backbone strategy in place for systems—one Enterprise Resource Planning (ERP) system for all needs—then an integration project will be necessary.

A complete solution must be considered to ensure success. A complementary and diverse combination of resources with systems-expertise and project management is required, as no individual or team can create the entire product or solution in isolation. Many sub-project efforts may be required, with a comprehensive plan to link all of the sub-projects into the final architecture.

Clarity of Functional Requirements

Understanding your organization's needs from a functional perspective will drive the e-learning architecture you put in place. To assure that your functional capabilities meet current *and* future needs, it is important to actually capture your understanding of these requirements in a detailed requirements document. It is critical to gain input and agreement on these requirements from the CLO level to the system administrator level. There are several areas to address in functional requirements definition, including, but not limited to: user experience, tracking and reporting requirements (see Chapter 6), organization structure, complexity of learning offerings, and accessibility.

Development and Integration of New Processes

This is an area that can easily be overlooked or delayed as you focus on systems implementation, but this is definitely not the approach to take for a successful implementation. It is essential to define your learning processes in the areas of demand forecasting, logistics management, learning management, and financial management. It is also critical to determine roles and responsibilities as you look at each of the newly defined processes.

Examples of process questions to ask include:

- Are learners able to self-select learning, or is it management directed?

- What is the relationship between learning and job performance assessment, compensation, or promotion?

- How is the budget for learning managed? Are there chargeback processes in place? Are they consistent through the enterprise?

- Are there different HR models for learning?

- Who approves e-learning attendance?
- What are the requirements for tracking and reporting?
- What current business processes are in place that must be supported by your technology solution?

Integrate e-Learning Courseware

If an LMS is in place, it will require underlying databases for recording and tracking activity.

The scale and mode of access will dictate whether these can be small local environments or high-end, enterprise-class systems. User and course data also needs to be integrated into HR or ERP environments. For example, a training catalog and registration system managed through an LMS may contain cost information that needs to be passed on to internal financial systems, and user information will need to be integrated with HR systems. The LMS may also contain varying degrees of workflow and triggering functionality for managing registration and administration processes.

To simplify the detailed tracking of online courses, registrations, score results, and similar data, standards have been developed that ensure that the LMS can interact in a standard manner with the vendor e-learning modules you have selected, whether these are computer-based training (CBT) or Web-based training (WBT).

It is important to have a standardized definition of the components and architecture of learning systems, as well as standardized interfaces among them, to ensure that:

- Re-usable content is of higher value, and greatly increases the incentive to develop educationally effective learning materials of professional quality.
- Content developed for one learning management system can be ported seamlessly to another.
- Limited or no restrictions exist with regard to compliance specifications for those companies who do large procurement of e-learning content.

These current standards are referred to as the AICC standards. (The *Airline Industry CBT Consortium,* formed in 1988 to standardize hardware used for training in the airline industry, has subsequently also moved into the standardization of learning management systems.)

New and more comprehensive standards are being developed by the IMS (Instructional Management System) project, a coalition of corporate, academic, and government partners originating from the 1997 EduCom *National Learning Infrastructure Initiative.* IMS' vision is to create a comprehensive open architecture and infrastructure for learning technologies (IMS 2000).

Another specification being widely used is Shareable Content Object Reference Model (SCORM) released on January 31, 2000. SCORM is a set of interrelated technical specifications built upon the work of the U.S. Department of Defense (DOD), AICC, IMS and Institute of Electrical and Electronic Engineers (IEEE) to create one unified content model.

Although all these technical specifications can be overwhelming, if tracking and reporting to stakeholders and learners is a business requirement, then a process for integrating or tracking the courseware must be established. Work with your Information Technology department to establish test platforms for new and existing content. Establish standard questions for vendors on their courseware, how it is developed, and the compliance they have achieved on AICC and SCORM. The technology infrastructure and system choices you have made will determine the specific focus of these questions.

If the content cannot be incorporated into an automated tracking process such as an LMS would provide, then establish a business process whereby the learner records and reports their results to learning administrators to register. If the content is hosted externally, then it will be necessary to explore what kind of tracking your vendor provides, and the types of reports that will be available about the use of the courseware as well as completions.

What Support and Maintenance Infrastructure Is Required for e-Learning Technologies?

As shown in Figure 5-8, there are three types of support required for learning systems:

- Technical
- Functional
- End User

Technical support can either be provided in-house or outsourced.

Application administration is generally provided by the IT department. This includes hardware such as servers, software installation set up, and maintenance of the appropriate databases. Other functions include upgrading the software to the latest version and transferring customizations, as

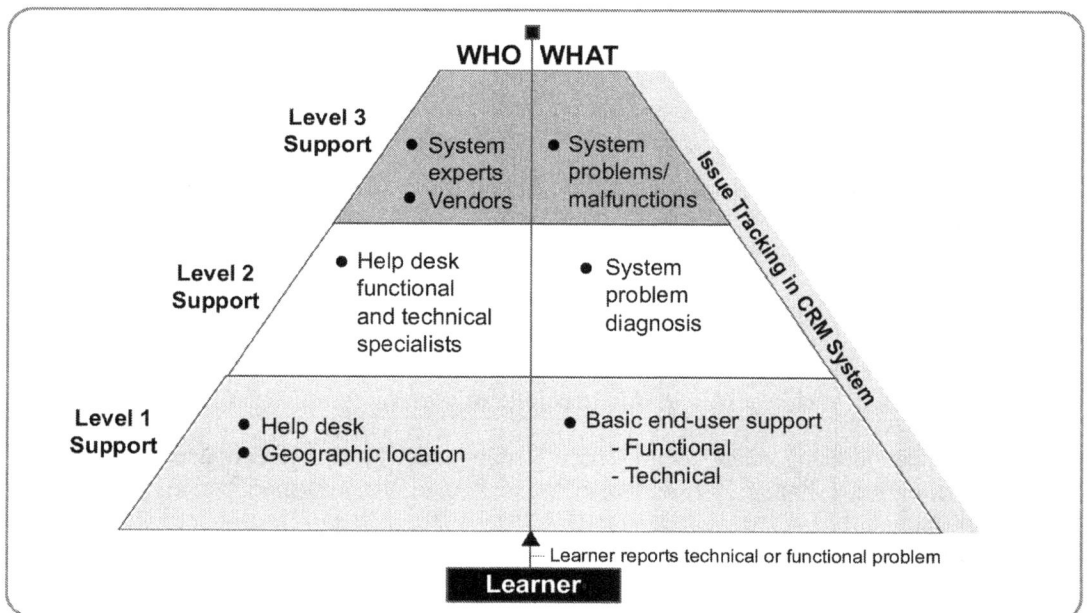

Figure 5-8: Three Levels of Technical Support for Learners

well as applying *patches and fixes*. Functional administration relates to the system itself and is generally handled by the department that *owns* the software.

As part of the support network, consider processes for evaluation of upgrades and timing, escalation paths and support systems to log issues for trend recognition.

Putting in place a SPOC (single point of contact) support capability—a one-on-one learning customer response system for handling e-learning related problems, questions, and inquiries—is essential. End-user support should be provided by a help-desk network. For successful approaches to forming a partnership with the IT department see Chapter 3.

It can be damaging if issues are logged at first level support, such as a help desk, and not appropriately escalated. Adequate training for all support levels will help to prevent this.

In the next chapter, the methods for measuring results of e-learning initiatives will further amplify how the data collected through these systems can support the business case for e-learning.

Lessons Learned

✓ Partner early with IT, HR, business, and operations departments for support and assistance

✓ Plan for an e-learning landscape by focusing on integration challenges (such as from learners/demand to e-learning applications to training content/supply)

✓ Leverage enterprise software platforms and balance with the capabilities and integration of best-of-breed applications

✓ Document and review existing business processes

✓ Compose a clear statement of work and manage it closely

✓ Define clear roles and responsibilities for the project

✓ Consider and evaluate all options with regard to your business needs

✓ Develop a clear communications plan

✓ Consider change management and the barrier it can represent

6

Does e-Learning Have a Credibility Problem?

Does e-Learning Make Business Sense?

What Gains the Commitment of People That Matter?

How Do You Design Blended Learning Programs?

What Makes e-Learning Technology Work?

How Do You Measure e-Learning Initiatives and Results?

What Does It Take to Work Successfully with Vendors?

What Motivates People to Engage in e-Learning?

How Do You Launch e-Learning to a Global Workforce?

Business Alignment

Design & Development

Deployment

How Do You Measure e-Learning Initiatives and Results?

The main themes for this chapter are:

- *Why Track e-Learning?*
- *What Can Be Tracked in e-Learning?*
- *Laying the Foundation for Tracking and Reporting*
- *Designing and Building Reports*

How Do You Measure e-Learning Initiatives and Results?

When embarking on the journey of e-learning, one of the most important steps is to track, measure, and report the e-learning activity. There are a myriad of items demanding attention, from building curricula through buying or building content, to constructing the infrastructure to make the content available to the intended audience. However, the important data, derived from accurate tracking and the related preparation of strategic and informative reports, drives the engine that supports ongoing improvement of e-learning initiatives, validates the business case, and engenders support for the overall effort.

If you have offered classroom learning and tracked data related to those activities, you are very familiar with the type of basic information that is collected. You may assume that much of what was collected and reported on in instructor-led training (ILT) will be applicable to e-learning. You may also assume that you will be able to implement your tracking and reporting strategy quickly and painlessly. As you start the process, it soon becomes clear that while there are some similarities to measuring classroom learning, there is much more that needs to be considered when measuring success with your e-learning strategy.

Why Track e-Learning?

There are numerous reasons for tracking and reporting e-learning, many of which are driven by the enterprise learning strategy and the role that e-learning plays in that strategy. Several examples illustrate why this information can be so critical.

- Measurements from online assessments and certification examinations provide evidence that employees are developing skills critical to the organization, such as improving customer service, fast launch of new products and services, application of new systems and business processes, sales force knowledge of products and services, and leadership development.

- Data on e-learning course completions can indicate that employees are in compliance with legal and regulatory mandates, as seen in the healthcare and accounting professions.

- Income generated as a result of customer and partner use of e-learning can be tracked.

- e-Learning usage can provide market intelligence, for example indicating which e-learning courses are used by potential customers.

- Data applicable to performance management can provide information used in year-end evaluations and discussions between manager and employee regarding development needs.

- Information on e-learning courses linked to organization competencies provides insights for human capital management and identifies competency gaps.

- Usage data can provide justification for the investment in e-learning courseware and/or infrastructure.

- Evaluation data can validate the effectiveness and efficiency of e-learning compared with a classroom learning approach.

What Can Be Tracked in e-Learning?

When considering what to measure in e-learning, you might find that you have more questions initially than you have answers. It is important to gain clarity on the answers you will require later to identify the types of questions you need to ask. These questions will provide the information required for the creation of a variety of reports.

While this chapter is on tracking and reporting of e-learning, it is strongly recommended to approach tracking with a long term goal of measuring business impact and return on investment (ROI).

e-Learning Evaluation Questions at The Hartford *

1. The course was informative.

2. The course met my expectations.

3. The pace was appropriate.

4. The training was appropriate for someone in my position.

5. I will apply what I learned at my work place.

6. I would recommend an online course to my friends/colleagues/acquaintances.

7. The course content and activities were appropriately engaging.

8. The course was easy to move through.

9. The objectives of the course were achieved.

Scale utilized: 1. Strongly Disagree, 2. Disagree, 3. Neutral, 4. Agree, 5. Strongly Agree.

*See Chapter 12: The Hartford Company

Figure 6-1 shows the five levels of e-learning evaluation recommended Donald Kirkpatrick and Jack J. Phillips. In addition, Level 0 (zero), e-Learning Participation, has been added as a **new level**. This chapter will focus primarily on Levels 0 through 4, as Level 5, return on investment, has been covered extensively in Chapter 2.

Level 0, e-Learning Participation, has evolved as a very important measurement level for e-learning. As a comparison, measurement of participation in face-to-face classroom events was never difficult. If a classroom course was developed, it was just a matter of scheduling the course and signing people up. Education professionals calculated the number of attendees and classroom days, and handed out paper-based course evaluation sheets (*Level 1*, Satisfaction) at the end of the class.

The world of e-learning is very different. By solely making e-learning courseware available, there is no guarantee that people will take and/or complete the courses. Therefore, an understanding of the level of participation in e-learning courseware is the foundation metric before anything else can be measured. Compared with classroom, there are a number of different ways to measure e-learning participation. This can include the number of hits, downloads, live plays, orders, unique users, live e-learning attendance, or overall usage. These definitions will be reviewed in the next section.

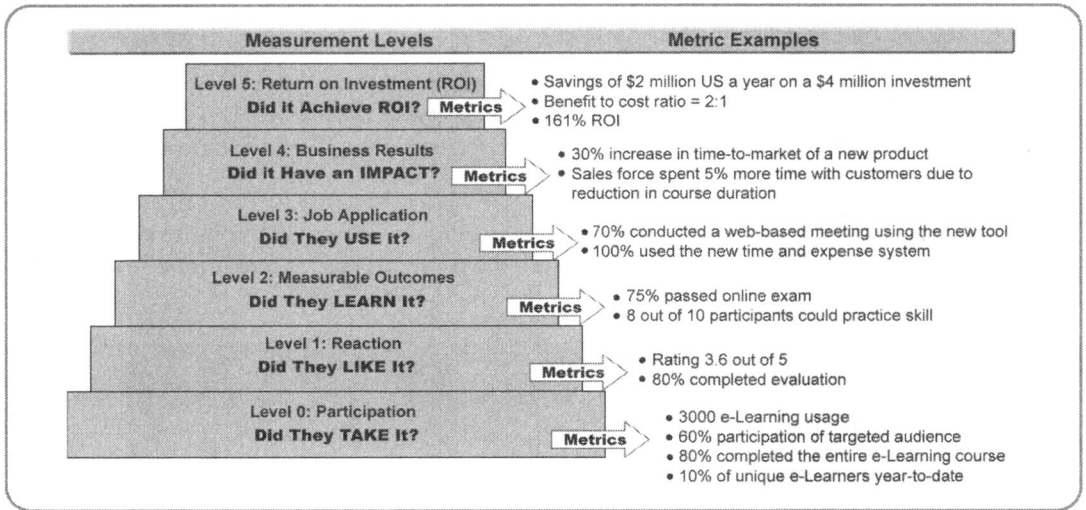

Figure 6-1: e-Learning Measurement Framework

Is it necessary to track all levels all of the time? No. In the early stages of defining an e-learning initiative, it is important to think through your measurement strategy. In some initiatives, you may decide to only focus on Levels 0 through 2. In other initiatives, you may focus on Levels 4 and 5. Table 6-1 provides guidelines for the recommended percentage of overall e-learning initiatives measured at each level.

Table 6-1: Recommended Percent for Measuring e-Learning by Evaluation Level	
Measurement Level	**Percentage of e-Learning Initiatives**
Level 0	100%
Level 1	100%
Level 2	70 to 100%
Level 3	30 to 70%
Level 4	20 to 30%
Level 5	5 to 20%

It is recommended that for every e-learning initiative you capture data at a minimum for participation and satisfaction (Levels 0 to 1); whereas you may only measure Level 4 results for 20 to 30 percent of e-learning, and Level 5 ROI for 5 to 20 percent of your e-learning initiatives. These decisions are based on the following questions:

- How much is being invested in this initiative?
- What is the shelf life of this initiative?
- What is the targeted number of expected participants in this initiative?
- How critical is this initiative? Is it directly aligned with business goals?
- What is the key stakeholder's perspective on the initiative?

Most organizations evaluate Levels 1 to 4 for a selected number of e-learning initiatives. However, many e-learning success stories are still focused on the results for Level 4 evaluation, primarily focused on the cost savings realized by utilizing e-learning in the place of physical classroom events. Despite energetic dialogue about ROI, most learning organizations have limited experience with ROI calculations. However, many involved in deploying e-learning initiatives intend to increase ROI measurements in the future to acquire or retain investment dollars for e-learning solutions. For more information on calculating the ROI of e-learning investments, see Chapter 2.

As with traditional classroom learning, completions are still an important metric to capture. However, there is one word of caution where e-learning differs significantly from classroom learning. Many people think that tracking completions is the only metric to truly measure success for a given program or class. When this approach is used, one of the most significant values of an e-learning strategy is missing, namely just-in-time learning, where the learner might only complete the aspect of the e-learning course that directly applies to their current work-related requirements.

> ### e-Learning Measurement at Cingular Wireless*
>
> *"Cost effectiveness was a big one. For example, to deliver the nine compliance courses to the entire organization costs about $1.45 per employee. That's about $0.16 per course per employee to deliver, which represents a 90 percent cost reduction in content delivery if we had to deliver it in an instructor-led classroom format."* – Rob Lauber
>
> *See Chapter 13: Cingular Wireless

With this in mind, there are many other points to consider. Much of what is tracked is dependent on an organization's approach to e-learning. Whether the overall philosophy is to track specific courses and/or certification programs, provide access to a library of courses for just-in-time or developmental learning, or a mixture of the above, numerous metrics must be captured in order to validate the learning strategy and inform the business case.

Laying the Foundation for Tracking and Reporting

As with any type of systematic processes and procedures put in place, it is important to build a foundation that provides clarity and consistency as the strategy moves forward. This is true of tracking and reporting for e-learning.

The following two fundamentals need to be addressed and clarified up front to implement effective tracking processes: First, the organization's *e-learning hierarchy*; and second, *the tracking categories, definitions, and units of measurement.*

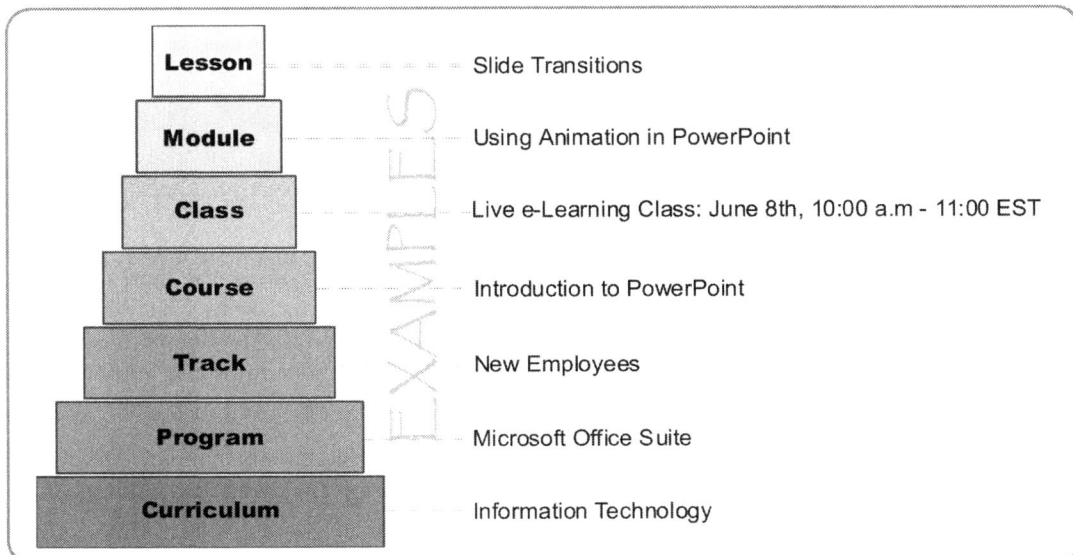

Level	Example
Lesson	Slide Transitions
Module	Using Animation in PowerPoint
Class	Live e-Learning Class: June 8th, 10:00 a.m - 11:00 EST
Course	Introduction to PowerPoint
Track	New Employees
Program	Microsoft Office Suite
Curriculum	Information Technology

Figure 6-2: Sample e-Learning Hierarchy Structure

e-Learning Hierarchy Structure: The learning hierarchy structure defines all of the components and levels the organization employs in e-learning programs.

Tracking can occur at any of these component levels depending on the reporting needs. Once the organization's hierarchy structure is determined, it needs to be mapped to the learning infrastructure solution, including learning management systems, externally hosted content providers, or internal content delivery systems. This step in the process is critical to ensure data consistency and integrity across systems and vendors. The terms used in a hierarchy structure will vary depending on the learning model an organization has in place (e.g., university model), but the need for a hierarchy is applicable across all organizations.

An example of a hierarchy structure for e-learning is depicted in Figure 6-2, and these hierarchy terms are explained in more detail below.

- **Curriculum:** A plan of instruction that details what the learners are to know within a given subject. A curriculum spans a subject from basic to advanced skills or knowledge.

- **Program:** A group of one or more tracks created to meet specific objectives for a specific audience, or set of audiences. A program can cross curricula. Not all learning must be part of a program.

- **Track:** A group of course sessions, modules, lessons and/or learning objectives within a program. Tracks may cross curricula. Not all programs have a need to define tracks, but tracks must be part of a program.

- **Course:** A group of modules, lessons, and/or learning objects targeted at a specific audience by level or interest and selected to meet specific learning objectives.

- **Class:** A particular delivery of a course at a specific day and time. This is also applicable for live e-learning (synchronous).

- **Module:** A group of lessons that support the achievement of one, or a few closely related, learning objectives.

- **Lesson:** A group of learning objects that support achievement of one learning objective.

- **Learning Object:** A package of content and any related activities that addresses a single idea or topic, supporting achievement of only one learning objective. They are the smallest chunks of material that are still recognizable as learning.

Tracking Categories, Definitions and Units of Measurement: This is one of the most important fundamentals to address prior to building any reports and sharing data with stakeholders. It is important to engage the learning and/or human resources leadership in the development of these categories to ensure their understanding, agreement, and support of the terminology and units of measurement.

Figure 6-3 is a suggested example of categories, definitions, and units of measurement. Deciding which of these are applicable to the organization's e-learning strategy is a critical second step.

Completion: Complete an entire learning object, class, or course. This can be tracked in multiple ways depending on the systems in place. In many cases, completion is indicated by achieving a certain percentage in an assessment. It is important to determine what percentage is necessary for passing an assessment.

Download: The retrieval and storage of content to a local computer for offline use. Determining the frequency for counting a download for a particular learning object, or course, is essential. Depending on the infrastructure stability, a user might start to download the same course more than once if connectivity is an issue. For example: One or more downloads per learning object/course, per user, per day/week/month.

Hit: Access to a learning object by a user. This should be recorded each instance. (This is similar to counting 'hits' to a web page.)

Live Play: Access of content via a live, continuous connection where no part of the content is stored locally. A user may access the same learning object or course within the same day or week. Selecting the frequency for counting a live play for a particular learning object/course is another important step. For example: Count one (or more) live play per learning object/course, per user, per day/week/month.

Order: Tracks when a user places an order within a learning management system or content management system for a learning object/ course. An order is counted only once.

Unique User: Number of learners who have participated in any e-learning activity. A unique user is counted only once in a designated time period (monthly, yearly). It is common to measure unique users monthly and yearly.

e-Learning Usage: A total of the metrics that are determined to be applicable in an organization. For example: A total of downloads, live plays, orders, and completions for a designated time period.

Live e-Learning (Synchronous): Online learning events or capabilities that occur, or are used at the same time.

Ancillary e-Learning: White papers, mentoring, chats, or recorded live sessions. Track orders and hits in these categories.

Figure 6-3: Example of e-Learning Categories, Definitions, and Units of Measurement

How to Track Data

A primary tool used for tracking learning activity is a global learning management system. As mentioned in Chapter 5, a learning management system can be within the internal infrastructure, or can be a vendor-hosted solution. It is important to ensure that the systems not only support the hierarchy structure and tracking definitions, it must also support the organization structure from a discipline/division and geographical perspective. It is essential to work with content providers to ensure that all learning objects are built to AICC or SCORM standards. Also, the ability to track at the learning object level, not just the program or course level, needs to be ensured.

Once the infrastructure and systems are in place, data can be tracked in the following categories:

- Classroom learning
- Live e-learning (synchronous)
- e-Learning (e-learning orders, live plays, downloads, completions)
- Other learning products (includes electronic study guides, reference materials, CD-ROM learning)
- External vendor learning

All of the above can be tracked utilizing functionality in a learning management system, either in-house or by an external vendor.

Designing and Building Reports

Reports go far beyond just providing information or statistics to an intended audience. They are an opportunity to further the e-learning strategy and are the foundation for demonstrating the business impact and measuring ROI.

There are two questions to consider when starting to design and build reports.

- What data/information does the organization and/or stakeholder want to know?

- What data/information do I want the organization and/or stakeholder to know?

Reporting e-Learning at Austrade*

Reporting mechanisms have provided senior management with a clear picture, showing a greater degree of work output from the staff and improved efficiency in responding to clients. With supporting systems, 91 percent of the organization is using e-learning, which is being seen as increased productivity and competency in the workplace.

See Chapter 14: Austrade

It is essential to incorporate the answers to both of these questions when building reports, ensuring that the reports are a useful tool in driving the e-learning strategy. The Learning and/or Human Resources organization needs to spend time addressing the second question. As with any strategy, taking the time to identify the key messages important to the stakeholders, and building reports to do just that will definitely pay off.

Steps to Design and Build Reports

1. Identify the stakeholders and audience for the reports and understand their needs.

2. Know the goals of the stakeholder. Be clear about their specific targets as well as those that have been set for the learners and the organization. This will impact how data is presented.

3. Identify the reporting parameters, such as key information needed, frequency of report, and distribution of the information (who receives what). Build in the answers to the two questions above.

4. Know the data! Be clear on what is tracked, where it is tracked and what it means. Based on the internal systems, utilize the tools available (for example, Excel, reporting software such as Crystal Reports, or an LMS).

5. Determine data needed for specific reports and ensure the integrity of that data. In other words, do the requisite homework. Make sure that the data is accurate regardless of the story it tells.

6. Build a prototype of the report and gain agreement with the stakeholder on the final design.

7. Standardize and document the process and automate it wherever possible, as these reports may be needed on a regular basis.

8. Verify the report information within the learning organization.

9. Analyze report results and take actions based on what is now known.

Identify and build standard, cyclical reports, so that the organization becomes very familiar with the concepts, terms, and metrics of e-learning. Consider some sort of learning dashboard or scorecard to drive the e-learning strategy. It can be very valuable to show e-learning and classroom learning data to measure progress as the organization shifts from an e-learning to a blended learning culture.

Table 6-2 depicts data-sorting by geographic location. Depending on the learning management system, there may also be options to sort by organization structure, level, or program/course.

Table 6-2: Example of an e-Learning Report: Calculations Monthly or Year-to-Date				
e-Learning Metrics	Americas	Asia-Pacific	Europe Middle East Africa	Total
e-Learning Usage	3,000	1,500	2,000	6,500
Unique e-Learning Users	700	200	400	1,300
e-Learning Completions	2,100	1,050	1,400	4,500
Unique Users as a Percentage of Headcount	41%	29%	51%	40%

There are new and/or improved reporting tools available in the market today that can enhance your reporting capabilities significantly. Whether you use standard tools such as Crystal Reports, Excel or Access, it makes sense to explore some of the new software that is available to help track and measure ROI. Many of the LMS vendors are introducing new programs with improved reporting functionality as well. Using the proper tools will allow you to spend more time on strategic analysis versus the manual processes of gathering the data and building the reports.

Harnessing the Power of Tracking and Reporting

Once reporting is in place, it is important to collaborate with key stakeholders and the recipients of your reports to ensure their needs are being met. When valuable, accurate data is provided and the audience becomes more educated in analyzing this data, be prepared for new requests and additional interests. Work with the stakeholders to identify gaps between expected and actual results. As a strategic business partner, work with your senior executives and learning champions to address the gaps. Continue to track and report on progress.

e-Learning tracking and reports have proven a valuable tool for business leaders and champions of e-learning initiatives to further drive usage and completions of e-learning, to measure the effectiveness of courses and programs in equipping employees to achieve important strategic goals and to plan for the future.

In the next chapter, methods and approaches for engaging the support of your strategic partners will be explored.

Lessons Learned

✔ Develop a tracking and reporting strategy, and have processes in place to capture the data needed. These are critical to the overall success of e-learning.

✔ Invest the time in strategy-level discussions within learning and with key stakeholders.

✔ Address all levels of measurement for e-learning including Level 0: e-Learning Participation.

✔ Don't expect that tracking and reporting of e-learning is simple and easy. Often the opposite is true. It requires a combination of knowledge, resources, time, and a commitment to getting it right to be successful.

✔ Ensure that resources in the reporting area are knowledgeable in e-learning and have a strong database skill set.

✔ Realize that reporting is an ongoing process and not static.

✔ e-Learning does not possess the same attributes as classroom learning and should not be tracked and reported as such.

✔ It is critical to educate the stakeholders and leadership in understanding the hierarchy structure, terms, categories, and definitions.

✔ Hierarchy structure, terms, and definitions differ from vendor to vendor. Share the internal information right away when working with vendors to avoid confusion and data not tracking appropriately.

✔ Always ensure data integrity prior to releasing any results. Your reputation and trust in the learning organization depend upon it.

CHAPTER

7

Does e-Learning Have a
Credibility Problem?

Does e-Learning Make Business Sense?

What Gains the Commitment
of People That Matter?

How Do You Design Blended
Learning Programs?

What Makes e-Learning
Technology Work?

How Do You Measure e-Learning
Initiatives and Results?

**What Does It Take to Work
Successfully with Vendors?**

What Motivates People to
Engage in e-Learning?

How Do You Launch e-Learning
to a Global Workforce?

Business
Alignment

Design &
Development

Deployment

What Does It Take to
Work Successfully with Vendors?

The main themes for this chapter are:

- *Why Do I Need Vendors?*
- *How Do I Select the Right Vendor for My Specific Learning Solution?*
- *How Do I Know I'm Not Paying Too Much?*
- *How Do I Establish Successful Vendor Partnerships?*

What Does It Take to Work Successfully with Vendors?

As most organizations embark on their quest to become an e-learning provider, they inevitably turn to an evaluation of vendor capabilities to complement their own internal resources and talents. Five to ten years ago, this was a fairly straightforward endeavor. A limited number of vendors, each with its clearly defined scope of services and products, made it fairly easy for an organization to map its own specific needs to the products available. Content offerings were also limited and focused primarily on technology skills required in a typical Information Technology environment. Learning management systems (LMS) were rudimentary at best, in an environment primarily monopolized by one or two primary vendors. Given their own limited experience in developing e-learning strategies, most vendors did not presume to provide strategic professional services to potential clients; rather, they focused solely on implementation and deployment of services.

Clearly, the vendor landscape, as we knew it, has rapidly evolved. As more and more organizations understand the value and appeal of an e-learning migration at some level, the potential e-learning providers recognized the true potential in this fledgling industry. As discussed in Chapter 1, e-learning has experienced exponential growth. However, IDC has also identified that from 2002 until 2006 business skill e-learning content will also grow at remarkable rate of 49 percent, as more vendors use simulations, multimedia, and mentoring to reinforce skill areas that had previously been addressed only through classroom training and mentoring. By 2006, the e-learning services forecast a potential marketplace now populated not only by traditional content and technology providers, but also by most professional services and consulting organizations eager to take advantage of a promising market niche in an otherwise prevalent economic slowdown.

The impact of this explosive growth and constantly expanding range of products and services has an enormous impact on the potential buyer.

> "The e-learning industry is not only in a nascent phase, but is also in a state of some confusion. Much debate exists on the future role of the learning infrastructure players, and on the convergence of e-learning infrastructure software with the other enterprise software categories and vendors-ERP, CRM, and HRM to name a few. What attracts no debate is the continuing criticality of learning content, learning solutions and high-quality learning and knowledge experiences and tools for your employees."
>
> Greg Priest, Chief Strategy Officer of SkillSoft

Why Do I Need Vendors?

As more and more organizations migrate to e-learning as part of their overall enterprise learning strategy, they realize the importance of *time-to-implementation* in successful strategies. Transforming content, technology infrastructure, and the overall culture of your organization is not an easy task. However, effective use of vendor capabilities to assist in escalating your time-to-implementation, and therefore to demonstrate a rapid return on your e-learning investment (ROI), will be key to making e-learning a success in your organization.

Many ask, *Can't I build my own custom content and technology infrastructure to support my e-learning strategy?* You could, but probably at a much higher cost and a much longer time frame than resulting from leveraging successful vendor partnerships in your implementation efforts. The core expertise of Global 5000 organizations is their core, their own industry, and the unique markets and customers they serve. Thus, those organizations interested in establishing e-learning initiatives have seen the importance of engaging vendors whose core competence is e-learning.

By picking the right vendors and solutions, you will be able to:

- **Jumpstart the availability of new and expanded content for your end users in a multitude of technology and business skills areas.** By quickly mobilizing an engaging, well-organized e-learning curriculum, the organization makes significant strides in *selling* end users on the value of an e-learning strategy and gains management commitment to the development of intellectual capital in their valuable human resources.

> **e-Learning Strategy at Invensys Foxboro***
>
> Stay with the organization's core competencies. If you do not have the expertise to develop or deliver e-learning, then partner with those who do.
>
> **See Chapter: 17, Invensys Foxboro*

- **Rapidly implement a technology platform which will facilitate effective access and use of custom and off-the-shelf e-learning content.** Experienced e-learning vendors have spent years perfecting access mechanisms and interfaces that will engage and interest end users in their initial foray into the e-learning arena. Vendor solutions enable organizations to benefit from those capabilities, while in parallel being able to customize the interface to reflect the organization's identity and priorities. In addition, only through rapid implementation of rigorous technology architecture can an organization begin to quantify the value-add associated with its e-learning initiatives, and therefore prove the business case to management and leadership.

- **Embark on parallel paths of content, technology, and infrastructure initiatives** which, in tandem, can accelerate and optimize your *time-to-market* for your overall e-learning strategy.

Optimizing vendor relationships is only one component of a successful e-learning strategy. The decision is not as easy as *build-versus-buy*; it is rarely an either/or decision. The most compelling reason to adopt a vendor partnership strategy is that it provides immediate credibility and availability to end users, while at the same time giving the learning organization time to assess and implement their custom content and technology initiatives.

> **Use of Vendors at Black & Decker Corporation***
>
> Use external professionals to build the first program so you have an expert show you the way and give you an opportunity to determine what resources you need for future projects. This quickly builds great success and allows time to develop internal capabilities that are cost effective.
>
> ** See Chapter 13: Black & Decker*

How Do I Select the Right Vendor for My Specific Learning Solution?

As shown in Figure 7-1, even with all of the broadband changes in the e-learning industry, most e-learning vendor offerings still fall into one of the three key elemental areas of an e-learning solution:

- Content
- Technology
- Services

Courseware
Resourceware
Simulations
Asessment/Competency

Content

IT Content
Soft Skills/Business Content
Vertical Content
Academic Content

LMS
Authoring Tools
Live Delivery/
Meeting Software
Knowledge
Management
LCMS

Technology

Services

Customer Implementation
Support
Online Mentoring
Hosting
Custom Development
Software Integration

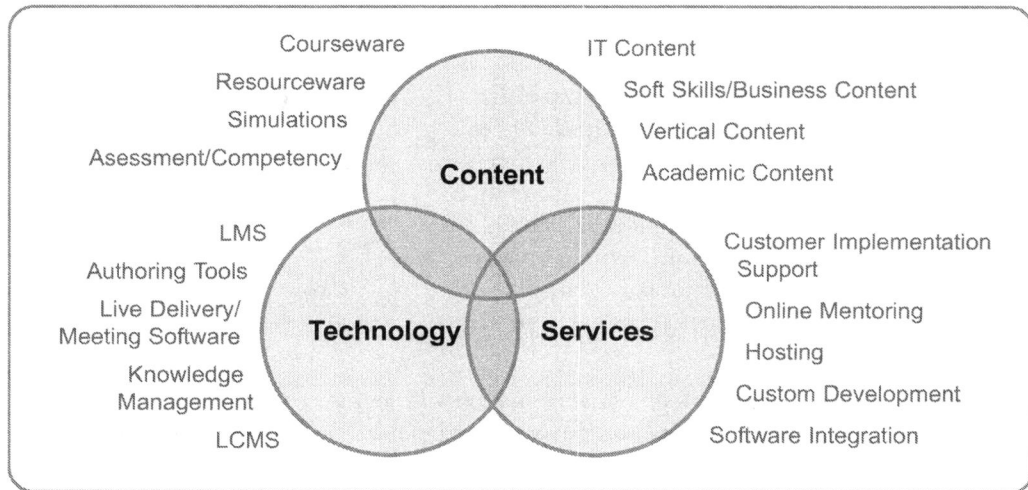

Figure 7-1: View of the e-Learning Industry

Some vendors, particularly the larger and more mature e-learning providers, profess to offer products and services in all three of these areas. The challenge in selecting the best vendor partners, for any given organization, is to accurately determine your goals and objectives in each of these areas, and then map those requirements to available offerings in each of the three categories.

The proliferation of vendors in each of these three areas has certainly escalated over the past two to four years, as has the scope and breadth of the range of products in each of the areas. For example:

- Content is not only broad business- and technology-based content, but also includes deeper vertical content in specialized industry and competency areas, such as financial services, healthcare, e-business, and certification curricula.

- Technology includes not only traditional learning management system offerings, but now also includes more avant-garde niche players, specializing in unique development capabilities, such as games software, interactive simulations, and sophisticated live e-learning tools to further expand the boundaries of the traditional e-learning solutions portfolio.

- Services now include not just implementation and deployment, but also the full spectrum of complete lifecycle e-learning strategy development and deployment, tracking from concept, through vendor selection, to migration and ROI assessment.

To begin the vendor selection process, your learning team needs to perform a full assessment on the organizational gaps which exist in each of the above three areas; prioritize those in the context of available resources, including financial funding, people skills, and leadership support; and identify the highest priority gaps that vendor partners can and should fill.

Selecting e-learning content

Before an organization can even begin to consider evaluating vendor content, it must develop a high level blueprint of subject areas, levels of skill and knowledge required, and target audiences in the organization for whom the e-learning offerings are being developed. This blueprint may be referred to as a *Learning Model.* By mapping major content requirements in the Learning Model against vendor offerings in vendor content area, the organization can identify the extent to which standard libraries can fulfill major organizational needs and requirements.

Typical questions may include:

- Are we trying to acquire an entire library, or a narrower, smaller subset of courses to fulfill a specific learning need?

- What are the demographics of our proposed audience? Global versus national, localization, multiple delivery options? (See Chapter 9.)

- Does the courseware operate in multiple delivery environments?

- Is content customizable in terms of our ability to repurpose modules or objects for custom use in our organization?

- Is there an easy-to-use mapping inherent in the content library which assists new users in navigation through the various content areas?

- Is there a sophisticated search facility for those users who are not quite sure which course content would be appropriate for their needs?

- Can users pre-assess their capabilities, and test-out of components of the courseware in which they are already proficient?

- Does the vendor provide a variety of interactive mechanisms to engage the user, including simulations, sample assessment questions, and multimedia experiences?

- What is the growth plan for this specific vendor? Do their future areas of concentration map to the strategic areas of interest for the organization?

Identifying the correct e-learning technology

Before an organization can select vendor products and services in technology areas, it must have a detailed understanding of its existing technology architecture, and current technological capabilities and restrictions. Bandwidth restrictions, audio/visual streaming limitations, server capacity, firewall restrictions, and support capabilities are all critical to understanding integration possibilities and probabilities for both content offerings and for technology platform opportunities with any given vendor. Whether you are seeking to acquire a major new technology component (a new LMS or LCMS) or just to accommodate new content within your technology architecture, such as providing easy access for users, an in-depth understanding of the existing technology platform is a must.

Key questions include:

- What is the targeted bandwidth level to deliver the content?

- What is the differentiation between download versus liveplay options? (See Chapter 6.)

- What player requirements are associated with content?

- How are learning pathways and the organization's learning model accommodated in the vendor's LMS/LCMS?

- Are the products industry compliant, for example, AICC/SCORM?

- Do you have a sandbox option for pre-acquisition testing, that allows an exploration of functionality and capability in the organization's environment?

- What is the interoperability performance between the vendor's products and those of the other major vendors? Does the vendor have standard interfaces?

- What is the vendor's commitment to keeping up with version changes on other vendor products in terms of these standard interfaces?

An entire Request for Proposal (RFP) process could be, and probably should be, devoted to the acquisition of additional technology components within any organization's technology domain. For the purposes of this chapter, however, we limit this discussion to relatively high level concerns.

Constructing appropriate e-learning services

Services is a very broad term, covering a full lifecycle of consulting and advisory services, including but not limited to:

- Custom development of proprietary content

- Implementation assistance associated with procurement of a new or upgraded technology platform, such as an LMS, an LCMS, or custom-developed interface

- Hosting of custom or off-the-shelf content for customers who do not have the bandwidth to host content internally

- Integration services focused on assisting customers in acquiring, implementing, and integrating an array of vendor content and technologies

- Strategic planning and evaluation services to assist customers in planning and launching effective e-learning initiatives

As you evaluate potential vendors to fill in gap in your specific Content, Technology, and Services requirement areas, it is critical to look first at product and service fit to your purposes and functionality, and then at the vendor themselves. While many vendors profess to support excellence in all three of the areas above, true *one-stop-shopping* is very rare. Over the past few years, the more progressive players in the e-learning industry have reaffirmed the importance of focus, and are concentrating their efforts in the content, technology, or services arena. There are, of course, still areas where the circles overlap:

- Most major content providers provide some level of technology platform to launch and access their courseware, as well as implementation services to assist new customers in rolling out courseware in a new environment.

- Most major technology providers provide implementation services assistance to customize their products for the user environment, as well as integration services to join existing content with the new technology platforms.

- Most major services providers have formed alliances with various content and technology providers to facilitate easier integration recommendations and expedite mapping of customer requirements to various vendor offerings.

Whether you choose one vendor for a specific need, or multiple vendors to fulfill a variety of needs in all of the above areas, the most important factor is to be very clear on what you believe you need and what product/service capabilities are most critical to the success of your e-learning initiative.

If you are new to e-learning, it's important to network with other companies who have had experience establishing successful e-learning initiatives. Insights from other organizations that are further along the path of e-learning implementation can help a company new to e-learning to develop a solid sense of important criteria in selecting the right e-learning partners.

> **Selecting Multiple e-Learning Vendors at 3Com***
>
> Do not hesitate to work with multiple vendors to complete a program. Vendors who say they do everything are often more expensive and less experienced than where you need the expertise.
>
> ** See Chapter 17: 3Com*

How Do I Know I'm Not Paying Too Much?

Too much is a very relative term. Obviously for any major financial outlay, a rigorous evaluation should include a comparison of various pricing options among a short list of options. But that is only the first step of the contracting *dance*. Most vendors, who are truly interested in partnerships and not just sales, will be responsive to creative and flexible pricing arrangements and alternatives. The best e-learning initiatives are usually the result of significant co-investment by both vendors and customers in the program success. Ultimately, business relationships where there is a one-sided risk equation—all risk for the vendor and no risk for the customer—rarely result in e-learning programs that succeed and deliver business results.

First, you need a clear understanding of what is included in the proposed pricing agreement.

✓ For Content and Technology acquisition, what level of customization and implementation assistance is included in the quote? What may appear to be a much less expensive alternative may in fact become much more costly if every hour of implementation assistance is billed at standard rates, rather than included as part of the due diligence of the vendor.

✓ What kind of commitment is the vendor willing to make to ensure that their solution works in your environment? As an example, some vendors are willing to take only X% (10 to 20 percent) of their contract price up front, and the remainder on successful implementation. While this seems trivial, in reality, the truth is that with inconsistent levels of compliance with industry standards, it can easily take six to nine months to integrate new components into your existing architecture. Will your contract start at that point, or have you given up six to nine months of use/access?

✓ In some cases, vendor proposals seem prohibitively high, but the functionality extremely attractive. Most established vendors are willing to consider and/or propose creative pricing arrangements that might be more attractive to your organization based on your current economic profile. Alternatives might include:

▫ Scaled pricing levels for the first few years of implementation, giving your learning organization time to institutionalize e-learning.

- Pilot programs to *test the waters* for the vendor products prior to full-scale commitment and implementation.

- Availability of a *sandbox* environment for interim testing and integration evaluation prior to signing on the bottom line.

In reality, the truism *You Get What You Pay For* is typical also with vendors. High quality, dependable content and platforms do not come cheap, but the rewards of a solid partnership and long term success more than outweigh the relative cost.

> **Cost-Effective Vendor Relationships at The Hartford***
>
> When buying content from an external vendor, thoroughly investigate whether it is more cost-effective to buy a large site license or use a pay-per-view approach.
>
> *See Chapter 12: The Hartford*

How Do I Establish Successful Vendor Partnerships?

Successful vendor partnerships are long term commitments—both parties should be in for the long haul. Like any relationship, it takes a significant amount of effort on both sides to make it truly successful. There are, however, a number of critical success factors to making vendor relationships work:

1. **Establish the Account Team.** Effective teaming is essential in vendor relationships. The Account Team should comprise technical skills and customer relationship management skills. There should be a point person on both sides to ensure that your needs are understood by the vendor and that the vendor is well represented in your organization.

2. **Take Responsibility as a Team.** As a working team, establish the initial project plan and accept joint responsibility for the successful implementation of the project plan. Clearly identify respective responsibilities and issues. Agree on due dates and deliverables. Over the tenure of the contract, additional projects and initiatives will continue to be added to the charter of the Account Team. Projects should be jointly prioritized and incorporated into the overall vendor strategy and implementation plan.

3. **Avoid *Pointing the Finger.*** Over time, there will be issues, such as slipped deadlines and missed deliverables due to a number of factors, including changing priorities on both sides, technology shifts and upgrades, and platform issues. Prompt elevation of issues to the Account Team and effective brainstorming as to the optimal, expeditious solution of those issues is best. Nothing erodes vendor relationships more quickly and more effectively than an *us versus them* mentality. Expend your efforts in finding creative solutions rather than assigning blame.

4. **Communicate, Communicate, and Communicate.** In many long-term vendor relationships, there is a strong possibility that both organizations will undergo some level of change over time in terms of strategies, technology, leadership, and priorities. Regular communication is absolutely critical to smooth relationships. On a regular basis, the joint account team should review priorities, address issues, identify additional areas of interest, and share changes in overall direction and strategy.

5. **Recognize the Value of Partnership.** Partnership is not an insignificant word. It means celebrating joint accomplishments together, and defining additional areas in

which both firms can work together to make each other successful. Opportunities may include:

- Joint development of initiatives that can be mutually beneficial

- Expansion of the existing scope of the relationship to include additional initiatives that have evolved as a result of the accomplishments to date

- Joint marketing in terms of references, testimonials, case studies, and success stories, directed to both internal and external audiences in each organization.

6. **Plan for the Future.** Keep abreast of vendor new product/solution release dates and upgrades, and ensure that your own planning for those upgrades begins relatively early. Involve your IT group and the Account Team in these discussions as well, and focus on changes on your user groups and how those will be communicated.

7. **Understand that Customization Requires Maintenance and that You Must Pay for It.** Customization is frequently attractive and desirable, but with all vendors providing upgrades to their standard decks on a regular basis, any customizations you implement will also have to upgraded and integrated, frequently at your own cost. Customization for the sake of minor cosmetic changes should definitely be evaluated in terms of their long-term value. For more substantial customization efforts, be sure both the vendor and your customization team maintain clear documentation of the work done, such that they can map to changes required due to upgrades and changes in baseline vendor products.

8. **Participate in Vendor User Groups and Forums.** You are not alone. Vendor user groups and forums frequently provide great opportunities to learn from others' experiences and find additional ways to utilize vendor products/solutions in your own environment. Collaboration is profitable on both sides. User groups can be leveraged to provide development forums, realizing substantial economies of scale if common deliverables can be identified.

9. **Participate in Executive Advisory Boards/Chairman's Councils.** At the strategic level, for those vendors with whom you maintain a substantial relationship, it makes sense to participate in leadership councils where decisions are discussed as to vendor direction, strategies, and tactics. Key client input is of high importance to vendors, particularly where those clients have a long-term commitment to their products and solutions.

10. **Have Fun!** Teaming with a vendor whose skills strongly leverage your own, and with whom you can achieve significant progress, can be an exhilarating experience for you and your team. Never lose sight of what you bring to them, and what they bring to you. Partnerships are never easy, but they are always worthwhile.

Most major e-learning vendors have tools and methods that are the result of hundreds and/or thousands of experiences with working with joint vendor/customer teams.

While the landscape of e-learning vendors can be challenging, the good news is that the best e-learning vendors are usually very interested in, and committed to, the success of their customers, because they know the success of their customers is critical to their future reputation and growth as partners.

For most e-learning initiatives within Global 5000 business organizations, you will likely find yourself working with multiple vendors to put together the strongest solution for your own organization. The right vendors for you will probably be the ones with the strongest capabilities and track record within the areas of e-learning products and services you have identified as the most critical to the success of your e-learning initiative.

Both you and your selected vendor(s) must make a significant commitment to providing the right resources and the right investments in your program success. Selecting the right vendors/products/services is only the initial step to a successful e-learning initiative. Making that partnership work, ensuring the right resources are deployed, and reaping the necessary return on investment from each e-learning initiative requires a level of structure, commitment, and dedication well beyond *signing on the dotted line.*

Now that you have built it, *will they come?* This is a driving question in the field of e-learning initiatives. The only success is when the learners benefit from what is being provided, and when their learning needs to become more knowledgeable and productive are satisfied. In the next chapter, several approaches to ensuring the engagement of your learning community in the e-learning that programs provide will be explored.

Lessons Learned

✔ Leverage the core e-learning expertise of successful e-learning providers to jump-start your e-learning strategy.

✔ One-stop shopping capability in e-learning vendors is very rare; focus on the vendors with the strongest capabilities and track record within the areas of e-learning products and services that you deem the most critical to the success of your e-learning initiatives.

✔ Let your e-learning vendor(s) work actively with you as a partner; e-learning initiatives which create a one-sided value proposition are rarely successful.

✔ Map vendor capabilities and technology requirements to your own business and technology platforms; ensure that proposed vendor solutions are realistic given your current environment.

✔ Expect creativity and flexibility in vendor pricing arrangements; vendors interested in a true long-term partnership will be happy to comply.

✔ Share responsibilities, milestones, and successes; work together to overcome adversity and resistance.

✔ Establish a bi-directional flow of communication; ensure that vendors are aware of changes in your strategies and infrastructure, and that you are aware and have input to changes in theirs.

CHAPTER

8

What Motivates People to Engage in e-Learning?

The main themes for this chapter are:

- *e-Learning Enablers*
- *e-Learning Drivers*
- *e-Learning Motivators*

What Motivates People to Engage in e-Learning?

e-Learning is becoming more popular as an effective method of disseminating information and knowledge across the employee base in companies. However, it continues to be challenging to fully engage all employees in the productive use of the available e-learning offerings.

Companies have generally neglected to promote the benefits of e-learning to their employees and played down the fact that the shift to e-learning represents a large organizational cultural change. It needs to be demonstrated to employees that e-learning is not about cost-saving, but more about delivering improved training benefits to the individual worker.

Many, familiar with classroom training in the corporate environment:

- Regard non-traditional (non-classroom) learning as less valuable and less prestigious
- Miss the face-to-face interaction with facilitators and fellow learners
- Find that they need to employ more discipline and self-motivation to start and complete e-learning courses

Different audiences show evidence of differing adoption rates. Many older employees are resistant to e-learning, not having grown-up with technology as a normal part of their routine. Pew Internet & American Life point out that the current college-age generation, who grew up with the personal computer, is now heavily wired on campus and relies on the Internet in every dimension of college life.

Many colleges not already pursuing online courses are integrating the Internet into everyday campus life, and are using the Web to augment textbooks and to assist communication. Their study found that 86 percent of U.S. college students use the Internet, compared to 59 percent of the overall U.S. population. Students claimed that the Internet is essential to their academic and social lives. According to Marc Prensky, members of Generation Y, or the *digital generation*, learn differently, are generally more comfortable with Internet technology, are more visually orientated, and generally learn by discovering and doing, thus becoming good candidates for e-learning applications.

What Factors Impact Involvement in e-Learning?

Three important factors contribute to the successful engagement of learners in e-learning-enablers, drivers, and motivators.

e-Learning Enablers

The following e-learning enablers must be effectively implemented to ensure access and usage.

- The right e-learning technology infrastructure and support
- Time allocated for e-learning
- Affordable investment and demonstrated return on investment
- Existence of an organizational e-learning culture

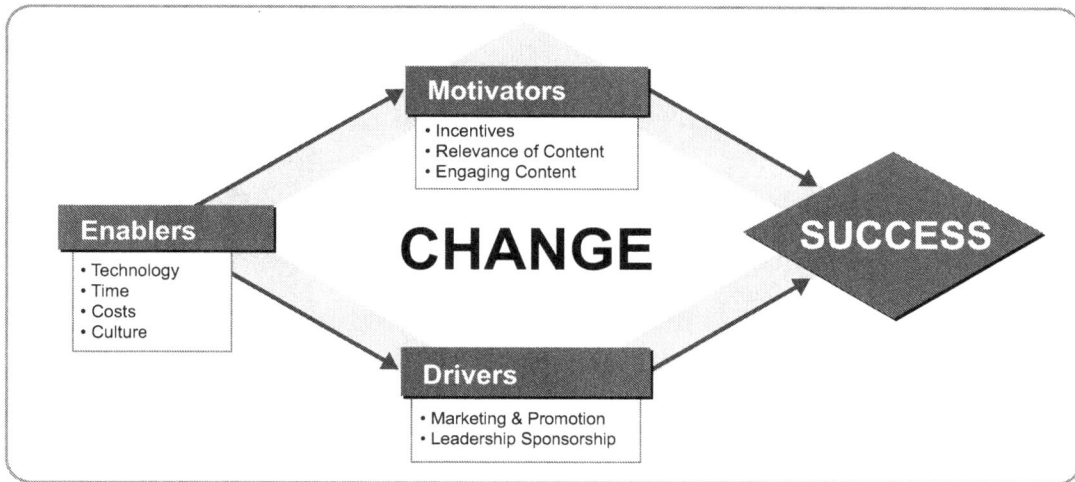

Figure 8-1: Factors That Impact Involvement in e-Learning

e-Learning Technology and Infrastructure Support

Because learning technology is still maturing, significant technical issues can be encountered by the learner. It is therefore important to identify risks, to anticipate contingencies, and to identify the constraints and limitations of systems and tools.

Although it is important to keep in mind that this is essentially a learning project, and not an information technology project, the Masie Center emphasizes that the supporting technology infrastructure for e-learning is an enabler and one of the primary factors affecting successful deployment, along with ongoing support in the development and deployment of e-learning content.

Modern e-learning courseware often dictates the use of broadband technologies to fully support the functionality. Individuals are drawn to e-learning by multimedia streaming services, such as *always-on* Internet access. Adequate clock speed, processor capabilities, and unimpeded access via broadband to a corporate intranet, both from within the corporate environment and from home, encourage the use of corporate e-learning. Online learning today extends a company's training environment into their employees' home environments, and thus support for the home technology infrastructure needs to be factored into help desk support capability.

In-Stat/MDR has found that U.S. households find the cost of broadband is still a problem, and as a result, fewer than 33 percent of U.S. households will subscribe to a broadband service by 2006. According to In-Stat MDR, 42 percent of dial-up subscribers claim they have no need for broadband service, while 32 percent believe that the technology is too expensive. In contrast, only 8 percent reported that broadband was not available in their area. A limited subscriber base is a potential barrier to the uptake of home-based corporate e-learning. Thus, companies may choose to provide alternatives which can support off-network learning, such as providing courses on CD-ROM, with assessments being available online in the office.

An important bridge from face-to-face classroom teaching to e-learning is live e-learning. Live e-learning tools, such as Centra, Interwise, WebEx and Mentergy support the use of *virtual classrooms*, and are designed to work on the basis of minimal bandwidth, although they fully support

VoIP (Voice Over Internet Protocol). However, their true functionality, in capabilities such as application sharing, are best utilized at higher bandwidths. Most of the live e-learning tools do not require substantial, or difficult desktop configuration, and are intuitive and easy-to-use.

> **Building e-Learning Technology Familiarity at Prudential Financial***
>
> When deploying e-learning that people will attend from their desktop, spend time in the beginning teaching people how to use the technology.
>
> *See Chapter 13: The Prudential*

The likelihood of ongoing interest in e-learning has been found to be heavily influenced by a positive and worthwhile first learning experience being and worthwhile. Limitations in bandwidth, formats, and sometimes browsers can make an implementation and successful adoption difficult. Nothing discourages users more than a defective or restrictive infrastructure, and a single exposure to a defective technological infrastructure may be enough to act as a disabler to future exposure.

From an ongoing support perspective, it is important to provide learners a single point of contact for assistance and ongoing global technical support for learning tools and technologies. It is also critical that the learning technology infrastructure track and support progress, and thus be employed to provide follow-up capability through course completion.

Allocated Time for e-Learning

For many learners, one of the overriding negative aspects of participation in, and completion of, e-learning is the perceived lack of approved, allocated time during work hours in which to complete the learning.

In the classic model of learning, the line between time for training and for work were clearly delineated. Managers provided approval for an individual to attend classroom training, and workers left the workplace to attend the class. In many modern organizations, e-learning is readily available as part of the work environment, and requires limited, or no approval from superiors. The challenge for many is that they have to schedule their e-learning during working hours, where it can be construed as being unproductive, and where they can also be distracted by everyday working activities, such as telephone

> **A Blended Model of Manageable Learning Chunks at Unilever***
>
> In e-learning, 'little bits of small are better than three bits of big.' Big files that take a long time to download and complete discourage people from engaging. If it is small enough, people will fit it into the day.
>
> * See Chapter 15: Unilever

calls and e-mail. These individuals may then choose to consider to, or be forced to, complete e-learning at home after working hours.

Time for learning seems to be less of an issue when the learning is broken into smaller, manageable modules. The design of learning content (see Chapter 4) highly influences this element. Studies indicate that providing content in *learning chunks*, which can be completed in a single sitting, seems to encourage both learning retention and the probability of e-learning completion.

Instructor-led live e-learning has the disadvantage that it requires attendance at a certain time. However, live e-learning sessions can be recorded, edited, and stored as alive e-learning objects for later use as many times as needed by those unable to attend the original online session.

Many companies have experienced success with e-learning initiatives by establishing *e-learning laboratories:* secluded, private spaces equipped with appropriate learning technologies and high-speed access to the corporate intranet and to external Web sites.

Affordable Investment and Demonstrated Return On Investment

Companies are increasingly demanding a return on investment (ROI) on their learning costs (see Chapters 2 and 6). What constitutes the cost of an e-learning infrastructure? Primarily it consists of the purchase, or design and building of courseware and ongoing maintenance costs. Also, the people and management costs in a *design and build environment* form a high proportion of overall cost, and many companies are reaping the benefit of outsourcing e-learning program coding to offshore vendors. The infrastructure costs can be substantial, with the implementation of learning management systems (LMS), supporting hardware, as well as interfacing costs for linking the LMS with the corporate human resource management, financial, and other corporate systems. Help desk support for both hardware and software also is an important cost element. In addition, the construction of in-house learning laboratories and associated hardware can be expensive.

> ### When and Where? The Time and Place for e-Learning at Austrade*
>
> The agency created space within the office for e-learning that eliminated interruptions, whether it was a separate cubical location or hanging up a sign that alerted fellow workers that an employee was engaged in e-learning and their learning time was to be respected.
>
> *See Chapter 14: Austrade*

Where are the savings? Through deployment of e-learning courseware and live e-learning teaching, companies may reduce, or even possibly entirely eliminate expenses related to classroom training and travel expenses incurred in classic, face-to-face training programs, and can impact the opportunity costs by reducing the time learners are away from their office and their daily jobs.

As discussed in Chapter 2, it is important that the learning function be aligned with the business goals and have an impact on the business. It needs to be beneficial to the organization and either reduce core processing costs, or enhance corporate profit, and ideally both. How is this *learning business* run? In some cases, course costs are allocated to departments, and many times this can be done electronically by interfacing the LMS, human resource and financial systems. A possible advantage of this approach is that the learning budget is not held centrally, but decentralized across departments. The disadvantage can be that consolidation is required to provide the full cost of learning, or that the full cost of learning is never apparent.

In many of the companies interviewed for this Fieldbook, formal approval processes exist for face-to-face training. Some companies have carried this process forward into the e-learning environment. However, this approval requirement can act as a barrier to *always-on, always-available,* unrestricted e-learning opportunities. Learners may be prevented from taking the lead in their professional development, a critical aspect of the e-learning culture.

Existence of an Organizational e-Learning Culture

There are two major contributors to the learning culture of an organization: the national culture, as discussed in Chapter 9, and the corporate culture.

Globalization has become a driver for economic prosperity for many individuals and companies, which operate both nationally and across national borders. e-Learning has played an important role in the supply of learning globally. The importance and impact of national cultures on the uptake of e-learning may be reduced over time as the globalization and localization of e-learning content becomes more widespread.

Global Reach estimated that some 64 percent of the total global online population was from non-English speaking zones, or the equivalent of 403.5 million non-native English speaking Internet users. Twenty-six percent of Internet users have an Asian language as their first language. Chapter 9 examines this, as well as various other factors in multicultural adoption of e-learning in more depth.

Within a national culture there are multiple corporate cultures. Many corporate cultures are now rooted in increasingly information and knowledge-based industries. Information-rich organizations are increasingly distributed across countries and even continents. In this twenty-first century reality, the classic method of face-to-face training is thus less feasible than in the past.

What is corporate culture, and how does it affect the success or failure of e-learning? According to Neuhauser, Bender, and Stromberg, corporate culture "is a major component of the infrastructure engine that drives the organization in the direction it has set for itself. Culture is often defined as the way we do things around here. If the way a company does things does not match its business strategy, the culture wins every time. No matter what a company says it intends to do, the way people actually behave, think, and believe determines what really happens."

This implies that dictates, or mandates, which are not supported by the right sponsors, or which do not match the business culture, are doomed to failure. A half-hearted, or poorly sponsored e-learning program, that does not support true business or individual needs will probably not be accepted by the majority of the learners, who would resist it en-masse.

Corporate culture is thus an e-learning enabler, or disabler. William C. Symonds offers as an example the e-learning experience of the U.S. Army, which since January 2001 has had approximately 10,400 soldiers taking online courses and earning degrees online from 24 participating colleges: "Students at eArmyU, as its known, receive a free laptop and printer and 100 percent of their tuition. No wonder the Army expects enrollment to hit 80,000 by 2005 as it takes the program Army-wide."

The technology maturity of the e-learner and their willingness to complete e-learning is influenced by the work environment—their corporate culture. The headquarters or country of origin of the organization may also play a role in corporate culture and subsequent adoption of e-learning.

The mainstream adoption of e-learning appears to have started with global IT firms such as Cisco Systems and IBM Corporation, and moved from there to professional services firms, and subsequently to other organizations and industries. Thus, we have seen that large American multinationals are more likely to utilize e-learning across their global operations.

e-Learning Drivers

Organizations can drive e-learning by engaging leaders in their organization as sponsors and by increasing awareness through mounting a sophisticated and comprehensive marketing and promotional campaign

e-Learning Promotion and Marketing

Ideally learning should be embedded in work processes, and workers should be aware of how in-the-moment access to e-learning can enable them to improve their performance and effectiveness on-the-job. On-going marketing and promotional efforts associated with e-learning courses have been shown to be highly influential in attracting and retaining learners. Many programs have been successful only because of this type of intense marketing and promotion.

Examples of e-learning promotion and marketing activities include:
- e-Mails
- e-Cards
- Webinars
- e-Newsletters, outlining availability of e-learning programs
- e-Learning kick-off meetings
- Videos
- Learning portal communication
- Learning posters in offices
- Learning laboratories
- Learning-related live presentations
- Repetitive demonstration/ marketing videos in company lobbies, bistros, cafeterias
- Direct networking with various stakeholders
- Live and live e-learning training sessions
- Frequent e-learner incentive programs

Some of the companies featured in the cases included in this Fieldbook present e-learning as just one part of the company's overall learning strategy, emphasizing it as an additional dimension in a blended learning approach, and not simply as a replacement for traditional classroom-based learning. Many prefer to feature e-learning as another communication vehicle to disseminate information quickly, with the aim of improving the effectiveness of the learner. Various studies have shown that a rich multimedia, multi-channel learning offering strongly appeals to learners, thus reducing the need to explain why a particular approach may be a good one.

This positive spin in marketing and an emphasis on the personal motivation to engage in e-learning is important.

Many different means can be employed to communicate and advertise e-learning messages to all levels in the Firm. One useful tip is to find synergies with other internal communications, and to utilize these as far as possible. Examples include using every meeting to communicate the message, advertising in internal newsletters and intranet Web pages, and employing e-learning tools in meetings. Some companies successfully utilize live e-learning tools in meetings, and this exposure encourages further use, as learners develop enthusiasm about their first exposure to the tool.

A few companies have achieved great success in e-learning initiatives by precisely targeting the learner with the right learning product at the right time. Deloitte Consulting targets the selection of courses to particular levels of the client service practitioner base, allowing the learner to choose to take only the learning they need at that level, when they need it.

When launching a new e-learning program, it may be useful to target early adopters who will market a program on an ongoing basis once they are finished. Some companies find it useful to start the rollout of a program with a small pilot group, and later to extend it to a broader customer base.

> ### e-Learning Promotion and Marketing at Oracle Corporation*
>
> "The 18-month Oracle DBA certification usually has a positive impact on a person's earnings and position in the workforce, and personnel wanted to shorten the average cycle time to complete the program. Oracle based its value proposition on time-to-certification and the resulting e-learning Fast Track program took less time overall, and disrupted people's schedules less."
>
> *See Chapter 17: Oracle*

Leader Sponsorship and e-Learning Champions

Learning should be related to a specific context, be challenging, and result in development and change. The business impact of an e-learning program needs to be very clear before commencement. To ensure top-level buy-in, establishing the business impact of a program should be a key element of the program marketing plan.

Who best drives or assists with the marketing campaign?

Various studies have found that the level of leadership commitment reinforces the strategic importance of the program. It is also useful to note that employees pay more attention to the person or people who are either their immediate supervisors, or well-known and respected individuals among the senior executives. These are the individuals who should sponsor e-learning initiatives, by leading, driving, and monitoring progress.

> ### Gaining Leader Sponsorship of e-Learning Initiatives in INSEAD OnLine Client Programs*
>
> Without top management support and sponsorship, any e-learning initiative will not succeed. When learners know that their leadership is backing a program, they will engage.
>
> *See Chapter 15: INSEAD OnLine*

e-Learning Motivators

These are the things which drive and motivate the learner to utilize the available e-learning.

Ultimately, learning is up to the learner.

David Butcher argues that the advantage of e-learning is that "it democratizes the opportunity to develop yourself, and that this is very in tune with some of the underlying ideals of the organization." Butcher uses the catchy term *just-for-me* learning.

The Masie Center states that, "Ultimately the largest cost and benefit drivers for e-learning acceptance is the learners own desire to obtain new skills." Building accountability on the part of the learner, as opposed to holding the training department accountable, is critical for the successful adoption of e-learning.

A positive approach and self-motivation on the part of the learner greatly reduces the need for *negative incentives,* such as mandating a program and linking it to a performance evaluation system. This motivational approach is strongly influenced by many elements, including:

- Individual incentives to take and complete e-learning
- Relevant and engaging e-learning content

Incentives to Take and Complete e-Learning Programs

So what's in it for me, the learner?

To answer that question honestly, every e-learning program or initiative has to support a strategic business objective, or answer a specific business need relevant to the learner. The business impact must be clear to the learner, their superior, and the sponsor, and the managers and sponsors must continually ensure that employees are aware of how e-learning courses can contribute to their personal development and growth in the company.

Learning that allows speedy application of new skills, or behaviors on the job, results in immediate payback, and encourages continued learning. In support of the *just-for-me* approach to learning, some companies involve senior executives in championing and coaching practitioners to prioritize and define their learning requirements. In more mature learning environments, the development of individual, *just-for-me* learning plans should be encouraged.

Customers sometimes require that their vendor staff be certified. Certification is often viewed and treated as an incentive to e-learning. Externally recognized or accredited certification is viewed in the marketplace as being an addition to important job skills, and is often in demand by employers. Many certifications can be achieved through blended learning programs, and some may be achievable exclusively through e-learning programs.

The Masie Center suggests that full participation in e-learning tended to occur only when courses were tied to performance reviews, for example, when the approved learning plans are closely monitored and rewarded. e-Learning completion can be linked to performance reviews.

In addition, both the design and delivery process can stress the benefit of personal growth and development. At Deloitte Consulting, subject matter experts are often employed in the content design process, regardless of their geographic location. Many subject matter experts have experienced tremendous personal growth as a result of this recognition.

Many companies have even used direct incentives to improve uptake. These vary from small non-monetary incentives to bonuses.

e-Learning Uptake Improved by Incentives at McDonald's Corporation*

Restaurants in the McDonald's pilot that offered inexpensive prizes or promoted restaurant-to-restaurant competitions achieved higher penetrations than restaurants that did not.

* See Chapter 14: McDonald's Corporation

Development, Deployment, and Maintenance of Relevant and Engaging Content

"e-Learning material has to be compelling and highly engaging. People need to be lured into the experience," according to Tom Graunke, CEO of KnowledgeNet, and this is amplified by a statement made by Robert McGarvey "When it is compelling, it will find an audience."

Creating a compelling and effective e-learning experience is primarily about instructional design. Designing an effective, engaging, and interactive blended learning experience focuses on the content, and not exclusively on the technology.

Both ease of use and overall program quality, two factors affecting uptake, are influenced by the design. Many companies stress the importance of quality program content design and development. This results in both enhanced uptake, or an uptake with less resistance, as well as in reduced ongoing costs, as the design may be replicated later in other initiatives, resulting in less expensive and more efficient rollouts.

A blended course design appears to greatly improve user acceptance, and this is described in depth in Chapter 4. Blending in live e-learning delivery provides benefits.

- They typically feature two-way audio, text, and graphic interactions similar to a classroom session.
- Communication tools, such as messaging and chats are inherent in most products.
- Interactions, such as speaking and asking questions are prompted by electronically *raising hands*.
- Online surveys can be done real time.

Embedded collaboration and interaction capability facilitates better e-learning. Many companies have achieved success by including Web seminars, virtual teaming business projects, Web dialogue, commentary, and chat rooms in their blended offerings.

Programs with longer durability often need periodic updates to content in order to remain current. This is an easily neglected factor, and one which can greatly influence the learner's perception of quality.

Integrated design using the full spectrum of inexpensive broadband may serve as a major motivator to all but the most resistant learner. Multimedia usage, such as in-dash Internet radio channels and MMS-enabled mobile telephones, may mean that individuals receive more innovative learning, and it is pushed out to learners in many more ways.

> **Updates to e-Learning at Prudential Financial***
>
> When budgeting for the development of a new program, be sure to include in your plan how often and to what degree maintenance of the program must be performed.
>
> ** See Chapter 13: Prudential Financial*

Given the removal of other more obvious, restricting factors, personal motivation has always been the primary challenge in learning and ongoing development, and will remain the primary driver for acceptance of a learning opportunity.

In the next chapter, the cultural adaptations necessary to foster and encourage the use of e-learning will be discussed.

Lessons Learned

✔ PC familiarity should never be assumed; provide an optional orientation before any e-learning activity.

✔ Allocate time for e-learning where possible; ideally implement a formal policy.

✔ Give credit for approved learning that learners do at home/offsite.

✔ Encourage learning in 'short bursts' where possible. Anything helps!

✔ Market, market, and market!

✔ Keep in mind those whose native language may be different from the delivery language. They may have more difficulties than most.

✔ Understand and target the correct audience in marketing efforts.

✔ Find the learning champions in your company and use them to drive e-learning.

✔ Make sure the content is relevant to the learning customer.

✔ Link learning to performance where possible.

✔ Provide incentives if possible, particularly when an audience is new to the process or technology.

✔ Track data, and use it to boost performance.

✔ Design or buy the best quality learning that can be afforded.

✔ Revise outdated material regularly if it is due for redelivery.

CHAPTER

9

How Do You Launch e-Learning to a Global Workforce?

The main themes for this chapter are:

- *Key Drivers for Cross-Cultural Adoption of e-Learning*

- *e-Learning Culture Prints*

- *Crafting a Multicultural e-Learning Strategy*

How Do You Launch e-Learning to a Global Workforce?

Innovations in technology and increasing global access to the Internet are pushing relentlessly toward a seamless, digital world of 'e'. Today, e-learning, is becoming available in countries where lack of access to the Internet has hindered growth in the past. A growing number of organizations, including the case organizations featured in this book, such as: Deloitte Consulting, McDonald's Corporation, Unilever, and Austrade, among others, have already successfully implemented e-learning programs to their workers in many countries around the globe, or are currently in the process of expanding their global e-learning capabilities.

According to IDC, the corporate worldwide e-learning market will grow from approximately US$9.1 billion in 2003 to approximately US$24 billion in 2006. The largest growth opportunities in e-learning is forecasted for the Europe/Middle East/Africa (EMEA) region (see Table 9-1). The UK leads this region and Germany is expected to make a comeback and will soon overtake the UK in terms of spending. In absolute numbers, the largest market for e-learning still is the Americas, and this market will grow at a compounded annual growth rate of 36 percent.

The greatest growth in the Asia Pacific region is anticipated in China. However, currently Japan is the largest e-learning market in Asia and according to IDC more companies in Japan are adopting e-learning to reduce costs and increase employee competencies.

Table 9-1: Worldwide e-Learning Market Forecast 2003 – 2006 in Million USD					
Region	2003	2004	2005	2006	2001-2006 CAGR (%)
The Americas	7,296	10,316	14,252	18,943	36.7 %
Asia Pacific	900	1,048	1,263	1,550	14.9 %
Europe Middle East Africa	934	1,422	2,186	3,243	49.8 %
Total	9,130	12,786	17,701	23,736	35.6 %

Source: IDC, 2003

 It is important to note however, that the global e-learning market estimates were even higher at the end of the nineties. Since that time, a number of organizations have experienced successes but also failures with the implementation and adoption of e-learning across cultures, leading to lower than expected growth.

Two questions arise out of this rapid growth and the related experiences in e-learning:

- What are the key drivers that can enhance cross-cultural adoption of e-learning?
- What are the key elements required to create a successful multi-cultural e-learning strategy?

Key Drivers for Cross-Cultural Adoption of e-Learning

Although Internet access is growing expo-
nentially around the globe and the access
to e-learning through Web-enabled
resources is spreading with 24/7 availability, attention must be given to the cultural
adaptation of e-learning to enhance
acceptance, utilization, and completion of
e-learning courses. Fundamentally, there
are five drivers which have an impact on
the adoption of e-learning worldwide, as
shown in Figure 9-1.

All of these need to be functioning well to
support the learner in a successful e-learning experience, and yet if the first four
drivers are in place, without consideration
of the last pillar-the cultural dimensions-
the execution of the e-learning strategy
could still be hindered.

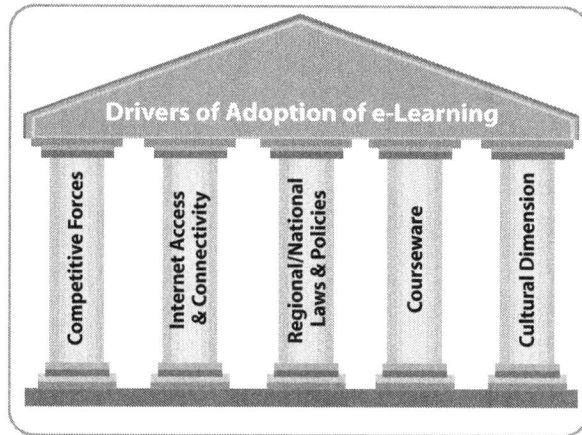

Drivers of Adoption of e-Learning

Competitive Forces

Internet Access & Connectivity

Regional/National Laws & Policies

Courseware

Cultural Dimension

Figure 9-1: Drivers of Global Adoption of e-Learning

The First Driver: Competitive Forces

As discussed in Chapter 2, e-learning implementations are driven primarily by the need for organizations to become more competitive and drive shareholder value. The dynamic, competitive global business environment requires higher standards of quality, lower costs, efficient responsiveness
to customers, targeted products within global market segments, and speedy flexibility to accommodate market changes.

These extraordinary pressures in the twenty-first century marketplace compel global and national
enterprises to:

- Reduce time-to-market for new products/services

- Increase sales effectiveness

- Deploy rapidly and seamlessly to geographically dispersed employees

- Build strong customer relationships

- Leverage investments in Customer Relationship Management (CRM) and Enterprise
  Resource Planning (ERP) implementations

- Align a global workforce to the strategic direction and develop related skills

- Comply with various national and international regulations and laws

As shown in the company cases featured in this fieldbook, e-learning solutions have proven to be
very successful in supporting the growth and development of the workforce to achieve these business goals.

The Second Driver: Internet Access and Connectivity

One of the key drivers and enablers for usage of e-learning is Internet access and connection speed. At the end of 2002, there were approximately 600 million people around the world with Internet access (see Table 9-2). As a comparison, this was only approximately 36 million in 1996. Interestingly, for the first time, Europe now has the highest number of people with access to the Internet.

The percentage of a national population with access to the Internet, called Internet penetration, differs significantly from country to country. Table 9-3 shows the top ten countries in Internet penetration.

In addition to access to the Internet, it is important to understand the impact of con-

Table 9-2: Number of People with Internet Access by Geographic Region	
Geographic Region	**Population in Millions**
Africa	6
Asia Pacific	187
Europe	191
Middle East	5
Canada and USA	182
Latin America	33
World Internet Access in These Regions	**Total: 605 million**

Source: NUA 2002

nectivity or access speed on the e-learning experience. Internet speed determines what types of e-learning programs can be engaged in on the Internet and has an impact on the effectiveness of the e-learning experience. High-speed Internet access is only used by a limited number of Internet users. A 56-Kbps dialup connection has become the lowest-common denominator in the U.S. In contrast, 26 Kbps is considered speedy in many countries.

However, improvements in the telecommunication infrastructure, the increase of wireless Internet solutions, cost-reductions in hardware and Internet access, and the general popularity of the Internet will increase the estimated number of people with Internet access and good connectivity to an estimate of 1 billion globally by 2005 (NUA 2002).

This then becomes a market of a billion potential e-learners around the world.

Table 9-3: The Top 10 Countries in Internet Penetration at End of 2002		
Country Ranking	**Country**	**Internet Penetration in the Population (%)**
1	Iceland	69.8
2	Sweden	65.6
3	Denmark	60.0
4	Hong Kong	59.6
5	US	59.1
6	Netherlands	58.0
7	UK	56.8
8	Norway	54.4
9	Australia	54.3
10	Canada	52.7

The Third Driver: Regional and National Laws and Policies

National laws and policies can have an enormous influence in the adoption of e-learning.

The European Community has published the eEurope 2002 Action Plan, which has committed all the member countries to equipping every citizen with the skills needed to live and work in the information society. They are also providing a European diploma for basic Information Technology skills, including a decentralized certification procedure.

> **Internet Savvyness in the McDonald's Corporation Workforce***
>
> One of the questions we asked online during participant registration was: How often do you use the Internet? We found out that among our employees there was more computer savvyness outside the U.S., than inside the U.S. For example, only 7 percent in Brazil had never used a computer, compared with 26 percent in the U.S.
>
> ** See Chapter 14: McDonald's Corporation*

Other countries where national laws and policies have a favorable impact on e-learning include Sweden, Singapore, and Italy. Sweden and Singapore are establishing nationwide broadband access, which makes these countries ideal for testing broadband e-learning approaches. While in Italy, government initiatives allow citizens to deduct the cost of Internet access and telephone charges from their taxes, resulting in 18 million citizens being connected. In Asia, the Japanese government is providing major subsidies to all Japanese workers to learn new skills online. (IDC 2003)

In some cases, current existing laws have unintended consequences on Internet access and applications in e-learning. Some labor unions in Europe are very apprehensive about access to personal data. For example, there is resistance to the results of an assessment or test being transmitted over the Internet to a learning management system. Germany has excellent Internet access, but names and test scores are not transmitted over the Internet because of existing 'safe harbor' regulations. Awareness of these difficulties, however, allows the application of remedies through specific policies to provide a secure technology environment.

In the cultural adaptation of e-learning initiatives, it is helpful to understand and appreciate the impact of current laws, regulations, and policies that will influence the success of your efforts.

The Fourth Driver: Courseware

Learning must be engaging, motivational, and fun to foster commitment and completion. This is covered extensively in Chapter 4 of this Fieldbook. However, to make e-learning attractive across the globe, language and culturally corresponding look and feel are highly important.

An analysis of the 100 major languages indicates that English is spoken as a native language only by an estimated 5 percent of the global population. In contrast, the residents of English speaking countries currently make up about 40 percent of the Internet user population. Fortunately for e-learning developers, there are a growing number of global companies who have decided to adopt English as their business and learning language. In addition, some countries such as Singapore, Malaysia, and Hong Kong (China) are dominated by English speaking enterprises.

However, there is a growing need to have learning content available on the Internet in languages other than English. It is predicted that 36 percent of all Internet users in 2003 will prefer to use a language other than English, for example:

- 84 percent of online users in Japan prefer to use Kanji

- 75 percent of the online users in Latin America prefer Spanish or Portuguese
- 52 percent of the online users in Europe prefer a language other than English

Besides language translation, there is also a recognized need to provide e-learning that corresponds to the national business culture, and a growing e-learning industry segment is dedicated to this localization of Internet interfaces and e-learning content. Content that especially benefits from such localization includes:

- Development of soft skills, such as interviewing, leading meetings, conducting presentations, and sales skills
- Policies/procedures/laws where it is very important that people understand the subtleties in their home language
- Foreign language training

Elements within e-learning courseware that are often localized include:

- Visuals
- Colors, the meaning of colors can vary by culture
- The characters and appearance of people and environments
- Sound
- Language
- Flow or order

> "The overwhelming predominance of English on the Internet sharply limits its usefulness for most Chinese. Much more Chinese-language content and much faster network speeds will be needed to make the rich multimedia information of the Internet accessible and attractive to the great majority of Chinese Net users."
>
> Source: US Embassy Beijing, 2002

The Fifth Driver: Cultural Dimensions

The fifth pillar is one of the most important considerations in the adoption of e-learning.

What is the definition of culture? Culture is a shared set of learned assumptions, values, and behaviors developed over time, which influence thoughts, feelings, and day-to-day actions. The core of culture is formed by values. It is recognized that there are various groups who can share a culture, for example, engineers share a professional culture. However, in this discussion of e-learning adoption, the focus will be on nation or state culture.

Geert Hofstede has identified and researched four dimensions of culture that have a significant bearing on adaptation of new approaches. These cultural dimensions of difference can point to explicit issues in design and actions that can support the adaptation, and may speed the adoption, of e-learning. Selected dimensions of difference from Hofstede's research are illustrated in Figure 9-2. The potential impacts these dimensions might have on the design and deployment of e-learning programs are enormous (see Figure 9-3).

> "The export of ideas to people in other countries without regard for the values context in which these ideas were developed can be observed in the domains of education, and in particular, management and organization."
>
> Geert Hofstede, Software of the Mind, 1991

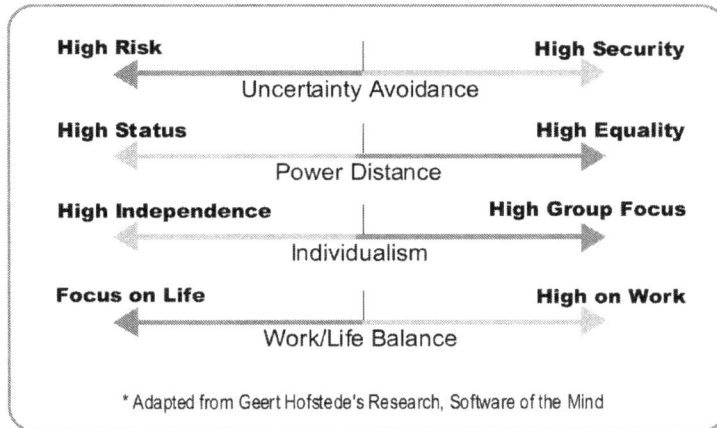

Figure 9-2: Dimensions of Cultural Difference

Explanation of the dimension and the potential impact on e-Learning adoption	
Dimension	Potential Impact on e-Learning Adoption
Uncertainty Avoidance: High Security Versus High Risk Indicates the degree to which one is comfortable with ambiguous situations and can tolerate uncertainty. High security cultures prefer formal rules.	The unproven field of e-learning can be seen in a high risk country as fun, motivational, interesting, but can be seen in a high security country as dangerous and risky.
Power Distance: Status Versus Equality A measure of the inequality between bosses and inferiors, and the extent to which this is accepted. High status countries are much more comfortable with a larger differential than high equality cultures.	In a high equality country, the equality between superiors and workers implies a feeling of knowledge being shared by all. Internet access and e-learning supports a high degree of equality in knowledge sharing. In a high status country, status differences require a 'sage on the stage' to teach what needs to be known. e-learning in this context might require a more directive teaching approach in design.
Individualism: Independence Versus Group The degree to which one thinks in terms of 'I' versus 'We'. Either ties between individuals are loose, or people are part of a cohesive group throughout their lives	In high independence countries, there is a sense of 'being in the driver's seat' of your career and work choices. Since e-learning is frequently an independent activity, cultures which value this trait would adopt e-Learning more readily. In a high group country, the success of the group is paramount. Team learning and group consensus building in the e-learning design would be valued in these cultures.
Work/Life Balance: Work Versus Life The degree to which achievement and success are more valued than caring for others and the quality of life. This dimension is also described as the relative masculine and feminine influences in the workplace.	People 'live to work', or 'work to live'. High work focus countries require recognition, sense of achievement, and certification. In a high life focus country, work related issues, including learning, would need to be managed within the context of the work day.

Figure 9-3: Dimension of Difference and Potential Impact on e-Learning Design

e-Learning Culture Prints

Culture Prints of five countries—United States, Brazil, France, Germany, and Japan—along the dimensions of difference, quickly reveal the potential opportunities and challenges in the design and deployment of e-learning programs and strategy.

The United States e-Learning Culture Print

An ideal e-learning Culture Print[1] of a society that would readily adapt e-learning might be that of the United States, and this could be the fundamental reason why U.S. companies and learners have adopted e-learning so readily (see Figure 9-4).

Americans adopted e-learning more quickly because the self-directed, personalized, on-demand, specific, peer-to-peer style of e-learning meets many of the cultural drivers already in place.

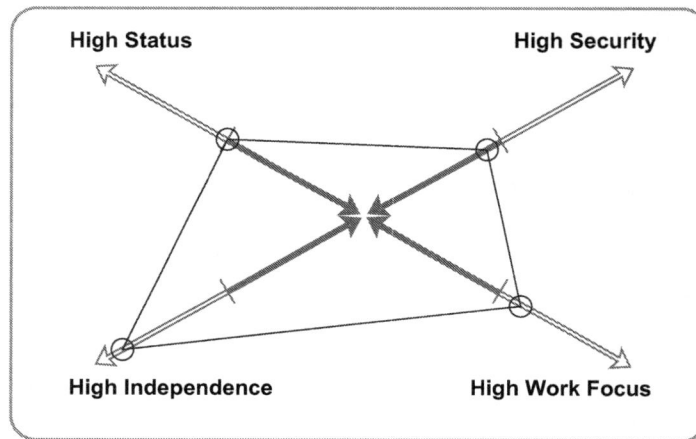

Figure 9-4: United States e-Learning Culture Print

Dimension	Impact
Mid-Range in Equality/Status	Accept content in learning not necessarily promoted or presented by a recognized expert or teacher, but also enjoy recognition for accomplishment.
High in Independence	Able to enjoy the independence of tailoring their 'MyLearning' portfolio, and pursuing their own path. Sense of career ownership drives interest in acquiring new skills.
High in Risk	Capable of taking risks in exploring something not completely proven, learning in Internet time and space.
Mid-Range in Achievement	Equally focused on work and life, able to both accept e-learning opportunities at work, but also will engage anytime/anywhere.

[1] All data for the Culture Print Graphics included in this chapter are adopted from Geert Hofstede, *Cultures and Organizations: Software of the Mind*, McGraw-Hill 1997.

However, the verbatim export of the above approach to e-learning may not work in every culture. The challenge in fostering global e-learning adoption is to effectively integrate the new learning approach with the embedded cultural values of the country.

Investigating the Culture Prints of the other four countries provides some snapshots of how e-learning methods, content, and approaches may be localize more effectively to engage the learner in an experience that recognizes and leverages their cultural drivers.

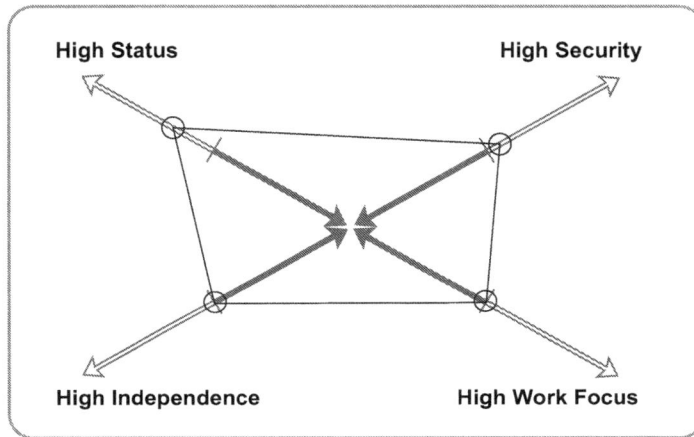

Figure 9-5: Brazil e-Learning Culture Print

As seen in Figure 9-5, the recommendations for e-learning initiatives in Brazil could focus on:

- **High Status:** Include the supervisor to engage the learner in e-learning, reward completion, and involve known subject matter experts visibly in presentations during online live e-learning sessions or in Macromedia Flash content

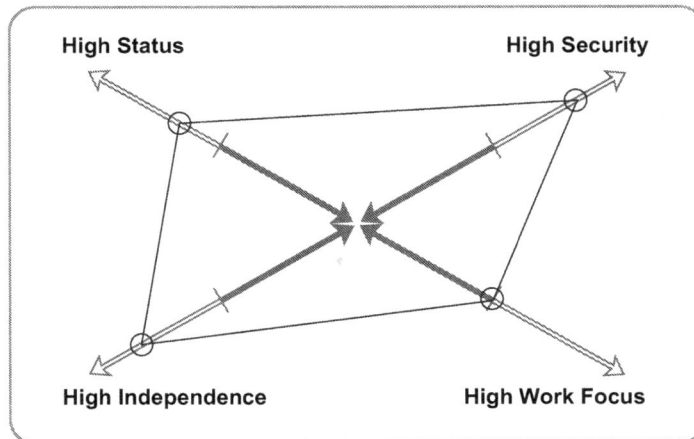

Figure 9-6: France e-Learning Culture Print

The selected recommendations (see Figure 9-6) for e-learning initiatives in France could focus on:

- **High Independence and High Status:** Use features such as MyLearning to enable workers to create and pursue their own learning pathways, while including the supervisor and recognized experts visibly in the promotion of e-learning initiatives and content

- **High Security/Low Risk:** Provide small early wins in the e-learning experience to develop confidence in the approach and value

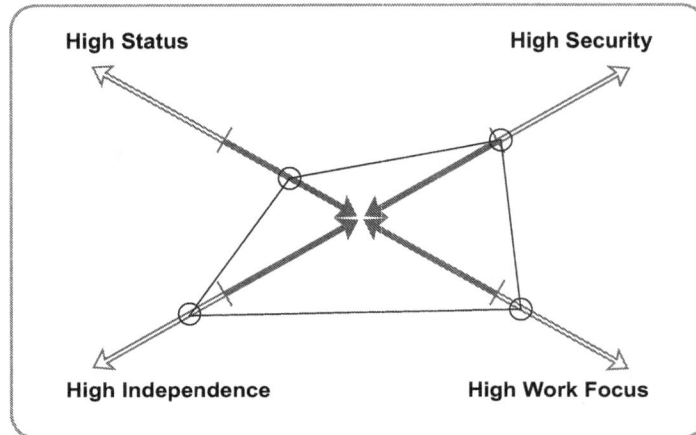

Figure 9-7: German e-Learning Culture Print

The selected recommendations (see Figure 9-7) for e-learning initiatives in Germany could focus on:

- **High Equality:** Share access and network knowledge across the organization through e-learning communities, using e-learning to foster exchanges of best practice

- **High Independence:** Provide universal access and linkages to multiple sources of e-learning opportunity

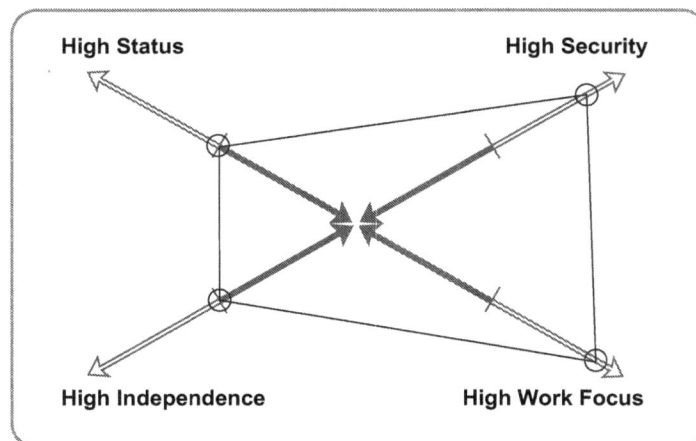

Figure 9-8: Japanese e-Learning Culture Print

The selected recommendations for e-learning initiatives in Japan could focus on:

- **High Work Focus:** Assign individual roles of leadership periodically within the group e-learning experience, where personal expertise is given an opportunity to be observed and commended. Assessments and certification may also contribute to the sense of achievement.

Crafting a Multicultural e-Learning Strategy

In the past, learners were brought out of their own environment to experience learning in a different place, perhaps even a different country. A critical aspect of e-learning implementation is that the learner remains very much in their own culture when engaged in the learning, with local cultural cues in full force around them. Micro-cultural issues that can be ignored when bringing learners out of their normal day-to-day life, must be embraced when pushing learning out through the Internet to the learner, who is sitting in their own office or home in Oslo, Osaka, Sao Paulo, Frankfurt, or Beijing.

Within the blended model of e-learning, there are significant opportunities to address these cultural dimensions, deliberately and effectively.

The considerations that should top your list as you move into a globalized e-learning strategy include:

- Ensure that the drivers of adoption of e-learning strategy, such as competitive forces, Internet access and connectivity, regional/national laws and policies, culturally adapted courseware, and cultural considerations, are part of your assessment.
- Review the impact of the dimensions of difference and the e-learning Culture Print for each country prior to a rollout of e-learning.
- Conduct your own organization cultural assessment to identify significant factors at play.
- Select and implement e-learning initiatives that link to cultural drivers.
- Engage people from different countries in the design and development of e-learning courseware.
- Have pilots in countries to test accuracy, cultural fit, and effectiveness of learning courseware. Let people observe the pilots and give feedback.
- Have a flexible curriculum that allows countries to pick and choose the learning content most valuable to them.
- Recognize that the time for completion of the course will differ because of language, learning, and cultural differences.
- Measure e-learning effectiveness in all of the countries you are serving and manage continuous improvements.

Lessons Learned

✔ Assess the need for e-learning content in the local language.

✔ Identify local e-learning delivery limitations, such as access to systems, compatibility of hardware and software, connectivity, and time for learning

✔ Start with e-learning pilots in new countries and integrate the feedback from a variety of cultures.

✔ Review the Culture Print for each country prior to a rollout of e-learning and make appropriate adaptations

✔ Conduct your own organizational cultural assessment to identify significant factors at play.

✔ Select and implement e-learning initiatives and methodologies that link to cultural drivers.

✔ Create an international glossary of terms.

✔ Ensure that the look and feel of the content and interface reflect culturally acceptable and familiar norms.

✔ Pay close attention to status, hierarchy, and reward systems in the deployment of the e-learning program.

✔ Make sure that the first experience is the best experience possible, as this addresses a variety of cultural values that cross many differences!

Part II:

How organizations are aligning
e-learning with business goals:
25 case studies from leading
organizations

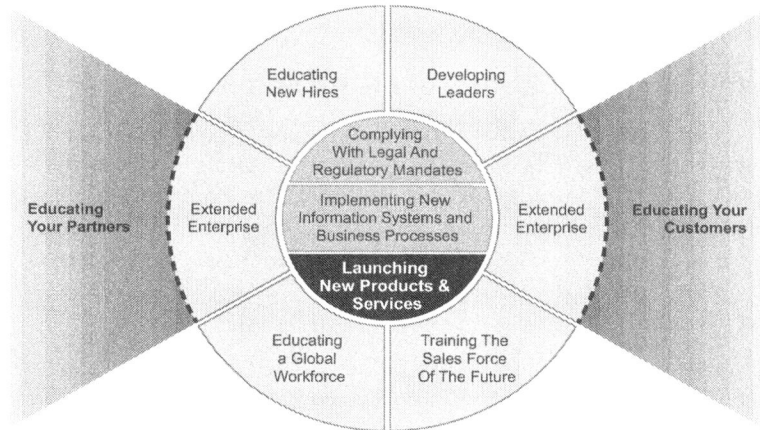

Educating
New Hires

Developing
Leaders

Complying
With Legal And
Regulatory Mandates

Educating
Your Partners

Extended
Enterprise

Implementing New
Information Systems and
Business Processes

Extended
Enterprise

Educating Your
Customers

Launching
New Products &
Services

Educating
a Global
Workforce

Training The
Sales Force
Of The Future

CHAPTER

10

Launching New Products and Services

The cases for this chapter are:

- *Deloitte Touche Tohmatsu*
- *STMicroelectronics*
- *Defense Acquisition University*

Introduction

Why Did They Choose an e-Learning Solution?

A critical success factor for most organizations today is the successful, speedy launch of new products and services. When launching new products and services, time-to-market driven by increasingly compressed product life cycles is critical to profitability. In many cases, the information about the new product or service is sought not only by employees, but also by extended partners, such as customers, vendors, and suppliers. From the employees, to the sales and distribution channels, and on through to the consumer, many diverse audiences must be reached and educated to successfully launch a new product, approach, or service.

However, rapid distribution of this knowledge through classroom training is impractical for a globally dispersed workforce, just as providing written brochures and manuals is inadequate to meet the needs of the extended partners outside the organization.

Using e-learning to address this need offers many benefits, such as:

- Rapid access for a geographically dispersed audience to the requisite knowledge
- Accurate positioning of the product or service
- Consistent quality in the level of service
- Dissemination of essential messages for successfully launching the product or service in the marketplace

This chapter presents three case examples of companies who developed e-learning programs to support the launch of new products and services. They include: Deloitte Touche Tohmatsu, a global professional services firm; STMicroelectronics, a global high-tech manufacturer; and a governmental agency, The United States Department of Defense, Defense Acquisition University (DAU).

All three organizations chose an e-learning approach to rapidly reach a broad audience with a consistent message and learning content. Also important to all three organizations was the need to maximize the capabilities and knowledge of subject matter experts to ensure a consistent message.

Rapid Deployment of Learning to a Broad, Geographically Dispersed Audience

As large global enterprises, the learners of Deloitte Touche Tohmatsu and STMicroelectronics are found in various locations worldwide. Likewise, although U.S. based, DAU learners are comprised of an extended audience of 9,000, including many outside their direct workforce of 500 employees. Although the content in these e-learning initiatives delivered varied significantly from methodology to technology to a certification program, all three organizations found that an e-learning approach afforded a cost-effective method for rapid delivery of the required learning to a broad audience in multiple locations.

The speed of learning completion is represented in the experience of Deloitte Touche Tohmatsu where they found that in addition to reaching their global audience, they effectively reduced the amount of time required to accomplish the goals of the training from 56 hours to 34. Similarly, DAU found that they were able to recapture over 300 work years annually through the efficiencies realized in applying an e-learning solution to the regulated certification requirements.

Essential Messages Delivered in an Effective Manner

Consistent content and messages were essential to the e-learning initiatives at all three case organizations in this chapter, whether they were launching a new product, service, or technology. One limitation of classroom learning, that they each recognized, is that the subject matter expert is only available to those who are able to attend in that moment, at that place. e-Learning enables the subject matter expert to convey clear, reliable content and knowledge over time and diverse geographies to multiple learners, in either live or self-paced e-learning formats.

At STMicroelectronics, self-paced e-learning components provided the foundation for understanding the technology, while expert online coaching sessions provided an opportunity to connect the learner with the right product subject matter expert for detailed questions about their extensive technical product line. At DAU, a decrease in the number of subject matter experts available, due to budgetary constraints and the retirement of the baby-boomer generation, limited their capacity in terms of the learners they were able to accommodate each year. By employing self-paced e-learning, enhanced by individual coaching from the subject matter expert faculty, DAU found that they were able to support more learners with the same number of faculty members, with no adverse impact on the learner experience.

The case organizations in this chapter each have many gold nuggets of experience to share that amplify the usefulness of e-learning solutions when launching new products and services.

Case 1: Deloitte Touche Tohmatsu

Company Facts and Figures

✔ **Industry:** Professional Services

✔ **Scope of Services and Products:** Provides assurance and advisory, tax, and consulting services

✔ **Estimated Number of Employees:** 119,000

✔ **Year e-Learning Introduced:** 1996

✔ **Offices and Locations:** 140 worldwide

✔ **Estimated 2002 Revenues:** US$12.4 billion

✔ **Website:** www.deloitte.com

✔ **Number of e-Learning Programs in Entire Curriculum:** More than 3,000

Introduction

When you think about using e-learning to launch a new product or service, you may visualize a course about a physical product with information on how to use the product and how to support the product among other product specifics. In the case of Deloitte Touche Tohmatsu's (DTT's) Express Methodology e-learning program, the product is a proven approach or methodology for performing a key group of consulting services.

The mission of DTT's Management Solutions (Solutions) group is to provide consulting services to rapidly growing mid-sized enterprises and larger organizations to help them improve their businesses

Why e-Learning?

DTT's Management Solutions group selected an e-learning approach to:

✔ Consistently deliver training on a core methodology to all practitioners globally at a lower cost

✔ Provide any time, any place access to the learning content

✔ Reduce the time-to-train to minimize time spent away from clients

results through process changes enabled by technology. One of their core consulting methodologies is called Express, which outlines Solutions approach for performing Information Technology (IT) Strategy, Package Selection, and Package and Technology Implementation projects. Solutions consultants use the methodology at every step in the consulting process to make their projects more productive and efficient. Therefore, providing effective training on this method is critical to ensuring the delivery of consistent and high quality services to their clients.

In 2001, Solutions launched a development project to create an e-learning approach for delivering learning on the Express Methodology. Moving from their seven-day, instructor-led classroom program, Solutions converted the learning experience to a blended e-learning program—titled *The Express Virtual Team Challenge*—containing 18 hours of self-paced and live e-learning, and a two-day classroom component.

How Was the Program Aligned with the Business?

Conducting IT Strategy, Selection, and Implementation projects for their clients is a major component of Solutions business. All consultants in all of the Solutions practices globally who provide these consulting services must be able to demonstrate proficiency in applying the Express Methodology on their projects.

Before the Express Virtual Team Challenge, only a small percentage of Solutions consultants were able to attend the seven-day, instructor-led training program due to the expense and the geographic challenges involved in program deployment, as well as the volume of the potential audience. Solutions identified e-learning as their answer to bridging the gaps of cost, volume, and geography in delivering this critical learning program to their consultants worldwide.

Using e-learning, they made the course available to all 8,000 consultants around the world. Solutions estimated that previously the learning was only available to a small percentage of their consultants. In addition, using an e-learning format alleviated inconsistencies and varying quality levels in delivering an instructor-led course.

Key Business Drivers

✓ The Express Methodology is one of Solutions' primary methodologies.

✓ Previously, Express Methodology training was only being delivered to a small percentage of the targeted learners through the instructor-led approach.

✓ Using an e-learning approach consistently provides access to key content for all practitioners globally.

How Was the Program Designed?

The Express Virtual Team Challenge is a blended e-learning program with self-paced e-learning, live e-learning, and classroom components. The design contains highly interactive elements including skill application through case studies, the opportunity to discuss project experiences, and group interactions for team exercises.

Self-Paced e-Learning

The self-paced e-learning course (see Figure 10-1), created in Macromedia Flash, contains five modules:

✓ Express: An Introduction

✓ Express: IT Strategy

✓ Express: Selection

✓ Express: Implementation

✓ Express: Case Studies

Each self-paced module has an assessment to measure the learning, and the results are tracked. Other interactive elements include: pre-concept quizzes with feedback that help the learner determine how much they know about the next topic; practice assignments such as drag and drop exercises; example scenarios where the learner makes decisions and receives feedback on their choices to reinforce key concepts; and links to the Express Methodology.

The Case Studies module presents exercises for the learner to apply the skills gained to a sample project. There are resources available to help the learners complete the interactive exercises, including client interviews, relevant industry data, and opportunities to ask an expert for information. In the case study exercises, the learners make decisions and receive feedback on their choices. They also create sample deliverables and compare their work to sample solutions.

Check It Out Online!
www.elearningfieldbook.com

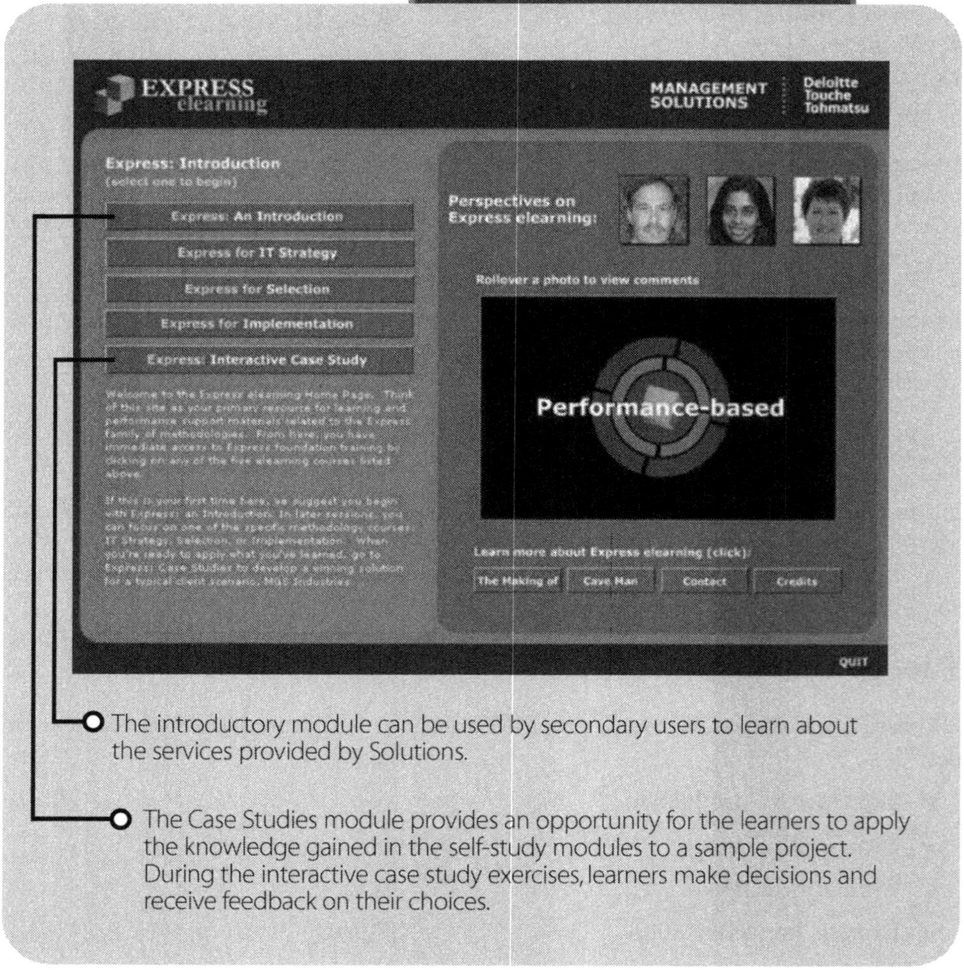

Figure 10-1: Express Methodology e-Learning Home Page

Live e-Learning

Once the self-paced modules were available online, Solutions created a live e-learning component to complement the self-paced course. They use live e-learning to:

✓ Actively manage participation in the course

✓ Add local project examples and additional case study exercises conducted in a virtual team environment

✓ Provide an opportunity for the consultants to interact with their peers and partners and senior managers focusing on these services

✓ Added a team challenge element to the Express Virtual Team Challenge program

Classroom

The new course design also retained a two-day, instructor-led component for extended learning on the Express Implementation module. In the two-day course, participants continue to apply the skills gained in the self-study modules by participating in a case study in a typical project environment. This component is delivered in a variety of flexible options for each location including a choice of live e-learning, a series of mini-sessions delivered over several days, or other approaches best suited to the needs of the local office.

Focused Development for a Global Team

To accomplish the goal of rapid design and development, while incorporating a global view of the content, the projects executive sponsor brought the designers, developers, subject matter experts, and prior course experts from various locations around the world to a central development site in Brussels, Belgium for four weeks.

Having the team together during initial development provided a highly iterative environment where the team members worked together on scope and design, broke into sub-teams to build the components, and regrouped for review sessions. This helped streamline development and decision-making, and provided an effective environment to prototype and incorporate feedback throughout the design process.

Solutions converted the instructor-led courses into storyboards for 18 hours of e-learning in four weeks with a team of 5.5 full-time resources. The Solutions' team views the approach as a significant time saver in the overall project, estimating that the storyboard process may have taken as many as seven months using another approach. Flash development for the project took an estimated 2,400 hours, and 100 additional hours were consumed in the testing, review, and approval process.

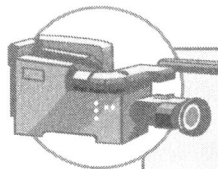

Media and Tools

✓ Macromedia Flash to develop the self-paced e-learning modules and assessments

✓ PlaceWare and Centra for the live e-learning components

✓ Audio of quotes from business leaders included in the self-paced e-learning modules

How Was the Program Deployed?

The Virtual Express Team Challenge is deployed both as an independent self-study e-learning program and as a facilitated group study e-learning program through Solutions knowledge management portal.

As an independent self-study program, the five self-paced e-learning modules are available online at any time.

In the facilitated approach, Solutions couples the self-paced e-learning modules with a live e-learning component for up to 20 participants per course. The goals of this blended approach are to:

✓ Facilitate the learning experience

✓ Add additional real-life project examples to the learning

✓ Include a networking and team dimension to the course

✓ Raise completion rates

This is designed to be implemented at the country or office level so that local project experiences can be included.

To select learners for the structured approach, the team reviews professional development plans to identify individuals who plan to take the course. They are sent an invitation from the national service line leader to participate. The invitation contains a link to an introductory Web site with a welcome from the national practice leader explaining the strategic importance for developing expertise in this area and the importance of committing to learning.

The site includes a game, called Who Wants to Be a Partner?, which introduces the course and its importance to the participants. Correct answers move the learners up the career path, and participants receive T-shirts on completion. The site directs the participants to complete the one-hour awareness module as a pre-session exercise and includes logistics information for the scheduled live e-learning components.

Following the pre-session, there are four scheduled live e-learning sessions. In the first session, the facilitator welcomes the participants, reviews the schedule and objectives, and establishes the exercise teams. The three remaining sessions, scheduled at one-week intervals, focus on the three Express modules: IT Strategy, Selection, and Implementation. Participants are asked to budget five hours for learning each week and to complete the corresponding self-paced module and online case exercises. Also, they are assigned additional case exercises to be completed with their virtual teams. These exercises are based on local project examples.

The facilitation team provide ongoing e-mail support throughout each week, and there is an online discussion forum for participants to exchange thoughts and ideas. The virtual teams present their exercise results online during the final session.

Marketing Approach

✓ Course posted on the knowledge management portal

✓ Consultants contacted through a direct e-mail to promote the course

✓ The executive sponsors promote the course with regional practice leaders

✓ Regional practice leaders identify and directly invite participants

✓ Course promoted through newsletter articles, news articles on the portal, and through presentations at various meetings

What Was the Business Impact of the Program?

Solutions estimates that the cost savings realized by conducting the Express Virtual Team Challenge through e-learning paid for development of the e-learning program within one year. In addition to cost savings, they reduced the time required to train from 56 hours to 34, effectively reducing the amount of time spent away from clients for both consultants and their instructors.

Learner Perspectives

✓ 100 percent of participants said the course increased their interest in using the DTT Express Methodology.

✓ 100 percent said they gained knowledge they can use immediately on the job.

✓ 71 percent said they gained knowledge that could have a long term impact on their career.

Converting the program to an e-learning format also benefits the learners as the program is now available online, any time to all learners—an important benefit for consultants, especially those who may not have had access to the instructor-led course.

The learner feedback for the facilitated approach combining the self-paced e-learning modules, the live e-learning sessions, and the expanded local case studies illustrates the impact and value that the program delivered to the learners:

✓ 88 percent prefer the structured approach to the entirely self-paced approach

✓ 88 percent value the team discussions

✓ 71 percent virtually met and learned from other Solutions professionals

In addition, the course completion rate was an estimated 84 percent using the facilitated approach.

Summary

Purpose: The Express Virtual Team Challenge e-learning course enables Solutions consultants to learn about one of the Firm's primary consulting methodologies-Express for IT Strategy, Selection, and Implementation—and to practice application of the methodology to projects.

Program Structure: The Express Methodology Virtual Team Challenge is a blended e-learning program that contains:

- ✓ Five self-paced e-learning modules
- ✓ A facilitated live e-learning component
- ✓ A two-day classroom component

Number of Learning Hours per Learner: 18 hours of e-learning and 16 hours of classroom learning

Total Number of Hours of Learning in the Program: 34 hours

Number of Learners:

- ✓ 3,000 primary learners worldwide—full course for consultants who deliver IT Strategy, Selection, and Implementation consulting services
- ✓ 5,000 secondary learners worldwide—opportunity for awareness- level learning by completing the Express: An Introduction module for those consultants interested in learning more about the services and service lines supported with the Express Methodology

Completion Requirements:

- ✓ This course is intended for all consultants who deliver IT Strategy, Selection, and Implementation consulting services

Media and Tools:

- ✓ Macromedia Flash
- ✓ PlaceWare
- ✓ Centra
- ✓ Audio recordings

Deployment Mechanism: The Express Team Virtual Challenge is deployed online through the DTT Solutions knowledge management portal

Lessons Learned

✓ The approach of bringing designers, developers, and subject matter experts together in a single location for focused development, streamlines the process and shortens development time. On The Express Virtual Team Challenge project, they used this approach for the design phase only. In a subsequent project, Solutions used the approach for both the design and testing phases. The development lifecycle for the second project was shortened further, and they plan to employ that technique for future projects.

✓ Solutions found that a large majority of participants prefer the structured, facilitated approach over an entirely self-paced learning approach. In addition to user satisfaction, this approach has led to a high course completion rate in a defined period of time. One suggested area for improvement is to expand the course time and live e-learning sessions to allow for reflection and discussion of the group exercises.

✓ From a technical perspective, Solutions worked with their IT organization early in their process to plan the development structure, deployment, and integration aspects. However, they did encounter an implementation challenge later in the process during installation of the development version of the course in the production environment. Although the issue was resolved, the lesson they learned is to not only consult with IT early, but also to consult with them on a detailed level throughout the development and testing processes.

Case 2: STMicroelectronics

Company Facts and Figures

- ✓ **Industry:** High Tech Manufacturing

- ✓ **Scope of Services and Products:** Developing and delivering semiconductor solutions across the spectrum of microelectronics applications

- ✓ **Estimated Number of Employees:** 43,000

- ✓ **Year e-Learning Introduced:** 1999

- ✓ **Offices and Locations:** 6 advanced R&D units, 39 design and application centers, 17 manufacturing sites, and 88 sales offices in 31 countries

- ✓ **2002 Revenues:** $6.36 billion

- ✓ **Web Site:** www.st.com

- ✓ **Number of e-Learning Programs in Entire Curriculum:** 10 in-house, plus off-the-shelf offerings

Introduction

A global independent leader in designing, developing, manufacturing, and delivering semiconductor solutions and microelectronics applications, STMicroelectronics began experimenting with e-learning in 1999.

Early in 2000, after benchmarking and trials, ST University, the corporate university of STMicroelectronics, deployed an e-learning infrastructure to help keep pace with a fast-moving microelectronics market.

A top priority was to deploy strategic sales and marketing programs within the frame of the ST University School of Sales and Marketing. Alain Bucher, e-learning Director of ST University remembers that in 2000, the market was booming. "To keep pace with this growth and increase our marketshare, we had to hire many new sales and marketing staff," says Bucher. "These people needed to be brought up to speed quickly in basic semiconductor technology and processes. We would not have been able to train them all on time using standard classroom training."

Given the market environment at the time and their business goal of increasing market share, STMicroelectronics developed the e-learning program *Fundamentals of Semiconductor Technology* to help new sales and marketing representatives rapidly attain a high level of competency in their field and work more effectively with customers and STMicroelectronics experts.

Why e-Learning?

STMicroelectronics selected an e-learning approach to:

- ✓ Train a large number of people at different locations throughout the globe

- ✓ Meet a rapid time-to-market cycle and reduce time-to-train

- ✓ Rapidly deliver consistent training that does not rely on the availability of classroom instructors

- ✓ Provide a tool to support company culture, which is a key factor in the company strategy and success

This launch was followed by complementary e-learning courses, enriching the sales and marketing curriculum and moving towards a blend of e-learning and traditional classroom training (see Figure 10-2).

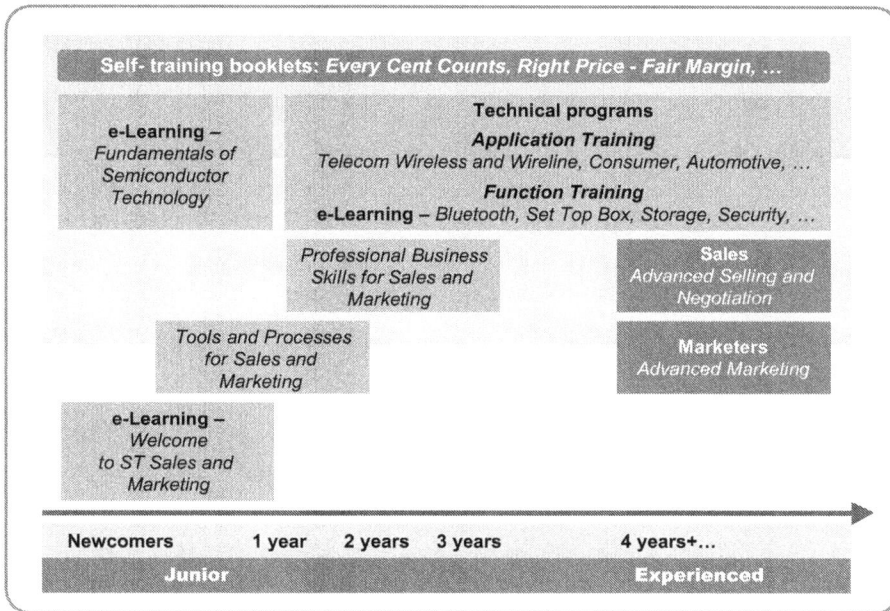

Figure 10-2: Sample of Blended Learning Curriculum

How Was the Program Aligned with the Business?

Prior to the development of e-learning at STMicroelectronics, basic sales and marketing trainings were conducted approximately once a quarter in a classroom at ST University. In addition, the portions of the sales and marketing seminar related specifically to semiconductor technology were taught by a peer engineer, as the owner of the know-how. This required the engineer to be removed from his or her current assignment to travel to the training location and deliver the class.

STMicroelectronics felt that reducing time-to-train was intrinsic to reducing time-to-market and gaining a foothold on increasing market share. With this objective in mind, they began to develop e-learning courses to meet their sales and marketing training needs.

Key Business Drivers

✓ Increase market share

✓ A marked increase in the sales and marketing work-force, who needed to quickly acquire common knowledge of semiconductor technology, processes, and STMicroelectronics solutions

✓ Rapid deployment of new products, requiring knowledgeable sales and marketing representatives

✓ An increasing desire to offer Internet-based training on new products to customers

The new e-learning program answered the key business drivers by coupling learners with the right subject matter experts and deploying knowledgeable sales and marketing staff to the field faster than was possible with the previous classroom-based training.

How Was the Program Designed?

Online Self-Study

The Fundamentals of Semiconductor Technology e-learning program is comprised of four courses, each approximately six hours in duration. They are:

✓ Course 1: Design Steps

✓ Course 2: Front-End Manufacturing Steps and Processes (see Figure 10-3)

✓ Course 3: Back-End Manufacturing Steps and Processes

✓ Course 4: Reliability and Quality Issues

The course content was designed according to standard instructional design methodology adapted to the e-learning medium. The full process ranges from needs analysis to course development and deployment to post-program evaluation and updating.

The content was developed in English using Macromedia software (Dreamweaver, Flash, and Fireworks). Each course includes Kirkpatrick Level 1 and 2 evaluations (satisfaction evaluation and pre- and post-tests) and interactive exercises to reinforce learning and retention.

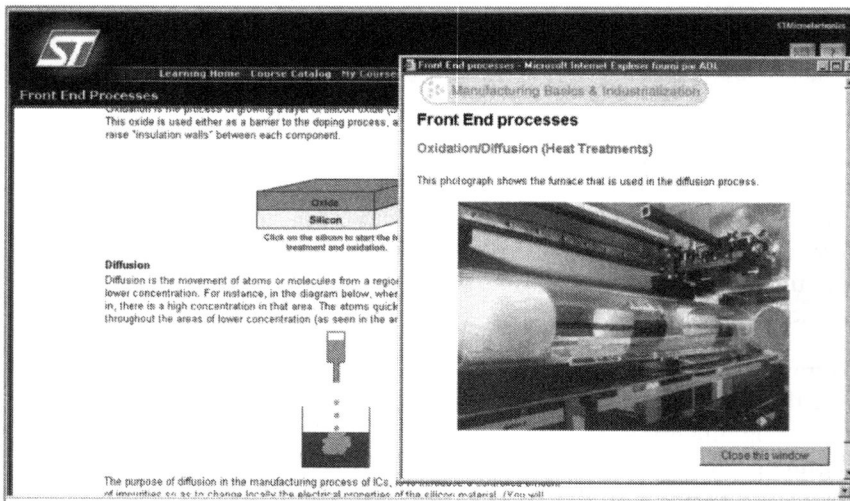

Figure 10-3: Sample of STMicroelectronics Course

Expert Coaching Online

In addition, online discussion forums are facilitated by STMicroelectronics experts throughout the course, allowing participants to ask questions and exchange knowledge. As part of the "ST Trains ST" program, STMicroelectronics experts are trained in online facilitation skills. They remain in close contact with participants, via phone, e-mail, discussion forums, or Microsoft's NetMeeting throughout the online session.

Putting It All Together

Early in 2001, STMicroelectronics began designing and developing the Fundamentals of Semiconductor Technology program using a combination of in-house developers and external contractors. STMicroelectronics estimates that has taken a dedicated staff of at least two full-time designers and developers between three to four months to complete 24 hours of instruction.

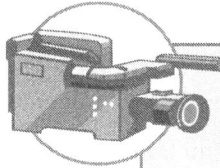

Media and Tools

✓ Macromedia software (Flash, Dreamweaver, and Fireworks)

✓ PeopleSoft's Human Resource Information System (HRIS) to track course registration, completion, and results

✓ IBM's LearningSpace (LS5) as a learning management system

✓ Pre- and post-tests developed and delivered using the LS5 application

How Was the Program Deployed?

STMicroelectronics deployed the Fundamentals of Semiconductor Technology program via the company-wide learning portal, the ST Learning Campus. Content is delivered as self-paced e-learning via IBM's LearningSpace 5 (LS5).

Personal coaching is provided via discussion forums in LS5, and learners in an identified group are encouraged to review materials at approximately the same pace. This fosters peer exchange of information and allows participants a window of access to top-level company experts.

A discussion forum, linked to a specific set of content, is kept open for a limited period of time during which learners review the content and post questions or responses to the forum, which is facilitated by a subject matter expert. Pre- and post-tests and course evaluations are delivered via the LS5 platform.

Marketing Approach

✓ A champion in the sales and marketing division of the company has taken a lead in developing internal promotion for the program.

✓ The program is advertised on the ST Learning Campus, a company Intranet site dedicated to training.

✓ Training managers for each site regularly e-mail identified learners regarding their participation in the program and post course promotion forms in their site information area.

✓ Repurposing the content to meet additional marketing objectives externally can potentially increase market acceptance of a new application or family of products.

This program is currently available only on the company's intranet system. However, STMicroelectronics is investigating the possibility of repurposing the content from other programs (such as Bluetooth) and deploying it via the Internet to support external sales needs and provide customers with additional training on specific products or applications.

What Was the Business Impact of the Program?

The primary advantage of using e-learning for STMicroelectronics has been the ability to bring high-quality content, developed by specialists in the topic area, to the workforce with greater frequency and speed than before.

Compared to a classroom course, STMicroelectronics estimates an e-learning course developed internally costs four times less per learner, while generating Level 1 and 2 evaluations are roughly equivalent to classroom costs. These cost savings have allowed STMicroelectronics to redeploy resources and enlarge its offering of sales and marketing training programs.

What are participants saying about e-learning?

- ✓ The e-learning courses are useful for my job.
- ✓ These courses provide an overall know-how about processes from the beginning to the end.
- ✓ There is insight in all-important steps of the design/manufacturing and quality process for low cost and with no travel needed.
- ✓ I like the flexibility to participate at the time I choose.
- ✓ Having training at my own desk is great.
- ✓ I like the possibility to learn important things even during a cost-saving period.

Though the actual return on investment has yet to be exactly qualified, STMicroelectronics already has evidence that their workforce is improving their skills and enhancing their knowledge faster and more consistently by adding e-learning courses to the School of Sales and Marketing curriculum.

Learner Perspectives

- ✓ Learners appreciate the more personal coaching they receive from subject matter experts using discussion forums.
- ✓ Learners feel comfortable and engaged taking the program in a coached format rather than in an entirely self-paced format.
- ✓ Learners like being able to organize their time.
- ✓ Learners are motivated to enhance their professional skills and overall qualifications.

Summary

Purpose: Provide newly hired sales and product marketing engineers a broad understanding of semiconductor manufacturing steps, processes, and quality requirements, as well as STMicroelectronics technical specificities, bringing them up-to-speed in basic semiconductor technology and processes.

Program Structure:

✓ The program is comprised of four courses, each approximately six hours long.

✓ A group of learners are encouraged to complete each course at roughly the same pace, fostering group discussion and exchange with STMicroelectronics experts.

✓ Additional coaching is provided both individually and via online discussion forums

Total Number of Hours of Learning in the Program: 24 hours

Number of Learners: Approximately 600 targeted learners globally

Completion Requirements:

✓ Complete all courses of the program online at roughly the same pace as peer learners

✓ Participate in discussion forums for each course of the program

✓ Pre- and post-tests and course evaluation

Media and Tools:

✓ Macromedia software (Flash, Dreamweaver, and Fireworks)

✓ Pre- and post-tests are developed and delivered using IBM's LearningSpace application

Deployment Mechanism:

✓ Web-based delivery via the company-wide learning portal

✓ PeopleSoft's HRIS System to track course registration, completion, and results

✓ IBM's LearningSpace as a learning management system

✓ Online discussion forums deployed using IBM's LearningSpace

Lessons Learned

✓ Rely on a good internal network of training managers to help deploy an e-learning philosophy enterprise-wide.

✓ Make precise specifications and procedures when working with contractors who may be assisting in e-learning development, especially if your content is highly technical.

✓ Ensure IT support for e-learning through internal service agreements.

✓ To deploy an e-learning infrastructure and approach enterprise-wide, you must have everyone seated at the table at the same time and gain broad acceptance from the beginning.

✓ Successful e-learning requires solid instructional design.

✓ e-Learning course evaluation level and completion rates depend largely on the quality of facilitation and coaching.

Case 3: Defense Acquisition University

Company Facts and Figures

✓ **Industry:** Public Sector

✓ **Scope of Services and Products:** Education for the Department of Defense Acquisition, Technology, and Logistics Workforce

✓ **Estimated Number of Employees:** 500+

✓ **Year e-Learning Introduced:** 1998

✓ **Offices and Locations:** Five regional campus locations within the U.S.

✓ **Web Site:** www.dau.mil

Introduction

Imagine yourself responsible for the continuing professional education of 132,000 public employees, where the leadership can change every four years, and you have the public's trust to spend tax payers' money efficiently. This is the environment of the Defense Acquisition University (DAU). DAU provides learning to the people who work in Acquisition, Technology, and Logistics for the Department of Defense. Over time, DAU has transformed from a traditional classroom-only setting to a corporate university, emphasizing Web-based training, performance consulting in the workplace, and forming strategic partnerships with university, industry, and professional organizations.

Why e-Learning?

The Defense Acquisition University selected e-learning because:

✓ They had 132,000 people all with yearly learning requirements for their career track.

✓ It was important to find a way to increase the effectiveness of learning.

✓ They wanted to maximize public employees' time in the office.

Learning is integrated throughout DAU and the workplace. This is seen in DAU's mission statement:

Provide practitioner training and services to enable the acquisition, technology, and logistics community to make smart business decisions and deliver timely and affordable capabilities to the war fighter.

Because of the need to reach more learners with quality learning, reduce classroom time, and increase the time people spend on the job, the University needed to optimize learning opportunities. To transform the classroom learning environment of the twentieth century to a learner-centric environment of the twenty-first century, DAU turned to e-learning.

The efficiencies and effectiveness of e-learning at DAU can be seen within their Program Management Career Track. For one course within the program track, DAU graduated four times as many students using e-learning as compared to traditional classroom learning, and they increased the quality of the learning experience by adding case-based scenarios.

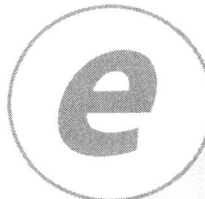

How Was the Program Aligned with the Business?

The Challenge

DAU was at capacity in terms of the number of learners they were able to accommodate per year, and they were challenged with a leaner workforce that needed to spend more time on-the-job and less time in the classroom. Workforce demographics were changing as well; the baby-boomer generation was beginning to retire and taking much knowledge with them. The DAU's learner community was also speaking up. They wanted to improve or obtain certain skills and also wanted to be more efficient in gaining those skills. This was further complicated by the fact that for each of the thirteen career tracks in acquisition, technology, and logistics, there is a continuous learning requirement of 80 hours every two years. Based on their career track, employees are required to be certified in certain areas within a specified time frame. Therefore, DAU needed to develop a learner-centered approach to education.

The Solution

DAU evaluated their classroom courses and developed a plan for transitioning the content for online delivery. DAU determined the courses that were best suited for the transition by reviewing the learning objectives, costs associated with the classroom version, and the projected return on investment. This transition to online delivery enabled DAU to increase the number of students attending a program, as well as decrease the time employees spent away from the job. For example, for the Acquisition 101 course of the Program Management Career Track, DAU was able to accommodate over 9,000 students online, where in previous years with classroom delivery, they could accommodate only 3,000 learners annually.

Key Business Drivers

✓ Increase the productivity of the employees

✓ Decrease the amount of time learners spend in classroom training

✓ Increase the number of learners served within the current DAU resources

✓ Provide just-in-time training that is effective as well as efficient

How Was the Program Designed?

The Program Management Career Track (see Table 10-1) is a certification program designed for a specific audience. This is a continuous learning program with completion requirements over an extended period of time. The track contains six courses and three different levels of certification plus a statutory required level for program management leadership. Progression through the track also includes formal education and real-life experience requirements that are outside the scope of DAU. When learners complete all six courses and the additional requirements, they receive the highest level of certification training in Program Management that the University offers.

Table 10-1: Courses for Program Management Career Track			
Level 1 Certification	**Level 2 Certification**	**Level 3 Certification**	**Statutory Requirement Level for Leadership Positions**
Acquisition 101	Acquisition 201	Program Management 352 Program Management 250	Program Management 401 Program Management 402

With each level of certification, learners become eligible for positions with an increasing level of responsibility. For those in leadership positions within program management, they are required by United States law to complete the entire track, including the highest level of certification. Courses are enhanced by a case study, tailored to a learner's individual needs.

The Move to Online Deployment

As shown in Table 10-2, the move from a classroom-based program to a blended learning program transformed the Program Management Career Track. The number of hours saved by changing the program deployment and the number of learners accommodated more than proved e-learning's return on investment for DAU.

Table 10-2: Learning Hours and Total Learners in Blended Learning vs. Classroom Learning			
Course	Classroom Duration	Online Duration	Annual Learners
Classroom-Based Program			
Level 1 Certification	64 hours	None	3,000
Level 2 Certification	120 hours	None	5,000
Level 3 Certification	560 hours	None	960
Total	**744 hours**	**0 hours**	**8,960**
Blended Learning Program			
Level 1 Certification	0 hours	25 hours	9,000
Level 2 Certification	30 hours	91 hours self-paced 24 hours in virtual group work	5,500
Level 3 Certification	232 hours	50 hours	700
Total	**262 hours**	**190 hours**	**15,200**
Quick Look at the Numbers:			
Total Learning Time: 744 hours vs. 452 hours		Total Learners: 8,960 vs. 15,200	

Program Development

During the design and development phase of an e-learning program, a DAU team conducts a needs assessment, determines content, and develops learning objectives in conjunction with a team from the career field. A full-time program manager is assigned to the project to make sure the program is successful. The program manager selects the appropriate subject matter experts to provide unique content while working with contractors on the instructional design, development, testing, deployment, and maintenance.

Online courseware is developed in accordance with DAU's e-learning technical specifications. Those specifications identify the design standards, SCORM requirements, Section 508 requirements (accessibility), and states which Web-based standards or technologies can or cannot be used. Because of the adherence to the SCORM standard, the e-learning content is re-useable within DAU's learning management system.

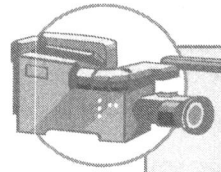

Media and Tools

✓ HTML

✓ JavaScript

✓ Macromedia Flash

✓ Forum

How Was the Program Deployed?

DAU Virtual Campus

The University's virtual campus is a custom-built learning management system called Operational Support System (OSS). The OSS is integrated with the student registration system that allows learners to search for and take e-learning courses and register for classroom-based learning. The University also has worked to develop strategic partnerships with other departments and federal agencies, as well as leading universities, private companies, and professional organizations involved in e-learning. One example is DAU's partnership with the Federal Acquisition Institute (FAI), where FAI funds the course development and DAU hosts the course and provides support for learners and instructors. The benefits began with sharing the costs of the development and deployment of the courseware, but also resulted in all Federal employees taking the same introductory course. Combining all this provides the Acquisition, Technology, and Logistics workforce with a world-class corporate university.

Program Management Career Track Deployment

The Program Management Career Track is an example of a blended learning approach. The University has taken a large program and reviewed the content piece-by-piece to determine the best deployment method. They have combined self-paced e-learning with live e-learning sessions and classroom learning. See Table 10-3 for the program components and delivery methods.

Course	Delivery Method		
	Self-Paced e-Learning	Live e-Learning	Classroom Learning
Acquisition 101	✓		
Acquisition 201	✓		✓
Program Management 250	✓	✓	
Program Management 352	✓		✓
Program Management 401			✓
Program Management 402			✓

Table 10-3: Program Component Delivery Methods

Because the Program Management Career Track is such a long and intensive learning program, the courses are distributed over an extended period of time, depending on the learner's service area and career track. Learners are given 60 days to complete each self-paced e-learning course. To keep track of learners and their progress throughout the program, DAU assigns an instructor who is responsible for supporting people through the course. When the instructor sees that someone has registered for a course but not progressed, the instructor is responsible for following up with the learner to determine the next steps.

Managing Learners through Blended Learning

When offering blended learning courses, the self-paced e-learning is offered within certain time frames to reduce the amount of time between the self-paced sections of the course and the live e-learning and/or classroom portions. For example, when learners sign up for the Program Management 352 course, they are first enrolled into the classroom part (PMT 352B). Approximately 80 days prior to the start of the classroom portion, the students receive an e-mail stating that they may begin the online portion of the course (PMT 352A). Learners then have 60 days to complete the online portion, which must be finished at least two weeks prior to the start of the classroom portion. If they have not completed PMT 352A, they will be dropped from the classroom course.

DAU has found that this approach of limiting the time between completion of the online and classroom components helps to enhance the classroom experience and reduce the amount of information that is lost due to the passing of time. PMT 352 is also the first course where DAU is leveraging the power of its learning management system in the classroom as well as online. Classroom courseware and material, exercises, and exams are all in the learning management system. Students have access to the classroom content at any time.

With the extreme mobility of the Acquisition, Technology, and Logistics workforce, DAU is making the availability of downloadable learning objects a priority. Internet connectivity remains a challenge for DAU participants, with issues such as bandwidth and firewalls. Learners are located throughout the United States, as well as at sea and at international posts. They need the ability to download content, review it in off-line mode, and then upload test scores or completion data. DAU is developing their next generation learning management system that will provide this mobile learning capability, eliminating the need to be constantly tied to the Internet, without giving up the benefits of access to the latest content.

Changing the Way DAU Works

As e-learning delivery began to increase for DAU, they realized that not only did they need to change the learning culture for the learners, they also needed to change the way people at the University approached their work. The effort to move into a more learner-centric organization meant DAU had to operate differently. Instead of classroom instructors, there was a need for e-learning facilitators to coach and monitor learner progress. DAU found that the same faculty could be readily engaged to support the classroom and the online courses. Because the courses are self-paced, DAU could support many more learners with the same number of faculty members.

The increased faculty to student ratio enhanced the learner experience. DAU found that the time e-learning facilitators spent individually with their learners increased over classroom-based training, and this felt more personal to the learner. Because of this increased time, DAU realized that online instructors require a different type of training and preparation so they have developed a faculty certification program that addresses these classroom and online training needs.

Communications for Launching the Program

The marketing efforts for the new e-learning and blended learning courses were an important part of DAU's success. Because the Acquisition, Technology, and Logistics workforce varies in age and background, DAU began reaching out to stakeholders with demonstrations of the new courseware. To advertise e-learning, DAU opened up communication channels to leadership and learners, and developed brochures that advertised courseware and the virtual learning center. DAU staff realized they had to communicate upwards to the Pentagon, as well as out in the field to their end-user audience.

Marketing Approach

✓ Communicating and demonstrating capabilities and efficiencies gained through e-learning to key leadership in the Pentagon

✓ Announcements on the organization's intranet portal front page

✓ Demonstrating program to learners to show that e-learning does help build skills just as classroom training does

What Was the Business Impact of the Program?

With the efficiencies realized through the re-design of the Program Management Career Track, Department of Defense acquisition, technology, and logistics organizations were able to recapture over 300 work years annually. DAU came to this figure by reviewing the amount of time saved with e-learning and the number of learners attending the courses. Because of e-learning, employees are spending less time away from the office and more time being productive in their jobs. In addition, DAU was able to accommodate a significantly larger number of learners and not increase DAU staff. They found that with a blended learning program, the cost per graduate decreased.

Learner Perspectives

✓ "[I appreciated] the ability to take the course online at my own pace with the help of the course book for notes and reference."

✓ 89 percent indicated that their learning objectives were met.

✓ "I saw great benefit in learning through real world-type situations instead of lectures."

✓ "[The course] touched on a lot of areas impacting acquisition that I had not previously been exposed to."

The University envisions a time when all learning is available to all people anywhere, anytime, anyplace. DAU is changing the way people learn, and they are using the available technology to help them do that.

Summary

Purpose: To bring quality learning to more people, reduce the amount of classroom time, and decrease the time people spend away from the job

Program Structure: Learning is offered via self-paced and live e-learning, as well as classroom learning. There are six blended learning courses offering four levels of certification:

- ✔ Level 1: Acquisition Fundamentals
- ✔ Level 2: Program Management Tools and Intermediate Acquisitions
- ✔ Level 3: Case-Based Program Management
- ✔ Level 4: Statutory Requirement Certification Level

Total Number of Hours of Learning in the Program: 190 e-Learning hours; 262 classroom hours

Number of Learners:

- ✔ 132,000 in the Acquisition, Technology, and Logistics workforce

Completion Requirements:

- ✔ Completing all four levels of certification is required for learner to hold one of the top program management leadership positions in the organization
- ✔ Completing lower levels of certification allows learners to become eligible for positions with increasing levels of responsibility

Media and Tools: The program includes these media types:

- ✔ HTML
- ✔ JavaScript
- ✔ Macromedia Flash
- ✔ Cold Fusion
- ✔ Forum
- ✔ Conference calls and e-mail

Deployment Mechanism: Deployed online through DAU's Corporate University, marketing approaches include:

- ✔ Communications to top leadership at Pentagon
- ✔ Buy-in from key stakeholders at the Department of Defense Acquisition, Technology, and Logistics
- ✔ Demonstrations to learners

Lessons Learned

✓ Requirements must be clearly defined.

✓ Course managers and subject matter experts must have sufficient time to support the project.

✓ e-Learning instructors require a different type of preparation and train-the-trainer session than classroom-based training.

✓ Good project management of the design, development, and deployment of e-learning is essential.

✓ Maintaining a production and quality review schedule and adhering to the work plan is important to preserve the intensity and integrity of the program

✓ Plan and budget for and incorporate content and technology upgrades (hardware and software) during the life of the program.

✓ Ensure that the infrastructure to support the program is in place.

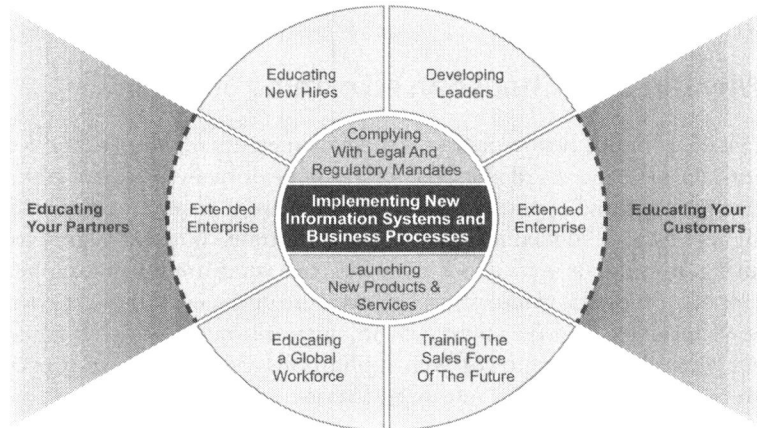

Implementing New Information Systems and Business Processes

The cases for this chapter are:

- *Wyndham International, Inc.*
- *Anglo Platinum*

Introduction

Why Did They Choose an e-Learning Solution?

Efficiency of business processes is the new measure of winners and losers. Process management is critical to the success of any business, as poor or badly managed processes drain resources and profits. Improved application of new information systems and related business processes produce higher yields, while reducing costs and cycle time. Whether highly technical industries, manufacturing, mining, or service industries, all companies are integrating new information systems that support products, platforms, solutions, customers, customer experience, revenue models, processes, value chain, logistics, supply chain, channels, networking, and research and development. In many cases, the strengths of Web applications are employed to support the integration of these processes to simplify and automate diverse functions.

e-Learning is a key solution to training employees in the application and uses of these new information systems and business processes. The use of technology-based learning itself mirrors the environment that is being implemented, while the rapid, standard roll-out of capabilities related to implementation of the new systems allows the investment to be leveraged more quickly.

Engaging learners in e-learning to develop understanding and capabilities in the implementation of software applications provides many benefits, such as:

- Speed-to-competency on new software and systems implementations
- Effective application of the software to business problems and issues
- More rapid return-on-investment for technology investments

This chapter presents two case examples of companies who developed e-learning programs to support the implementation of new information systems. They are: Wyndham International, Inc., an upscale, luxury hospitality and lodging company; and Anglo Platinum, the world's leading producer of platinum metals.

Both organizations chose an e-learning approach to reach a geographically dispersed audience, with learning on the use and application of new software that would enhance their business processes.

Efficient Training of Dispersed Learners on New Information Systems

Both Wyndham and Anglo Platinum needed to reach dispersed learners quickly to train them in new software as it was launched. In the case of Wyndham, the learners were located in their hotels around the world. The goal was to implement an information system that would benefit their customer loyalty campaign and provide a standard experience for all customers at every Wyndham property, based on their customer profile and preferences. On the other hand, Anglo Platinum wanted to reach their miners and 13 geographically dispersed business units, many of which were in remote, somewhat inaccessible locations. The new software was the implementation of SAP R/3, urgently needed to meet internal requirements and external mandates. In both organization cases, the staff needed hands-on experience with the software and input from subject matter experts as they applied the technology to their processes.

Different e-Learning Approaches Successfully Employed for Information Systems Training

Many employees in the Wyndham organization worldwide needed to be trained on the new software—a total audience of 3,500 potential learners at 165 properties. However, customization would be needed to accommodate the various property types and sizes. In addition, experimentation with the software application to a variety of local circumstances and challenges had to be integrated into the learning experience. To accomplish this, Wyndham's e-learning solution included a combination of pre-launch dialogue with local property management, followed by live e-learning sessions customized to local needs, during which the goal of the customer loyalty program was described, and hands-on application exercises were used and feedback given. Finally, they recorded the live e-learning sessions to make the learning available to additional employees. With this solution, Wyndham was able to launch the software realizing a 329 percent ROI on the first five months of training.

At Anglo Platinum, the choice was different, but just as successful. With a potential 4,500 SAP end users and a strong impetus provided by new legislation in South Africa to implement HRD activities on a broad scale, Anglo Platinum chose a blended model for learning. The blended model included classroom orientation where the objectives of the new system were described, self-paced e-learning with application activities and assessments, and video conferencing with subject matter experts demonstrating SAP transactions. This approach was so effective that Anglo Platinum is intending to employ e-learning to meet related objectives in the improvement of basic literacy, adult education, management development, and additional systems training.

In both case examples in this chapter, the ability to employ e-learning in the launch of new software systems ensured that the application of the software was meaningful to those required to execute the transactions, and also that the training in the software allowed the intended value of the system to be realized more quickly.

Case 1: Wyndham International, Inc.

Company Facts and Figures

✓ **Industry:** Hospitality

✓ **Scope of Services and Products:**
Owns, leases, manages, and franchises
hotels and resorts throughout U.S.,
Canada, Mexico, the Caribbean, and
the United Kingdom

✓ **Estimated Number of Employees:**
25,000

✓ **Year e-Learning Introduced:** 1999

✓ **Offices and Locations:**
Headquarters in Dallas, Texas with 165
property locations in the U.S., Canada,
Mexico, the Caribbean, and the United
Kingdom

✓ **Web Site:** www.wyndham.com

✓ **Number of e-Learning Programs
in Entire Curriculum:** 150+

Introduction

Wyndham International, Inc. is an upscale,
luxury hospitality and lodging company.
Based in Dallas, Texas, Wyndham owns, leases, manages, and franchises hotels and resorts in
the United States, Canada, Mexico, the Caribbean
and the United Kingdom.

At the heart of Wyndham's operating philosophy is
Wyndham ByRequest, an innovative guest loyalty
program that stresses personalization of each guest's
stay. To fully integrate the guest program across all
hotels and resorts, Wyndham needed a common
property management system that would track
guest profiles and preferences and also provide man-
agement with tools for customer relationship management, rate management, forecasting, and
report writing. With this in mind, Wyndham selected MICROS-Fidelio OPERA Enterprise
Solution.

Why e-Learning?

Wyndham selected an
e-learning approach to:

✓ Provide a cost-effective solution to deliver
a consistent message to 3,500 employees
at 165 locations

✓ Reduce training related expenses, such as
travel, facilities, and support

✓ Provide just-in-time, customized learning
and deliver more efficient information at
an accelerated pace

The OPERA property management system is a full-featured, Oracle-based system that presents
users with a familiar, easy-to-use Windows interface. With the OPERA Enterprise Solution
installed in every hotel, Wyndham would have the tremendous resources to further enhance the
experiences of their guests.

To successfully implement the new project management system, every employee at a Wyndham
hotel would need to attend training on the new software and how it would be used to support
the ByRequest program. Traditionally, classroom-based training would have been conducted on-
site at Wyndham's hotels. Given the challenge of reducing training expenses and meeting training

needs in a short period of time, the implementation team decided to use an e-learning solution for this project.

For Wyndham, using e-learning to conduct the training resulted in:

✓ Faster implementation

✓ Reduced training expenses

✓ Decreased training time

✓ Successful implementation of an integrated property management system that supports the Wyndham ByRequest program

How Was the Program Aligned with the Business?

The Challenge

Listening and responding to the needs of customers is the core of Wyndham's brand philosophy and characterizes their approach to hospitality. Wyndham developed a brand-wide initiative, focusing on empowering guests to customize their hotel experience by voicing their needs. Wyndham ByRequest invites guests to personalize each hotel stay to their own preferences and rewards them with meaningful and immediate perks during their stay. Much more than a guest recognition program, Wyndham ByRequest is a service philosophy integral to the Wyndham brand.

Within Wyndham's proprietary brand, there are three distinct hotel brands: Wyndham Hotels & Resorts, Wyndham Luxury Resorts, and Summerfield Suites by Wyndham. Approximately 30 percent of Wyndham properties are privately managed and franchised and were integrated with the company's central reservation or property management system. Wyndham needed a way to have all properties communicate with each other so guests could make arrangements for stays at other Wyndham locations while retaining their stay preference information.

The OPERA Enterprise Solution was implemented to seamlessly integrate all of Wyndham's technology initiatives, including a common property management system, a centralized reservations office, Wyndham ByRequest, and an upgraded Wyndham Web site. This new system would house the ByRequest personal profile information of guests, as well as handle transactions associated with hotel management, such as check-in, guest registration, and accounts payable for all Wyndham property locations.

As the new property management system was rolled out, it was vital to the success of the project to train employees about the system and demonstrate how it would support the Wyndham ByRequest program. So the challenge was how to quickly and economically train more than 3,500 employees at more than 165 property locations throughout North America, the Caribbean, and the United Kingdom.

The Solution

Previously, corporate personnel traveled to various Wyndham sites to deliver training sessions, which was costly in terms of travel for trainers and staff, lost work time, and facility expenses. In this case, the OPERA project team selected Centra and its collaboration technology to host live instructor-led, e-learning events.

Together with Centra, Wyndham could deliver training to learners in any location for virtually little expense, excluding employee time, initial development time, and Centra fees. In the first five months of the OPERA training program, Wyndham saved 329 percent using the virtual classroom technology compared with traditional classroom-based training.

Key Business Drivers

✓ Rapidly educate staff about a new property management system software and how it would support Wyndham's guest loyalty program

✓ Further enhance the guest experience at all Wyndham hotels and resorts

How Was the Program Designed?

The OPERA training program is a live e-learning event and is designed to allow the project team to interact with learners for more effective training. Handout materials accompany the live e-learning sessions and are sent to participants prior to the training event.

With a live e-learning platform, the project team has flexibility in scheduling sessions and the ability to record sessions. This is an important feature because hotel staff tends to be transitional, with an influx of staff during the peak season and a large number of part-time and flex-time employees. Employees who miss their training sessions or need refresher training can easily get access to content.

To ensure that training sessions are relevant for the audiences at the various Wyndham properties, the OPERA team designed courses by job function or task. During a six-month period, the team designed and developed ten courses: Reservations I, Reservations II, Front Desk, Housekeeping, Cashiering, TAP (Travel Agent Processing), Groups, Accounts Receivable, Night Audit I, and Night Audit II. Each course was designed to be delivered in three hours or less, allowing the team to easily pull together and break apart the content, based on the needs at a certain property. For example, an employee at a 1,200-room resort with multiple restaurants has different training requirements than that of an employee at a 400-room hotel. A live e-learning event could easily be modified to target the training needs for a specific group or department.

Prior to the property management system rollout, the instructors review the hotel's current system and mimic the conditions in the new system to assist with the transition. The instructors have found that this additional level of effort has paid big dividends with the participants in terms of making learning connections to the new system.

Course content was developed in PowerPoint and included new terms and concepts, as well as traditional classroom elements, such as brainteasers and quiz questions. The five trainers on the OPERA team, who developed the materials, also designed the program to include significant system demonstration time using application sharing via the live e-learning platform tool.

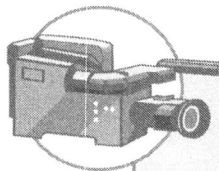

Media and Tools

✓ Custom content, developed in PowerPoint

✓ Video and audio

✓ Adobe Acrobat files and other Microsoft Office tools

✓ Classes delivered via CentraOne version 6.0

✓ Property management system training environment for instructor demonstrations and learner practice

Just as with traditional classroom-based training sessions, the program is designed so that participants can experiment with the new technology. Application sharing allows participants to work with the new system and perform transactions in a practice environment under the guidance of the instructor. The instructor can ask a participant to run a demonstration and then coach them remotely. During live sessions, instructors also provide time for participants to complete exercises. Participants, each working at their own computer, work through real-life scenarios in the property management training environment while the instructor is available for questions and help during the session.

How Was the Program Deployed?

The OPERA e-learning program was rolled out via the Wyndham International University Web site as properties upgraded their property management system. Wyndham houses the content and hosts the sessions on its servers using purchased Centra licenses.

As a site is ready to go-live with the upgraded system, instructors work with property managers to determine course requirements and employees schedules. Most classes are offered at least twice to accommodate different shifts and worker coverage. Sessions are also recorded for attendees to review content at a later date, or for employees who missed a session.

At the designated session start time, participants log into the live e-learning platform through the Wyndham International University Web site and then click the session link to join the instructor for the class. The instructors conduct the training sessions from Wyndham International headquarters in Dallas, Texas. Most learners participate from PC work stations at Wyndham property locations, but because the sessions are offered over the Internet, they could also participate in the live online sessions from any location.

Marketing Approach

✓ Program launch presentations were given at every location.

✓ Announcement packages, containing information such as required courses and class dates, were sent to each hotel location.

✓ Global leadership sent e-mails directly to all employees explaining the requirements and purpose of the program.

Learners wear headsets to communicate with the instructor and other class participants. This real-time feedback creates a very interactive learning experience.

What Was the Business Impact of the Program?

Because the upgraded property management system enables Wyndham properties to communicate and share guest preference information with each other, a successful employee training program was crucial to business. Successful training means that employees are better prepared to provide customized services for guests, which is at the core of Wyndham's brand philosophy.

By conducting the OPERA program as a live e-learning event, Wyndham realized a 329 percent return on investment in the first five months of training. e-Learning brought 3,500 geographically-dispersed employees up-to-speed in a short period of time without the travel, facilities, and support costs associated with classroom learning.

In addition to the monetary impacts this training program has had on the organization, the e-learning arm of the Wyndham International University took shape. Wyndham International University offers employee training on various topics from technology to risk management to benefits. Learning is offered through classroom sessions and self-paced or live e-learning sessions. e-Learning has now become a part of the Wyndham culture, with employees preferring to use a virtual learning format over traditional classroom offerings.

Learner Perspectives

✓ 98 percent of Wyndham's online participants have reacted positively to the e-learning solution.

✓ The recorded sessions add flexibility to help maintain work balance.

✓ One participant comments that "…e-learning has made it easier for me to obtain information when I need it, and it is targeted to my individual learning needs."

Summary

Purpose: To effectively train a geographically-dispersed audience about a new property management system while reducing training costs and travel expenses. The new system enhances the guest experience by supporting Wyndham ByRequest and improving communication between properties.

Program Structure: The OPERA project team, tasked with implementing the new property management system, designed and developed training materials by job role. In total, ten courses were developed and all were delivered via Centra's live e-learning platform.

Number of Learning Hours per Learner: 15 to 25

Total Number of Hours of Learning in the Program: 240

Number of Learners: 3,500 employees in 165 locations

Media and Tools:

✓ Custom content, developed in PowerPoint

✓ Video and audio

✓ Adobe Acrobat files and other Microsoft Office Tools

✓ Classes delivered via CentraOne version 6.0

✓ Property management system training environment for instructor demonstrations and student practice

Deployment Mechanism: Wyndham International University was the gateway used for the training sessions. Wyndham International University is hosted on a customized Centra platform located at Wyndham's Corporate Headquarters. Hotels ready for implementation attend the virtual training sessions.

Lessons Learned

✓ Just as with traditional instructor-led classroom training, include activities, such as brain-teasers and quiz questions, as well as time for breaks in virtual classes.

✓ Try to encourage more participation in synchronous sessions.

✓ Give participants more control during live sessions and make sessions more interactive.

✓ Recognize that there will be a learning curve with live e-learning sessions.

✓ Provide support materials for on-the-job reference.

Case 2: Anglo Platinum

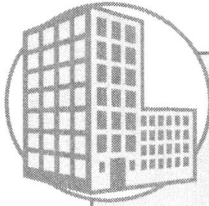

Company Facts and Figures

- ✓ **Industry:** Mining
- ✓ **Scope of Services and Products:** Largest platinum producer in the world
- ✓ **Estimated Number of Employees:** 65,000
- ✓ **Year e-Learning Introduced:** 2001

- ✓ **Offices and Locations:** South Africa
- ✓ **2002 Revenues:** US $2.3 billion
- ✓ **Web Site:** www.angloplat.com
- ✓ **Number of e-Learning Programs in Entire Curriculum:** 13

Introduction

The Anglo Platinum group is the world's leading primary producer of platinum group metals and is listed on the Johannesburg and London Stock Exchange.

During a recent SAP implementation, Anglo Platinum selected a blended learning solution to train 4,500 end users.

Anglo Platinum used this opportunity to pilot e-learning within the organization and in the process reviewed and revised their Human Resources Development (HRD) strategy. As a result of the success of the SAP project, Anglo Platinum is intent upon using e-learning to support basic literacy, adult basic education, management development, and compliance training in addition to systems training. They will also be using e-learning to support the next SAP upgrade. The overall strategic intention is to use e-learning to make learning available to people any time and in any place to increase productivity, to meet legal compliance requirements, and as part of their social responsibility to develop previously disadvantaged people within South Africa.

The rapidly expanding nature of the industry as well as national legislation, require HRD activities on a large scale. The traditional HRD approach cannot meet the demand, and has led to the emergence of e-learning as a solution.

Why e-Learning?

Anglo Platinum selected an e-learning approach because they needed to:

- ✓ Train 4,500 SAP end users
- ✓ Reach a geographically dispersed workforce in remote locations
- ✓ Access and on-board new business units quickly

How Was the Program Aligned with the Business?

The initial business driver of e-learning within Anglo Platinum was the implementation of SAP R/3 across 13 geographically dispersed business units, many of which are in remote locations. In addition, as a result of the business expansion program, there were a large number of new employees who required SAP training.

HR therefore had to adopt a training approach, which could be developed centrally and deployed nationally. The plan had to accommodate a large number of end users, with different levels of SAP experience and understanding of Anglo Platinum's business processes.

The SAP training also had to be delivered within a short period of time, and this resulted in the need to run multiple sessions simultaneously. There were also an insufficient number of trainers to deliver the training using a traditional classroom approach. The e-learning platform therefore enabled Anglo Platinum to use existing permanent employees to facilitate or act as mediators without incurring the cost of additional trainers.

The work environment also posed a number of challenges. At Anglo Platinum, many SAP end users are miners and spend a large part of their day underground. A flexible manner to train production personnel had to be introduced, while minimizing traveling and accommodation costs. The safety of personnel traveling over large distances was also a factor that was addressed through the use of an e-learning platform.

Key Business Drivers

✓ Keep pace with rapidly expanding business and the addition of new business units

✓ Provide for a longer rollout period

✓ Reach a geographically dispersed workforce in remote locations

✓ Meet demand with limited number of internal training staff

✓ Run multiple training sessions simultaneously

✓ Provide flexible training hours to meet requirements of the work environment

✓ Make provisions for refresher training

How Was the Program Designed?

The SAP Learning Program is a combination of a self-study e-learning component and a video conference workshop.

Program Structure—Two Levels of Learning

The first component of the program addresses theory and processes and provides an opportunity to perform transactions in a simulated environment. The objective of this component is for learners to gain an understanding of the system and also to understand why they need to complete various transactions. The activities include:

> ✓ An introduction and orientation session during which a facilitator explains the objectives and assists the learners with the first online learning activity.

> ✓ A self-paced e-learning session (see Figure 11-1) during which the learners are given headphones, and access to a number of online activities, including theory, practice, and assessment.

The second component focuses on various SAP transactions. The objective of this session is for learners to observe the facilitator completing a number of transactions on the actual SAP system and then to practice the exercises on their own. The activities include:

✓ An interactive video conference session explaining the process and the related transactions

✓ A self-paced exercise on the computer

In addition, specific online tests had to be successfully completed before learners could move on to subsequent sections.

Development Process

Media and Tools

✓ Video conferencing

✓ Macromedia Authorware

✓ iTutor

✓ AVI video files

✓ Quick reference guides

All courses were developed by Anglo Platinum staff. The team consists of four or five people, and at first it took approximately 200 hours to develop one hour of learning. This time has since been reduced to approximately 85 hours of development time.

In total, it took approximately six months to purchase the relevant hardware and software and develop two, two-day SAP courses and also pilot them. Anglo Platinum incorporated a number of tools and media into the design. The primary facilitation tool was videoconferencing, and the self-paced e-learning sessions were developed in iTutor and Macromedia Authorware.

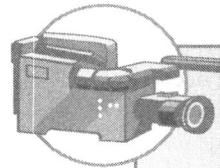

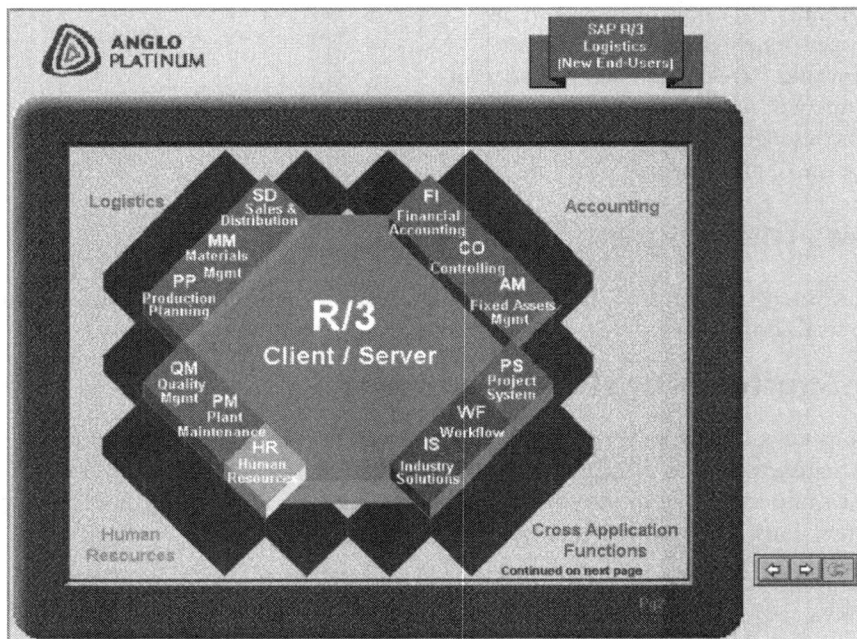

Figure 11-1: Learning Program Interface

How Was the Program Deployed?

For delivering the program, a host classroom was equipped with videoconferencing facilities and PCs. A number of remote classrooms were also equipped with PCs and linked to the videoconferencing facilities. Anglo Platinum initially tried to access the courses from a central server but found that the access time was too slow due to the large video and simulation files. They eventually loaded the courses onto individual PC hard drives.

During Day One of the two-day program, the learners in both the host classroom, as well as the remote classrooms, work through a number of self-placed e-learning modules. In takes the learners from five to ten hours to complete the program, depending on their level of SAP knowledge and PC literacy. One benefit of the self-paced e-learning approach is that all learners begin at the same level in terms of knowledge on Day Two of the program.

During Day Two, the learners in the remote classrooms are linked up to the host classroom. The objective of this session is to practice completing transactions within SAP. In contrast to the previous day, the learners now complete transactions within the SAP environment rather than in a simulated environment. A facilitator who is located within the host classroom guides the learners. The learners within the remote classrooms watch the facilitator on a large television screen. Moderators, located within the remote classrooms, assist the facilitator. Anglo Platinum selected the videoconferencing system as opposed to Web conferencing because of the higher quality and speed it presents.

Anglo Platinum has not purchased a learning management system. They use SAP's Training and Events module to record course attendance and test results. Because functionality is related to payroll, the learners are required to pass the test with a 100 percent rating before being accredited and gaining access to SAP.

A full training management session was held with the relevant people at the various mining sites before any training began. Several test runs were also conducted with various audiences to give the facilitators and moderators an opportunity to become familiar with the new delivery method. The moderators were people from the business unit HRD departments.

Anglo Platinum also decided on an unusual initial target audience. They selected the people who they thought would be most likely to resist the new delivery medium. The rationale for this was to try the new approach on a critical group of people, and then assess the validity of any criticism and make the necessary changes.

Once senior management was exposed to the approach, they actively supported and promoted the program. Prior to this, an executive business case was prepared and endorsed by the Executive HR Director and fully bought into by the HRD professionals.

Marketing Approach

✓ Training management session

✓ Test runs

✓ Critical target audience

✓ Senior management buy-in

What Was the Business Impact Program?

The pilot project was considered a huge success and the e-learning approach has been subsequently included in the HRD strategy as a major focus area for the delivery of all kinds of learning interventions.

By adopting an e-learning approach of this nature, Anglo Platinum was able to reach a wide audience quickly, reduce the costs associated with travel and accommodation, reduce the time away from work, allow learners to progress at their own rate, work accurately once back on the job, and increase productivity.

In addition, it was possible for a group of people, who may not have had an opportunity otherwise, to share ideas remotely and learn from one another.

Finally, the pilot was used as a proof-of-concept and gained acceptance from management as well as staff as an exciting alternative to traditional classroom training.

Since the SAP pilot, Anglo Platinum has also developed a number of soft skills and compliance programs and has received similar positive feedback. An extensive evaluation has been developed for learners to provide feedback on course content and delivery. The benefits have once again been instantly recognized by learners, in particular the enhanced way of learning.

It appears that the program was very well accepted, and that learners would welcome further e-learning opportunities. This ties in well with the Anglo Platinum HRD strategy to support basic literacy, adult basic education, management development, and compliance training in addition to systems training.

Learner Perspectives

✓ "I was really impressed with the e-learning process. I think this way of learning can save a lot of time and money in future. Well done!"

✓ "This kind of training is what we've been waiting for, and its immediate implementation will help so much."

✓ "I think all employees should complete the course. It was excellent with the new technology. It works great."

Summary

Purpose: Provide essential SAP training to 4,500 end users in a cost-effective way

Program Structure: The program consisted of a two-day session divided into two distinct phases:

✔ Theory and practice with simulation and assessment

✔ Hands-on practice using the SAP environment

Number of Learning Hours per Learner:

✔ Day One: Range between 6 and 10 hours

✔ Day Two: 6 hours

Number of Learners: 4,500

Completion Requirements:

✔ End users must pass assessment with 100 percent proficiency

Media and Tools:

✔ Self-paced e-learning

✔ Video conference

✔ Quick reference guides

Deployment Mechanism: The program is deployed in a host classroom environment, and at the same time, in multiple remote locations.

✔ Host classroom has PCs, a facilitator, and video conference system

✔ Remote classrooms have PCs, a moderator, and a television screen for viewing live video conference session.

Lessons Learned

✔ e-Learning is still very much in its infancy; therefore, there are very few people who can provide advice on how to approach a project of this nature.

✔ Understanding the culture and identifying what will work best is critical.

✔ Gaining senior management support early on in the process supports success.

✔ Developing a strong business case gains management support.

✔ A research and development pilot phase is critical to prove the concept to management.

✔ Providing the learners with enough support makes them feel at ease.

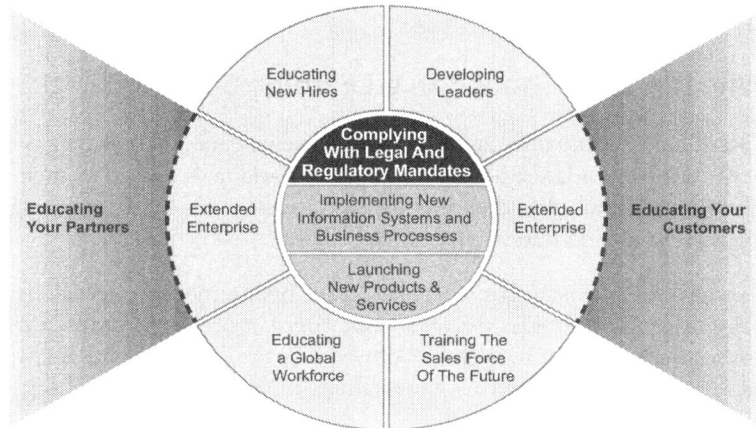

Complying with Legal and Regulatory Mandates

The cases for this chapter are:

- *The Home Depot*
- *BMW of North America, LLC*
- *The Hartford*
- *Wachovia Corporation*

Introduction

Why Did They Choose an e-Learning Solution?

Today, many companies are faced with the challenge of complying in a designated time frame with various standards, policies, regulations, and laws related to their business. Often, companies must demonstrate that their employees have completed training programs on the standards or regulations as a condition of their compliance.

Compliance with standards may be driven by internal or external factors. For example, in externally-driven scenarios, companies must conduct training to meet a requirement specified by a government or other regulatory body to be in compliance with a law or regulation. In internally-driven scenarios, companies may establish internal policies requiring training to meet a specific business objective.

Characteristics of successful compliance training include:

- Ensuring easy access for registration and participation
- Measuring the learner's skill development on the topic
- Tracking participation and other required data about the learners
- Reporting the results as required

This chapter presents four case examples of companies in diverse industries that developed e-learning to meet a compliance training need. They include: The Home Depot, the world's largest home improvement retailer; BMW of North America, LLC, distributor of BMW automobiles, motorcycles, and sports activity vehicles (SAVs); The Hartford, one of the largest insurance companies in the United States; and Wachovia, provider of complete banking services, brokerage services, asset management, wealth management, and innovative products for individual customers.

The four companies discussed in this chapter each successfully used e-learning in a different way to meet the challenge of training their employees on compliance issues, regardless of time frame, complexity, and content.

Ensuring Standards in Compliance Training

The regulations distributed by legal entities drives compliance training in a variety of industries as diverse as financial services and home improvement retailing. A critical issue is for all employees to receive standard training that achieves the goals of the compliance regulation. Equally important is that this can be verified by attendance and completion records kept by the company. In the case of The Home Depot, several safety and hazard regulations set by the United States Occupational Safety and Health Administration (OSHA) impact daily safety and operations. One aspect of these regulations relates to training over 90,000 Home Depot associates every two years in forklift truck safety. The Home Depot uses a blended learning approach because it is the most cost-effective way to train its large audience with a standardized curriculum. A side benefit in using e-learning to achieve this goal was that The Home Depot saved over 60,000 instructor hours compared to the former classroom training approach.

In the case of The Hartford, a new United States federal law, the USA PATRIOT Act of 2001, mandated that they rapidly train all employees who handle or monitor financial transactions to detect money laundering. An e-learning approach enabled The Hartford to deploy a learning experience to 6,000 employees quickly and effectively, meeting the compliance for financial institutions within United States federal law.

In both cases, all employees were reached with a standard curriculum, and registration and completion were tracked. Notifications were sent to employees and their managers via the learning management system when completion was delayed, or if there were employees who should attend and complete the course who had not as yet registered. This ensured complete compliance with the mandated regulation.

Employing e-Learning for Compliance with Internal Business Mandates

At times an internal issue is important enough to require a similar approach to compliance. BMW of North America uses e-learning for a compliance training program driven by internal business policies, standards, and codes of conduct. All 1,300 employees are required to complete this ethics and professional conduct training on a yearly basis as a part of their individual professional development plan. However, the learners are geographically dispersed. The use of e-learning enabled all employees, regardless of location, to complete the course within the required time frame, ensuring that 83 percent have completed the training in the first 11 months of it being offered.

Wachovia Corporation's experience combined an external regulatory requirement with an internal software roll-out. The company needed to rollout training in a new proprietary software to hundreds of users across the company. The software ensured that Wachovia could comply with government regulations that every account be reviewed once in each calendar year. Therefore, Wachovia had to train all trust administrators, portfolio managers, and their staff in a short period of time so that accounts could be reviewed prior to year end. With evaluation and assessment results indicating that the e-learning is equal in impact to that of the former traditional approach, a total of 1,300 employees have been trained in on-going monthly cadres.

These organizations have found that delivering e-learning to a large number of employees to ensure compliance with externally or internally driven mandates is the most efficient and effective way to engage, train, and track completions for the targeted learning audience.

Case 1: The Home Depot

Company Facts and Figures

✔ **Industry:** Home Improvement Retailer

✔ **Scope of Services and Products:** Retailer for over 40,000 home improvement items targeted to the do-it-yourself and professional markets

✔ **Estimated Number of Employees:** 290,000

✔ **Year e-Learning Introduced:** 2001

✔ **Offices and Locations:** 1500+ stores in U.S., Canada, and Mexico

✔ **Actual 2001 Revenues:** US $53.6 billion

✔ **Website:** www.homedepot.com

✔ **Number of e-Learning Programs in Entire Curriculum:** 14

Introduction

The Home Depot is the world's largest home improvement retailer and second largest retailer in the United States. Home Depot targets the do-it-yourself, and professional markets with a wide range of products, including lumber, building materials, floor and wall coverings, plumbing, gardening supplies, hardware, paint, and appliances. In addition to over 40,000 commercial products, The Home Depot also owns over 50 EXPO Design Center stores with showrooms featuring bath, kitchen, and lighting products.

With over 290,000 employees in 1,500+ stores throughout the United States, Canada and Mexico, a new Home Depot opens every 43 hours. This massive expansion coupled with a forever challenging, retail employee turnover rate, forced The Home Depot to re-evaluate its traditional instructor-led training model. Also because of the high turnover rate, The Home Deport needed to ensure that its sales floors continued to be safe environments for associates and customers.

Why e-Learning?

The Home Depot selected an e-learning approach to:

✔ Quickly train new sales associates on store safety and operations

✔ Provide a safe work environment for associates and customers

✔ Allow for flexible scheduling of sales associates on the floor in order to maintain high utilization

✔ Standardize training content for 290,000 associates in over 1,500 stores.

Additionally, The Home Depot is required to adhere to several safety and hazard regulations set by the Occupational Safety and Health Administration (OSHA) as part of its daily safety and operations. One OSHA regulation with which The Home Depot has to comply relates to safe forklift operations. The Home Depot has trained over 90,000 store forklift operators in safety regulations. Then, every year, The Home Depot chooses to re-certify its forklift operators.

The Home Depot's response to these challenges is an eight-hour blended learning program for initial certification and a three-hour blended re-certification learning program. In both cases, the e-learning portion of the program can be completed at the learner's own pace without interfering with their sales floor utilization.

How Was the Program Aligned with the Business?

The Home Depot faced several challenges in complying with the OSHA safety standard using its former instructor-led training model. The most immediate issues were cost and quality of training.

A subject matter expert from the field typically conducted the training. This meant that the company incurred an instructor cost as well as lost revenue because the instructor and associates were not working with customers. Also, the large associate population needing training, coupled with the high employee turnover rate, meant scheduling a substantial number of training sessions throughout the year. However, they were training and re-training 90,000 employees with a non-standardized curriculum. Therefore, learning largely depended on store subject matter experts' knowledge of standards and their teaching style.

The solution to these challenges was the Forklift Safety Course, a blended learning program. This approach allowed The Home Depot to standardize course content and delivery for each of its employees in all 1,500 stores. It also allowed them to maintain coverage on the sales floor by having the store human resources manager plan training times around employee's schedules when possible.

Key Business Drivers

✓ Deliver OSHA forklift safety requirements to over 90,000 associates with 100 percent compliance

✓ Lower cost of training by decreasing the number of total instructor hours, while maintaining coverage on the sales floor.

✓ Train and certify new associates in forklift safety in a cost-effective and timely manner while facing high employee turn over rates.

With the e-learning solution, The Home Depot cut its dependence on instructors in half. Therefore, they lowered expenses due to instructor cost and increased coverage on the sales floor. In addition, since the training was available at all times, new employees had on-demand access to the same training as veteran staff.

Essentially, this blended learning approach reduced costs and increased quality and accessibility.

How Was the Program Designed?

The Home Depot set high standards to introduce e-learning to their associates. They invested hundreds of development hours for each finished hour because they wanted to make the initial e-learning experience positive for a large audience and spark enthusiasm for future e-learning. To meet the objective of developing on-demand, standardized training, the forklift safety program contains two learning components—self-paced e-learning and hands-on coaching.

Self-Paced e-Learning

The first component is a four hour e-learning course that media production and programming staff from the information systems department designed in Macromedia Flash and 3D Max. By using 3D technology, the designers had complete control over the environment and could easily make virtual adjustments to create a uniform store environment. In addition, it allowed The Home Depot to start a virtual store library that could be re-used for other training. Instructional designers from the human resources organization developed the course content, which covers:

- ✓ Safety inspection of a forklift
- ✓ Types of forklifts and selection criteria
- ✓ Setting up barriers
- ✓ General education about operating a forklift safely

Subject matter experts from the field and safety department then reviewed and approved all content.

Assessment

To complete the e-learning component, the learners take an assessment on the course content. During this phase if learners answer a question incorrectly, they are taken back to the topic in the courseware. After reviewing the course topic, they are returned to the assessment where they can answer a similar question again. Once they successfully complete this assessment, they can move on to the second part of the program.

Hands-On Coaching

In the second component, learners complete a four-hour hands-on coaching course. They work with subject matter experts on the floor applying safety theory to practical scenarios.

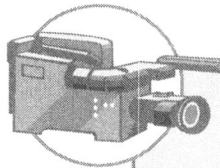

Media and Tools

- ✓ Macromedia Flash
- ✓ 3D Max
- ✓ Java-based learning management system

A custom-developed, Java-based, learning management system tracks completion results. The human resources manager then pulls status reports from the system to track the progress of individual associates and to allot more training time as needed. These reports can be used for competency verification during OSHA inspections.

How Was the Program Deployed?

As a condition of their employment, any associate who will operate a forklift is required to take this course. The store human resources managers monitor completion of the role-based curriculum. They work with the store scheduler to arrange specific times for associates to complete the training program.

All training is completed on-site. Though initially each store was annually scheduled to receive one computer dedicated to e-learning over the next two to three years, demand for, and the success of e-learning courses, sped deployment. Within the first year, The Home Depot issued each store up to three PCs dedicated to learning.

Within each store, the course is downloaded from the WAN to each store LAN using a proprietary caching mechanism. Using this controlled LAN-based learning environment allows The Home Depot to use higher end production value media and to easily update course content. Therefore, if content is revised and posted to the WAN, each store LAN will automatically be updated the next time a user launches the course. Associates then work through the four-hour e-learning course at their own pace. In addition, book marking functionality allows learners to leave the course at any time and pick up where they left off when they begin their next training session.

Once the course is completed, the human resources manager pulls a report that states which associates have met compliance regulations by completing the course. Another report provides information on those associates who still need to be scheduled to complete the course.

Marketing Approach

✓ All sales associates are assigned a role-based curriculum that requires them to complete specific courses within a specified timeframe.

✓ Each store has a full-time human resources manager who monitors associates' professional development and coordinates training sessions with the store scheduler.

To promote e-learning, The Home Depot plans to broadcast short commercials on their internal video channel to make all associates aware of e-learning opportunities. This would encourage associates to take steps toward their professional development and be proactive in meeting OSHA standards for compliance.

What Was the Business Impact of the Program?

The Home Depot delivered forklift training to more than 90,000 forklift operators, achieving 100 percent compliance with OSHA regulations in a little over one year. With their blended learning training program, The Home Depot made sales floors safer for employees and customers, as well as saving over 60,000 instructor hours and creating tens of millions of dollars in top line revenue opportunity. Since instituting the program, they have maintained annual compliance with lift truck certification, exceeding OSHA's requirement that forklift operators complete this training every two years.

In addition, an unanticipated benefit of the program is that its popularity has lead to improvements in the stores' operations processes. At the time that The Home Depot was implementing this new courseware, it was also working towards another goal—moving most inventory management tasks to the evening. By instituting the e-learning program, The Home Depot can offer convenient training times that align with the associates' evening work schedule, saving trainers valuable sales hours when stores are open to customers. In addition, the training program has enabled The Home Depot to limit most of its forklift operations to nighttime hours, so each morning stores look as if they are ready for a "grand opening."

Learner Perspectives

✓ Learners tackle complex subjects at their own pace during regular work hours, day or night.

✓ "…they should provide more training classes like this one."

✓ "…it makes getting a forklift license more efficient…no more waiting for a trainer and a class to be scheduled."

✓ "…the course has given me the confidence to carry out the necessary forklift operation and serve the customer better."

Summary

Purpose:

✓ To train and certify 90,000 associates on forklift operations and OSHA forklift safety procedures in a cost-effective and timely manner

✓ To standardize course content and course delivery so that it is available for new hires and for re-certification

Program Structure: Program is structured as a two-part blended learning experience with four hours of self-paced e-learning on in-store PCs. Then after successfully completing an assessment, learners work with subject matter experts for four-hour, hands-on instruction to apply safety theory to practical scenarios.

Number of Learning Hours per Learner: 8

Total Number of Hours of Learning in the Program: 8

Number of Learners:

✓ 90,000

Completion Requirements:

✓ Complete four hours of self-paced e-learning about forklift safety operations and OSHA standards

✓ Successfully complete assessment

✓ Complete four hours of hands-on instruction with a coach

✓ A learning management system tracks progress on individual associates so that reports can be used for competency verification during OSHA inspections

Media and Tools:

✓ Macromedia Flash

✓ 3D Max

Deployment Mechanism:

✓ Store PCs dedicated to learning

✓ Java-based learning management system

Lessons Learned

✓ **Build Executive Support**
The Home Depot e-Learning Team rapidly built support for e-learning among senior management by using video tapes to capture the e-learning experience and provide concrete examples in a user-friendly format.

✓ **Using Versatile Technology**
Creation of a virtual 3D store rather than using photography established accurate and consistent store settings that were easily developed into bandwidth friendly courseware using Macromedia Flash.

✓ **Create Audience Acceptance**
The Forklift Safety Course gained profound audience acceptance because The Home Depot set the initial production mark high by allocating ample funds and devoting hundreds of production hours to the project.

Case 2: BMW of North America, LLC

Company Facts and Figures

✓ **Industry:** Automotive

✓ **Scope of Services and Products:** Markets and distributes BMW automobiles, motorcycles, and sports activity vehicles (SAVs) in the U.S.

✓ **Estimated Number of Employees:** 1,300

✓ **Year e-Learning Introduced:** 1999

✓ **Offices and Locations:** Various locations in the U.S.; Corporate headquarters in Woodcliff Lake, NJ

✓ **Web Site:** www.bmwusa.com

✓ **Number of e-Learning Programs in Entire Curriculum:** 100

Introduction

Often, compliance training includes courses that support an externally-driven compliance objective. Examples are learning programs that educate employees about a new law or regulation, or programs that meet training expectations set by an external governing body.

At BMW of North America, LLC, compliance training is driven by internal policies, standards, and codes of conduct. All 1,300 employees are required to complete training as a part of their individual professional development plan. This training provides continuous learning opportunities to cultivate professionalism and reinforce the premium level of quality expected within the BMW workplace.

Why e-Learning?

BMW selected an e-learning approach to:

✓ Train learners who were geographically dispersed

✓ Quickly deploy learning in a cost-effective way

✓ Mirror how the learners develop their skills on a daily basis

In 1999, BMW of North America's Learning and Development Solutions team determined that e-learning needed to be a part of the corporation's overall learning strategy. To initiate this strategy, BMW implemented a THINQ learning management system and also integrated third-party e-learning content that was selected to mirror and support BMW's existing curricula. Then in 2002, BMW implemented Centra as their live e-learning platform, and this completely altered how learning took place for their employees.

One of the first classroom-based compliance training courses that BMW converted to a live online e-learning approach was the BMW Business Ethics program. Originally, the BMW Business Ethics program was a 90-minute instructor-led program, and a representative from BMW's Ethics Advisory Council co-facilitated the classroom session with a representative from the Learning and Development Solutions team. Classroom courses worked well for the 350 employees located at BMW of North America's corporate headquarters in New Jersey, but there was still a majority of employees to consider at all other BMW locations throughout the United States. It was not the best use of time and money to send two instructors to all locations to deliver training. In addition, the logistical challenge of conducting instructor-led sessions would take more time than was available to meet the deadline of training all employees within one year. With these factors in mind, learning leaders decided the solution was to convert the BMW Business Ethics course to a live online e-learning program.

How Was the Program Aligned with the Business?

In converting the Business Ethics course to a live e-learning experience, BMW wanted to ensure that the course remained aligned with the company's four core values. These core values are:

- ✓ Generate a culture of trust in the organization
- ✓ Provide orientation and direction
- ✓ Promote cooperation, teamwork, working with others, and working across borders and functional groups
- ✓ Realize responsibility

In addition, as reputation is a high priority business issue for BMW, it was imperative for the course to focus on employees making the right decisions within the company. Victoria Macdonald, training manager for BMW's Learning and Development Solutions group says, "[In the course] we talk about loss not just from a monetary standpoint, but loss in terms of reputation. [BMW] has an absolute sterling reputation, and we want to maintain that reputation."

Key Business Drivers

- ✓ Uphold BMW's core values: trust, orientation, teamwork, and responsibility
- ✓ Maintain BMW's sterling reputation
- ✓ Develop an understanding of BMW of North America's internal code of conduct

How Was the Program Designed?

The BMW Business Ethics course is designed as a live e-learning program. The course materials used in the original instructor-led session were outsourced to an external vendor who repurposed the course for delivery as a live e-learning event.

Using the live e-learning platform tool, online facilitators present real-life scenarios and conduct online breakout sessions to engage learners. The course includes:

- ✓ Guidance for acceptable professional behavior
- ✓ A model to make ethical decisions
- ✓ Examples of ethical dilemmas

    ✓ Suggestions for how to integrate business ethics in everyday work life

    ✓ Details about employees' roles in the Ethics Now Model

    ✓ An explanation of the BMW Code of Conduct

Three facilitators conduct each live e-learning session. The first facilitator is an external consultant, who focuses mainly on the technical aspects of the course delivery during the session, the second is a representative of the Learning and Development Solutions organization, and the third facilitator is a representative of the Ethics Advisory Council.

Each employee attends a live e-learning session from a computer at his or her workplace. Because it takes some time for all participants to log on to the system, those learners who are ready and waiting for the session to begin are instructed to use the whiteboard tool to share what business ethics means to them. This makes excellent use of the learners' time and allows for interactivity right from the start of the course.

Media and Tools

✓ Live audio, application sharing, and custom developed content

✓ Real-time Web collaboration sessions, presented using Centra's live online e-learning tool

An example of a scenario discussed in a breakout session is how failure to follow corporate procedures could negatively affect the company. By using a breakout session format, learners can interact, comment, and receive feedback on topics in real time.

An assessment, designed in a survey-style format and presented in segments, is also included with the course. Learners complete the assessment during their online session.

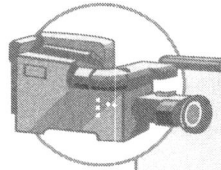

How Was the Program Deployed?

For the initial rollout, the BMW Business Ethics course was announced to staff via e-mail. Employees signed up for the class through the learning management system. First-time users attending a live e-learning session receive an e-learning kit, which helps transition learners from a classroom model to an e-learning model. Using the e-learning kit, employees can prepare for the course and learn more about other online learning opportunities. Kits include: headphones for the session, directions for accessing the course, a yellow tape sign that says "training in progress," a learning contract for the employee and his or her manager, and candy. The learning contract is an agreement stating that the online courses support the learning objectives established for the year and that interruptions should be kept to a minimum while attending an online session.

Marketing Approach

✓ BMW Business Ethics is a mandatory course.

✓ The learning management system provides class and date information and also facilitates registration.

✓ E-mail reminders are sent on a regular basis.

✓ Each person receives an e-learning kit.

✓ Employees receive training credits.

If the BMW Business Ethics course is the first exposure of the employee to the live e-learning tool, he or she took a 15-minute online preparation class that covered basic navigation of the tool.

As a follow-up measure to ensure that all employees complete the BMW Business Ethics course, e-mail reminders are sent via the learning management system to those who have not enrolled in a session. In addition, the course was recorded, so that new hires and employees who are unable to attend a live session can access the course to complete their training.

What Was the Business Impact of the Program?

Before 1999, few employees at BMW North America had experienced e-learning. As of 2002, almost 20 percent of the employee population completed an asynchronous course, and over 85 percent completed a live e-learning course. BMW believes that this number will certainly continue to grow. During the first 11 months of the BMW Business Ethics course, an incredible 83 percent of the target attendance goal was met.

Implementing an e-learning solution has changed the way employees learn at BMW. Employees are accepting the new technology and taking other business-related online courses purchased from an external vendor.

Learner Perspectives

✓ "I have to tell you, it was a wonderful way to take the training… I felt I was right there with everyone in the class… I really appreciate the opportunity to be able to attend classes this way. Thank you."

✓ "What a wonderful way to learn! I do not know what I was so unnerved about. Thanks for all your help."

✓ "I like technology and think it is a wonderful facility for learning."

Summary

Purpose: Compliance training at BMW of North America cultivates professionalism and reinforces the premium level of quality expected within the BMW workplace. The BMW Business Ethics course provides training to all 1,300 employees located throughout the United States so that they will:

- ✓ Understand the BMW Code of Conduct
- ✓ Use the Ethics Now Model to resolve ethical concerns
- ✓ Realize what constitutes acceptable professional behavior and what does not
- ✓ Recognize BMW's core values

Program Structure: A 90-minute live synchronous session, which includes:

- ✓ Breakout sessions and real-life scenarios conducted by three facilitators
- ✓ Assessments, which are presented in segments and discussed in detail

Number of Learning Hours per Learner: 90 minutes

Total Number of Hours of Learning in the Program: 90 minutes

Number of Learners: 1,300

Completion Requirements:

- ✓ Learners must complete the BMW Business Ethics course within one year from program initiation

Media and Tools:

- ✓ Live audio, application sharing, and custom developed content
- ✓ Real-time Web collaboration sessions, presented using Centra's live e-learning platform

Deployment Mechanism: Deployed on an ongoing basis though BMW's learning management system, THINQ. Marketing approaches include:

- ✓ E-mail sent to all employees at time of launch
- ✓ Reminder e-mails sent if employees have not enrolled in the course
- ✓ Recorded version available for review and for new hires

Lessons Learned

✓ Implement e-learning in small steps.

✓ Get to know your IT manager.

✓ Partner with a consulting firm that specializes in implementing learning technologies.

✓ Network with other professionals in the learning industry.

✓ Attend professional meetings to learn more about what other learning organizations and vendors are doing in the industry.

✓ Participate in professional organizations because they provide many benefits, such as technical skills and best practices needed to implement e-learning.

✓ Recognize that the role of training director has shifted to include skills of an IT director. Training directors now must be knowledgeable about implementing learning technology within their organization.

Case 3: The Hartford

Company Facts and Figures

✔ **Industry:** Financial Services

✔ **Scope of Services and Products:** Provider of investment products and insurance

✔ **Estimated Number of Employees:** 27,000

✔ **Year e-Learning Introduced:** 1994

✔ **Offices and Locations:** Nationwide in the U.S. with headquarters in Hartford, CT

✔ **Estimated 2002 Revenues:** US$15.2 billion

✔ **Web Site:** http://www.the hartford.com

✔ **Number of e-Learning Courses in Entire Curriculum:** More than 200

Introduction

The Hartford, one of the largest insurance companies in the United States, began supplying professional development and learning to its workforce via CD-ROM and LAN-based applications in the early 1990s. In 1994, as they moved away from their mainframe/dumb-terminal-based infrastructure to a PC and server/client-based infrastructure, they began to offer e-learning as a training alternative. As Dennis Finnegan, Director Assistant Vice President of Corporate Education at The Hartford explains, "Unfortunately, we were a Wang terminal organization, so e-learning was a bit of a challenge." Originally, all e-learning material was purchased from external vendors, but in recent years, The Hartford has built a small internal development team.

Why e-Learning?

The Hartford selected an e-learning approach to:

✔ Meet the learning objectives mandated by the USA PATRIOT Act in a minimum amount of time

✔ Easily track completion of the mandated course for possible auditing and reporting to Federal agencies

✔ Efficiently train a distributed audience of learners

✔ Control training costs

On October 25, 2001, the United States Congress passed into law H.R. 3162, the USA PATRIOT Act of 2001. Several sections of this law charge banks and other financial institutions with the responsibility to detect, prevent, and report possible money laundering activities as one method for combating international terrorism. The Training Council and the Chief Compliance Officer for The Hartford identified early on that the company may be affected by this law and sought to develop training for employees who may handle or monitor financial transactions as part of their standard job description.

How Was the Program Aligned with the Business?

At The Hartford, training initiatives and needs are overseen by a group of training leaders who report to a Training Council. When the USA PATRIOT Act was first signed into law, a training leader reviewed the regulation to determine possible training implications for The Hartford. Further review by the Training Council and the Chief Compliance Officer confirmed a training obligation that The Hartford would need to meet should Federal agencies choose to audit financial institutions.

In addition to complying with Federal mandates, The Hartford chose to build training to fulfill its own commitment to be a good corporate citizen by participating in practices and activities that monitor or combat international terrorism. Providing employees with training on how to spot and report suspect activity was The Hartford's response to this corporate obligation.

Key Business Drivers

✓ Complying with a Federal regulation requiring financial services companies to train employees about the provisions of the law

✓ Meeting a corporate commitment to support the new regulation

✓ Using e-learning as the most effective and efficient way to meet these goals

How Was the Program Designed?

The USA PATRIOT Act course is a 30-minute Web-based course, designed as self-paced e-learning. An internal team of three e-learning developers built the course in approximately 200 hours.

The objectives of the course (see Figure 14-1) are to:

✓ Understand the intent of the USA PATRIOT Act and its anti-money laundering provisions

✓ Be able to describe the basic elements of money laundering, as defined in the USA PATRIOT Act

✓ Be aware of The Hartford's requirements regarding the USA PATRIOT Act

✓ Understand the mechanisms for detecting and reporting suspicious activity

✓ Have a basic understanding of Office of Foreign Assets Control (OFAC) trade sanctions and regulations as they apply to The Hartford

Interactions, such as drag-and-drop questions (see Figure 14-2), were included throughout the course to engage participants.

The Hartford expects to leverage the shell or interface of the USA PATRIOT Act online course to develop several other courses in the future. There are also plans to expand the course to include a team-based classroom session that trains employees on using the electronic system that actually detects potential money laundering events.

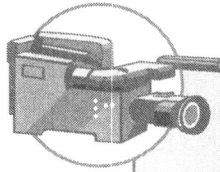

Media and Tools

✓ Macromedia Dreamweaver

✓ Microsoft Active Server Pages (ASP)

✓ A learning management system (LMS) designed by Desai Systems, which manages and administers the Hartford Corporate University

How Was the Program Deployed?

In the first phase of deployment, an e-mail from the Chief Compliance Officer was sent to all employees of The Hartford, notifying them about the USA PATRIOT Act and highlighting some specifics of the regulation. Employees who are directly responsible for financial transactions can access The Hartford's Corporate University and register for the online course. An external Internet site was also developed for other constituent groups, such as agent-brokers, to access the course. The target audience uses computer workstations and has access to the corporate intranet, so the course is not available for viewing offline, such as on a CD-ROM.

Marketing Approach

✓ An e-mail from the Chief Compliance Officer was sent to all employees about the new USA PATRIOT Act and notifying them that an online course was available for employees who handled financial transactions.

✓ As a reminder, when an employee registers for the course in The Hartford's Corporate University, a feature allows the learner to place an appointment in their Microsoft Outlook calendar for when they plan to take the course.

Periodically, the training leaders run reports to determine who has and who has not completed the course. The training leaders communicate directly with employees who have not completed the course and personally encourage them to do so.

What Was the Business Impact of the Program?

To date, approximately 6,000 employees of The Hartford have completed the USA PATRIOT Act online course. A major concern of the learning development group at The Hartford was not to exceed a training seat time of 30 minutes. Initially, when reviewing similar content created by external vendors, The Hartford could not find a course that was shorter than 60 minutes. By conducting a content analysis with input from the Chief Compliance Officer, The Hartford identified the critical requirements of the regulation, thereby designing a shorter training course that addressed the essentials. Following this approach, The Hartford met critical training needs without demanding a large amount of learner time. This has been well received by both learners and stakeholders.

Check It Out Online!
www.elearningfieldbook.com

Figure 14-1: Objectives of The Hartford's Compliance Training Course

Figure 14-2: A Sample Interaction

Other impacts of developing this course were that the internal learning development group at The Hartford increased its competence in building e-learning, and the project sponsor within the company saw a good example of the application of e-learning. This project sponsor, who was initially skeptical of an e-learning approach, has now become an e-learning champion within The Hartford.

Finally, the participants completed a learning evaluation as part of the course, and overall results (see Table 14-1) indicate that learners:

✓ Feel comfortable with the e-learning course

✓ Find the content appropriate

✓ Find the interactions engaging

✓ Would recommend the course to others

Table 14-1 : Results from Evaluation (Based on Approximately 1000 Learners)	
1 = Strongly Disagree 2 = Disagree 3 = Neutral 4 = Agree 5 = Strongly Agree	
1. The course was informative.	4.3
2. The course met my expectations.	4.1
3. The pace was appropriate.	4.2
4. The training was appropriate for someone in my position.	4.1
5. I will apply what I learned at my work place.	4.1
6. I would recommend an online course to my friends/ colleagues/ acquaintances.	4
7. The course content and activities were appropriately engaging.	4
8. The course was easy to move through.	4.3
9. The objectives of the course were achieved.	4.3
Overall Average	**4.2**

Learner Perspectives

✓ Learners view the course as being concise and pleasant to take.

✓ Learners view the course as being easy to access.

✓ Learners felt they were able to learn and retain what they needed to know about the regulation from the e-learning course.

Summary

Purpose: To provide an overview of the USA PATRIOT Act and the Office of Foreign Asset Control's requirements under the Act so that learners would:

- ✓ Understand the intent of the USA PATRIOT Act law
- ✓ Be able to describe basic elements of money laundering
- ✓ Be aware of The Hartford's requirements regarding the law
- ✓ Understand the mechanisms for detecting and reporting suspicious activity
- ✓ Have a basic understanding of trade sanctions and regulations as they apply to The Hartford

Program Structure: Each learning objective for the course is addressed as an individual module, each approximately 5 to 6 screens in length.

Total Number of Hours of Learning in the Program: 30 minutes

Number of Learners: Of the 12,000 targeted learners, 6,000 have completed the course so far.

Completion Requirements: Learners must finish all modules of the online course to get credit for completing the course.

Media and Tools:

- ✓ Macromedia Dreamweaver
- ✓ Microsoft Active Server Pages (ASP)

Deployment Mechanism: The course is deployed online through The Hartford's Corporate University, which is managed and administered through a learning management system designed by Desai Systems. Marketing approaches include:

- ✓ E-mail notification from the Chief Compliance Officer to all employees
- ✓ Reminders through individual's Microsoft Outlook calendar for taking the course

Lessons Learned

✓ Build a library of "success stories" that you can use to market the value of e-learning to leadership.

✓ Develop high-quality, interactive programs to help overcome resistance with learners who may remember the "bad old days" of computer-based training (CBT).

✓ Carefully review and judge promises offered by external vendors. Identify what fits best with your corporate culture and get commitment from vendors to work towards that.

✓ Complete a cost/benefit analysis to determine whether it makes more sense to buy courses or build in-house.

✓ When using external development vendors for the first time, select a low visibility project.

✓ When buying content from an external vendor, thoroughly investigate whether it is more cost-effective to buy a large site license or use a "pay-per-view" approach.

✓ Develop clear processes about who is responsible for decision-making, especially with regard to content. This is important if you will be relying on numerous subject matter experts (SMEs).

✓ Use media judiciously and verify that all media is educationally appropriate and necessary.

Case 4: Wachovia Corporation

Company Facts and Figures

✓ **Industry:** Financial Services

✓ **Scope of Services and Products:** Complete banking services, brokerage services, asset management, wealth management, and innovative products for individual customers

✓ **Estimated Number of Employees:** 84,000

✓ **Year e-Learning Introduced:** 1997

✓ **Offices and Locations:** Offices throughout the U.S. and more than 30 international offices; Headquarters in Charlotte, NC

✓ **Estimated 2002 Revenues:** US$19 billion

✓ **Web Site:** www.wachovia.com

✓ **Number of e-Learning Programs in Entire Curriculum:** 600+

Introduction

Learning new processes and procedures quickly is key for the employees of one of the United States largest financial services institutions. When Wachovia Corporation needed to rollout a new proprietary software course to hundreds of users across the company, they faced several challenges. First, Wachovia had to comply with government regulations that every account had to be reviewed once in each calendar year. Therefore, Wachovia had to train all trust administrators, portfolio managers, and their staff in a short period of time so that accounts could be reviewed prior to year end. Second, the training budget was shrinking. And finally, as this new software would change the way people work, because the paper process was completely eliminated and now automated, a collaborative and interactive environment was needed to effectively facilitate learning.

Why e-Learning?

Wachovia selected an e-learning approach to:

✓ Train hundreds of people in a short period of time to meet government regulations

✓ Reduce or eliminate travel, telecommunications, and facilities costs associated with classroom learning

✓ Bring together geographically diverse groups of people to interact and learn in a highly collaborative environment

Since approximately 1997, Wachovia, a full-service financial and retail brokerage company, has implemented e-learning as part of their overall learning strategy. "We do 3 to 3.5 million hours of training per year," says Scott Sutker, Vice President for Advanced Learning Systems at Wachovia. "And 50 percent of our learning is non-classroom."

For non-classroom based training, Wachovia uses media, such as CBT, WBT, CD-ROM, self-study workbooks, conference calls, satellite, and video. In addition, Wachovia also uses a live e-learning tool developed by Centra. In the case of creating training for the new software program, learning leaders at Wachovia decided that using the Centra tool would be their best solution for developing and delivering the course, Client Servicing Automated Regulation 9.

An online virtual classroom solution can provide "many features that mimic live classrooms, including real-time collaboration, feedback, breakout rooms, and evaluations." says Margaret Magner, Wachovia's Director for Professional Development for the Retail Investment Group. After the course was designed and developed internally, one online facilitator trained 800 employees from all over the United States within a three-month period—and no travel was involved for anyone.

How Was the Program Aligned with the Business?

The framework of Wachovia's learning organization is evident in their mission statement.

*We are strategists who provide learning and
development solutions that drive business results.*

Wachovia's training organization is a combination of centralized and decentralized training teams. It is decentralized to provide business unit expertise and focus, and centralized to increase efficiency and reduce redundancy for the entire corporation. The decentralized business unit training teams conduct needs analysis, performance consulting, and job-specific training delivery. They also provide the core of a Learning Council, which consists of training leaders from each of Wachovia's six major lines of business.

Wachovia's centralized teams research, recommend, procure, design, develop, and coordinate training products and services. The centralized unit, known as the Learning Strategy Group, also coordinates and conducts extensive post-training effectiveness and ROI measurement to ensure optimal learning effectiveness and business value.

In this case, a business unit was implementing a new software system and changing work processes in a major way. With the new automated work process, Wachovia could:

✓ Ensure that all trust accounts that required a review would actually receive a review

✓ Ensure that people involved in the process were adhering to the department's policies and procedures

✓ Save the corporation an estimated $1.5 million in paper costs alone

Key Business Drivers

✓ Rapidly training all trust administrators, portfolio managers, and their staff to understand an in-house system application that combines imaging and workflow systems into one automated process, the benefits of the automated process, and their role(s) in the process

✓ Complying with Federal regulations that govern trust departments to meet an annual review deadline

✓ Updating employees' customer service skills, which are integral to the bank's success

The business unit leaders met with the central Learning Strategy Group to identify the learning need, and the central group then determined the media platform, course objectives, timelines, and design of the course.

How Was the Program Designed?

The Client Servicing Automated Regulation 9 course is designed to be delivered as a 90-minute live e-learning event on the company intranet, as part of Wachovia's Virtual Campus. Using the Centra authoring product, instructional designers created a highly interactive course, which included real-time audio, application sharing, custom developed content in PowerPoint, polling questions, an evaluation, and an assessment. Then using the Centra virtual classroom application, an instructor could schedule and offer the same course as many times as needed and still be able to tailor the live session to a particular audience.

The focus of the course is to introduce trust administrators, portfolio managers, and their staff to a new in-house system application and process, demonstrate the benefits of the new process, providing guidance as to their role(s) in the process. The course contains:

✓ An introduction to an in-house designed application that combines two previously separate systems to be accessible through one automated process

✓ Information about who will be impacted by the automated process

✓ An explanation of the expected cost savings by using the automated process as compared to the previous 182-step manual and very paper-intensive process

Media and Tools

✓ Live audio, application sharing, custom developed content in PowerPoint, polling questions, an evaluation, and an assessment (all designed within the Centra authoring tool)

✓ Real-time Web collaboration sessions, presented using Centra's virtual classroom application and accessed through Wachovia's internal learning portal

✓ Messages about other key benefits for the new process, including being able to ensure that people involved with the process were adhering to the trust department's policies and procedures

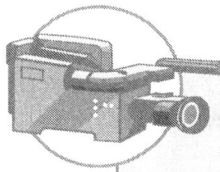

How Was the Program Deployed?

Wachovia's corporate-wide learning portal, called the Learning Connection, provides access to training and education for all employees. The Learning Connection was created from the marriage of legacy Wachovia's Center for Learning and legacy First Union's First University. Courses range from new-hire orientation to senior management mentoring, from technical training to macroeconomic investment strategies. Learners can access the library of courses, class schedules, their grades, and the Virtual Campus all from the Learning Connection.

Marketing Approach

✓ Reminders sent to employees and their supervisors via e-mail

✓ Successes from the pilot test used to market the training in the organization

Wachovia delivers the Client Servicing Automated Regulation 9 course as a live e-learning event through the Virtual Campus (see Figure 14-3). In the initial rollout, about 800 employees had to complete this course within a specific time period to meet federal mandates. These employees were contacted by e-mail and scheduled for specific online sessions. Typically, 15 to 20 learners at a time participated in an instructor-led live e-learning session from either a PC at their desk or one located in a multimedia center in their office.

At the end of the course, learners must complete an assessment. Results are sent to a database, and a multitude of reports can be run based on the course. Wachovia is in the process of implementing a more robust learning management system to better manage certification and regulatory compliance.

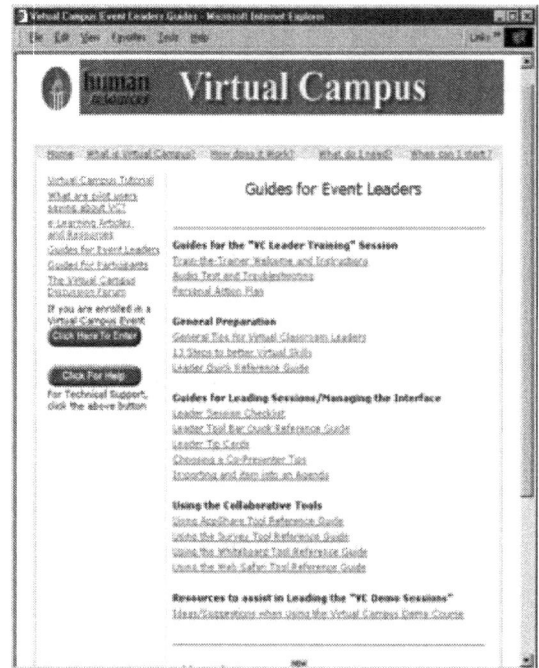

Figure 14-3: Wachovia Corporation's Virtual Campus

What Was the Business Impact of the Program?

Approximately 800 employees completed the course in the initial rollout. Since then, online instructors have delivered the course to an additional 500 people, and are continuing to conduct monthly classes for new users and as a refresher for current users. The cost savings was an important impact of this program. An estimated $425,000 that would have been spent on travel, room cost, and other classroom-related expenses was saved by conducting online training sessions.

An evaluation is included within the course to capture feedback from learners. More than 90 percent have given favorable ratings.

Another benefit of the online training is the time savings. For classroom training, participants often would travel for more time than the class would last. "That's pretty inefficient," says learning generalist Karen Thompson, Assistant Vice President and Trust Officer at Wachovia. "And our data shows that the learning is equal to that of the traditional classroom, if not more effective."

Learner Perspectives

✓ "Very interesting format. Easy way to reach many in various locations."

✓ "I enjoyed this type of learning process. Time was used to good advantage taking the course in the office."

✓ "This was an excellent introduction into the automated Reg. 9 process."

✓ "This course was expertly presented and an excellent way to cover a new and technically demanding subject."

Summary

Purpose: To introduce a new propriety software and process to trust administrators, portfolio managers, and their staff so they would:

- ✔ Understand the benefits of the automated process versus the paper/manual process
- ✔ Understand the new workflow and their role(s) in the process
- ✔ Comply with Federal regulations
- ✔ Adhere to departmental policies and procedures

Program Structure: An e-learning module delivered as a real-time online instructor-led session that included:

- ✔ An introduction to an in-house designed application
- ✔ Information about who will be impacted by the automated process
- ✔ An explanation of the expected cost savings by using the automated process
- ✔ Messages about other key benefits for the new process

Number of Learning Hours per Learner: 1.5 hours

Total Number of Hours of Learning in the Program: 1.5 hours

Number of Learners: 1300 to date

Completion Requirements: Primary learners are required to complete the course to meet an annual review deadline.

Media and Tools:

- ✔ Audio
- ✔ Custom-developed content in PowerPoint
- ✔ An assessment and evaluation
- ✔ Application sharing

Deployment Mechanism:

- ✔ Live e-learning delivery via the corporate intranet

Lessons Learned

✔ Ensure that you have support from senior management.

✔ Build a working relationship with IT.

✔ Gain buy-in from decision makers that e-learning is effective.

✔ Keep your focus on making an impact on business and on real business issues.

✔ Start small and do pilot testing.

✔ Communicate successes and demonstrate ROI to show the rest of the organization that e-learning works.

✔ Select the right media tool for what you are trying to accomplish.

✔ Familiarize the participants with transition from classroom learning to a virtual class. Discuss the differences between classroom learning and a virtual class, as well as the etiquette for virtual classes.

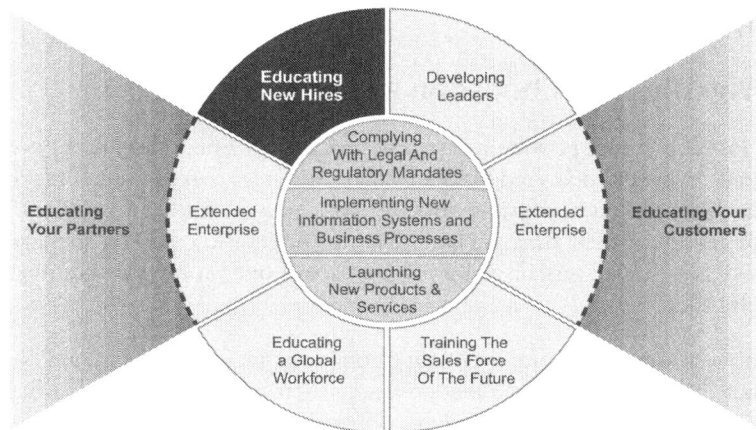

13

Educating New Hires

The cases for this chapter are:

- *Black and Decker Corporation*
- *American Skandia*
- *Cingular Wireless*
- *Prudential Financial*

Introduction

Why Did They Choose an e-Learning Solution?

Most companies provide new employees a short orientation within the first two days of employment, typically delivered by the human resources department. This orientation generally focuses on the completion of paperwork, a tour of the facilities, and a review of the benefits package. Depending largely on a person's role, this orientation may be as short as two hours or as long as two days. This is usually followed by one-on-one training with a manager or co-worker in specific job tasks.

However, as companies experience periods of rapid expansion and contraction, they have found that this approach can be inadequate to their needs. Increasingly, they must quickly bring new employees up to full productivity, while in some cases meeting government regulation requirements. In addition, company's want to ensure in the new hire's mind that they made the right choice in selecting this employer, and that their ability to excel in their job is assured by on-going training and development.

Employing an e-learning solution addresses a number of challenges in new hire training:

- Access can be provided to the learning whether the size of new hire group is one or two in an office, or a few hundred
- Job-skill training allows the new employee to become productive faster
- The number of facilitators to deliver the training is not a limiting factor
- Errors during on-the-job trail period can be reduced
- Consistent delivery of content regardless of employee location can be assured
- New content can be quickly updated and distributed

This chapter presents four company case examples where e-learning provided a platform for training new hires and for assuring a quality result. They include: Black & Decker Corporation, a leading manufacturer and marketer of power tools and accessories, hardware, and home improvement products; American Skandia, a financial services company offering a wide range of products including variable annuities and mutual funds; Cingular Wireless, a provider of wireless voice and data communications; and Prudential Financial, an insurance and financial services company.

These organizations, for a variety of business reasons, chose to revamp their entire new hire orientation approach, each employing a blended model to deliver just-in-time learning combined with hands-on application and coaching or mentoring.

Engaging New Workers from Day One through e-Learning

One of the important drivers in the move into e-learning solutions was the need to provide adequate, engaging learning from the first day of employment, regardless of the number of employees joining the company on any given day or in any place. At Black & Decker in the past, a new hire received a binder and several weeks later attended a classroom session, many times never having looked at the binder. Now, when a person joins they immediately receive a welcome packet with their user ID and access instructions to the Black & Decker University Learning Portal where they find and begin their training program. The immediacy of the e-learning is augmented with on-the-job coaching by their manager. This learning is engaging, complete, and provides the skills for learners to do their jobs well.

Cingular Wireless offers new hires a similar immediate immersion into the culture and goals of the company through an e-learning approach. The first day, new hires are welcomed by the people in their location and then given a tour of the workplace. Next, they are coached through logging onto the Web site called Joining the Team to begin their e-learning about the company, their development opportunities, and benefits. There they also engage in nine compliance courses and can return and refer to the content as often as they need to.

New Hire e-Learning Simulation Coaching to Achieve Higher Job Performance

In situations where job performance is an immediate concern, e-learning simulations combined with mentoring and coaching provide a safe environment to learn, be assessed, and receive feedback on performance. Prudential Financial's new hire orientation for Call Center employees is delivered in a seven-week blended program that gives many opportunities to practice transactions and master the information. Through online simulations and instructions, new hires learn about products, processes transactions, procedures, and systems, finally receiving live calls targeted at their current learning level. Using this approach, Prudential has been able to reduce call handle time by teaching best practices to new hires through simulations and feedback.

The American Skandia new hire program also combines e-learning with coaching to achieve higher performance in the required NASD Series 6 license examination. New hires formerly achieved an average 60 percent pass rate on the exam, below the national average. Using a blended model of e-learning with online practice exams and coaching, these new hires now average a 90 percent pass rate on the examination and are better equipped to assist customers adequately with the over 100 financial products American Skandia offers.

All of the case companies have found many unexpected benefits from their blended model orientation programs. The availability of the Web-based learning is used as an attractive recruitment tool. In addition, the frequency that 'graduates' return to the learning to review and refresh their knowledge has been noted. Finally, all find that the use of e-learning to support new hire orientation allows easy and inexpensive upgrading and revisions of content as the company changes and grows.

Case 1: Black & Decker Corporation

Company Facts and Figures

✔ **Industry:** Consumer/Commercial Products

✔ **Scope of Services and Products:** Manufacturer and marketer of consumer grade and professional-grade brand power tools and accessories

✔ **Estimated Number of Employees:** 22,700

✔ **Year e-Learning Introduced:** 1998

✔ **Offices and Locations:** Products and services marketed in more than 100 countries; Manufacturing operations in 11 countries

✔ **Estimated 2002 Revenues:** US$4.3 billion sales

✔ **Web Site:** www.bdk.com

✔ **Number of e-Learning Courses in Entire Curriculum:** 100

Introduction

The Black & Decker Corporation is a leading manufacturer and marketer of power tools and accessories, hardware and home improvement products, and technology-based fastening systems. Their commercial (professional-grade) brand, DEWALT is sold through major building product suppliers and retailers, such as The Home Depot, Lowe's, and Sears. Each year Black & Decker's Power Tools and Accessories business in the U.S. hires about 150 new sales representatives for their commercial product line. Traditionally, these new employees would spend two weeks attending classroom training at Black & Decker's headquarters in Towson, Maryland. In 1998, Black & Decker University (BDU) created a Web-based course that according to Matt DeFeo, Vice President of Training and Recruiting, demonstrated that "e-learning is very powerful, even with a fairly modest course design."

Why e-Learning?

Black & Decker selected an e-learning approach to:

✔ Provide self-study courses for new employees to complete within their first 60 days with company

✔ Provide base knowledge for learners prior to attendance of hands-on training in the classroom course

✔ Invest in employee development because this will translate into higher retention and better earnings

✔ Reduce travel expenses associated with classroom courses

In 2001, BDU decided to remodel their new hire classroom-only program to a blended learning program. The DEWALT Field Marketing Training Program now combines 16 e-learning courses with both on-the-job training and classroom instruction. The team that designed the DEWALT Field Marketing Training Program is part of the Sales and Marketing group, which is responsible for the development of sales and marketing employees from the time they join the company through promotion to senior level positions. Other groups are responsible for delivery of training to employees in areas such as manufacturing and business administration.

How Was the Program Aligned with the Business?

This e-learning program is aligned with four significant business objectives for the Power Tools and Accessories business. These objectives:

✔ Provide product knowledge and sales skills

✔ Integrate new hires rapidly into the sales force

✔ Develop leaders

✔ Increase skill sets faster to drive market share and profits

The alignment with the business is best explained by Jeff Davis, Director of e-Learning at BDU. "We select bright college graduates who can be future leaders within the organization," says Davis. "We then teach them not to be the best carpenter, but to have the confidence and credibility to convert one of our targeted end users over to the DEWALT brand."

Many new hires have never used commercial power tools and have little experience with the building trade. This program teaches not only the features and benefits of DEWALT tools but also the application of the tools in the accomplishment of various activities on a job site. This may include the cutting of rafters, the framing of a house, or the installation of drywall. It is important that new sales people know the technical specifications of the tools (knowledge) and how customers may use the tools more effectively than competitors' products (application).

Another goal is to move people quickly from learning to doing. With the original classroom program, Black & Decker would wait until a large number of new people were hired before scheduling a course. Often this would delay training for new employees as much as three months. By implementing e-learning for much of the fundamental knowledge, the business was able to begin training sales people during their first week on the job.

Some benefits of moving fundamental knowledge to a blended learning course include reducing the time in the classroom, reducing travel costs, and returning sales people to the field sooner.

Many people who participate in this program will be the future sales and marketing leaders of Black & Decker. It is critical to long-term company success that new hires are well grounded in the company's products, and that they understand how Black & Decker goes to market. Says Davis, "We need our new hires to be knowledgeable about our users, their needs, and how DEWALT products meet their needs."

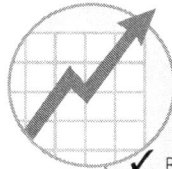

Key Business Drivers

✔ Drive sales for the organization

✔ Reduce time-to-market and rapidly make new sales people effective in the market

✔ Rapidly develop new hires for management positions in the company

✔ Become a world-class sales and marketing university

How Was the Program Designed?

The original classroom-only program consisted of a binder with reference materials that was sent to new hires when they joined the Power Tools and Accessories business. Within their first three months, each new sales person attended a two-week classroom course at BDU. Often the new hires would show up for the class not having opened the binder. Says Davis, "The new hires may have never even touched a power tool in their life, and many do not know the difference between a jig saw and a reciprocating saw."

This original classroom course was 80 percent instruction using PowerPoint presentations, to go over facts, figures, and market information, with the remaining 20 percent actually spent using some tools.

The new blended program contains four distinct components:

- ✓ e-Learning, which consists of a pre-assessment, 16 self-paced e-learning courses, and a post-assessment
- ✓ On-the-job training, which involves field experience, such as meeting customers at job sites under the guidance of experienced sales people
- ✓ Classroom training, with one week of hands-on application training and a final exam
- ✓ Mentoring, which involves the application of knowledge in the field with one-on-one mentoring, followed by a final online assessment

The new program expertly blends e-learning, practical field experience, classroom training, and manager feedback. This combination helps to quickly develop effective sales people. Today, when a person joins the business, they immediately receive a welcome packet with their user ID and access instructions to the BDU Learning Portal. This packet also directs them to logon to the university and begin the program.

The first two components of the program, self-paced e-learning and on-the-job training, are completed simultaneously. For the e-learning component, learners first complete a self-paced course that orients them to the learning program and other online resources, such as the knowledge management system, the product information database, and links to the company's Web sites. The learners then complete a pre-assessment that tests them on fundamental knowledge covered in the program. Then over the next 30 days, learners complete 16 self-paced e-learning courses, augmented with work completed in the field with their managers. At the end of the 30 days, learners complete a post-assessment. Participants must complete this e-learning portion and pass a post-assessment before attending the classroom learning.

In the second step, on-the-job training continues with two to four weeks in the field, so that learners can apply their new skill sets at job sites. "They become more knowledgeable about our customers, what their needs are, and how we can impact that customer," says DeFeo. "DeWALT has a method of growing the business. We want to be where contractors buy, work, learn, and play."

The first two steps of the DeWALT Field Marketing Training Program prepare new sales people for the third part of the program—classroom training. When new hires arrive at BDU's training facility, they have gained foundational knowledge and customer experience that helps strengthen their learning in the classroom. Each part of the program builds on the previous part and is evaluated by testing and personal feedback.

The redesigned classroom training is a total reversal of the old program. Eighty percent of the time is spent discussing and using the tools to build real-life applications. Participants now cut a rafter and then fasten the rafter to a truss system. Each activity is now an example that reflects how a customer would use a DEWALT tool on a job site.

The remaining 20 percent of the course is spent in the classroom, reinforcing the hands-on activities though interactive discussions with the instructors. Game shows, quizzes, and other activities are used to reinforce key concepts, terminology, and facts. The implementation of e-learning for knowledge delivery allows the classroom instruction to focus on the application of the knowledge, which greatly improves retention and creates time for skill development.

In the fourth part of the program, learners go back out to the field and apply concepts from the classroom. Field managers reinforce what was studied in the classroom. After approximately 30 days, the new hires complete a follow-up assessment, which covers the key learning points from all four components of the program.

How Was the Program Developed?

To build this blended program, the Power Tool and Accessories business selected a full service vendor, Vuepoint, which provided key capabilities such as:

✓ Content development tools and services

✓ Learning content management system

✓ Implementation services

✓ Instructional design

✓ Standard proven design methodology to rapidly develop programs with consistent quality

"BDU was able to create 16 e-learning courses in less than a year and overhaul the classroom content in large part through our partnership with Vuepoint," says DeFeo. "They guided the BDU staff through an instructional design model, ROPES (Review and Relate, Overview, Present, Exercise, and Summarize), that we used to identify how to present the information in ways that work best for the learner."

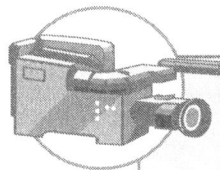

Media and Tools

✓ Vuepoint authoring tool

✓ Vuepoint learning content management system

✓ Macromedia Flash

✓ Toolnet, product knowledge repository

The project team for both the 16 e-learning courses and the revised classroom course was composed of 15 subject matter experts from Black & Decker, three to four developers, and a program manager from Vuepoint.

Black & Decker found that a key element of e-learning design is that content that changes frequently should be kept outside the e-learning course. This reduces the time and expense of making constant updates to courses.

"We tried to build the content so that it has a longer shelf life," says Davis. "Concepts are taught from a foundational level, and we use an internal database called ToolNet for specific information. For example, the amps on a tool or the rpms on a motor are referenced in the database. This allows specifications to be kept current through links in the course."

How Was the Program Deployed?

BDU learning portal (www.bduniversity.com) is used to provide general information. Once learners enter their user ID and password (see Figure 13-1), they have access to their own personal learning portal where they can view their courses. At this point, the learners are in the Vuepoint learning content management system, where they can:

✓ Check the calendar of upcoming events at the university

✓ View their course transcripts

✓ Register for upper level courses

✓ Access various other functions, based on user's profile

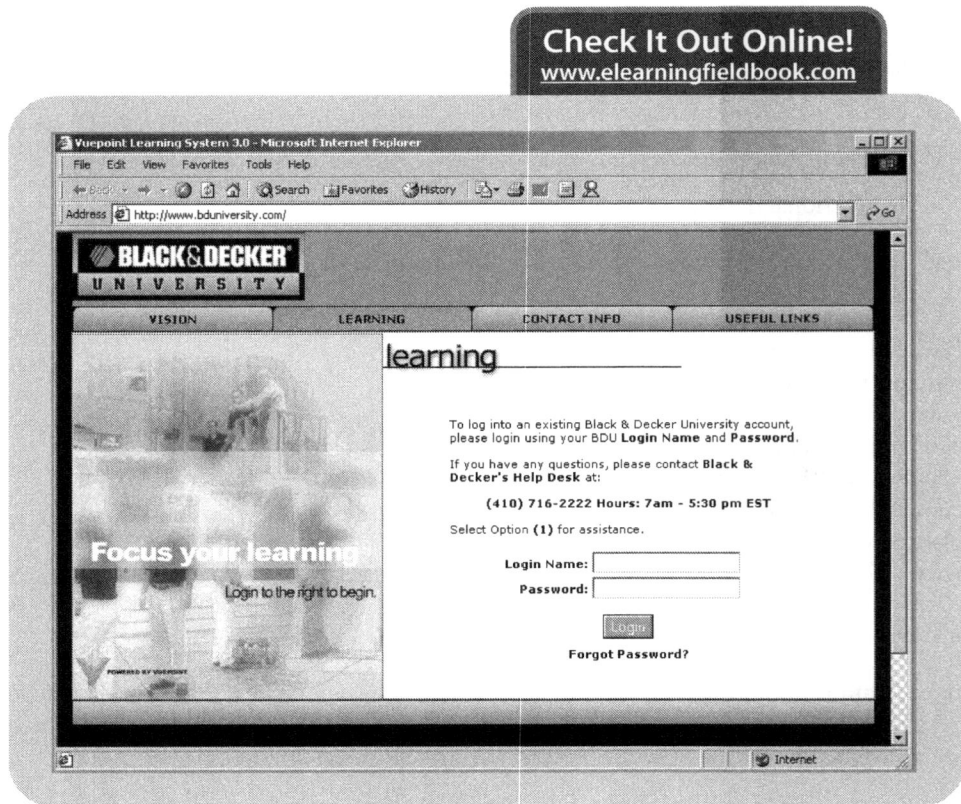

Figure 13-1: Black & Decker University Login Screen

Black & Decker uses the PeopleSoft HR system. One of their goals is to link Vuepoint with PeopleSoft so that they can transfer attendance records from the Vuepoint system to PeopleSoft on a weekly basis. This will greatly reduce the manual maintenance of user profiles.

Marketing Approach

✓ Market Black & Decker University as a key element of the recruiting process

✓ Provide information and course instructions in the new hire welcome package

✓ Reach existing employees through e-mail and office campaigns

✓ Demonstrate learning portal at major meetings

Marketing of the program was divided into three audience targeted campaigns: new hires, existing employees, and company management. When new hires join the company, they receive a packet that includes access instructions and their user ID for the BDU portal. This learning portal has been incorporated into the recruitment process as one of the benefits of joining Black & Decker. When new hires receive the packet, they generally have already seen a demonstration or overview of the portal.

Existing employees also have access to the portal and the e-learning courses. An awareness campaign, Kick Off Your Learning, was developed to introduce them to the program. Because it was launched in the fall of 2001, the campaign used a football theme and included give-aways, such as a new mouse pad delivered to each person's desk.

To introduce management to the program, two kiosks were set up at major sales meetings. These kiosks contained demonstrations of the virtual campus. Another marketing tool was created by wrapping the first module of the Black & Decker history course in a Marcromedia Flash video. This video was sent out as a teaser to employees, encouraging them to go online and take an e-learning course. This campaign has resulted in 100 percent of new hires attending the e-learning courses and wide acceptance by management for the longer training period.

What Was the Business Impact of the Program?

"This program has been phenomenal," says DeFeo. "It has revolutionized the way we train today. New sales people are experiencing a faster time-to-market with new knowledge and skills. In addition, our retention rate has doubled over the past year."

By using e-learning, the classroom experience has changed from 80 percent content presentation to 80 percent hands-on experience in the use of products. Content has been brought to life through interactions that are fun and engaging and managers have been given the opportunity to reinforce content in the field. "Initially, we saved a lot of money; we will save more this year, and in about two and a half years, we will have recouped our costs," says DeFeo.

Says DeFeo, "An unexpected benefit of the e-learning courses is that after completion, many people are going online to view the basic courses because we all forget so much over the years. Having information at our fingertips has been fantastic because binders, books, and flyers are outdated the day they are sent out."

The Power Tools and Accessories business took the time to totally overhaul their traditional two-week classroom new hire program, converting it into a blended program combining e-learning, practical application on-the-job, classroom experiences, and manager coaching. This extended the learning period from two weeks to over twelve weeks but allowed training to begin immediately. The implementation of e-learning also allowed the business to move hard costs that were spent on travel into learning development and delivery. By having the learner alternate between knowledge acquisition and application, Black & Decker has built a powerful program that is exceeding their goals for retention and rapid integration of new employees into the sales force.

Summary

Purpose: To move people quickly form learning to doing

Program Structure: The new blended program contains four distinct parts:

- ✓ A pre-assessment, 16 e-learning courses, and a post assessment
- ✓ Two to four weeks of field experience, meeting customers at job sites with experienced sales people
- ✓ One week of classroom training with a final exam
- ✓ Application of knowledge in the field with one-on-one mentoring, and then a final assessment

Number of Learning Hours per Learner:

- ✓ Eight hours e-learning, minimum
- ✓ 40 hours classroom, combined with on the job coaching

Total Number of Hours of Learning in the Program: More than 60 hours

Number of Learners: 1,000 in sales force

Completion Requirements:

- ✓ 16 e-learning courses with a post-assessment
- ✓ Classroom course with a post-assessment

Media and Tools:

- ✓ Macromedia Flash
- ✓ Audio recordings
- ✓ Classroom presentations
- ✓ Hands-on lab activities

Deployment Mechanism: Vuepoint's learning content management system, which:

- ✓ Links to a company portal
- ✓ Provides access to all e-learning courses
- ✓ Manages classroom registration
- ✓ Tracks course completion

Lessons Learned

✔ Use external professionals to build the first program so you have an expert show you the way. This then provides an opportunity to determine what resources you need for future projects. Plus, this quickly builds great success and allows time for developing internal capabilities.

✔ Tie content to direct application in the field.

✔ Create presentations of the content for customers and sales managers to motivate learners.

✔ Have your Information Systems community involved from day one.

✔ Be prepared that for the short term, there is a huge people and time commitment needed to create a successful blended learning program-but the payoffs are phenomenal

Case 2: American Skandia

Company Facts and Figures

✓ **Industry:** Financial Services

✓ **Scope of Services and Products:** Money management services; Provider of long-term investment products for businesses and individuals

✓ **Estimated Number of Employees:** 7,000 globally; 800 in the U.S.

✓ **Year e-Learning Introduced:** 2000

✓ **Offices and Locations:** Based in Connecticut; Represented in 22 countries on five continents

✓ **Web Site:** www2.americanskandia.com

✓ **Number of e-Learning Programs in Entire Curriculum:** More than 1000

Introduction

American Skandia is a company that provides a wide range of financial products in areas such as variable annuities and mutual funds. They are in a highly regulated industry with licensing for new employees and annual National Association of Securities Dealers, Inc. (NASD) continuing education requirements.

The approach that American Skandia took to provide learning to all employees was to build a corporate university, American Skandia University (ASU). Launched in March 2000, and using a combination of classroom training, internally developed e-learning, in-field coaching, and job aids, ASU provides training for all employees. Third-party content from Securities Training Corporation is used for industry-specific online training. Additional training areas such as desktop applications and professional skills are offered via content from Element K and SkillSoft, respectively. The ASU:

Why e-Learning?

American Skandia built its corporate university to:

✓ Offer a diversity of learning options better suited to the varied adult learning styles

✓ Standardize, track, and monitor all training efforts

✓ Bring people up-to-speed consistently and quickly with higher skill levels than they had in the past

✓ Support the rapid rollout of new products and systems

✓ Is organized into five colleges similar to a university model with multiple colleges/specializations under the university umbrella to address needs of a business unit or enterprise-wide core competency

✓ Has several online courses that are used to satisfy 100 percent of the annual Firm Element portion of the NASD continuing education requirement for the maintenance of an employee's Series 6 license

✓ Is a portal on American Skandia's intranet and all American Skandia employees have access to the e-learning modules located on this Web site

When new employees join American Skandia, they attend a three-day Orientation Program called Beginnings. If they are a new hire in the Variable Annuity or Mutual Fund customer service areas, they continue with a five-week program called Foundations, first launched in April 2000. This case study examines the Foundations program in detail.

How Was the Program Aligned with the Business?

American Skandia is a leader in the financial services industry, which is highly regulated. All registered representatives in a sales capacity, or in the customer service arena, or in other key roles around the firm must pass an entry level exam according to NASD regulations. The Series 6 license is an industry threshold, and is American Skandia's requirement for continued employment in several customer service roles. The primary business driver for the Foundations program was to teach new employees about the:

- ✓ Financial services industry
- ✓ Proprietary software systems
- ✓ Features and benefits of American Skandia products
- ✓ Policies and procedures of American Skandia
- ✓ Skills necessary to provide superior customer service

Additionally, certain employees must pass the NASD Series 6 license examination. Given this critical business driver, ASU built a multi-phased approach to support learners to achieve a higher first-time pass rate than the national average (65 percent in 1999) and the American Skandia benchmark average of 60 percent.

The approach included giving participants in the Foundations program a self-study schedule, self-study materials, online practice exams, a two-day review class, and small group coaching sessions to increase success with the Series 6 examination. In the first year, the first-time pass average improved to 76 percent. Recent classes have seen a general class pass rate average of 90 percent or above. Program participants are motivated to pass because if they are not successful in obtaining their license within the first six months of employment, they must be redeployed to an area where licensing is not required or be terminated. This also results in lost recruiting and training costs for the firm.

Key Business Drivers

- ✓ Provide excellent customer service in an increasingly complex financial services market by providing effective initial training, and on an ongoing basis during product launches

- ✓ Increase the first-time pass rate for the NASD Series 6 License.

- ✓ Provide ongoing training required to meet the annual Firm Element NASD continuing education requirement

"We need new employees to be up-to-speed more quickly and with greater skill levels than in the past," says Rebecca Ray, Ph.D., Senior Vice President and Director of Training at American Skandia. "We have more than 45 variations of variable annuities and more than 86 funds in 24 different fund families. Our new employees have so much to learn and master in such a short period of time that we have to give them several ways to learn, and support them during the critical first few months of employment, for them to be prepared when they go to the customer service desks."

How Was the Program Designed?

The five-week Foundations program has four main components. Participants spend approximately 50 percent of the training day in an instructor-led classroom setting; 30 percent in simulation labs, which mirror the customer service floor; 10 percent on self-study reading materials; and 10 percent in self-paced e-learning. Knowledge assessments are threaded throughout the program. This blended approach to new hire training also uses e-learning modules as part of the lab in the classroom training. So the combination of e-learning courses, simulations, and online tests make up at least 40 percent of the program.

When participants are in the simulation lab, they work on fictional accounts and are monitored by trained coaches (highly skilled employees from the customer service desks) and receive feedback and coaching. The coaches, as well as the instructors, then listen in as trainees begin to take live calls. Tape-recorded calls are replayed, analyzed, and critiqued. Trainees take many knowledge assessments throughout the simulations to confirm that they are mastering industry concepts and proprietary information systems.

In building the curriculum for this program, all of the classroom materials were created in-house and augmented with third-party self-study courses and online modules. The Series 6 self-study materials as well as the industry-specific online modules were purchased from the New York City-based Securities Training Corporation (STC). These materials provide a strong foundation for understanding the industry, as well as how variable annuities products work. American Skandia's in-house instructors became certified through STC so that they could deliver the two-day, instructor-led Series 6 review class.

"We have an Advisory Committee on both the variable annuity and the mutual fund side, and they review materials, processes, and procedures," says Ray. "They sit in on classes, and in many cases, help deliver much of the instructor-led modules. We put them all through subject matter expert training so that they feel comfortable in the role of the occasional trainer.

The Corporate Training Team of ASU created (with the help of subject matter experts) the online reference tools for day-to-day use by all customer service employees. These American Skandia-specific modules on products and funds (Product Snapshots and Product @ A Glance) are online, dynamically linked documents that are, in essence, an electronic performance support system.

Additional online modules for Microsoft Office applications and desktop skills, and professional development were provided by Element K and SkillSoft. Quia and Trainersoft products were used to develop online tests.

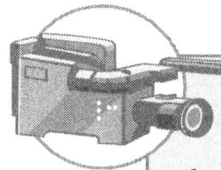

Media and Tools

✓ DKSystems' OnTrack for Training learning management system

✓ Securities Training Corporation for financial service industry content

✓ Element K for desktop skills

✓ SkillSoft for professional skills

✓ Quia and Trainersoft for knowledge assessment

How Was the Program Deployed?

The program is tracked and monitored via American Skandia's learning management system—DKSystems' OnTrack for Training. "OnTrack is the backbone of our American Scandia University Web site," explains Ray. "Employees register for courses and get their transcripts online. We schedule, track, and monitor course and module completions."

OnTrack and all of the learning resources are available at ASU's site on the company Intranet. Each of the five colleges in the ASU offers specialized curriculum paths for a specific population.

New employees first experience online learning in the new hire orientation. Says Ray, "In the Beginnings program, we take them right into the PC labs and have them log on so that everyone knows how to get to the university site."

What Was the Business Impact of the Program?

American Skandia experienced a number of measurable benefits from the new programs. "Originally, we had a 60 percent pass rate at American Skandia," says Ray. "After our new program was put in place, we began to have pass rates of 85 to 90 percent, which beats the national average."

The program also has a big impact on the learners. This program greatly reduced learner stress relative to passing the Series 6 license examination. This is in part due to periodic assessments given throughout the program and a series of practice tests taken prior to writing the certification examination. Additional benefits can be seen in the increased scores on the various online knowledge assessments from week-to-week during the Foundations program.

From a learning perspective, 97 percent of the participants stated in their course evaluations that they enjoyed the online learning experience, and many preferred this method of learning for desktop applications in particular.

Learner Perspectives

✓ Learners were more successful, not only on the knowledge assessments within the program, but also more likely to pass the NASD exam upon completion.

✓ The new blended learning approach greatly reduced learner's anxiety regarding the certification exam.

Summary

Purpose: To bring new hires up-to-speed consistently and quickly, and also improve pass rates on NASD Series 6 license exam

Program Structure: Blended learning program combining classroom, simulations, e-learning, and mentoring

- ✔ Hands-on experience (application) in simulation labs using proprietary systems with coaching and feedback
- ✔ Instructor-led and supervised online learning
- ✔ Print and online self-study
- ✔ Self-paced online module completion
- ✔ Observation and feedback as well as on-line knowledge assessment is integrated throughout the program

Number of Learning Hours per Learner: Five weeks

Total Number of Hours of Learning in the Program: More than 200 hours

Number of Learners: 20 to 25 per class, ongoing

Completion Requirements:

- ✔ All new customer service employees must complete the program
- ✔ 90 percent knowledge assessment rates must be maintained throughout the course

Media and Tools:

- ✔ Simulations
- ✔ Element K courses
- ✔ SkillSoft courses
- ✔ Quia and Trainersoft for assessments

Deployment Mechanism:

- ✔ Internal company portal
- ✔ DKSystems' OnTrack for Training learning management system

Lessons Learned

- ✔ Delivering product update training directly to employees desktop through e-learning courses quickly became part of an effective deployment strategy.
- ✔ Partnering with subject matter experts at every phase is critical.

Case 3: Cingular Wireless

Company Facts and Figures

✓ **Industry:** Telecom

✓ **Scope of Services and Products:**
Provides wireless voice and data communications

✓ **Estimated Number of Employees:**
More than 34,000

✓ **Year e-Learning Introduced:** 2000

✓ **Offices and Locations:**
U.S. and Puerto Rico;
Headquarters in Atlanta, GA

✓ **Estimated 2002 Revenues:**
US$14.7 billion

✓ **Web Site:** www.cingular.com

✓ **Number of e-Learning Programs in Entire Curriculum:** More than 200

Introduction

The Learning Services Team at Cingular Wireless was faced with a challenge—create an orientation process for the newly formed company that would not only help new employees feel welcome and a part of the Cingular team, it would also provide a consistent experience regardless of work location, job function, or hire date.

Cingular Wireless was formed in 2001 through a joint venture between the wireless divisions of SBC and BellSouth. Each parent company had its own unique culture and new hire program. One goal was to create a single new hire experience that reinforced the combined company culture and business strategy.

Why e-Learning?

Cingular Wireless selected an e-learning approach to achieve:

✓ Consistency of message

✓ Common employee experience

✓ Timely dissemination of information and resources

✓ Reliable tracking and reporting capability

✓ Flexible completion time frame

The solution Cingular chose was the blending of traditional Human Resources (HR) first-day meetings with a series of activities, events, and e-learning courses designed to meet both business needs and organizational compliance and regulatory needs. The launch of this new orientation process was scheduled to coincide with the transition of employees from the two parent companies into one company—Cingular Wireless.

The first step Cingular Wireless took, after identifying key stakeholders' criteria for success, was to conduct a full needs assessment that included surveying internal and external groups regarding their new hire orientation experiences. Cingular collected data on the key elements in a successful orientation from both a new employee and business perspective. They looked at what contributes to creating a great first impression, and what contributes to creating a less then ideal experience.

"What we learned is that the experience starts from day one and that sometimes when an employee has to wait days or weeks before they begin an orientation, the experience is not as great as it could have otherwise been," says Betty Cotton, Manager of Employee Development. Another finding of the company's research was that new employees often feel overwhelmed with the amount of information they receive during traditional HR orientations, with little time to digest the content.

It was determined that a blended approach with a strong e-learning focus would be the best solution. This solution would allow orientation and training to start immediately, provide consistency of message, a common employee experience, and timely dissemination of information and resources. Says Cotton, "Employees are located in various Cingular offices across the country, and we were aiming for as close to a consistent process as possible for our employees to experience their orientation and learn about Cingular."

New employees are introduced to the orientation and guided to the various orientation components through an interactive Web site called Joining the Team. The Web site and all e-learning courses are completed within the first 30 days of employment and are accessed and tracked from Cingular's learning management system.

How Was the Program Aligned with the Business?

A number of key business drivers are directly related to the new program. "At the time Cingular was formed, we had 12 different brands, and our operations were very decentralized," says Rob Lauber, Executive Director of Learning Services. "One of the strategic initiatives of the company going forward was to create a consistent employee and consistent customer experience that would reinforce a new employee's belief that they made the right choice in joining Cingular."

Cingular recognizes that their long-term growth and ability to provide exceptional products and services is directly related to their ability to attract and maintain a skilled and diverse work force. In training, this equates to providing adequate access to the knowledge and skills associated with a person's job. A key element of e-learning is that content is delivered consistently at all locations and available at any time.

"Culturally we were trying to make sure that we got the same kind of messages and the same kind of experiences across to employees regardless of where they were located and regardless of the function that they worked in," says Lauber. Another reason Cingular Wireless decided to convert much of the orientation content to e-learning is because new hires are coming in at different times throughout the month, and this way orientation could start immediately for the new employee.

The online aspect of the orientation eliminated potential delays in training and the

Key Business Drivers

- ✓ Help employees contribute to Cingular's growth and profitability
- ✓ Communicate Cingular's policies and procedures and help new hires recognize the importance of complying with these policies and procedures
- ✓ Reinforce the new hires' belief that they made the right choice in joining Cingular
- ✓ Provide a consistent message and employee experience regardless of location, job function, or hire date
- ✓ Provide a flexible orientation process that supports the HR staffing model

costly travel expenses associated with traditional classroom courses. Also, the use of the Web site and e-learning courses reduced the number of classroom instructors needed from the HR department. "We wanted a process that would require fewer HR professionals to deliver and maintain," says Lauber. "The process would also encourage more interaction between the new employee and the hiring manager."

Another key business driver is the ability to track and report on employees' completion of compliance courses. "This was a major factor in our decision to use e-learning versus CD-ROM in deploying the orientation program. Tracking completion through the learning management system provides an excellent way for managers to ensure that their employees have completed the orientation and compliance courses and also take corrective action if they have not. Although CD-ROM would allow for more media-rich online content, completion could not automatically be recorded and tracked.

How Was the Program Designed?

The Learning Services team, along with HR and management, know it is important for new hires to be welcomed to the company by people and not a computer. So the new employee is greeted and welcomed to Cingular Wireless by co-workers, their manager, and local HR and leadership. Following these introductions the employee receives a tour of the work facilities and is guided through the process for logging into the learning management system and enrolling for, and starting, the online components of the orientation.

Media and Tools

✓ Lectora by Trivantis: Online training authoring tool

✓ Macromedia Flash

✓ Centra e-collaboration tool to communicate and share online components with leaders, management, and HR

✓ Docent: Learning management system to deploy online courses and track results

✓ Zoomerang to develop, administer, and gather participant feedback

The online elements of the orientation are located on a Web site called Joining the Team. This site is designed to introduce new hires to Cingular's culture, commitment to diversity and professional development, safety, and benefits. The site also serves as a central point for the entire orientation experience. New employees can go to job aids, activities, and many Cingular resources, such as the HR portal Web site and Cingular communications. Most importantly, the Joining the Team site introduces and directs new hires to the online compliance training courses they will be required to complete. "The Joining the Team site is a great way to communicate the importance of the compliance training and easily direct our new employees to these courses for completion," says Cotton.

Each compliance training course is designed to be no more then 30 minutes in length. The courses present very concise and direct content, which makes it easier for new employees to assimilate information at a time when so much is coming their way. Plus, smaller courses can be completed in the time frame of a busy work day.

During the orientation experience, new employees also learn about the internal structure of Cingular Wireless through an online, interactive tour called Inside Cingular. This tour introduces new employees Cingular's business strategy and leadership team. Photos of the executive team are included so new hires can put faces with the names they will hear or see often.

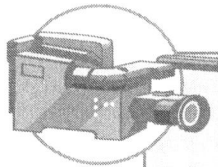

Throughout the orientation, there are opportunities to engage with managers, coworkers, and HR. "Employees are given tips and encouraged to perform certain activities around networking with their manager and peers," says Lauber. For example, a new employee and his or her manager is expected to meet face-to-face to discuss job expectations and work responsibilities.

All course design for the orientation program was completed internally. Two vendors were used to develop media, such as graphics and Macromedia Flash animations, and also program both the Web site and compliance training. For the online components, Cingular required vendors to use Lectora, an authoring and publishing software program by Trivantis. Says Cotton, "We wanted the ability to easily update and maintain the content in-house."

How Was the Program Deployed?

The Learning Services team identified a deployment strategy that was simple, fast, cost-effective, and allowed for tracking of participant's completion. During the design phase, the team concluded that a CD-ROM approach was not the best delivery method because:

✓ Duplication and distribution would be costly

✓ Tracking of scores and completion would prove almost impossible

✓ Timely distribution of CD-ROMs would be challenging

✓ Access to a CD-ROM could be more challenging for many employees than access to an Internet site

✓ Version control for course material would be difficult

Deployment through Cingular's learning management system was identified as the best option. This option allowed new employees to easily and quickly enroll, access, and track all of their courses from one location. Plus, it was easy to connect new employees to the online evaluation that was developed and deployed through Zoomerang. These evaluations allowed for quick access to participants' reactions and feedback to the orientation.

To help ensure the orientation process was successful, the Learning Services team needed to market the process and get buy-in from senior leadership, management, and HR. This was achieved through multiple marketing and communication techniques that took place before, during, and after the deployment of the orientation program.

Marketing Approach

✓ Joining the Team resource guide given to managers

✓ Centra Web conferences to update leaders, managers, and HR

✓ E-mail announcements

✓ Articles in company online newsletter

✓ On-site demonstrations

During the design and development phase, Web conferences deployed by Centra were held with the Senior Leadership team. These conferences were an opportunity for the Learning Services team to provide updates on the status of the overall development effort, which helped set expectations, answer questions, and ensure that the team continued to move in the right direction. In addition, open houses were scheduled to coincide with regional leadership meetings to ensure that there would be maximum participation in the orientation program. "We traveled to

regional offices and call centers and provided an opportunity for the leadership teams to see the welcome video, interact with the online Web site and courses, and ask questions about the orientation process," says Lauber.

For management, the purpose of marketing the orientation process was not only to gain buy-in, but also to communicate the critical role managers play in the orientation process. A resource guide was developed to help managers guide and support new employees through the process. This guide provided checklists, job aids, and information sheets, along with recommended schedules for completing the orientation within the 30-day time frame.

Finally, for HR, buy-in was essential because of the important role they play in the orientation process and, for most, the new program represented a significant change from the way orientation was conducted in the past. To achieve this buy-in, members of the HR team were identified to participate on the orientation implementation team. Their role was to help develop the deployment strategy, review and provide feedback on content and support materials, and communicate the process within their region. This collaboration not only helped determine recommendations for deployment and strengthen the orientation content, but it also helped HR get excited about this new process.

What Was the Business Impact of the Program?

Cost effectiveness was an important impact of the program. "To deliver the nine compliance courses to the entire organization costs about $1.45 per employee, says Lauber. "That's about $0.16 per course per employee to deliver, which represents a 90 percent cost reduction in content delivery if we had to deliver it in an instructor-led classroom format," explains Lauber. Costs were also impacted by a reduction in employee hours required for HR to support the delivery of the program. "Given the large number of the employees that we hire in a given period, it would have been extremely difficult to meet our goals with the number of HR staff that we have," adds Lauber.

Although the program is longer than the original orientation, it is spread out over four weeks allowing new employees the opportunity to absorb the material at their own pace. "Previously, we had received feedback that our orientation had too much information, people could not remember it, they could not process it, and often times they would leave the orientation feeling as though they had been overloaded with content," says Lauber "So by going in this new direction, employees learn in a way that is more consistent with how adults usually process information, and they always can go back and refer to the material as many times as they need to."

Learner Perspectives

✔ "Very enlightening and educational"

✔ "Online training allowed me to backtrack if I needed to access information again."

✔ "User friendly"

✔ "The orientation was very informative and thorough."

Summary

Purpose: To build a blended learning solution that provides a consistent orientation experience for all new Cingular Wireless employees as soon as they begin employment, regardless of their job type or work location

Program Structure: The orientation program included:

- ✓ Interactive online tour
- ✓ Self-paced e-learning courses
- ✓ Face-to-face networking
- ✓ Online evaluation

Number of Learning Hours per Learner: 8 to 12

Total Number of Hours of Learning in the Program: 8 to 12

Number of Learners:

- ✓ Varies based on the number of new hires

Completion Requirements:

- ✓ All new employees must complete the orientation within the first 30 days of employment

Media and Tools:

- ✓ Lectora by Trivantis
- ✓ Macromedia Flash
- ✓ Centra
- ✓ Zoomerang

Deployment Mechanism:

- ✓ Central Web site portal for all courses
- ✓ Docent learning management system

Lessons Learned

- ✓ Test underlying infrastructure as thoroughly as possible to ensure that all aspects function as intended.

- ✓ Run a sample group through complete program to validate communications, system inter-action, and user acceptance. This helps catch problems before launch that can be easily fixed, as well as maintains learning's credibility.

- ✓ Involve management early on in decision making process so that they are advocates for the program.

- ✓ Operate a question and answer line so that managers, subject matter experts, and HR delivery team can answer questions and quickly eliminate confusion.

Case 4: Prudential Financial

Company Facts and Figures

✓ **Industry:** Insurance and Financial Services

✓ **Scope of Services and Products:** Offers life insurance, property and casualty insurance, mutual funds, annuities, pension and retirement related services and administration, asset management, securities brokerage, banking and trust services, real estate brokerage franchises and relocation services

✓ **Year e-Learning Introduced:** 1999

✓ **Offices and Locations:** Headquarters in Newark, New Jersey

✓ **Estimated 2002 Assets:** Approximately US$556 billion in total assets under management and administration

✓ **Web Site:** http://www.prudential.com

✓ **Number of e-Learning Programs in Entire Curriculum:** More than 100

Introduction

Prudential Financial companies serve individual and institutional customers worldwide and include The Prudential Insurance Company of America, one of the largest life insurance companies in the United States. The Individual Life Operations Business Unit was one of the first at Prudential Financial to venture into e-learning when in1999, they launched a new seven-week blended learning version of the Life Operations Call Center New Hire Training Program.

Why e-Learning?

Prudential Financial selected a blended e-learning approach to:

✓ Provide consistent delivery of content in process and procedures

✓ Provide simulations of transaction systems to practice job activities

✓ Improve quality of call handling through use of exams and coaching incorporated within the training

"The program combines over 100 call center simulations into classroom learning, mentoring sessions, live call sessions, and self-study," says Suzanne LeVan, Director of Learning at Prudential Financial.

Typical transaction requests processed by call center employees include beneficiary change, report of a death claim, change of address, dividend payouts, loan applications, and cash surrenders. The seven-week program gradually improves how new hires handle these calls from customers. By using this approach for training, new hires are not overwhelmed by the volume of content, and they are given many opportunities to practice transactions, which greatly increases their retention of information presented in the program.

How Was the Program Aligned with the Business?

Customer Service Assistants (CSAs) in the call centers are the first line of contact with Prudential Financial's customers. "One of our main business goals is to provide quality service and information to our customers," says LeVan. With this in mind, the learning objectives of the Life Operations Call Center New Hire Training Program revolve around skill development in providing service to customers and also in handling all types of customer transactions.

Prior to the program's deployment, Prudential Financial faced a number of challenges in training new hires. Says LeVan, "We found that because training was dispersed in several locations and delivered by various instructors, there was a challenge with having consistency in our process and procedures."

Call Center employees must fully understand the types of products that Prudential Financial sells and all transactions related to those products. "We are an insurance company," says LeVan. "Employees must understand all the various types of portfolio products that we have so when our customers ask a question, we provide accurate information and quality service."

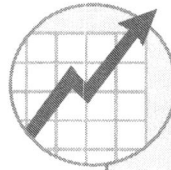

Key Business Drivers

✓ Provide quality service and accurate information to customers

✓ Provide consistent delivery of content to all office locations

✓ Train Customer Service Assistants (CSAs) in the handling of hundreds of transaction types

How Was the Program Designed?

The program was designed and developed by members of the Prudential Financial learning team working with subject matter experts. The simulations were first designed in a storyboard or "spec" format and then final content was developed using Macromedia Authorware.

There were fifteen people, both full- and part-time, working on the initial project team. This team was supplemented with contract programmers, who did the initial work and also transferred knowledge to internal developers. The total program took about one year to design and develop.

New hires participate in the Life Operations Call Center New Hire Training Program for a period of seven weeks. Sixty percent of the program time is self-paced e-learning and forty percent is instructor-led classroom learning. The program begins with an instructor-led classroom orientation session about Prudential Financial. Then within the first few days, new hires meet with their mentors, and listen to customer calls to get a sense of types of calls to expect. Then back in the classroom, through online simulations and instructions, new hires learn about products, processes, transactions, procedures, and systems. "Each day the learners are working through simulations, coming back together for debriefing sessions, and then participating in classroom instruction," says LeVan. "They are learning through simulations how to take various types of calls, and then we direct live calls targeted at their current learning level."

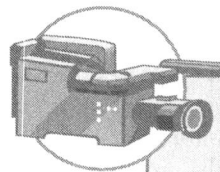

Media and Tools

✓ Macromedia Authorware

✓ Knowledge Planet, a hosted learning management system

✓ Vendor-provided generic training courses

During the seven-week program, most calls are monitored by coaches, who provide on-going feedback and instruction. Learners gradually increase their skills to take more complex levels of service calls and transactions. "Each week builds on the next so by the end of the seven weeks new hires are totally competent in taking the full range of service calls that are handled in our call centers." says LeVan. "Assessments are also built into the program and tracked."

Additional generic soft skill classroom courses are also completed during the program, and at the end of the program, self-paced e-learning courses, such as project management, are available to supplement the learning experience. As part of the quality control for course development, all learning materials that contain any product information are reviewed by Prudential Financial's compliance department for approval. "This is very to us important from a risk management perspective." says LeVan.

How Was the Program Deployed?

The original 14-week classroom-only course was delivered at central locations throughout the United States. Now the new seven-week blended learning program is accessible at four Prudential Financial offices and is deployed through Knowledge Planet, a hosted learning management system. New hires attend the program at one of four dedicated call centers, and these centers are set up with special training rooms that provide access to the more than one hundred simulations and allow mentors to monitor the handling of calls.

Mentors track a new hire's progress through the program using Prudential Financial's learning management system. Says LeVan, "We analyze online test results, how many people had certain questions wrong, or if they had to go back and do additional work on certain points." Learners must pass each assessment with 90 percent or above, and employees are also monitored and evaluated based on Prudential Financial's criteria for call handling and quality. They are all required to meet certain standards prior to leaving this controlled learning environment.

The program does not require internal marketing because new employees immediately join the program when they start work at Prudential Financial. However, during the recruitment process, the program is used as a marketing tool, with major details of the program shared with prospective employees. It is also fully described in the new hire packet.

Marketing Approach

✓ During recruitment process for new employees, major details of training program are shared

✓ Program is described in new hire packet

✓ Excitement is built about the program by demonstrating some simulations during the first-day orientation session

What Was the Business Impact of the Program?

Prudential uses a number of criteria when evaluating new employees. One criteria is call handling time. For example, it may take on average eight minutes for a new employee to handle a customer call. "One impact of the new program is that we were able to reduce our call handle time because employees learned the best path through simulations and feedback," says LeVan.

Within four weeks after graduation new hires might need to be down to a six-minute call handling time. Says LeVan, "We meet those measures through the simulations and the quality measures after graduation." Level Three criteria is measured after eight to ten weeks on the job, and this level is defined as having a direct impact on the business.

Learner Perspectives

✓ Learners were able to achieve call handle time goals because they experienced the best path through simulations and feedback.

✓ Learners were excited by the quality of the simulations.

Summary

Purpose: To provide consistent delivery of content for call center process and procedures and to provide simulations of transactions for practice in handling job functions

Program Structure: A blended learning approach, which combined:

✓ 60 percent self-paced e-learning using simulations

✓ 40 percent instructor-led classroom learning

Number of Learning Hours per Learner: 7 weeks

Total Number of Hours of Learning in the Program: 7 weeks

Number of Learners: 4,000 since launch

Completion Requirements:

✓ All new call center employees are required to attend program

✓ Pass all exams with 90 percent or above

Media and Tools:

✓ Simulations developed in Macromedia Authorware

✓ Monitored call handling in a controlled environment

✓ Vendor-provided generic training courses

Deployment Mechanism:

✓ Deployed in dedicated call centers

✓ Hosted by Knowledge Planet learning management system

Lessons Learned

✓ When budgeting for the development of a new program be sure to include in your plan how often and to what degree maintenance of the program must be performed.

✓ When building training for company systems, work closely with the owners of the systems to understand their plans for system enhancements and modifications.

✓ Spend the time to understand and select the authoring tools that will be used to build the programs and ensure that the one selected is part of the specification when selecting vendors to assist in the building of content.

✓ If you are building a department capable of creating and maintaining e-learning, work out the roles, responsibilities, job descriptions, job grades from an HR perspective before hiring the employees.

✓ When deploying e-learning that people will attend from their desktop, spend time in the beginning teaching people how to use the technology and how best to learn from e-learning.

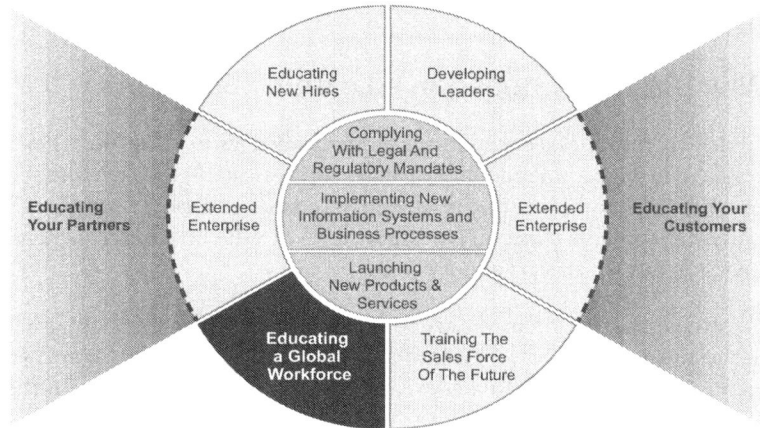

CHAPTER

14

Educating a Global Workforce

The cases for this chapter are:

- *Deloitte Consulting*
- *McDonald's Corporation*
- *Austrade*

Introduction

Why Did They Choose an e-Learning Solution?

Global organizations experience unique challenges in educating their workforce. To compete successfully in highly volatile, increasingly sophisticated global markets, companies must align the entire global workforce to the highest standards of service, knowledge, and capability, as customers and clients expect a consistent level of value, no matter where they come into contact with the company's products and services.

To attract and retain customers and clients, companies competing with a global strategy must harness the advantages of locations, but skill all the individual workers with similar content, learning, and coaching to achieve the requisite capability levels. In the traditional approach to training and learning, it has been found that a globally diverse workforce poses a variety of implementation barriers. However, recently, the dramatic operational improvement to be realized by using the Internet and e-learning to support delivery of high-quality learning to a diverse global workforce has been validated.

Deploying consistent, valuable e-learning to a global workforce, while allowing for localization of content to meet cultural norms, provides significant competitive advantages, such as:

- Rapid, global new skill development on mission critical capabilities
- Standardization of customer brand experience, wherever they are in the world
- Localization of content to meet specific cultural requirements
- Improved customer satisfaction through better qualified employee capabilities

This chapter presents three case examples of organizations with a global learning roll-out challenge that they addressed through an e-learning solution. They include: Deloitte Consulting, the world's largest, privately-owned management consulting firm; McDonald's Corporation, the world's leading food service retailer; and Austrade, the Australian Trade Commission, a small but highly global organization.

All three organizations found that an e-learning approach clearly provided important support in the deployment of skill development for their global workforce, whether the learning involved knowledge workers, customer service associates, or governmental employees.

Achieving Consistent Global Capabilities through e-Learning

One of the major challenges of global organizations is to ensure that their global workforce provides a consistent level of experience to their client or customer. To accomplish this using the traditional, classroom approach was practically impossible, as expense and time costs were insurmountable in a global roll-out of learning. To overcome these obstacles, Deloitte Consulting utilized a blended model of e-learning to skill their practitioners with the new suite of SAP extended enterprise products. These knowledge workers already were highly skilled in SAP applications; however, having the new capabilities was mission critical for Deloitte Consulting, to strengthen their on-going competitive global market position. Using a e-learning portal, all practitioners were able to access three levels of learning: vision and strategy, localized where relevant; an overview of the mySAP.business suite of products; and e-learning on each of the products, where Deloitte Consulting-specific content was combined with content provided by SAP AG. This e-learning was rapidly deployed to 5,000 learners in 33 countries with an estimated cost savings of 70 percent.

A similar experience employing an e-learning solution was realized by Austrade. Australian businesses anticipated quick, professional responses to their inquiries about opportunities to conduct business around the globe. The traditional approach to IT training at Austrade for their globally dispersed offices was expensive and slow, too slow to meet the quality standards expected by, and the requirements of these clients. With the use of the intranet, and a suite of e-learning programs provided by SkillSoft, Austrade was able to provide globally accessible training on 34 modules, leading to certification in Microsoft IT skills and competencies. The outcomes have benefited the clients as well as the bottom-line. Annual client-satisfaction surveys indicate that Austrade's approval rating has improved from 75 to 90 percent, while the IT training costs were reduced from AU$1 million to AU$225,000.

Relevance of Localization and Rewards for Engaging in Global e-Learning

Importantly, the ability to localize content is easily factored in to an e-learning solution. McDonald's Corporation has a global, largely transitional workforce, made up of many young people who need crew training to do their jobs competently, with a standard of service excellence expected by McDonald's customers worldwide. Efficiency, cost-effectiveness, and the ability to track completions in delivering this training were paramount to McDonald's in the pilot of their e-learning strategy.

However, the learning designers also knew that the global enterprise would need to accommodate translation of the content, and localization of the e-learning. Thus, a deliberate choice was made to utilize off-the-shelf development tools and software, so that the training content could be easily translated and localized by representatives in many countries. In addition, to engage workers in the learning, they instituted a reward and incentive program. Inexpensive prizes and restaurant-to-restaurant competitions gave the e-learning experience a local context. Results after the pilot in the countries of Canada, Brazil, Taiwan, Australia, and the United Kingdom indicate that 85 percent of learners found e-learning had improved their overall training experience.

All three organizations found that they were able to reduce costs, speed the time-to-capability, and accommodate local requirements by using an e-learning solution for global workforce training.

Case 1: Deloitte Consulting

Company Facts and Figures

✔ **Industry:** Professional Services

✔ **Scope of Services and Products:**
Management consulting services

✔ **Estimated Number of Employees:**
20,000

✔ **Year e-Learning Introduced:**
1996

✔ **Offices and Locations:**
34 countries

✔ **Estimated 2002 Revenues:**
US$3.5 billion

✔ **Web Site:** www.dc.com

✔ **Number of e-Learning Programs in
Entire Curriculum:** 3000+

Introduction

Deloitte Consulting, as a global management consulting firm, relies on the knowledge and experience of their people to deliver value to their clients. Companies hire consultants because they need access to specific knowledge, ideas, and best practices. Therefore, keeping their consultants ahead of the knowledge curve is not just a strategic business objective—it is a strategic business imperative.

Deloitte Consulting has more than 20,000 professionals in 34 countries. Given their global scope and size, highly mobile audience, and need for rapid deployment, Deloitte Consulting uses e-learning to help meet their learners' needs. Deloitte Consulting's overall e-learning strategy integrates custom content development, partnering with leading content providers, live e-learning, and an enterprise-wide learning management system.

Why e-Learning?

Deloitte Consulting selected an
e-learning approach
because they needed to:

✔ Deliver 10 to 14 hours of learning to 5,000 mobile learners worldwide in less than six months

✔ Rapidly deploy the learning content as time-to-competency/market was a critical requirement

✔ Minimize the time needed for the training to reduce the time away from clients

✔ Provide a continuous learning environment that includes periodic updates to content

One example is Deloitte Consulting's SAP e-Learning Program about SAP AG's new product suite, mySAP.business suite. The mySAP.business suite is an e-business platform that contains a family of e-business solutions, services, and technologies that companies use to manage their entire value chain across business networks. Deloitte Consulting offers consulting services to its clients on the mySAP.business suite platform and products through a core technology practice area including more than 5,000 practitioners. With the release of SAP's extended enterprise product suite, Deloitte Consulting needed to bring practitioners up-to-speed and provide strategic business information regarding the Deloitte Consulting practice area—fast.

To meet the unique learning needs, the program combined vital Deloitte Consulting specific content related to the firm's vision and strategy for Deloitte Consulting's SAP consulting practice area with the key information about SAP's new strategies, markets, and products (see Figure 11-1).

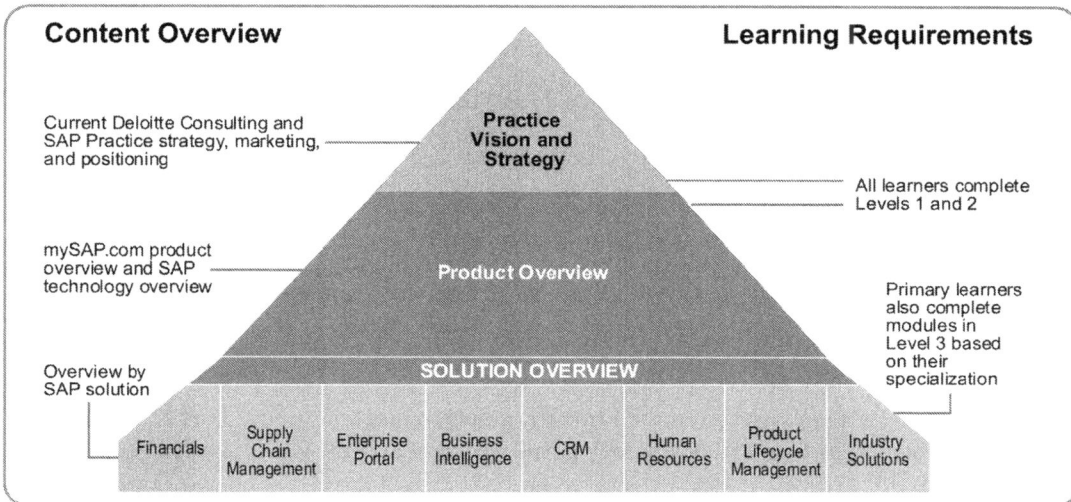

Figure 11-1: Overview of Deloitte Consulting's SAP e-Learning Program

How Was the Program Aligned with the Business?

Deloitte Consulting developed the SAP e-Learning Program to support one of its strategic business objectives in their core technology consulting arena:

Be a worldwide leader in SAP implementation and new SAP solutions

Providing learning for its consultants is a principal tool in supporting this strategy. The decision to develop the program was initiated by the top global executives in Deloitte Consulting's technology practice. They identified the learning need and worked with the learning organization to develop the program concept.

The drivers and objectives led to an e-learning program design that encompasses three levels of learning packaged within a flexible structure with variable content paths.

Key Business Drivers

✓ Rapidly tool and retool practitioners who were highly skilled with prior SAP product sets with the skills and knowledge needed to implement and consult on the new platform to bring value to clients–including an overview of the product suite as well as detailed learning on areas of specialization

✓ Educate practitioners about SAP's strategies, vision, and market positioning

✓ Build awareness of, and focus on, the Deloitte Consulting practice vision and related strategies

How Was the Program Designed?

The SAP e-Learning Program is a Web-based, self-study program. It combines custom developed content specific to Deloitte Consulting with standard learning modules developed by SAP AG for use by their clients and partners to learn about the technical platform and specific solutions within the mySAP.business suite product.

Program Structure—Three Levels of Learning

The program contains three learning levels. **Level 1** (see Figure 11-2) focuses on the Deloitte Consulting Practice Vision and Strategy and contains:

✓ An introduction to the e-learning program

✓ An update on Deloitte Consulting's related practice vision and strategy

✓ A discussion of the business strategies from each global region's perspective (Americas, Europe, and Asia-Pacific-Africa)

✓ Key related messages from the firm's top executives including the Chief Executive Officer (CEO), global technology practice leaders, and the Chief Learning Officer (CLO)

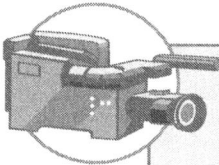

Media and Tools

✓ Content was custom developed in Macromedia Flash 5.0

✓ A game called IES Quest developed in Macromedia Flash and was a fun approach for reinforcing the learning objectives for Level 1.

✓ Multiple media types are used to present information and media types were selected based on the source of the information and the potential level of maintenance required for the content type. Included are:

• Videos
• Audio clips
• Macromedia Flash screens
• PDF files
• Links to Web sites

✓ Assessments were developed in Saba Publisher to measure learning achievements and to act as the completion milestone for each level of the program.

✓ Licensed standard content from SAP on the product technology was used in an e-learning format as a recorded session presented through InterWise, a distance learning tool.

Check It Out Online!
www.elearningfieldbook.com

IES Practice Vision and Strategy - Microsoft Internet Explorer provided by Deloitte Consulting

IES Deloitte SAP
e-Learning Program   LearningEdge   Deloitte Consulting

IES PRACTICE VISION & STRATEGY

Welcome

Introduction

Thoughts from Leadership

Reading Room

Assessment

Perspectives

Paul Horowitz   Doug Downing   David Moore

Process

About the Program   IES Quest

Glossary   Credits

QUIT

All three levels of the program are presented in a **common interface.**

The program includes **videos and audio clips** of the global practice leaders sharing their perspectives on the practice vision and strategy.

The welcome includes a videotaped interview with Deloitte Consulting's SAP Practice leaders in a **talk-show** format.

IES Quest is an **interactive game** in which players follow a gameboard to answer questions and earn points with the goal of becoming an IES Quest Master. Using a database, all IES Quest Master's names are posted to the first screen of the game.

Figure 11-2: Interface for Deloitte Consulting's SAP e-Learning Program

Level 2 provides an overview of the entire mySAP.business suite product including the technology platform and SAP's product strategies.

The SAP product suite is an enterprise-wide and extended-enterprise solution. Previous versions contained function-specific applications, and practitioners generally specialized in a product area within the overall platform. The new platform, mySAP.business suite, while continuing to provide function-specific areas, is more highly integrated and collaborative. Practitioners now needed to expand the scope and depth of their knowledge on the platform overall. This was one of the key learning objectives of Level 2 of the e-learning program. Level 2 contains:

- ✓ A definition of mySAP.business suite, an overview of the product suite, and its position in the market

- ✓ An introduction to SAP's policies and the drivers behind the product strategy

- ✓ An overview of the product's technical infrastructure

Perspectives from Deloitte Consulting leaders on the product and underlying technologies

Level 3 contains the Solution Overviews organized as eight learning modules, one for each component in the mySAP.business suite product suite. Learners select the modules for their specialization from the eight areas covered. They are also encouraged to explore other modules to expand their mySAP.business suite solution knowledge base.

The content in this level continues the combined perspectives, including Deloitte Consulting-specific content and standard learning content from SAP. In addition, there are links to key external content and Web sites, such as industry analysts, and also links to related supporting materials, such as articles, white papers, and presentations.

The content in the Level 3 modules is presented in such a way that the learner can select their own path. The interface points out the required components and describes the optional content with context on how it may apply.

Distributed Development Process—Saving Costs and Time

The development team for this project included:

- ✓ 1.0 project manager
- ✓ 2.5 instructional designers
- ✓ 3.0 developers
- ✓ 0.5 other roles such as technology infrastructure designers

One business approach that the development team used to maximize resources, reduce development costs, and strategically deploy development expertise within the project team was to use contract resources to build a portion of the course.

The contract resources had technical expertise in the tools used on the project including the Macromedia suite, graphics tools, and related programming tools. The contractor's significantly lower costs per hour for development allowed the project team to deploy internal technical resources to lead the high level design and use the contracted resources for the time intensive development tasks. With a difference of between 60-80% cost savings per hour, the team was able to shorten the development timeline and reduce costs overall.

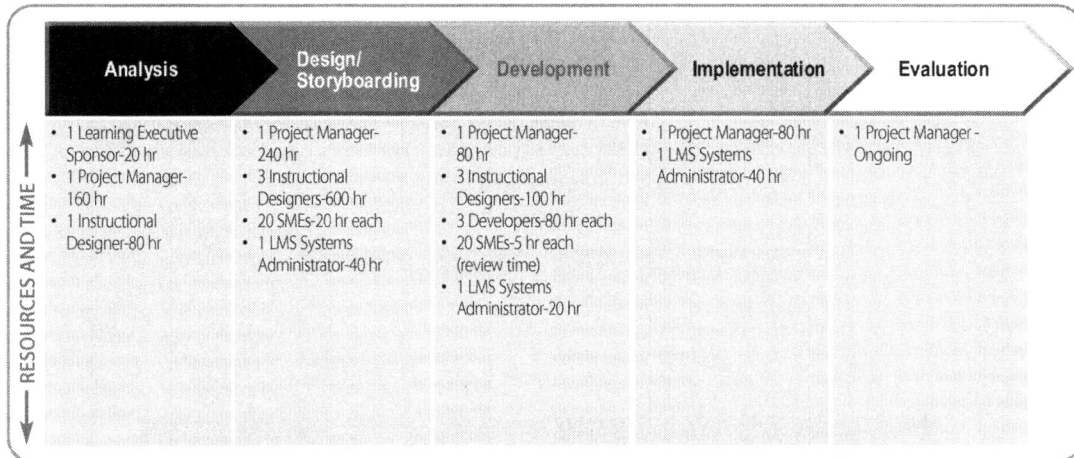

Figure 11-3: Resources and Time for Deloitte Consulting's Development Process of the SAP e-Learning Program

How Was the Program Deployed?

Deloitte Consulting deployed the SAP e-Learning Program online through its firm-wide learning portal. The backbone of the learning portal, called the Learning Channel, is the Saba learning management system.

Deloitte Consulting uses a tool they developed called Learning Pathways (see Figure 11-4), accessible through the learning management system, to illustrate curricula and provide guidance on recommended learning within their overall catalog of courses. They packaged all modules of the SAP e-Learning Program in a Learning Pathway to demonstrate how to progress through the three program levels, including Level 3 which has a variable path depending on the learner's specialization.

Learners use the SAP e-Learning Program Pathway to access and launch the modules, and to track their completion status. This mechanism also provides a structure for management reporting.

Learner Requirements and Management Reporting

For the SAP e-Learning Program, the primary learners must complete all three levels of the program and the secondary learners must complete Levels 1 and 2 of the program within a six-month period. To reinforce the learning requirement and to monitor progress, a weekly summary report is generated through the learning management system to identify the number of learners who have:

✓ Completed each program level (Levels 1, 2, and 3)

✓ Completed the entire program

✓ Started the program

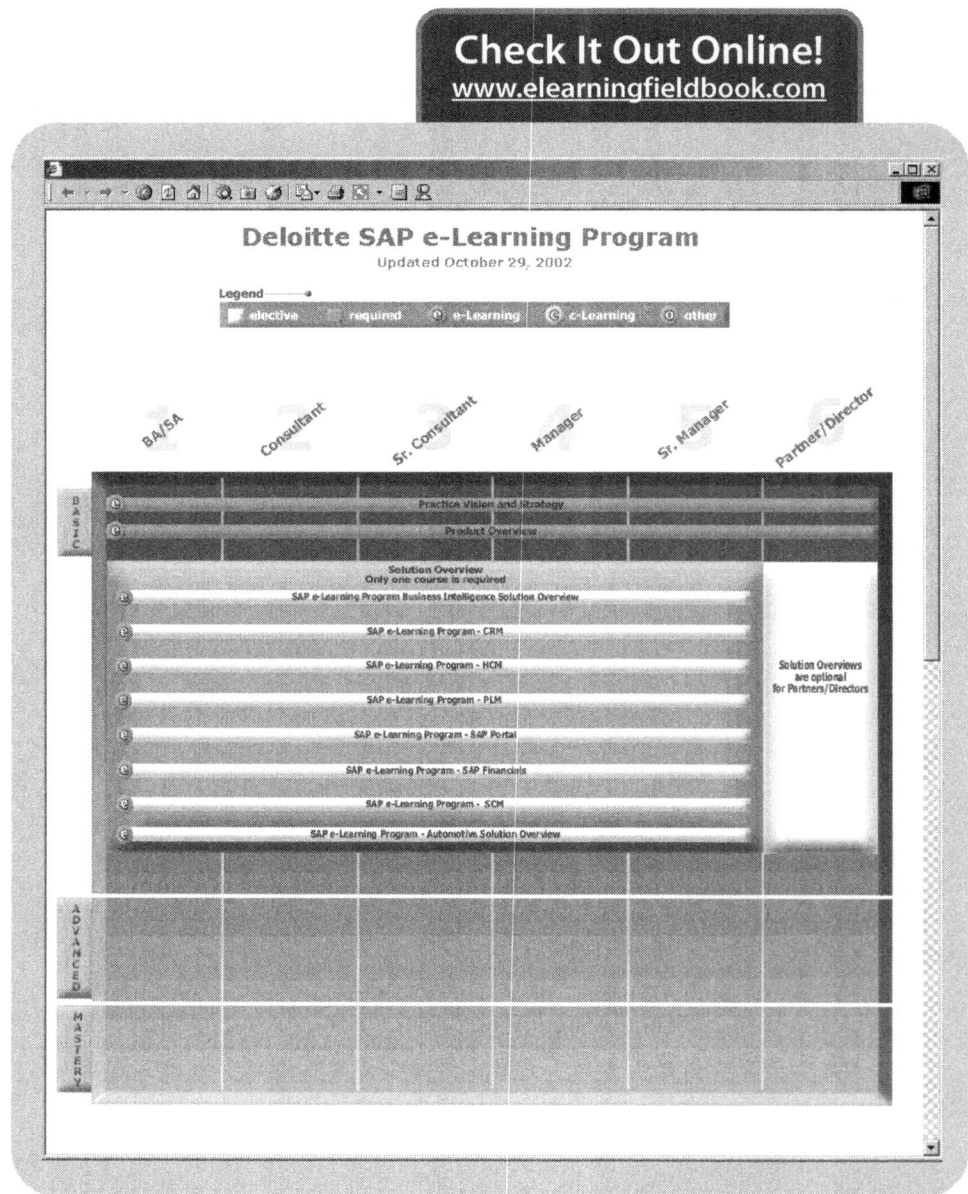

Figure 11-4: Learning Pathways

Deloitte Consulting's learning leadership monitors the participation and results through the management reports. In addition, the top leaders in the technology consulting practice area also review the reports and actively monitor the progress against the completion goals on a weekly basis. This level of leadership commitment in managing the results reinforces the expectations of the learners and demonstrates the strategic importance of the program.

Another motivator that Deloitte Consulting implemented is the policy that learners cannot attend SAP classroom learning until they complete the SAP e-Learning Program. This provides an incentive to complete the program for learners who need to drill-down to additional levels of detail on mySAP.business suite and also better prepares the learners for the next level of training.

> *"I found the SAP e-Learning Program extremely helpful in getting me prepared and giving me the background for the... [classroom course]. Having more programs that "copy" the SAP e-Learning Program structure will benefit staff at, I believe, a relatively low cost to the firm."*

Communications—Launching the Program

To launch the program, a detailed communication plan was developed that included multiple levels and types of communications.

The first level of communication prepared the global learning organization and the global technology consulting practice with the information they needed to support the program implementation and launch. This included communicating the program structure, purpose, objectives, approach, and requirements.

A variety of materials were also prepared to launch and market the program with the learners.

Marketing Approach

✔ Program launch presentation at every local office

✔ Global leadership e-mails direct to learners explaining the requirements and purpose

✔ Announcements on the Firm's intranet portal front page

✔ Regional leadership e-mails direct to learners offering regional perspective on requirements

✔ Posters in all 34 local offices promoting program

✔ Established "grass roots" champions at the local level to monitor participation and encourage participation through positive peer motivation

What Was the Business Impact of the Program?

Although Deloitte Consulting is only partially through the targeted lifecycle of the SAP e-Learning Program, the business impacts of the program from both the learner perspective and firm leadership perspective can begin to be identified through the comments and feedback received so far.

Learner Perspective

The SAP e-Learning Program includes an evaluation to capture the feedback from the learners regarding their experience with the course and the relevancy of the content in the course to their jobs.

In considering the statement, "This course will help me do my job," 81 percent indicated that the course will help on the job (see Figure 11-5).

In considering the statement, "My learning objectives for the course were met," a total of 89 percent indicated that their objectives were met (see Figure 11-6).

In addition, comments submitted through the evaluation and other channels highlight the learner's perceptions related to the impact of the course. Some of the impacts highlighted are that the course:

✔ Provides an efficient method for keeping up to speed in a rapidly changing landscape

✔ Helps differentiate Deloitte Consulting from its competitors

✔ Better prepares learners who are planning additional classroom training, thus maximizing the investment in the subsequent classroom experience

Firm Leadership Perspective

As stated, the program is still early in its lifecycle. However, some of the currently identifiable impacts from the leadership perspective at this point include:

✔ The course was developed and deployed to more than 5,000 learners in 33 countries. The process for developing and deploying the program as e-learning extended the learning opportunity to a much larger group than could have been trained through a classroom approach from a cost, time, and logistical perspective. In addition, the learners were exposed to a broad set of content, including the customized Deloitte Consulting content. The estimated cost savings in using this approach are projected to be approximately 70 percent.

✔ Investing in the development and deployment of this program demonstrated commitment and investment by Deloitte Consulting in the professional development of its people. This is important to the firm for knowledge building in this core consulting area and is a particularly important aspect in attracting and retaining highly talented consultants.

Learner Perspectives

✔ 81 percent indicated that the course will help them with their job.

✔ 89 percent indicated that their learning objectives were met.

✔ "… [This program] differentiates us from our competitors…"

✔ "…extremely helpful in getting me prepared and giving me the background for the [classroom course]."

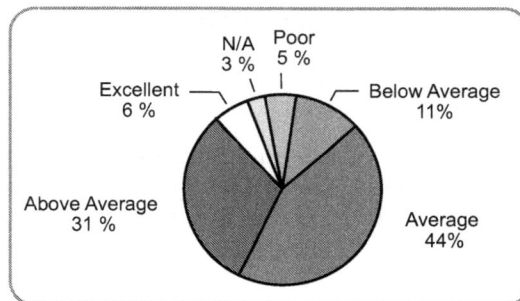

Figure 11-5: Learner Responses—Help Do Job

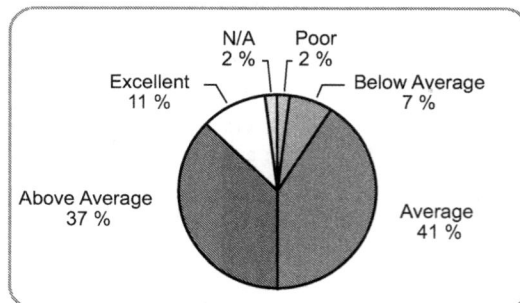

N/A 3 %
Poor 5 %
Excellent 6 %
Below Average 11%
Above Average 31 %
Average 44%

Figure 11-6: Learner Responses—Objectives Met

N/A 2 %
Poor 2 %
Excellent 11 %
Below Average 7 %
Above Average 37 %
Average 41 %

Deloitte Consulting's SAP consulting practice is highly rated by external evaluators of the consulting industry, including Gartner, Inc. In addition, in 2002, SAP AG confirmed Deloitte Consulting as a Partner at the highest level of accreditation in all countries around the world. Although these achievements cannot be directly attributed to the impact of the SAP e-Learning Program, it is clear in this case that learning, and specifically programs like the SAP e-Learning Program, is an invaluable tool in pursuing the stated business strategies.

One learner summarized the impact of the program by saying:

"I think that initiatives like this help us to differentiate ourselves from our competitors. The speed of change within the SAP landscape should require us to repeat this sort of update on a yearly basis. The way of e-learning proves to be a good addition to classroom learning to me..."

Summary

Purpose: To provide a self-study e-learning opportunity for Deloitte Consulting technology consultants to learn about the:

- ✓ New mySAP.business suite platform and products
- ✓ SAP strategies and markets
- ✓ Deloitte Consulting practice strategies and vision for the related consulting practice

Program Structure: 10 e-learning modules grouped into three learning levels:

- ✓ Level 1: Practice Vision and Strategy
- ✓ Level 2: Product Overview
- ✓ Level 3: Solution Overviews (eight modules)

Also Included are custom-developed modules and vendor modules and materials.

Number of Learning Hours per Learner: 10 to 14

Total Number of Hours of Learning in the Program: 45

Number of Learners:

- ✓ 2,500 primary users world-wide
- ✓ 2,500 secondary users world-wide

Completion Requirements:

- ✓ Primary learners are required to complete all three levels of the program in six months (for Level 3, based on their specialization, learners choose at least one of the eight modules)
- ✓ Secondary users are recommended to complete Levels 1 and 2

Media Used: The program includes these media types:

- ✓ Custom developed interface and content in Macromedia Flash 5.0
- ✓ Recorded Interwise courses purchased from vendor
- ✓ Video and audio clips
- ✓ Adobe Acrobat files
- ✓ PowerPoint files
- ✓ Assessments created in Saba Publisher

Deployment Mechanism: Deployed online through the Firm's learning portal, which is based on the Saba learning management system for registration, course access, and tracking. Marketing approaches included:

- ✓ Program Launch presentation at every local office
- ✓ E-mails direct to learners and regional leadership
  - Announcements on the Firm's Intranet
  - Posters in all 34 local offices promoting the program
  - "Grass roots" champions

Lessons Learned

✓ To participate in the program, learners navigated to Deloitte Consulting's Learning Channel and selected the SAP e-Learning Program Pathways. The team indicated that it would have been helpful to automatically register the target audience to reinforce the learning requirement. Using a "push" approach to distribute the learning content rather than a "pull" approach may have helped increase the initial participation in the program.

✓ Budgeting the SME time needed for the project was a challenge. Although the number of hours estimated was accurate, the time extended over a much greater period of time than was projected.

✓ Building a game took more hours than planned due to design issues and considerations around the database functions and firewall requirements.

✓ Deloitte Consulting practitioners are highly mobile. Often practitioners are accessing the program through slower speed dial-up connections. Although the team tested the design for performance for variable connection types, they would also consider creating offline viewing options for future development. They did provide the course on CD for offline use to learners with connectivity challenges.

Case 2: McDonald's Corporation

Company Facts and Figures

✓ **Industry:** Food Service

✓ **Scope of Services and Products:**
Quick Service Restaurants

✓ **Estimated Number of
Employees System- Wide:**
1.7 million

✓ **Year e-Learning Introduced:**
2001

✓ **Offices and Locations:**
30,093 restaurants worldwide;
Home Office in Oak Brook, IL, U.S.

✓ **2001 Revenues:** US$14.8 billion

✓ **Web Site:** www.mcdonalds.com

✓ **Number of e-Learning Courses
in Entire Curriculum:**
Restaurant crew curriculum: 25 courses
Restaurant manager curriculum: 4 courses

Introduction

McDonald's Corporation is the world's leading food service retailer with more than 30,000 restaurants around the world serving more than 46 million customers each day. McDonald's vision is to provide the world's best quick service restaurant experience satisfying more customers, more often, by delivering superior quality, service, cleanliness, and value. McDonald's employees are key to achieving this vision.

McDonald's has more than 1.7 million employees around the world. The largest group of employees within the McDonald's system is crew members in entry-level positions in the restaurants. Crew members are often teenagers or young adults, many of them entering the work force for the first time. It is not uncommon for young employees to take advantage of higher education opportunities or to transition to employment outside of McDonald's. (U.S. Secretary of State Colin Powell is one such example.)

Why e-Learning?

**McDonald's developed an
e-learning strategy to:**

✓ Provide consistent and convenient
training to all employees globally

✓ Provide a cost-efficient method of training

✓ Increase efficiency of training

✓ Track employee training paths

✓ More efficiently update training
curricula

McDonald's also provides employees with career growth opportunities. Many of the corporation's senior executives began their McDonald's career by serving customers at the front counter and the drive-thru window. With so many entry-level employees working in their restaurants, training is a critical link to providing superior customer service. McDonald's trains approximately three million new employees each year.

In 2001, McDonald's developed an e-learning strategy to benefit the business and address global training needs. (This strategy won McDonald's the MASIE Center's Pioneer in Innovation Award for e-Learning Strategy.) The strategy included conducting a variety of e-learning pilots.

To make the greatest business impact, the first e-learning pilot focused on crew members in restaurants in each geographic region of the world. This was followed by a pilot for regional mid-managers and then a pilot with restaurant managers using personal digital assistant (PDA) technology.

This case study focuses on the first pilot deployed in six countries (Canada, Brazil, Taiwan, Australia, the United Kingdom, and the United States) during a six-month period.

How Was the Program Aligned with the Business?

From the company's beginning in 1955, training has been a major emphasis for McDonald's Corporation. Their first Operations and Training manual was written by McDonald's founder, Ray Kroc. In 1961, McDonald's established Hamburger University as its restaurant management training center. Graduating only 12 students that first year, McDonald's has more than 65,000 graduates today. Training for crew members, however, usually takes place in the restaurant where they work.

McDonald's Commitment to Our Employees states that employees will have the resources they need to serve the customer, be provided the tools they need to develop personally and professionally, and be allowed time for training. To achieve this, McDonald's needed an efficient and cost-effective method to provide a consistent training experience to crew members worldwide. McDonald's also wanted the ability to track training and performance verification.

Key Business Drivers

✓ To improve quality and service delivered in the restaurants

✓ To quickly update training on products and services

✓ To improve recruitment and retention of employees

✓ To record and monitor training and verify results

✓ To provide an outstanding customer experience with every visit to a McDonald's restaurant

How Was the Program Designed?

Traditionally, crew training takes place in the restaurant where the new crew member works. McDonald's has developed a Crew Development Program for this purpose that includes videos, booklets, and shoulder-to-shoulder training with a crew trainer to learn the tasks associated with each work station. Job aids such as station guides (diagrams located at each station graphically depicting how to perform particular tasks related to that station) are also utilized. When the training for a station is completed, a crew member's competency for that station is verified by the crew trainer against a set of observable performance criteria detailed in the Station Observation Checklist.

For the initial e-learning pilot, content was converted from the existing Crew Development Program and also from shift management training. Later, next generation e-learning for crew training also included an online animated tutor named "MEL" (an abbreviation for McDonald's e-learning). MEL assists the employee through a course in a similar manner as a crew trainer in a traditional training session (see Figure 14-1).

Figure 14-1: Course with Online Animated Tutor

Figure 14-2: Example of e-Learning Course

The titles of the e-learning courses in the pilot include Hospitality, Cleanliness, Sanitation, and Food Safety, Beginning Service, Advanced Service, and Lot and Lobby. These titles were retained from the traditional Crew Development Program content to provide consistency. Courses vary in length from 20 to 35 minutes and are all self-paced (see Figure 14-2). Proven instructional design principles were applied to all content. Interactive exercises and quizzes are included throughout each course. There is a test at the end of each course, and test scores are automatically recorded in a database that is accessible via a secure reporting application.

McDonald's supports training solutions that blend traditional training methods with e-learning programs. Crew members using e-learning courses also receive shoulder-to-shoulder training (although data shows that e-learning reduces the amount of shoulder-to-shoulder training that is needed) and still have their performance at each station verified by a crew trainer against a set of observable performance criteria. A later pilot included an application for scoring this verification directly on a PDA.

e-Learning courses were initially developed in English and then localized for Chinese, Portuguese, and Spanish. The Chinese and Portuguese versions were used in Taiwan and Brazil, respectively. A large percentage of McDonald's U.S. restaurant employees are Spanish-speaking, so both English and Spanish versions were available in the U.S. pilot.

Program development was outsourced to a vendor working under the guidance of the McDonald's e-learning team. The process is estimated to have taken 3,000 hours to develop four hours of e-learning course material.

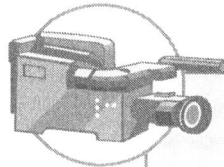

Media and Tools

✓ Macromedia Flash

✓ HTML and DHTML

✓ Java

✓ Java Script

How Was the Program Deployed?

In McDonald's global system, approximately 80 percent of the restaurants are owned and operated by independent franchisees. The remaining 20 percent are owned and operated by McDonald's Corporation. The pilot program was conducted in both franchisee- and corporate-owned restaurants. The pilot involved 36 restaurants and 845 employees in six countries. Crew members accessed the courses via the Internet on a computer, usually located in the crew training or break room. Most of the pilot restaurants had broadband Internet connectivity, but a number with a dial-up connection were included so that data could be compared between different connection speeds. (Survey data clearly indicates a higher level of satisfaction with Internet connectivity among those who had broadband connections versus those with a dial-up connection.) Although the pilot ended in March 2002, access to the con-

Marketing Approach

✓ Executives in each pilot market communicated their endorsement of e-learning to restaurant employees.

✓ Some restaurants used rewards as incentives for employees.

✓ e-Learning leadership traveled to the pilot markets to be involved in the kick-off and initial orientation.

✓ Employees were made aware that they were involved in a cutting edge training initiative.

tent remains available to crew members in several of the pilot restaurants. Other restaurants are already using enhanced, next generation e-learning content developed after the pilot.

During the pilot, McDonalds used the development vendor's reporting system. This enabled McDonald's to generate a variety of reports, such as usage, test scores, and completion percentages.

What Was the Business Impact of the Program?

Pre- and post-pilot surveys were conducted with crew members and managers in the pilot markets. Data collected from those surveys includes such information as:

- ✓ 85 percent reported e-learning improved the overall training experience
- ✓ 83 percent reported e-learning will improve employee recruitment and retention
- ✓ 83 percent reported e-learning did not negatively impact other restaurant operations
- ✓ 82 percent reported e-learning integrated well with existing training programs

Managers in all pilot markets mostly agreed that new crew members using e-learning had better skill development than crews using traditional training only. For example:

- ✓ 80 percent reported that the crew displayed more confidence
- ✓ 81 percent reported crew more quickly and successfully completed the verification requirements of the Station Observation Checklists
- ✓ 76 percent reported that crew required less shoulder-to-shoulder training
- ✓ 83 percent reported that crew displayed improved interactions with customers

Results from the pilot program have shown that better trained crew members are more confident about their skills, allowing them to perform better, which in turn improves customer satisfaction.

Reduced employee turnover results in a significant savings in training costs, as even a two percent reduction in turnover has the potential of saving tens of millions of dollars given the size of the McDonald's workforce.

e-Learning has also proven to be very beneficial when new restaurants open, particularly in remote areas where there is limited access to experienced trainers. Reports from newly opened restaurants that used e-learning prior to the opening indicate that those restaurants develop a core of well-trained and confident employees more quickly than would traditionally be the case. As a result, new restaurants reach full operational potential sooner. In these scenarios, the lack of an existing core of experienced crew members to transfer knowledge to incoming employees is largely nullified because e-learning usage transfers that knowledge to the new crew.

With the success of the pilot programs, a new expectation has been set throughout the McDonald's system to develop other training initiatives to be delivered by e-learning.

Learner Perspectives

- ✓ 86 percent stated that they learned a lot from the courses
- ✓ 85 percent stated the computer location provided convenient access
- ✓ 90 percent stated that McDonald's should continue to develop e-learning

Summary

Purpose: The crew pilot content introduces entry-level training skills to new crew and basic management skills to more experienced crew on the following topics:

✓ Hospitality: Teaches proper interaction with customers

✓ Cleanliness, Sanitation, and Food Safety: Teaches safe food handling basics and other sanitary practices

✓ Beginning Service: Teaches basic responsibilities when serving customers

✓ Advanced Service: Teaches advanced responsibilities when serving customers

✓ Lot and Lobby: Teaches how to care for the inside and outside of the restaurant

✓ Managing People, Equipment, and Products: Teaches about organizing employees during a shift, correct operation of equipment, and proper handling of products

✓ Basic Management Skills: Teaches introductory techniques to potential managers

Program Structure:

✓ 20 to 35 minute self-paced courses with interactive exercises and quizzes and a test at the conclusion of each course

Number of Program Hours per Employee: Approximately 4 hours

Total Number of Hours per Program: Approximately 4 hours

Number of Pilot Program Participants: 845

Completion Requirements: Crew members complete a test at the end of each course and then their performance of learned tasks is observed and verified by a crew trainer against a set of observable performance criteria.

Media Used: The program includes these media types:

✓ Macromedia Flash

✓ HTML and DHTML

✓ Java

✓ JavaScript

Deployment Mechanism:

✓ e-Learning courses were Web-based and delivered over the Internet

Lessed Learned

✓ Build alliances with internal information technology groups. e-Learning is a learning initiative and should be managed by learning professionals. However, as a technology-enabled learning solution, e-learning also requires the involvement of technical resources to be successful.

✓ Involve the target country in the localization process. The target market will not utilize courseware that is not well localized, so it is important to have strong local involvement throughout process.

✓ Use off-the-shelf development tools and software that are readily available rather than proprietary resources. Training content in a global corporation requires localization and modifications to make it appropriate for different countries. Using off-the-shelf tools to create programs allows representatives in other countries to more efficiently modify the original content than if proprietary tools are used.

✓ Maintain close control of your project if it is outsourced to a vendor. Clearly communicate your objectives and expectations to ensure that the vendor knows the expected deliverables.

✓ Conduct a thorough quality review of all materials before deploying (and do not assume vendors identified all quality issues in their review). In a corporation as large as McDonald's, sending out erroneous information has the potential to reach more than a million people.

✓ Use incentives to motivate and encourage e-learning participation. Restaurants in the McDonald's pilot that offered inexpensive prizes or promoted restaurant-to-restaurant competitions achieved higher participation rates than restaurants that did not.

✓ Obtain executive management support and have senior executives communicate and demonstrate approval of the e-learning strategy.

Case 3: Austrade

Company Facts and Figures

✓ **Industry:** Australian Federal Government

✓ **Scope of Services and Products:** Trade Advisory and Facilitation

✓ **Estimated Number of Employees:** 997 (509 in Australia; 488 dispersed globally)

✓ **Year e-Learning Introduced:** 2000

✓ **Offices and Locations:** 90 offices in 60 countries

✓ **Estimated 2002 Revenues:** AU$213 million

✓ **Web Site:** www.austrade.gov.au

✓ **Number of e-Learning Programs in Entire Curriculum:** 56

Introduction

There is much research data that indicates e-learning is only successful and affordable in large organizations. But Austrade, the Australian Trade Commission, is an excellent example of how a relatively small yet highly global organization has leveraged available vendor technology and content, combined with an intensive marketing campaign, to achieve extremely high e-learning usage rates among their employees.

Why e-Learning?

Austrade selected an e-learning approach to:

✓ Leverage an existing strong IT platform with a complete intranet that serviced every office in the organization

✓ Provide a consistent message and make training available to all offices

✓ Reduce training costs

Austrade is an agency of the Australian federal government that helps Australian companies win overseas business for their products and services, and assists foreign businesses in sourcing goods and services from Australia by taking advantage of Austrade's comprehensive networks and databases. They offer practical advice, market intelligence, and ongoing support (including financial) to Australian businesses looking to develop international markets, provide advice and guidance on overseas investments and joint venture opportunities, and help put overseas businesses in contact with potential Australian suppliers and investors.

Recognizing that the Internet is reshaping the global marketplace and transforming corporate strategies, Austrade established the Information Age Project to leverage Internet technology to better serve their clients. This included investing in the skills, training, and career development of employees through the Austrade Institute, a virtual structure that utilized the existing company intranet.

How Was the Program Aligned with the Business?

Between 1995 and 1997, fast-paced technology advances, such as upgrading Microsoft Office 95 to 97 and Microsoft Windows NT Server 3.1 to 4.0, propelled the infrastructure platform forward but training did not follow. By 1999, the office managers and regional IT coordinators were indicating that staff was deficient in IT skills and competencies due the lack of targeted training. Many staff member spent much of their time trying to find out how to do things.

Training at that time was classroom-based, with a number of differences in training policies and availability of training between each office. There was a need in the organization to develop consistent skills on a global basis, not only in IT and software application areas, but in general business, interpersonal, and specialized business process skills.

Key Business Drivers

✔ Need for consistent training across entire organization

✔ Availability of training for all offices regardless of location

✔ Comply with management directive that IT skills needed to be benchmarked to a recognized standard

Using the existing company intranet, e-learning was selected as the global training solution in June 2000, with SkillSoft (formerly SmartForce) chosen as the vendor to supply a broad curriculum of e-learning courses from their library. A customized portal was implemented in September of the same year.

e-Learning was funded originally as an IT special project, essentially offering the e-learning solution to the local offices for free. It is now funded centrally as a learning and development initiative on an ongoing basis, with no charge to the regions other than the time their staff applies to it.

How Was the Program Designed?

The first e-learning offered was a certification program of Microsoft IT skills and competencies. Thirty-four modules were launched on the first release. SkillSoft was chosen to deploy courses as it gave greater flexibility for future add-ons. As of 2003, there are 56 modules, with the addition of more technical courses for LAN administrators, 10 interpersonal courses, and two customized courses. Austrade is also moving beyond the generic SkillSoft modules to customized modules about their export procedures and business processes.

The courses are downloadable, giving the employee the option of completing training at home or while traveling. For SkillSoft assessments, the Austrade Institute provides internal certification and the Microsoft Office Specialist Accreditation Center provides global certification.

None of the courses or certification programs were compulsory as it was felt it would alienate employees and create a greater degree of resistance to e-learning. The program was deliberately designed to be "softer" to get a maximum amount of buy-in. Austrade believes this approach has actually enabled and allowed people to feel comfortable with online learning without added pressure on the learner. However, managers were encouraging staff to write into their performance agreements that they would get to a certain level or achieve a certificate, and had the option of using training as a required measure to improve an employee's skills if they felt it was necessary.

A major component to making the program successful was the creation of an environment that fostered the development of an e-learning culture. This was a challenge due the global nature of the organization and the diverse cultural viewpoints on learning in the various office locations. A high degree of flexibility was given to the local offices to encourage training. Some of the solutions to creating this new learning environment included:

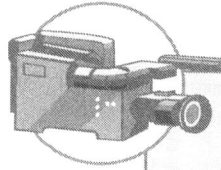

Media and Tools

✓ Self-paced learning on Austrade's Intranet

✓ SkillSoft library of courseware

✓ Customized courses

✓ Creating space within the office for e-learning that eliminated interruptions, whether it was a separate cubical location or hanging up a sign that alerted fellow workers that a co-worker was engaged in e-learning and their learning time was to be respected

✓ Providing incentives to complete e-learning, such as receiving a certificate, tying completion to bonus incentives, and making training part of the question and answer process during performance reviews

✓ Public recognition ceremonies for the awarding of certificates by upper management

✓ Supervisors lending out their own laptops so that direct reports without laptops could take e-learning courses at home

✓ Management support of a company policy that allowed for 30 minutes per week of e-learning while on the job

How Was the Program Deployed?

SkillSoft serves as Austrade's learning management system and also provides generic courses. A Web content development course and a customized Microsoft Outlook course were developed by other vendors. Austrade is also using a course development tool to create some of their own courses.

Access for courses is through Austrade's intranet, rather than the Internet due to limited bandwidth and connectivity issues. Sixty of the ninety offices had only 16 to 32K bandwidth; other offices were basically dial-up sites who phoned via modems in on-demand to get their e-mail and use the internet. So because of the limited bandwidth, which varied depending upon the office location, Austrade replicated their training environment on the Intranet to every site and hosted all the courses on that site's local server. This made maintenance and upgrades, which are done weekly, very slow. Updates are on CD-ROMs which are mailed weekly to the office LAN administrator, who then updates the information on the local server.

Marketing Approach

✓ Each regional executive general manager ran the launch.

✓ Preliminary information was initially sent out as a personalized flyer.

✓ E-certificates at competency and advanced competency level in IT skills were offered so people had something to strive for.

✓ Monthly reports to local office managers were provided in the first year stating who had done which modules for that month.

✓ Prizes were awarded for the first person in some offices who completed their certificate.

✓ Articles and photographs were placed in staff newsletters.

✓ Special ceremonies were held to present certificates to learners.

Job positions were assessed to develop a set of modules employees should be capable of at various levels, such as intermediate or power user. This way, everyone knew what skills they should have, and what training they would need. Learners had the option of taking a competency test for each level. If they passed the test, they were deemed competent at that level and could move to the next level. If they failed the test, they had do go back and complete the relevant parts of that course and then were allowed to take the test again.

Summary reports go to senior management so they can see who has used e-learning, what courses were taken, how many tests were attempted and passed, and how many learners earned competency certificates. Reports can be generated at all levels so the managing director can clearly see if progress is being made.

What Was the Business Impact of the Program?

In annual client satisfaction surveys, Austrade's approval rating improved from 75 percent to over 90 percent. Clients are receiving a more professional-looking product in a much quicker turn-around time.

Reporting mechanisms have provided senior management with a clear picture showing a greater degree of work output from the staff and improved efficiency in responding to clients. With supporting systems, 91 percent of the organization is using e-learning, which is being realized in increased productivity and competency in the workplace.

There has been a significant return on investment. In 1995, there was an IT training staff of five and a travel budget over a million dollars, plus each office had their own training budgets. In 2000, total IT training costs were approximately $225,000.

The current training infrastructure will support the move of all offices to a 128K minimum bandwidth at the end of 2002, with most offices going to 256K in 2003, allowing for true Internet-based e-learning and central administration of courseware.

Summary

Purpose:

✓ To provide consistent training to all offices in all countries

✓ To ensure all employees have the same access to training

Program Structure:

✓ Utilize the company intranet and the SkillSoft library of courseware to provide IT Certification programs and interpersonal skills training

Number of Learning Hours per Learner: Varies

Total Number of Hours of Learning in the Program: Varies

Number of Learners: 900

Completion Requirements:

✓ Completion of all modules and passing of tests to achieve competency

Media and Tools:

✓ SkillSoft library of courseware

✓ Customized courses

Deployment Mechanism:

✓ Company intranet

Lessons Learned

✓ Reach out to local offices for more initial buy-in prior to the launch stage. An office champion can help to encourage learning from the beginning.

✓ Start up in some offices was slower than others. Add a "getting started" package and session to the launch, and have someone in the local office kick it off.

✓ Need to upgrade infrastructure to support true remote access to e-learning for all offices.

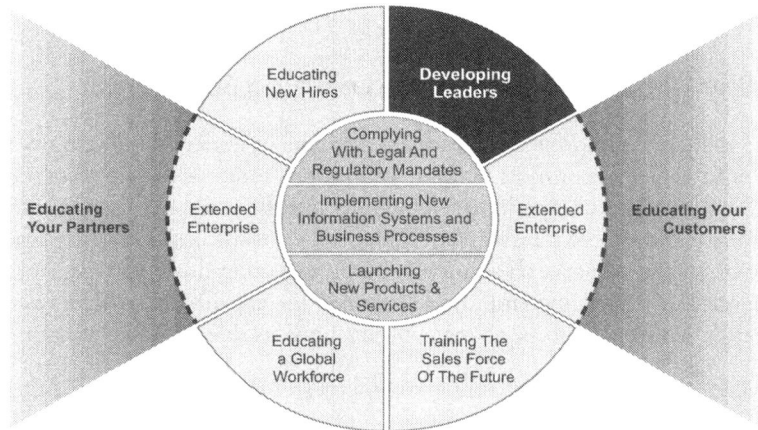

Developing Leaders

The cases for this chapter are:

- *Unilever*
- *INSEAD OnLine*
- *Babson College*

Introduction

Why Did They Choose an e-Learning Solution?

In the past, economic downturns meant cuts in leadership development. However, the opposite is found to be true in most major organizations today. They are recognizing that the turbulence of global markets, competition, geopolitics and the economy requires focused, skilled leadership to survive and succeed. Leadership development is increasingly being regarded as the platform needed to grow and improve the business. No longer an exclusive privilege of senior executives, leadership development is being employed to embed the capabilities to achieve strategic goals, organize innovative business projects, change culture, and cascade competencies throughout the organization.

Major companies are pursuing key themes in the development of their leaders. To maximize the link between leadership capabilities and strategy execution, leader-led development is being used to engage senior executives in the training and coaching of the next generation of leadership. In addition, the use of team business projects during leadership programs focuses participants on strategy execution while solving real-time problems and challenges. Also, a learning continuum for leadership development is also being pursued by most organizations, as they have found that the need to embed behavioral change, and new strengths and perspectives requires more than a one-week event. Finally, the importance of selected external partners is seen as a critical cornerstone.

To accomplish this intensive, on-going leadership development over a period of time with busy, geographically dispersed executives and managers, is a daunting task. However, those organizations who have used e-learning in a blended model for leadership development have found that this approach supports:

- Maximum leverage of the time executives have available to engage in learning
- Virtual teamwork on business and individual projects
- Online coaching and mentoring by senior executives
- Experience in online collaboration promoting post-program virtual work

The three organizations in this chapter have all been deeply involved in the creation of e-learning solutions for leadership development. They include: Unilever, a global producer and supplier of consumer goods and food; INSEAD OnLine, a top business school in Europe and Asia, which provided custom leadership programs for a major pharmaceutical company; and Babson School of Executive Education, a leading U.S. business school, which built an online MBA program for Intel Corporation.

A Blended Model Extends the Leadership Development Continuum

An intensive work environment, daily business challenges, global communications and input—the business environment of global leaders allows little flexibility or time to invest in learning and development. Indeed, how can learning be extended for leaders beyond a week-long event, or meeting? How can leaders be skilled to lead an organizational culture transformation? What can leaders do to drive a new strategic focus? These were the challenges that were met by Unilever in their Leaders into Action program. Unilever determined that a new strategic direction and related culture change was required for global growth and profitability. Working with external partners, Unilever's learning organization designed a learning continuum that engages learners in a leadership development journey to achieve this transformational change.

Using a blended model approach, this leadership journey alternates between online collaboration, virtual teamwork and coaching, and face-to-face classroom sessions. Senior executives are involved as coaches, both online and in the face-to-face events, as well as in the funding approval of the final business project proposals prepared by the participants. Results have been extraordinary. Business projects created by the virtual teams during the program have identified millions of dollars in opportunities and have led to successful new ventures. In addition, virtual, cross-boundary teamwork is becoming a way of doing business, a critical capability for this global company.

INSEAD OnLine also found the power of the blended model in ensuring that meeting time involving top scientists of a global pharmaceutical firm became more valuable, preparing them to address new approaches to innovation in their clinical drug evaluation processes. Prior to the meeting, these scientists engaged in a Web-enabled forum and in targeted e-learning on technological innovation. This supported better use of the costly and highly valuable face-to-face meeting time, as the scientists were able to use the pre-meeting insights and collaboration to engage in creating new initiatives.

Leadership Development Contributes to the Recruitment and Retention of Leaders

Intel Corporation was concerned that the best engineers they had recruited, frequently left after taking a leave-of-absence to attend company supported, off-site MBA programs. However, they also realized that these busy, young leaders needed to balance work lives with personal life, and that MBA programs delivered over years in evening classes were not attractive to the 'best and the brightest'. Turning to Babson's School of Executive Education for support, they engaged the school and Babson Interactive in the creation of a highly successful blended model MBA program that met the needs of these next-generation leaders. Face-to-face, monthly sessions at three Intel locations, were linked and supported by virtual classes, online teamwork, coaching, and projects, which engaged the participants in continuous learning over a period of 27 months. A key benefit to Intel was the virtual teamwork on targeted business projects selected by the company, and the presentation of these projects to senior executives during the program. Intel found that the ratings of the blended MBA were as high, or higher than the ratings of the students engaged in the traditional Babson MBA program.

In every case, the use of the blended model engaged very busy executives, both as participants and coaches, in an intensive, value-adding leadership development journey.

Case 1: Unilever

Company Facts and Figures

✔ **Industry:** Packaged Consumer Goods

✔ **Scope of Services and Products:** A global producer and supplier of fast-moving consumer goods in the Food and Home & Personal Care categories; Major brands include: Lipton, Breyers, Magnum, Q-Tips, Dove, Hellmann's, Skippy and Mentadent

✔ **Estimated Number of Employees:** 265,000

✔ **Year e-Learning Introduced:** 1997

✔ **Offices and Locations:** Dual headquarters in Rotterdam, Netherlands (Unilever NV) and London, UK (Unilever PLC)

✔ **2001 Revenues:** Worldwide turnover in 2001 was €52 206 million

✔ **Web Site:** www.unilever.com

✔ **Number of e-Learning Programs in Entire Curriculum:** Specific number of e-learning courses not available, but e-learning utilized throughout global enterprise on variety of topics and issues

Introduction

Unilever is a global company headquartered in two European countries. Employing 265,000 people, Unilever has two parent companies—Unilever NV and Unilever PLC—which, despite being separate businesses, operate as a single unit with the same board of directors. Following the announcement of a new strategic direction in 2000, Unilever was restructured into two global divisions, Foods and Home & Personal Care.

Over the past 20 years, Unilever operated in distinct and separate units, departmentalizing their work, thinking, and processes. This worked well in the past, but it became apparent that many smaller brands were competing successfully against Unilever in important markets, chipping away growth and share value.

The new strategy launched in 2000, called the Path to Growth, embraced a new organizational structure focused on building an enterprise culture.

Why e-Learning?

Unilever has been using e-learning approaches since 1997. They have:

✔ Accumulated experiences and best practices

✔ Supported initiatives and built capability through investments at the global level

✔ Fostered organization-wide change initiatives such as the launch of a new leadership competency model, delivered through an online training program so that global content could be:

- Blended with local workshops or best practices

- Localized with languages and examples

- Supported by online content from Harvard Business School

The cross-boundary structure allowed for improved focus on foods and home and personal care activities at both the regional and global levels. This structure also supported faster decision-making and strengthened Unilever's capacity for innovation by more effectively integrating research

into the divisional structure. The regions (with the operating companies) are the driving force behind Unilever. They are the key interface with customers and consumers, providing quick response to the needs of local markets.

With this strategy, organization, and culture, Unilever could leverage its global operations specifically to support its major brands. This demanded an entrepreneurial and innovative style of leadership and new perspectives from Unilever's top team.

The challenge was posed to the Learning Center of Excellence for Unilever Global to build an innovative and sustainable way to both empower Unilever leaders and to support the behaviors demanded by the new business strategy. In addition, the new leadership behaviors had to be embedded through experiences and applied by the leaders to real work and projects to ensure measurable impact on the business goals.

The result is the *Leaders into Action* program, a five-month leadership development journey. Delivered in a blended model that balances online work with face-to-face classroom sessions and coaching, each of five modules is driven by a headline activity to keep the participants focused and engaged. The program combines the following three critical aspects of the leader role:

✓ Personal leadership development

✓ Individual projects, in both personal growth and business improvement

✓ Business projects working in teams

How Was the Program Aligned with the Business?

Unilever had recently launched a new leadership competency model aligned with the five-year Path to Growth business strategy. The most important focus for senior leaders at Unilever was the goal of leading a deep and broad organizational change, transforming Unilever to embrace an innovation-driven enterprise culture.

The Learning Center of Excellence for Unilever Global realized that developing this new global leadership style and business capability required creating a learning program that would engage the learners to:

✓ Gain a deep self-awareness on personal leadership competencies and areas for growth and development

✓ Investigate insights, knowledge, and opportunities and then reflect on these leadership capabilities outside the normal limitations of business life

✓ Get individual coaching for support to change and grow

✓ Connect with internal Unilever senior management coaches, so that there would be direct relevance to Unilever goals and challenges

✓ Experience working in virtual, global teams

✓ Do real work on innovative and growth- and opportunity-oriented business projects

✓ Present new business proposals to sponsors who "can sign the check" and fund the proposed initiatives to grow the business

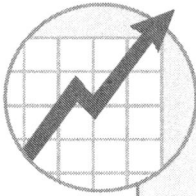

Key Business Drivers

Unilever was determined to innovate and grow, and leverage across brand, geographic, and company boundaries. Their new strategy was named Path to Growth and embraced six key strategic elements:

✔ Build an enterprise culture

✔ Reconnect with consumers

✔ Pioneer new distribution channels

✔ Focus on brands

✔ Develop a world-class supply chain

✔ Simplify

How Was the Program Designed?

Four Acres, Unilever's Senior Management Training Center, realized that the traditional approach to leadership development—where participants would engage briefly in a leadership development event rather than a developmental journey—would not adequately meet the leadership requirements posed by the new strategy.

To impact and basically change a leader's perspective and embedded way of doing things required a learning experience that extended over time and one which required skilled application of the learning to their work. It was determined that a continuum of leadership development was needed, a journey that combined individual growth and team-based business projects.

AsiaWorks was selected as an external partner to assist in the design of the overall blended model and to facilitate the coaching that would be integral to the five-month learning continuum. AsiaWorks has worked with over 100 organizations in areas such as teambuilding, leadership, change management, vision and strategy development, core value definition, creativity, customer service, interpersonal skills, and personal motivation.

It was recognized in the beginning of the design phase that there would be great value in starting the experiential learning and community dialogue before the participants came to the residential program. Also, the need to support virtual work in the intersessions between the face-to-face events required a medium that could support learning over a five-month timeframe. Initially, this online module was supported by an internal Web site, which posed technical and staffing challenges for the organization. For example, the scope of program offerings expanded immediately after the successful pilot delivery from a proposed three programs per year to ten.

Thus, the Learning Center sought a partner who could manage and support a learning community. Communispace was selected to provide a Web-enabled learning community tool which fosters the learning journey that begins with a virtual, experiential module, continues in the support of virtual teamwork during the program, and encourages the graduates to engage in learning beyond the program itself.

How Was the Program Deployed?

Thirty participants are selected to attend each program. The selection process is intense and competitive. The first communication is a welcome registration e-mail that directs the participant to the online learning community with their first assignment.

A tutor team consisting of a program manager and internal coaches are involved from the beginning to the end of all program modules. Senior Unilever managers, who act as internal coaches, are graduates of the Leaders into Action program and are required to attend an intensive coach training.

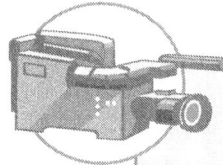

Media and Tools

✓ E-mail

✓ Teleconferencing

✓ Web-enabled forums

✓ Web-based learning community

✓ Online assessments

Leaders into Action Program

Module 1 (see Figure 15-1) supports immediate immersion into learning. The purpose of the module is to have the participants look outside-the-box, to give the freedom to explore, and to build the community of leadership learning.

There is no concept of pre-work in the look and feel of this module—the work begins with registration e-mail and it contains the first assignment. Every week there are new assignments, termed "blind corner" assignments, as they are never easily anticipated by the participants what direction might be taken. The assignments direct them outside their normal work and life to do research, analysis, and reflection on various issues. Some examples of assignments for Module 1 include:

- ✓ Interview a graduate of the program about their experiences and post your findings.

- ✓ Watch the *Dead Poets Society* and post what you observe about leadership and which leadership model you prefer and why.

- ✓ Define the individual business project you want to work on during the Leaders into Action program.

- ✓ Interview a futurologist, your children, or a politician about the future, and post findings.

Participants post their findings and comment on each other's postings in the community to create natural conversations that are very powerful. Coaches observe and collect data and impressions to use during Module 2.

Module 2 is a residential program that focuses on rigorous leadership development, combining self-awareness, self-assessment, coaching, and classroom sessions. In addition, each participant defines two individual projects, one focused on personal development, and one focused on business improvement. Also, each participant is assigned to work with a team on a business proposal.

Module 3 supports continued learning and application to real work, keeping the participants engaged and in action on personal and team project deliverables. Virtual supports, such as teleconferencing, online meetings, and e-mail, in addition to other virtual team supports are utilized.

Module 1: **Opening the Mind**	Online; 1.5-month duration; coaching and facilitation; experiential learning; blind corner assignments
Module 2: **Leadership Development**	Residential; 10-day duration; leadership development, self-awareness, and individual and team coaching with AsiaWorks; initial work on individual and team business projects
Module 3: **Project Planning and Implementation**	Online; 2.5-month duration; teamwork on business projects and individual projects; supported by online community and coaching, teleconference, and online meetings
Module 4: **Project Presentation and Learning Consolidation**	Residential; 8-day duration; teamwork project presentations to panels and sponsors; learning consolidation
Module 5: **Graduate Learning Community**	Online; continuing communication and learning

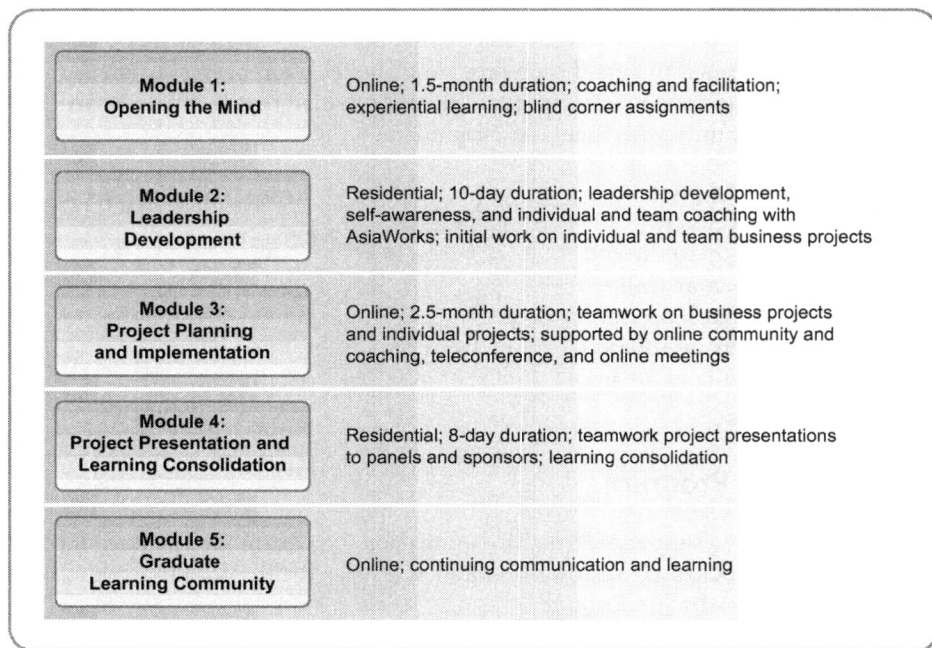

Figure 15-1: Overview of Leaders into Action Program Modules

Harvard Business School materials on virtual work techniques are available online, and the coaches are actively involved, assigned to a team and to individuals for virtual coaching throughout this module.

The highlight of **Module 4** is Panel Day, when top level board members, who have the authority to fund the business projects and proposals of the teams, hear team presentations for innovative approaches to enter new markets and launch new business processes.

Module 5 supports the virtual learning continuum, keeping the graduates engaged. The circle of leadership context and development is fostered with new materials and insights.

What Was the Business Impact of the Program?

The success of the Leaders into Action program in supporting the execution of the new business strategy is evident in the demand to increase the number of offerings for the program. It has changed from the annual plan to deliver the program three times for 30 participants each time to an annual plan of delivering a total of 12 program offerings in FY '03, ultimately engaging 360 senior managers from around the globe.

In addition, 100 percent of those enrolled to date have completed the entire five-month learning journey of Leaders into Action. Finally, a new participant group has requested to engage teams from discrete business units, such as a global brand leadership team and a Board of Directors. They recognize the value of dedicated time to grow as leaders while working on a selected high priority project that will improve and grow the business.

The impact of the Leaders into Action program in founding a leadership enterprise culture has been extremely positive. Some examples are:

✓ Innovative and entrepreneurial projects developed by teams during Leaders into Action have abounded. One project proposed entry into a new country with a major Unilever brand. This was identified as a six million Euro opportunity, and the teamwork on this project was noted as speeding up the entry into the market by six months.

✓ Managers are now familiar with using technology to support learning, and it has become now a standard in the launch of organization-wide change initiatives.

✓ Virtual, cross-boundary teamwork is becoming a way of doing business

✓ Individual participants have expressed positive personal leadership changes that are being noted in annual performance appraisals.

✓ As a result of participants' attendance in the program, scored development improvements under their Leadership Growth Profile have been noted in the key leadership competencies prescribed for effective leadership at Unilever.

✓ Unilever's Path to Growth business strategies are clearly visible in the results created from the program.

Learner Perspectives

✓ On individual growth: "I now believe that anything is possible-the Leaders into Action program has shown me over and over again how far people can go."

✓ On peer learning: "Honest feedback from a friend or colleague has more impact than feedback from a third party."

✓ On blended learning: "The combination of virtual and residential working reflects the way we are increasingly working together at Unilever."

✓ On leadership focus: "It's different from any other course I have experienced. It is not focused on knowledge transfer, but on who you are as a leader."

✓ On application to work: "In the implementation of a single European portfolio for 17 countries, I use what I learned in the Leaders into Action program every day, and I couldn't have done such an effective job without it."

✓ On cultural transformation: "We are seeing evidence of this happening already. Operating companies are beginning to invest more in coaching."

✓ On business impact: "I could never have imagined we would have achieved so much in the project to develop branded street food for markets in Central America."

Summary

Purpose: To support the development of a leadership enterprise culture while enabling leaders to execute the Path to Growth strategy.

Program Structure: The blended model engaged participants, who represented the most senior managers at Unilever, in a learning journey over five months, alternating online learning with face-to-face modules, in a highly integrated approach and requiring application of learnings to real personal and business challenges.

Number of Learning Hours per Learner:

- ✔ 5 months overall
- ✔ 18 days face-to-face learning
- ✔ Interim virtual learning

Total Number of Hours of Learning in the Program:

- ✔ 396 tutor hours for Leaders into Action for individuals
- ✔ 348 tutor hours for Leaders into Action for teams
- ✔ Both programs have an approximate 13-week period of applied learning in the work place

Number of Learners in Each Offering: 30

Completion Requirements:

- ✔ Finish all modules
- ✔ Define and implement three projects with relevant deliverables presented to coaches and stakeholder panel

Media and Tools:

- ✔ E-mail
- ✔ Teleconferencing
- ✔ Web-enabled forums
- ✔ Web-based learning community
- ✔ Online assessments

Deployment Mechanism:

- ✔ Web-enabled learning community
- ✔ Face-to-face classroom sessions
- ✔ Coaching, both virtual and face-to-face
- ✔ Team and individual projects

Lessons Learned

✓ Begin the program with an online community where one can develop the thinking and dialogue prior to the face-to-face program.

✓ Fully immerse the participants in the program with the first message and give it the look and feel of immediacy, with no option but to engage.

✓ 'Off-the-shelf' learning content in a blended model should be offered for use at the discretion of the end user, but not as a required component of the program.

✓ Reliability and ease of use of the technology is extremely important to top level participants.

✓ Internally managed Web sites to support learning communities can pose more administration problems than an internal learning staff can generally support, so it is best to outsource this aspect of a blended model.

✓ Relevance of the learning is only valuable if linked to application of real work.

✓ Involving internal graduates of the program as coaches is very valuable; however, intensive learning on coaching skills is mandatory for success.

✓ In e-learning, little bits of small are better than three bits of big. Big files that take a long time to download and complete discourage people from engaging. If it is small enough, people will fit it into their day.

✓ By using online capabilities, relationships can be built without meeting face-to-face.

✓ There is still work to be done in developing capabilities, techniques, and tools that support a virtual, global, networked company.

Case 2: INSEAD OnLine

Company Facts and Figures

✓ **Industry:** Academic institution dedicated to business education

✓ **Scope of Services and Products:** Offers online management development courses and customized e-learning blended solutions to corporate clients

✓ **Estimated Number of Employees:** Standing and affiliate faculty: 145
Visiting faculty: 46
Staff members: 616

✓ **Year e-Learning Introduced:** 2000

✓ **Offices and Locations:** INSEAD has twin campuses in Singapore and Fontainebleau, France

✓ **Estimated 2002 Revenues:** Non-profit institution

✓ **Web Site:** www.insead.edu/

e-Learning capability is employed primarily in executive education through INSEAD OnLine at: www.inseadonline.com

✓ **Number of e-Learning Courses in Entire Curriculum:** 13

Introduction

INSEAD OnLine was established as a separate legal entity in September 2000 to explore the opportunities offered by e-learning, to innovate in leveraging INSEAD knowledge and research for corporate clients, and to advise a strategy and approach to e-learning at INSEAD, a leading global business school.

INSEAD OnLine began with three overarching mission objectives:

✓ Innovate traditional learning methods with blended learning

✓ Provide access to INSEAD and its professors via off-campus learning programs

✓ Motivate managers and strengthen global networks

Focusing on existing corporate clients, the objective of INSEAD Online is to build expertise in providing executive education solutions that go beyond the boundaries of a formulaic one-week experience on campus.

Why e-Learning?

In serving its corporate clients, INSEAD is dedicated to establishing and supporting global learning networks in all of its initiatives.

✓ Global companies must quickly develop management capabilities on new concepts and changing issues, rapidly cascading these messages to all the other managers in a global context without the delays and obstacles inherent in limits to time and geography.

✓ Existing corporate clients want off-campus access to the teaching and learning available through INSEAD's faculty and research.

✓ The traditional approach of week-long, face-to-face learning programs for managers and executives was inadequate to meet the demand for rapid and deep organizational learning.

✓ The venture into e-learning was seen as a key to extending the boundaries of learning and as a critical method to build a global network of learners and knowledge.

To bring content into an e-learning format, INSEAD OnLine engaged in collaboration with four e-learning partners and worked closely with faculty to digitize content in engaging, interactive online modules. During the first two years, content was developed in three approaches:

✓ Stand-alone e-learning courses

✓ Business simulations

✓ Web-enabled collaboration platforms to support blended learning

INSEAD OnLine also engaged two technology partners in the implementation of their e-learning strategy.

Currently INSEAD OnLine has the following 13 e-learning courses:

Management and Organization

✓ Managing People/Managing Yourself

✓ Managing People/Managing Others

✓ Managing Technological Innovation

✓ Supply Chain Coordination

✓ Leadership

Finance and Accounting

✓ Assets and Liability Management

✓ Financial Accounting for Managers

✓ Introduction to Financial Statements

Strategy

✓ Industry Scan

✓ Fundamentals of Web Strategies

✓ Globalization

✓ Managing for Shareholder Value

Marketing

✓ Customer Relations Management

After this first two years of successful innovation and experience gathering, INSEAD OnLine was integrated into INSEAD Executive Education so that a fully realized leveraged, model applying all learning and faculty resources could became the standard offering and approach to learning.

The INSEAD Corporate Blended Program

The INSEAD Corporate Blended Program is the focus of this case. The head of clinical drug evaluation in a large, multinational pharmaceutical firm became interested in fostering thought

Check It Out Online!
www.elearningfieldbook.com

Insead OnLine

INSEAD OnLine - Home - Microsoft Internet Explorer

File   Edit   View   Favorites   Tools   Help

Back   →   Search   Favorites   History

Address   http://www.inseadonline.com   Go

INSEAD OnLine

Approach   Partners   Solutions   About Us   FAQ

Online Courses
▸ Complete Course List

Blended Learning
▸ Coached Programmes

Business Simulations
▸ World Business Challenge

Executive Toolkit
▸ InterAct Platform
▸ Login to InterAct

Product Summary
▸

For an overview of our online learning solutions, click on the icon

Executive Development

e-Learning

Internet

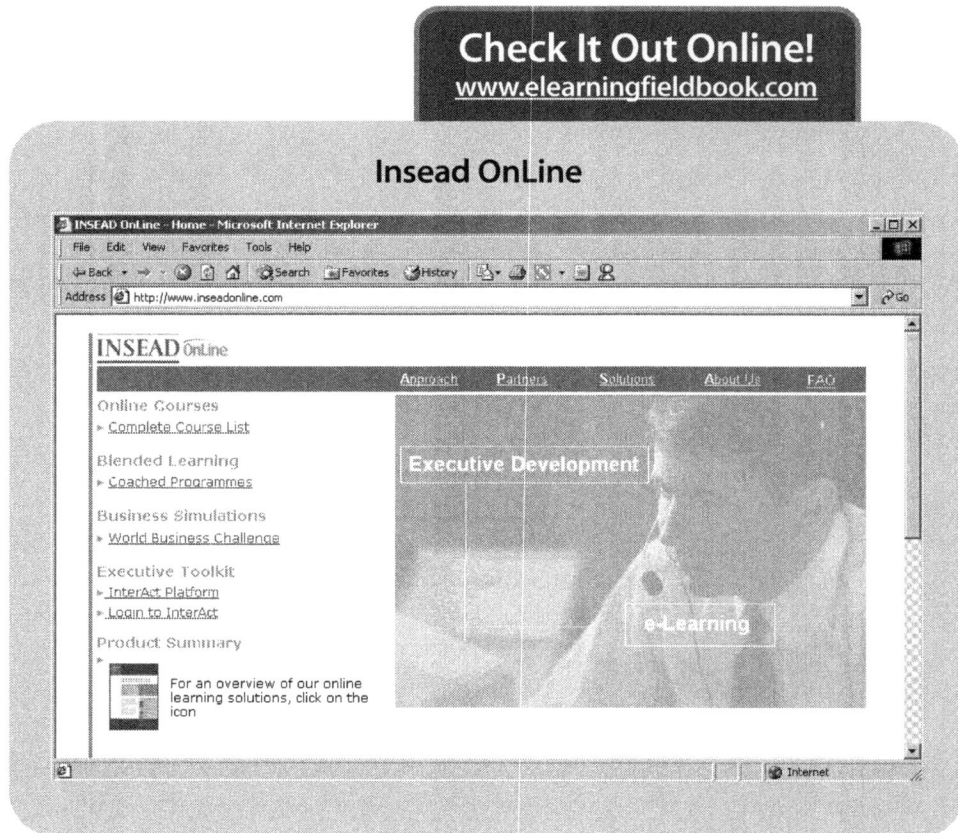

about innovation in clinical drug research. The purpose was to develop some insights and dialogue among the scientists on the innovation process and how it could be improved.

This learning program would precede a regularly scheduled monthly team meeting run by videoconference to four locations throughout the world. The virtual learning program was planned as a pre-requisite to stimulate new insights about innovative processes, and to support and enhance the dialogue during the meeting. Because the 27 scientists were located in geographically dispersed areas, INSEAD OnLine proposed a blended model approach to the learning, utilizing the Managing Technological Innovation e-learning course combined with collaboration on a Web-enabled platform.

How Was the Program Aligned with the Business?

For both of the partners in this initiative the business drivers needed to be met for real success.

INSEAD OnLine is interested in consistently exploring innovations that support the INSEAD global learning networks and in meeting corporate partner requirements in ways that offer the best learning solutions.

For the pharmaceutical firm a virtual approach that leveraged the experience, insights, and network of their scientists to create new methods and processes across geographies would benefit the business in several ways:

✓ Enhancing performance overall through a community of learning and experience

✓ Engaging scientists in the topic of the meeting prior to the actual face-to-face time, making the meeting more productive

✓ Improving the processes for clinical drug evaluation resulting in bottom-line results

Key Business Drivers

INSEAD OnLine Business Drivers

Working with the pharmaceutical company on the blended model provided the opportunity to meet the primary business drivers to:

✓ Create innovations in e-learning for corporate clients

✓ Build experience in implementing e-learning solutions with INSEAD faculty and staff

✓ Maximize and leverage corporate participants learning time

Pharmaceutical Company Business Drivers

Prior to the monthly meeting, a pre-meeting learning program was launched to:

✓ Prompt out-of-the-box thinking

✓ Engage the scientists in an exchange of ideas, challenges, and insights

✓ Utilize and leverage INSEAD faculty thought leadership to provoke thinking about change and support the learning and outcomes

✓ Prepare for a deeper discussion during the upcoming meeting

How Was the Program Designed?

A unique aspect of the request was that the learning initiative was not conceived as a stand-alone event, but as a critical prelude to a regularly scheduled meeting. In this case, the regularly scheduled meeting fulfilled the face-to-face component of the blended model in learning and the pre-meeting e-learning aspect extended and enriched the face-to-face meeting.

INSEAD OnLine utilized the e-learning courseware and Web platform capability that had been built over the preceding two years. Combining these e-learning approaches and leveraging their experiences in applying a blended model, INSEAD worked closely with the company's vice president of clinical drug evaluation and INSEAD faculty members to design a pre-meeting learning experience that would meet the business objectives.

The program is an example of a blended program and four different components:

✓ Briefing: With professor and/or professional coach

✓ Individual e-learning: Personal study of stand-alone material

✓ Online exchange: Virtual group working and discussion

✓ Workshop or meeting: Face-to-face session with professor

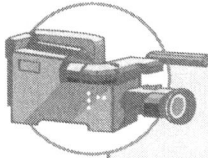

Media and Tools

Media and tools include:

✓ Video conferencing

✓ Streaming Video

✓ Simulations

✓ Live e-learning

✓ Web-enabled collaboration

Vendors include:

✓ CognitiveArts

✓ FT Knowledge

✓ ICUS Software Systems

✓ Academee

✓ Docent

✓ Centra

How Was the Program Deployed?

Working with the vice president of clinical drug evaluation, whose top level sponsorship was critical to the success of the pre-meeting learning program, and the designated company management liaison, INSEAD OnLine created a four-step approach to stimulate innovative thinking through e-learning prior to the meeting.

1. Welcome e-Mail Message from the Vice President

To indicate top level support for the initiative, participants received first an e-mail from the Vice President of Clinical Drug Evaluation stating the purpose for provoking new consideration of issues related to innovation and the learning objective for the program.

In addition, this e-mail directed the participants to those aspects of the e-learning course that would be most relevant to their work, the URL for the Web site, and their password.

2. Collaboration on the Web-Enabled Course Platform

The course Web site included photos and voice messages from each of the four leaders of the course:

✓ Arnoud De Meyer, the INSEAD faculty member, who is the thought leader behind the e-learning course entitled Managing Technological Innovation

✓ The vice president of clinical drug evaluation

✓ Adam Cohen, an external online learning coach

✓ Jens Meyer, INSEAD adjunct faculty

The left navigation bar gave the participants access to the e-learning course, resources and readings, participant profiles, the communication tools, and discussion forum.

3. The e-Learning Course

This e-learning course, Managing Technological Innovation, is one of the 13 existing e-learning courses available from INSEAD OnLine. Most participants finished this course in separate, individual sessions over a period of 5 to 6 hours.

In the use of this content for the pharmaceutical firm, the fact that some of the modules were not relevant to the drug research industry needed to be made explicit to the participants. This was addressed in the welcome e-mail from the vice president, indicating that there were a few modules that were interesting but not specifically relevant, and identifying and recommending that the participants focus on the modules that would be most meaningful and valuable to them.

4. The Pre-Meeting Assignment

Upon conclusion of the e-learning course, participants were asked to consider their own issues and challenges in their experiences with innovation.

The questions posed were:

✓ What are your key innovation challenges?

✓ How could we be doing things differently?

Responses were posted to the discussion forum, and commented upon by other participants. Finally, these postings and related comments were summarized by the faculty into a document that identified five key issues with specific content that supported the deeper dialogue during the planned, monthly video conference meeting.

What Was the Business Impact of the Program?

For INSEAD OnLine:

✓ This innovative approach blending e-learning into a normally scheduled meeting of senior scientists created new opportunities to leverage pre-meeting time through virtual learning and collaboration. Whereas in the past meetings, the pre-meeting is not generally considered learning territory, this opened new avenues to foster learning that meets corporate needs for faster, global, compact, and relevant learning that immediately can be applied to workplace realities.

✓ This model of blending meetings and learning proved valid and is proposed to other INSEAD corporate clients and HR professionals.

For the pharmaceutical firm:

✓ One participant commented, "Today's training videoconference was valuable. It gave insight into operational processes, new perspectives on strategies and objectives, and useful information regarding innovation in relation to economics."

✓ The success of this blended model has led the company to consider rolling out this type of e-learning to 27 other business units.

Summary

Purpose: To foster innovation and change while accessing insights and experiences through collaboration among the global clinical drug evaluation scientists:

✓ Improve the innovation processes

✓ Engage all in thinking out-of-the-box

✓ Share experiences and insights prior to a regularly scheduled monthly meeting

Program Structure: The blended model, including top level email communication, an e-learning module, Web site and pre-meeting assignments, enabled a geographically dispersed business unit to engage virtually and exchange challenges and experiences.

Number of Learning Hours per Learner: 6 to 8 hours

Total Number of Hours of Learning in the Program: 6 to 8 hours

Number of Learners: 30

Completion Requirements:

✓ Complete e-learning course

✓ Post answers on assignment to the course Web site

✓ Attend video conference meeting

Media and Tools:

✓ Video conferencing

✓ Streaming video

✓ Simulation

✓ Live e-learning using Centra

✓ Web-enabled collaboration

Deployment Mechanism:

✓ Welcome e-mail from vice president

✓ e-Learning course

✓ Collaboration on course Web site

✓ Assignment posting and commentary on course Web site

✓ Video conference meeting

Lessons Learned

✓ Without top management support and sponsorship, any e-learning initiative will not succeed. Managers are busy people, when they know that their leadership is backing a program they will engage.

✓ e-Learning typically poses technology challenges to first time users. These need to be dealt with effectively and efficiently to ensure that the technology doesn't become the issue, but that the content is the focus.

✓ Take-away readings supporting the online learning are very important. Participants want references and readings.

✓ Course Web site collaboration is valuable both prior to the face-to-face event and afterward as a communication tool. For Forum postings, participants use profiles, teamwork, assignments, readings, resources, and e-mail links.

✓ Alumni of corporate programs can be engaged in virtual teamwork simulation projects competing against other teams.

✓ Engaging individuals in e-learning to cover theory and fundamentals prior to face-to-face events can maximize the more expensive classroom time.

✓ Pre-classroom assignments and collaborative exchanges prior to face-to-face events assist the participants and faculty in focusing on the key issues and challenges of the group.

✓ Building content into quality, interactive, online e-learning takes a lot of time and is expensive, thus custom e-learning solutions require innovative blended models leveraging existing e-learning content.

✓ Expense in time and money advocates for investing in e-learning solutions that will be used more than once.

✓ A compelling learning reason, or very specific project, is needed to bring people together virtually, and this needs to be explicitly considered and promoted as integral to an e-learning solution.

Case 3: Babson College

Company Facts and Figures

✓ **Industry:** Academic Institution dedicated to business education

✓ **Scope of Services and Products:** Offers Bachelors and Masters degrees, and executive education

✓ **Estimated Number of Employees:** 208 Faculty

✓ **Year e-Learning Introduced:** 2000

✓ **Offices and Locations:** Wellesley, Massachusetts, U.S.

✓ **Estimated 2002 Revenues:** Non-profit organization

✓ **Web Site:** www.babson.edu/

✓ **Number of e-Learning Programs in Entire curriculum:** Babson College offers a public blended Fast Track MBA, in addition to custom e-learning capabilities to corporate clients.

Introduction

Babson College entered the world of e-learning in January 2000 through the formation of Babson Interactive, LLC, a distance-learning, for-profit company with Babson College as the sole shareholder. The notion was to establish a small company that could be more responsive to the marketplace and which could leverage Babson's wealth of knowledge and courses to deliver e-learning. This capability would be applied in both the Graduate School and in the School of Executive Education. Babson Interactive provides interactive learning experiences through its expertise in curriculum creation, project and program management, and technology implementation.

Immediately upon the founding of Babson Interactive three major projects were launched.

✓ The Babson Intel MBA program

✓ A suite of business simulation products

✓ A multi-media CD-ROM on Corporate Entrepreneurship

Why e-Learning?

Babson's School of Executive Education (SEE) believes that the classroom experience is the focus of learning; however, it builds on proven strengths to deliver custom e-learning executive education programs, which provide corporate clients with:

✓ Distance learning solutions needed to concurrently teach executives, middle managers and front-line managers around the world via online courses

✓ Capability to build learning beyond the boundaries of the classroom

✓ Reach to extend training from select executives to broad numbers of key managers

✓ Cost-effective ways to disseminate information, provide specific skill-building training, and the ability to build global communities

The Babson Intel MBA Program

The Babson Intel MBA program is the focus of this case. This innovative MBA program, which is very closely aligned with the Babson full-time, two-year MBA program, uses the same content and the same number of sessions comprising the standard MBA. It combines face-to-face, live and self-paced e-learning, and simulations in a blended learning model.

In addition, great effort was made both by Intel Corporation executives and Babson faculty to ensure that the Intel MBA program is:

✓ Integrated with Intel strategic business drivers

✓ Applied to real work projects and initiatives

✓ Supported by the presence of Intel executives during the intersessions and in guiding the work team projects

The learnings gained by Babson during the design, development, and delivery of the highly successful Babson Intel MBA program have been leveraged to create a new blended model MBA now offered to the public. It is called Babson Fast Track MBA.

How Was the Program Aligned with the Business?

As in all partnerships, the business drivers of both organizations must be considered and embraced to ensure success. In the design, development and delivery of this ground-breaking MBA program, both Babson College and Intel Corporation were focused on important, discrete strategic goals that were supported by the collaboration.

Babson School of Executive Education, a leader in entrepreneurship, recognized immediately the opportunity to build capacity in a new venue for teaching and learning. e-Learning offered ground-breaking innovations and capabilities for traditional institutions of learning to meet the requirements of their corporate clients through geographically unlimited, multi-media approaches to learning design and delivery. In addition, the learning curve offered to faculty and staff by engaging in an aggressive e-learning initiative enabled Babson to quickly develop an embedded interest and experience in delivering learning in this new methodology.

By offering a viable alternative to Intel's policy of sending people to full-time and part-time MBA programs, Intel sought to keep their best people, reduce attrition, and become more attractive when recruiting the best engineers. Intel wanted to be recognized as one of the best corporations for top engineers to work and to learn. Their strong belief was that the ability to offer an internal MBA from a recognized academic institution would offer a competitive edge in recruitment and retention.

Company policy offered their best employees a leave of absence to participate in two-year traditional MBA programs. Intel found that frequently once those who chose this option completed their degrees, they left Intel entirely. By helping the top employees to balance their workload while completing an MBA from a brand institution, Intel hoped to retain these high performers.

In addition, by forming a cohort of advanced, highly-motivated students within Intel, they offered a program that built cohesion, integrated learning with Intel issues and projects, and achieved synergy that benefited the company and the participants.

Check It Out Online!
www.elearningfieldbook.com

Fast Track MBA

Babson College - Babson College - Ranked #1 among all business schools for entrepreneurship

File   Edit   View   Favorites   Tools   Help

Back   Search   Favorites   History

Address   http://www2.babson.edu/babson/babsonhpp.nsf/public/homepage   Go

+ Entrepreneurship Celebration
The April 8th celebration includes graduate and undergraduate business plan competitions, student business fair, and keynote by Ben Cohen of Ben & Jerry's Homemade on social entrepreneurship.

+ Family Biz Study
Study by Babson, MassMutual, Raymond Institute and other partners shows that family businesses are experiencing robust growth despite the poor overall economy.

undergraduate | MBA | executive education | alumni | entrepreneurship | international | women's leadership   search

BABSON
COLLEGE

about babson | academics | athletics | events | jobs | newsroom

contact | site map

start here
Admission
   Undergraduate
   Graduate/MBA
   Executive Education
Alumni
Business Community
Educators and Researchers
Parents and Families
Faculty and Staff
Current Students

Fast Track MBA

Babson launches the Fast Track MBA program, the first-of-its-kind online/onsite MBA program in New England, integrating traditional onsite classroom instruction with distance and interactive learning. Enables students to obtain the MBA in just 27 months. Tailored for executives with a minimum of five to seven years of work experience.   Based on the successful Babson custom MBA for Intel Corp. employees.

Internet

O The Babson Fast Track MBA – A Powerful Opportunity

Highly motivated individuals now have a unique opportunity to develop their careers while sharpening their business acumen and broadening their educational horizons. In 27 months–just a few months longer than a full-time MBA program–students will earn a graduate degree from one of the nation's top business schools, while remaining on the job. They will continue to earn their full-time salary and benefits.

This hybrid-format MBA program provides a combination of in-person and online instruction, pairing the most up-to-date virtual learning technologies with the most innovative business curriculum. Students learn from top educators, business leaders, and perhaps most importantly, from their colleagues. By joining with fellow MBAs, participants will significantly expand their network of contacts–sure to be of great value for building a career.

Key Business Drivers

Babson College

Babson College differentiates itself in its approach to business education by:

✓ Offering integrated streams of learning rather than courses

✓ Focusing on entrepreneurship

✓ Seizing opportunities to be innovative in learning

Intel Corporation

Intel realized that an internal MBA program would support:

✓ Recruitment and retention of the best engineers in the world

✓ Work-life balance for these employees in meeting both work requirements and educational aspirations

✓ Better return on investments in higher education than Intel was realizing by sending individual employees out to participate in part-time MBA courses

How Was the Program Designed?

Intel approached Babson College to collaborate with them in developing a branded, world-class MBA program in an innovative format for their internal, high-potential employees.

The first approach was by a small group of young Intel engineers who were given a charge to find and develop an MBA program. The result of the first meeting was a decision by Babson to go to Arizona and spend a day talking to prospective candidates and the senior sponsors. Ultimately, the size of this group was too small initially to pursue the opportunity, and the proposal went on the shelf.

Then a top-level Intel human resources executive charged with the effort to create corporate-wide educational programs including an internal, customized MBA, approached Babson again and subsequently became the internal advocate of the program.

In the beginning of this venture, Babson's School of Executive Education was very new and inexperienced in e-learning, and did not have existing frameworks and models to apply. However, in the entrepreneurial and innovative spirit, they realized that the only way to become expert was to jump in to this new field. To produce high quality learning experiences, they engaged partners knowledgeable in the field of e-learning. They also determined that the design and delivery of the customized MBA must be of the same high quality and rigor of the traditional full-time MBA. It was anticipated that this look and feel alignment with the traditional degree program would satisfy both the concerns of the Babson faculty about the academic rigor of the new venture and meet or exceed Intel's requirements for a top-level MBA program.

Babson Intel MBA Design Parameters:

Similarities to Babson's Two-Year MBA

✓ **Faculty Oversight Committee**
Reviews the design and quality of the program and reports back to the faculty at large, ensuring a religious rigor to the traditional MBA program

✓ **Student Profile**
25 to 30 years old; Five to ten years work experience; good grades; GMAT scores of Intel internal students slightly higher

✓ **Assessment Tools**

- Same assessment tools as in the two-year MBA: Written case studies, exams, and formal presentations

- Exams sent to Intel by Babson; monitors hired and the exams collected and returned to Babson for grading; presentations done in video conference and recorded for grading by the Babson faculty

✓ **125 Instruction Days**

- Equivalent to the two-year MBA

- 62 intensive, face-to-face instruction days, 2.5 days per month over 25 months

- 63 instruction days in intersession, intensive individual and team learning supported by live and self-paced e-learning.

✓ **Content streams rather than courses**
Content delivered in an integrative way, with one case being taught from multiple points of view in one day.

✓ **Evaluations**

- Same evaluation as in two-year MBA

- 17-question evaluation of faculty, content, relevance, and teaching materials

Innovations to Babson's Two-Year MBA

✓ **Projects relate to real work**

- Students integrate learning into project assignments on the job

- "We do real work, not homework."

✓ **Visibility to senior management**
Senior managers sponsor the projects and view the presentations of the teams

✓ **e-Learning**

- CD-ROM is the backbone of the program, with syllabi and learning objectives week-by-week

- Interactive video cases with interviews with executives, investors, and employees

- Web forums using series of questions posted to different teams, critiques, and comments on each other's postings

- Multimedia course overview

- Web-enabled seminars and presentations

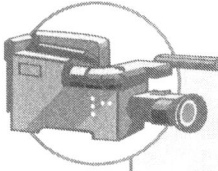

Media and Tools

- ✓ Multimedia CD-ROM
- ✓ Video conferencing
- ✓ Streaming video
- ✓ Macromedia Flash
- ✓ Simulations

- ✓ Live e-learning using CentraOne
- ✓ Web-enabled forums
- ✓ Voice-over PowerPoint
- ✓ Voice-over financial analysis and spreadsheets
- ✓ Web casts

How Was the Program Deployed?

The first cohort of 33 Intel students began the Babson Intel MBA program in May 2001, and 31 finished their MBA in June 2003.

Over the course of 27 months, 2.5 face-to-face classroom sessions are held each month. These classroom sessions offer integrated streams of content and are delivered each session by up to three full-time Babson College faculty working in teams. Rotating among three Intel office locations in Oregon, California, and Arizona, all students and faculty travel to the designated location to attend.

The Curriculum is delivered in four modules as follows:

✓ **Module 1: Introduction/Opportunity Recognition**
- Creative Management in Dynamic Organizations
- Law (continues throughout all four modules)
- Leading in Dynamic Organizations (organizational behavior)
- Effective Teams

✓ **Module 2: Opportunity Assessment**
- Competitive Strategy and Assessment
- Data Analysis
- Financial Impact of Business Decisions
- Managing Cash Flows
- Market, Environment, and Industry Adjustment
- Market Opportunity: Definition and Assessment

✓ **Module 3: Managing and Sustaining a Business**
- Designing Marketing Systems
- Decision Support Systems
- E-Business
- Information Systems for Managers

- Managing and Valuing Cash Flows
- Strategic Cost Systems
- Technology and Operations Management

✓ **Module 4: Managing Growth in an Uncertain Environment**

- Entrepreneurship
- Financial Strategy
- Managing in the Global Economy
- National Business Systems

For three weeks of each month between the classroom sessions, the students engage through online, virtual collaboration in individual and team study, and in application to work and real issues. For example, one team is asked to interview some of their own legal staff or to meet with the marketing or finance executives; individuals use the media-rich CD-ROM materials to master financial analysis; participants engage in faculty seminars delivered in live e-learning sessions, in video conference presentations, and in Web-enabled forums with related assignments, postings, commentary, and dialogue.

What Was the Business Impact of the Program?

For Babson College the business results were highly satisfactory.

✓ The faculty is on-board with the notion that a blended delivery model for a degree program is a viable and valuable alternative to full-time, classroom-based learning.

✓ The increased understanding, experience, and capability at Babson to support the internal development of e-learning materials have greatly improved.

✓ The lessons learned have guided the launch of the Babson FastTrack MBA.

✓ The expanded opportunity to consider geographically remote markets for Babson degree programs has become a reality.

✓ Babson College is being recognized as a leader in learning innovations. Financial Times has quoted Babson as 'leading the way' in providing interactive online education for executives through Babson Interactive.

✓ Intel Corporation launched the second Babson Intel MBA program cohort in January 2003.

The program evaluations submitted by the students indicate that the satisfaction with the learning experience equaled, and in some cases exceeded, the evaluations submitted by full-time MBA students.

Learner Perspectives

Intel Corporation Learner Perspectives

✓ Almost no attrition, only two students did not finish the program

Students appreciated:

✓ Relevance of the program to every day work

✓ High visibility to senior management

✓ Peer learning

✓ Integrated view of the company

✓ Quality of the program with full-time faculty

Module 1 Student Feedback by Subject Area:

Topic	Rating*	Delivery
Leadership	4.6	100% face-to-face
Creativity	4.4	67% online
Entrepreneurship	4.7	43% online
Ethics	4.0	100% online
Accounting	3.7	67% online
Law	4.4	60% online

* On a 5 point scale, with 5 being excellent

Summary

Purpose: Engage e-learning in a blended model to provide Intel high potential employees with an MBA program from a branded educational institution to:

✔ Support recruitment and retention of the best talent

✔ Assist in work-life balance issues

✔ Improve return on educational investments

Program Structure: The blended model enabled the faculty to engage the students in face-to-face sessions, as well as through Web-enabled learning, media-rich CD-ROM based learning and other distance and e-learning techniques, extending the learning into workplace realities and issues.

Number of Learning Hours per Learner: 1,000

Total Number of Hours of Learning in the Program: 1,000

Number of Learners: 31

Completion Requirements:

✔ Finish all coursework and pass multiple assessments and examinations similar to the rigor and manner utilized in the two-year MBA program at Babson College

Media and Tools:

✔ Multi-media CD-ROM

✔ Video conferencing

✔ Streaming video

✔ Macromedia Flash

✔ Simulations

✔ Live e-learning using CentraOne

✔ Web-enabled forums

✔ Voice-over PowerPoint

✔ Voice-over financial analysis and spreadsheets

✔ Web casts

Deployment Mechanism:

✔ Face-to-face classroom sessions

✔ e-Learning supported by CenQuest and CentraOne

✔ Project teamwork

Lessons Learned

✓ Always gain the commitment of the company senior executives at the beginning of the engagement, defining clearly the mutual commitments: what the company is prepared to do; what the institution is prepared to do; roles and responsibilities in marketing; and commitment of senior executives to sponsor work-related projects.

✓ Cover the basics of the content in face-to-face sessions to develop the context, to present what is being learned and why it is important, and to gain the student commitment to the learning at the launch of each new topic.

✓ Cover lecture-type material in Web seminars, not wasting valuable face-to-face time.

✓ Use e-learning capabilities for deeper, intensive learning in small groups or individually.

✓ Voice-over spreadsheets are an especially powerful tool to teach finance and decision systems.

✓ Dramatized cases and simulations are impressive; however, can be a waste of money. They look pretty, but students click through them because they can read faster.

✓ Web Forums are best when a variety of assignments are given to different groups, each group presents findings, and then comment on and critique each others results, followed by introducing just-in-time cases and articles to support dialogue.

✓ Some faculty prefer traditional face-to-face delivery, and the best performers in this environment may not be the star performers in the manager of learning role required in the e-learning environment. They manage the process rather than being on the podium leading the class.

✓ Don't underestimate the cost of moving content into a digitized delivery mode.

✓ Blended solutions do not need to be a 50/50 split between classroom and e-learning. In some cases it can be 20/80.

✓ Residency and evening MBA programs can be made more efficient through the use of e-learning.

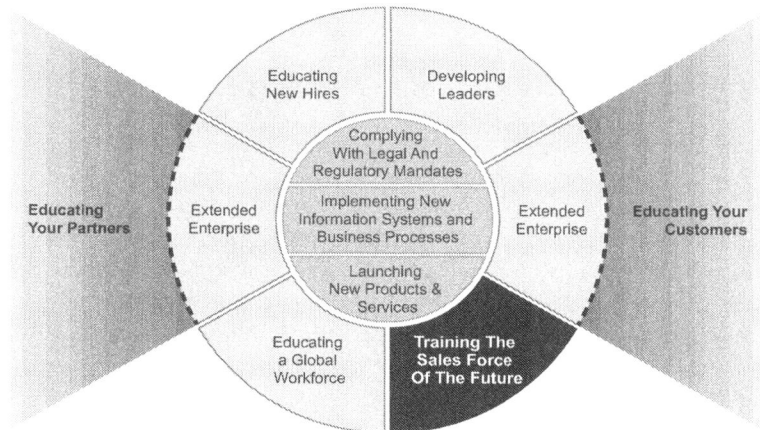

Training the Sales Force of the Future

The cases for this chapter are:

- *The Iams Company*
- *JPMorgan Chase*
- *Liberty Group*

Introduction

Why Did They Choose an e-Learning Solution?

A sales force is a major investment for most companies, and to grow the business requires that this sales force focus on market opportunities, be knowledgeable about the products, and skilled in selling to customers. During the high-growth 1990s many sales people could simply take orders, without expending much effort or becoming expert in product knowledge and sales techniques. Now, the twenty-first century reality is a highly competitive sales environment, and most sales people are challenged in this context to acquire new sales and attract new customers. Companies who during the past decade neglected to keep sales skills current are finding that they must quickly energize and train their sales force to move them out of their former order-taking mode.

However, this sales training must include more than learning about the sales cycle and selling skills because increasing gross revenue is only half the battle. Unless costs are simultaneously controlled or reduced, the sales effort may produce fewer profits than before. Managing the average cost-of-sale should be a major objective for every sales organization. An additional concern is the need to increase the number of transactions and the value of each transaction. Value selling models, such as building the customer relationship using a consultative approach, are now the state-of-the-art for the sales process. The sales force must be able to handle customers quickly and efficiently in less time, while ensuring that the value and profitability of each transaction is maximized.

An e-learning solution assists skill development for the sales force, while keeping an eye on the cost-of-sales bottom-line by:

- Distributing product information and learning in a cost-effective and timely way
- Engaging subject matter experts in focused learning, thus freeing up their time to be engaged with customers
- Ensuring accreditation of specific sales force groups, such as agents
- Equipping the sales force to engage customers in deeper, broader relationships with additional products and services

The three companies in this chapter utilized e-learning approaches to ensure that their sales force had adequate product knowledge and customer opportunity focus to increase the level and value of sales. They include: The Iams Company, a producer of premium dog and cat food and pet care products; JPMorgan Chase, a major financial services company; and Liberty Group, a financial services company based in South Africa.

Using e-Learning to Support Timely, Cost-Effective Sales Training

Knowing the product and being able to describe its benefits and value to customers is a critical capability in the sales force. The individuals who know the most about the product and how to convey its importance to potential and existing customers are the top sales performers themselves. Taking these subject matter experts out of the field to deliver training has serious opportunity costs that few companies can support over the long-term. Thus, it is critical to leverage subject matter expert knowledge without negatively impacting their ability to be active in current sales. The Iams Company recognized this need and found that an e-learning blended model solution provided important, accurate, product information to their sales force, while efficiently utilizing the time of the veterinarians who were needed in the field.

Initially, the Iams' veterinarians delivered classroom training for the three required sales courses, but now this foundational training on pet nutrition, label reading, and product knowledge has been reorganized into self-paced e-learning. This is followed by live e-learning workshops conducted by the veterinarians and research nutritionists, focused on applied nutrition. This content can be rapidly changed to accommodate changes in the market and new product information, ensuring that the content is always timely and relevant. Finally, the blended model includes self-paced e-learning available to the customers and consumers who buy Iams' products, extending the sales impact of e-learning beyond the sales force into the marketplace.

Ensuring the Sales Transaction Value Through Product Knowledge

JPMorgan Chase and Liberty Group both provide financial services products and realize that each customer is a potential source for new business. However, the sales force training challenges that they chose to meet with an e-learning solution were quite different. JPMorgan Chase has 17 unique financial businesses, which they needed to serve with up-to-date product knowledge and training. Especially important to JPMorgan Chase were their consumer bankers, who are responsible for 80 to 90 percent of the customers who enter the Chase network. To ensure that the information customers received at the point of entry was adequate and accurate, and to foster additional sales to these customers was of critical importance. With subject matter expert input, Chase developed seven individual product-specific assessments tied to self-paced, product e-learning modules. Every two to three weeks a new assessment and module were rolled-out to the consumer bankers. Within a few months, this Product Knowledge Assessment Process was launched to more than 1,000 bankers in 500 branches. Chase soon found that customer satisfaction in the targeted market area increased from 75 to 80 percent.

Liberty Group also experienced a need to disseminate accurate product knowledge to their internal sales force of 2,500, but also needed to reach an extended sales force of 2,000 contracted individuals and 6,000 brokers. Using a blended model, within 6 months almost all of the 2,500 Liberty agents had completed the accreditation examinations, and an additional 250 are completing the program each month. Results they are realizing include increased market share and new business.

These organizations recognized that sales training on product features, benefits, and value would increase sales, the efficiency of each transaction, and the potential value of each customer. All organizations successfully implemented an e-learning solution to achieve these goals.

Case 1: The Iams Company

Company Facts and Figures

✓ **Industry:** Consumer Products

✓ **Scope of Services and Products:**
Produces and sells premium dog and cat food and pet care products

✓ **Estimated Number of Employees:**
2,500

✓ **Year e-Learning Introduced:** 1994

✓ **Offices and Locations:**
17 office locations worldwide

✓ **Estimated 2002 Revenues:**
US$1.2 billion

✓ **Web Site:** www.iamsco.com

Introduction

To build upon their tradition of attaining business success through developing people, The Iams Company identified a need to educate their employees, consumers, and business partners (such as distributors, retailers, veterinarians, and breeders) about the importance of dog and cat nutrition. As a result, The Iams Company established Iams University and also designed a three-phase Applied Nutritional Science program that today incorporates both live and self-paced e-learning with classroom learning.

Phase 1, a requirement for all professionals at Iams, has three self-paced, e-learning modules covering dog and cat nutrition, label reading, and product knowledge (see Figure 16-1). It is an expansion of the first e-learning project launched at Iams in 1994. Initially, the three courses in this phase were facilitated by Iams' veterinarians in a classroom environment reaching every employee. Iams University determined that this was not the best use of the veterinarians' time and enlisted a team of learning experts to design and develop the program that is now in place.

Why e-Learning?

The Iams Company selected an e-learning approach to:

✓ Formalize their education process

✓ Eliminate stand-up instruction for employees company-wide

✓ Give Iams' veterinarians more time for field calls

✓ Train a distributed audience of learners

✓ Reduce training time

✓ Enable sales force to stay in the field

✓ Reduce travel costs associated with training

The first component, key to educating staff about the nutritional requirements of dogs and cats and the appropriate products to use during a particular stage in the animal's life, also lays the groundwork for the instructor-led classroom session in Phase 2 of this blended learning program.

The **Phase 2** instructor-led classroom learning was planned with the sales force in mind. This second phase builds on the three self-paced prerequisite modules in Phase 1 and moves the sales force to the next level of nutritional knowledge and application. Conducted by Iams veterinarians and research nutritionists, the content in these sessions is driven by market trends. This classroom

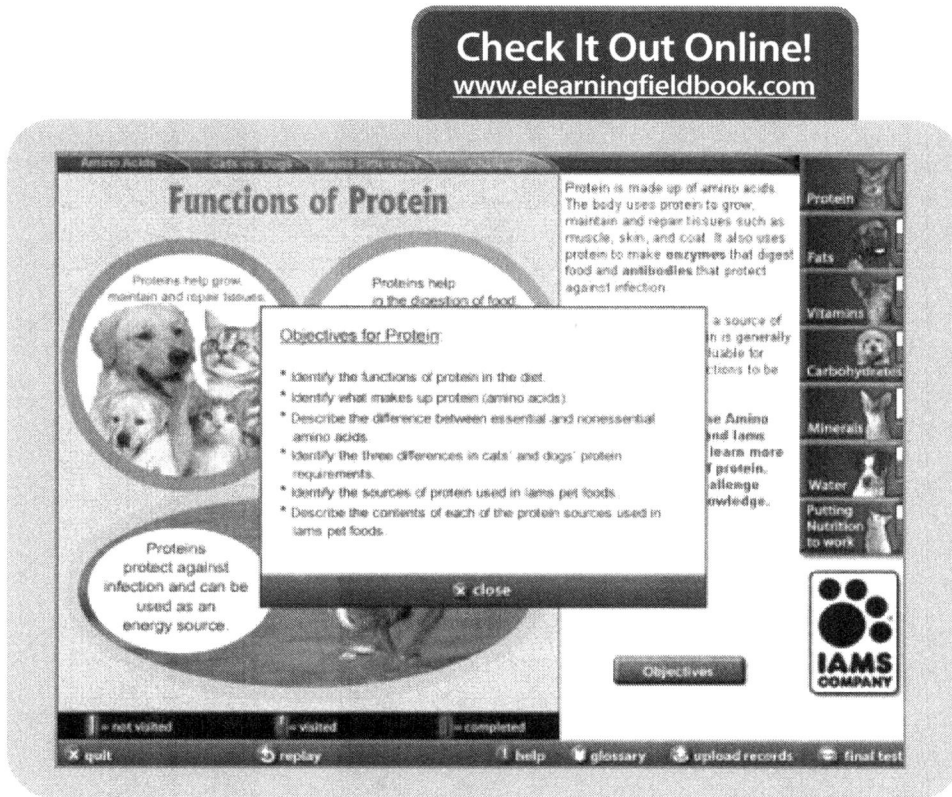

Figure 16-1: Phase 1-Foundations in Nutrition Module

phase, conducted twice annually, is generally two hours in length and focuses on applied nutrition and also how to use this knowledge during sales calls. Recognizing that each person has a different level of understanding, Iams is currently working to establish a baseline level in Phase 1 that would equalize participants' learning in preparation for Phase 2.

Live online learning sessions are another component of Phase 2. Course content is specific to trends in the market place, new product launches, nutritional advances, and research relevant to existing products. These monthly sessions, delivered through a live e-learning platform tool by veterinarians, scientists, and senior sales and marketing persons within the organization, are available company wide and are typically 1.5 hours in duration.

A sub-set of Phase 2 is a self-paced module targeted specifically toward the Veterinary Sales team and focuses on disease management. Delivered as self-paced learning via CD-ROM, this module helps sales teams understand how veterinarians diagnose and medically treat specific diseases or conditions. Also included are how these diseases or conditions can be nutritionally managed and which Iams products have been formulated to meet the nutritional needs of the animal impacted by the disease or condition. The disease management module includes 18 diseases or conditions and takes learners an average of 20 minutes per disease to complete.

Phase 3 is self-paced e-learning that reaches beyond the sales group to the customers and consumers who buy Iams' products. This phase mirrors the courses in Phase 1; however, slight modifications have been made to meet stringent regulatory requirements. Iams University provides direct Internet access to this external group, and these courses have been well received.

Before The Iams Company's Applied Nutritional Science program was introduced, much of the nutritional education at Iams was informal or on-the-fly, with an end goal of teaching as much as possible, whenever possible. For all Iams' efforts, it was still difficult to achieve, or sometimes even recognize, this goal. The Applied Nutritional Science program helped Iams formalize their education process. Employees now have a starting point, and there are checkpoints along the way to meet educational requirements and professional expectations.

How Was the Program Aligned with the Business?

The Iams Company's Applied Nutritional Science program is an integral part of the firm's strategic plan of moving from the category of mere dog and cat food to nutritional healthcare for pets—unyielding in their conviction that nutrition makes a difference. Iams is passionate about dog and cat nutrition and in their commitment to educate employees, customers, and consumers about the benefits of their products.

The Iams Company believes that if people are not thinking about how nutrition can make a difference in their pet, they will not spend money on the premium products Iams produces. To be successful in selling Iams' products, it not only requires that all Iams' employees understand the importance of nutrition, it is equally important that Iams educates the consumers and professional influencers.

Key Business Drivers

✓ Create a sales force knowledge base about nutrition

✓ Maintain passion about dog and cat nutrition with a continuing commitment to educate employees, customers, and consumers about the benefits of The Iams Company's products

✓ Find the most effective and efficient way to transfer nutritional information to all employees

The Applied Nutritional Science program supports Iams' corporate strategy to build and leverage organizational and operational excellence. By association, each employee is viewed by the general public as a dog or cat expert—a sales person. Iams feels strongly about professional development and education both inside and outside of the organization. Participation in this program enables an Iams employee, when asked, to make recommendations about pet care and nutrition.

How Was the Program Designed?

The Iams Company's Applied Nutritional Science program was designed as a three-phase series using live and self-paced e-learning along with an instructor-led classroom session. Program duration for the Phase 1 self-paced learning is approximately 2.5 hours. Phase 1 is followed by targeted, monthly live e-learning sessions as well

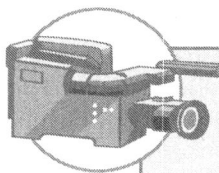

Media and Tools

✓ Macromedia Authorware

✓ Macromedia Dreamweaver

✓ Macromedia Fireworks

✓ Macromedia Flash

✓ HTML

✓ JavaScript

✓ Adobe Photoshop

✓ Centra Symposium

as classroom learning that reinforces and expands the concepts taught in the e-learning modules. The third phase of the program rolls out slightly modified versions of the Web-based programs and is directed to Iams' customers and consumers.

The Applied Nutritional Science program was designed and developed in approximately ten months by a nine-person internal team comprised of the Iams University e-Learning Group, Sales and Marketing College, subject matter experts, and regulatory affairs in collaboration with external vendors.

How Was the Program Deployed?

Courses are available on the company's intranet (see Figure 16-2) and on CD-ROM. For Phase 1, tracking the user's progress is immediate if there is a direct connection through the intranet. When a test is completed using the CD-ROM, progress is tracked on the user's hard drive, then uploaded to the system the next time the user logs in.

Deployment of Applied Nutritional Science program for new hires is through The Iams Company's formal initial orientation. This program is again introduced during a quarterly orientation for all employees. Managers also reinforce learning goals and expectations with employees and incorporate them into the employee's development plans. Field sales employees receive notification in their initial packets from Human Resources, and when they receive their laptops they are also given a CD-ROM containing Phase 1 of the Applied Nutritional Science program.

Marketing Approach

✓ Internal communications

✓ Manager-to-employee discussions

Figure 16-2: Example of Iams University Curriculum

What Was the Business Impact of the Program?

With the implementation in Phase 1 of the three self-study courses, Iams has reduced the learning period for each participant from a total of 8 hours instructor-led training to 2.5 hours of self-paced e-learning. Results of pre-and post-testing show that along with reducing the learning period, participants using e-learning have either retained or exceeded the knowledge gained as compared to the previous instructor-led training. e-Learning has eliminated the travel involved to get to a central location for classroom training and also reduced the number of days the sales force is out of the field for the training sessions. This program has also allowed Iams to roll out product information more quickly and to a wider audience.

The self-paced, e-learning courses have also given valuable time back to the veterinarians, who were the facilitators of classroom learning. Now they are available to train the sales force in more advanced topics during Phase 2 of the program and educate consumers and the professional influencers with regard to The Iams Company's products.

The Iams Company believes that this program, coupled with others that are in development, has brought to the forefront that Iams University has the skills to impact efficiencies and the bottom line.

Learner Perspectives

✓ Experienced sales people say that they wish that this program had been available when they started at Iams.

✓ New hires are impressed with the short period of time it takes them to absorb all the information.

✓ Learners are saying that e-learning:

- "...helps me feel more knowledgeable and confident..."
- "...has increased my credibility..."
- "...sessions are quick, concise, and informative..."

Summary

Purpose: Provide employees, consumers, and influencers information on dog and cat nutrition focusing specifically on:

- ✔ Foundations of nutrition
- ✔ Label reading
- ✔ Product knowledge

Program Structure: A blended learning model in three phases:

- ✔ Phase 1: Self-paced e-learning via Internet or CD-ROM
- ✔ Phase 2: Instructor-led classroom session and live online sessions that expand on knowledge gained from Phase 1 modules
- ✔ Phase 3: Self-paced e-learning via the Internet

Number of Learning Hours per Learner: Approximately 15 to 20 hours for each sales person per year. However, market conditions can impact the number of live online sessions in Phase 2.

Total Number of Hours of Learning in the Program:

- ✔ Phase 1: 2.5 hours
- ✔ Phase 2: 12 to 16 hours per year
- ✔ Phase 3: Variable

Number of Learners:

- ✔ Phase 1: 2,500
- ✔ Phase 2: 300
- ✔ Phase 3: Worldwide consumer base

Completion Requirements:

- ✔ Phase 1 required for all employees; Module assessments completed either directly online or from a CD-ROM and results are uploaded when user signs on again to the system
- ✔ Phase 2 classroom learning required for sales force; Live Web-based sessions available to all employees
- ✔ Phase 3 available to customers and consumers

Media and Tools:

- ✔ Macromedia's Authorware, Flash, Fireworks, and Dreamweaver
- ✔ HTML
- ✔ JavaScript
- ✔ Adobe Photoshop
- ✔ Centra Symposium

Deployment Mechanism:

- ✔ CD-ROM
- ✔ Intranet
- ✔ Internet

Lessons Learned

✓ Partner with IT from the start to ensure that the technical infrastructure can support the tools selected and the intended rollout plan.

✓ Align all the different initiatives in the beginning of the project and work together for the end result.

✓ Ensure subject matter experts understand their role and the impact on the project if they don't follow through.

✓ Start with the bigger picture and narrow it to several smaller projects.

✓ Be sure of any external regulatory review processes that might differ from internal review processes that are in place.

✓ Maintain a separation in the design and development processes.

✓ Evaluate functionality and capability of existing systems for tracking and reporting purposes.

Case 2: JPMorgan Chase

Company Facts and Figures

✓ **Industry:** Financial Services

✓ **Scope of Services and Products:**
17 unique financial services companies

✓ **Estimated Number of Employees:**
100,000

✓ **Year e-Learning Introduced:** 1997

✓ **Offices and Locations:**
Operations in 59 countries; Headquarters in New York

✓ **Estimated 2002 Revenues:**
US$3.4 billion

✓ **Web Site:** www.jpmorganchase.com

Introduction

JPMorgan Chase was faced with a tremendous challenge in bringing quality e-learning to its 100,000 employees worldwide. Mergers, acquisitions, and consolidations within the banking industry resulted in a multinational, multi-state organization with disparate learning methodologies. Within the 17 unique financial businesses at Chase, there were 14 distinct training departments.

In 1997, under the leadership of the current Director of e-Learning at JPMorgan Chase, leaders from each of the training departments convened to discuss the concept of alternative delivery methods. Their discussions centered on how to deliver training to individuals who were geographically dispersed, and how to increase their level of expertise and knowledge quickly so that they could be competitive within the industry. The group hammered out ways to align funds and resources, and create one strategy for the organization instead of fourteen separate strategies.

Why e-Learning?

JP Morgan Chase selected an e-learning approach to:

✓ Explore alternative delivery methods

✓ Deliver training to a geographically dispersed group

✓ Quickly and efficiently transfer knowledge so that individuals are better positioned

✓ Reduce cost across the organization

✓ Increase people's access to learning

As roles were defined and processes put into place, Chase created successes in developing content, rolling it out to small populations, and collecting feedback. This helped them to understand how the technology infrastructure worked, how to reduce costs across the organization, and how to increase learners' access to learning.

To analyze need and to facilitate learning development, Chase created the Decision Support Tool—a tool that not only gave them significant media attention, but allowed 350 learning professionals within the organization to share a common language (see Figure 16-3). This tool, through a series of questions, helps determine the best learning vehicle for a particular learning event. It has changed the way people think as they:

✓ Consider e-learning solutions

✓ Balance the shelf life and costs of a program

✓ Build programs that are managed and maintained by internal resources

This tool, in conjunction with other e-learning support tools, allowed Chase to develop and implement a self-paced Product Knowledge Assessment Process to help their consumer bankers, or sales force, to become more comfortable in selling products to their retail business clients. Initially, the process consisted of an online assessment only. However, it has now become a combination of assessments plus development opportunities for approximately 1,000 professionals.

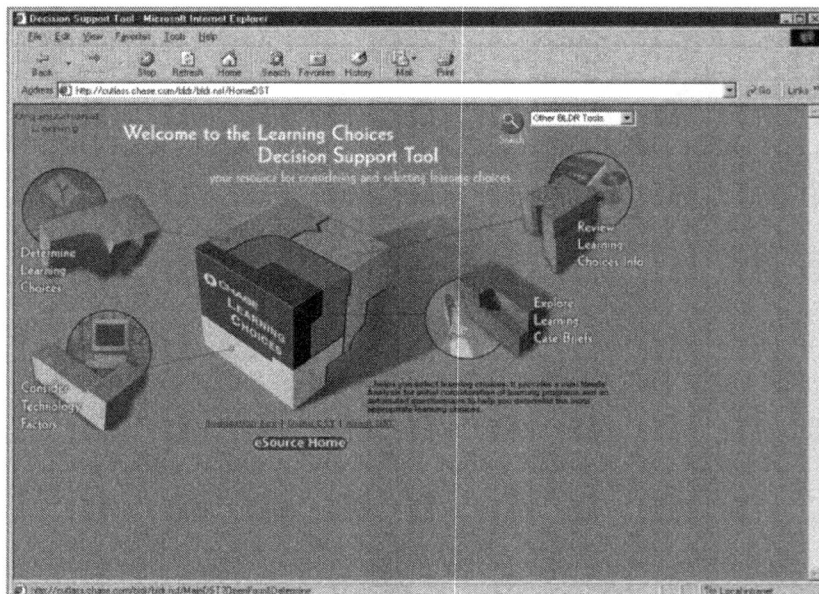

Figure 16-3: Decision Support Tool

How Was the Program Aligned with the Business?

The Product Knowledge Assessment Process was developed to support JPMorgan Chase's Six Sigma initiative called Customer On-Boarding.

This project outlined that one of the drivers for successful customer on-boarding was knowledgeable employees. The seven-module assessment process and associated e-learning programs were established to help the consumer bankers become comfortable discussing the range of products offered by Chase and enable them to cross-sell products and services effectively.

Because their consumer bankers are responsible for bringing 80 to 90 percent of customers into the Chase network, they wanted to make sure that the customers were receiving the correct information at the initial point of contact.

Key Business Drivers

- ✓ Educate employees
- ✓ Enhance employee performance
- ✓ Improve customer satisfaction
- ✓ Ensure opportunities were not missed for customer on-boarding
- ✓ Ensure customers receive accurate information
- ✓ Strengthen customer relationships

How Was the Program Designed?

The Product Knowledge Assessment Process is a Web-based, self-paced set of e-learning programs. It was designed and developed by an internal team consisting of people from the learning community, Human Resources, a project leader from the Six Sigma team, and the Information Technology group. The program was championed by the senior executive of the Six Sigma initiative.

Assessment questions were written by a core team of subject matter experts within the organization. What followed was a very rigorous review by teams who verified product content, geographic accuracy, and role or competency expectation.

It is not possible to be exact in calculating the number of hours spent designing this program. The entire assessment process took about seven months to develop and implement. The core team comprised of about eight people and additional resources were added and removed as the project moved into the various stages.

Program Structure

The program contains seven individual product-specific timed assessments. The assessments are used to establish the learner's baseline of product knowledge, which identify areas that require development. Learners complete the assessments using their desktops in a controlled environment to ensure equity across the process. Assessment scores are tracked, and learners with a development need are directed to Chase's internal learning portal, LearningConnect, to enroll in online e-learning in the required areas.

Each product learning module is approximately 30 minutes in duration; quiz results are not scored and learners can check their progress in a particular area by re-taking the assessment specific to that module. This however, is done on a scheduled, controlled basis, for example, every six months.

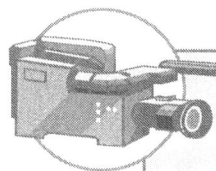

Media and Tools

- ✓ Questionmark Perception assessment tool
- ✓ Macromedia Dreamweaver
- ✓ Macromedia Flash
- ✓ HTML

How Was the Program Deployed?

Product assessments were rolled out in phases every two to three weeks to consumer bankers with at least three months of service.

To support the assessments initially, online e-learning programs were built in parallel, by leveraging the classroom training content for consumer products and converting it to Web-based learning. The learning was organized by the various topics within the assessments then uploaded to LearningConnect, where learners accessed the learning modules.

Marketing Approach

✓ Weekly market updates

✓ Identify certain key points of the program to discuss during established meetings

✓ Market on company's intranet site

With the assessment process established and key areas of learning developed, Chase is now able to evaluate the transfer of knowledge and related job performance of their professionals.

Product module completion is required if an assessment identifies a particular area of study as a development need. Learners are notified of completion deadlines and managers and coaches are assigned to assist individuals in fulfilling learning requirements.

What Was the Business Impact of the Program?

The Product Knowledge Assessment Process was launched to more than 1,000 consumer bankers in 500 branches located in four states.

Developing this program helped Chase realize that in the past they did not have a rich, disciplined approach to assessing existing training, instituting development initiatives, and delivering product training. They now have a focus they did not have before, with training directly linked to the performance management process.

Learner Perspectives

✓ "It was a great way to let me know areas I needed to brush up on."

✓ "It helped to give me a better understanding of our products."

✓ "I liked the Web-based functionality because I was able to take the modules when it was right for me."

Additional impacts on the business from this program are:

✓ The opportunity to build key relationships within the company and build credibility as a learning organization

✓ A sharp jump in the number of people requesting and participating in the product-related online e-learning programs

✓ The Scorecard, which is a tool used by Chase to evaluate consumer bankers, shows an increase in the accuracy and amount of key information being shared with customers

✓ Customer satisfaction within the targeted market segment has increased from 75 to 80 percent in some areas

Summary

Purpose: To provide a self-paced e-learning opportunity that would enhance Chase's consumer bankers' product knowledge and enable them to:

✓ Give customers the correct product information at the initial point of contact

✓ Recognize opportunities to bring new customers to Chase

✓ Expand their relationship with existing customers

Program Structure: Seven product assessments and e-learning modules related to a specific product

Number of Learning Hours per Learner: 3.5 hours

Total Number of Hours of Learning in the Program: 3.5 hours

Number of Learners: 1,000

Completion Requirements:

✓ Learners must complete all job- and geography-specific assessments and the associated e-learning modules if there is an identified development need

Media and Tools:

✓ Questionmark Perception assessment tool

✓ Macromedia Dreamweaver

✓ Macromedia Flash

✓ HTML

Deployment Mechanism:

✓ Internal Web- based learning platform, called Learning Connect

Lessons Learned

✓ Building the link with the internal Six Sigma initiative enabled Chase to focus on learning development resources and gain the support of a business champion.

✓ It is important to identify resources early in the process.

✓ Communication with all levels of the organization is imperative for executive buy-in.

✓ Plan a rollout strategy to minimize the impact on the business.

✓ Do not assume that all users have the same level of computer skills.

✓ Help desk support is crucial to success of any online program rollout.

✓ Make sure your technology infrastructure can support your rollout.

Case 3: Liberty Group

Company Facts and Figures

✔ **Industry:** Financial Services

✔ **Scope of Services and Products:**
Provider of investment, life insurance, retirement, disability, and health insurance products and solutions

✔ **Estimated Number of Employees:**
4,000

✔ **Year e-Learning Introduced:** 1999

✔ **Offices and Locations:** Main office in Johannesburg, South Africa

✔ **Web Site:** http: www.liberty.co.za

✔ **Number of e-Learning Programs in Entire Curriculum:** 25

Introduction

The Liberty Group, one of the largest insurance companies in South Africa, provides a comprehensive range of insurance products to both corporations and individuals. As such it relies heavily on an extended sales force to market a wide range of products to a diverse target audience throughout the country. The extended sales force consists of approximately 2,500 sales consultants employed by Liberty with an additional 2,000 contracted individuals and 6,000 brokers.

Why e-Learning?

Liberty selected an e-learning approach because they needed to:

✔ Assess the current skill levels

✔ Train a large geographically dispersed audience

✔ Provide accreditation to meet new legislative requirements for agent licensing

In June 2001, Liberty implemented an accreditation program for their extended sales force. This was a result of various factors including the high number of new agents joining the company each month, frequent product launches and the escalating costs of training the sales force. In addition, a new policyholder protection regulation had been introduced in South Africa that required all agents to be licensed and accredited to sell insurance and other financial products.

To meet the needs of the diverse group of learners, the program combines:

✔ Self-paced learning modules that present theoretical knowledge

✔ Regional facilitated workshops that focus on marketing-related knowledge and skills

✔ Accreditation exams

Depending on the level of experience, the sales consultants complete all parts of the program, or in some cases, they can qualify to complete the exam only.

How Was the Program Aligned with the Business?

The overall goal of this e-learning program was the accreditation of the sales force in line with the insurance industry's new legal requirements for policyholder protection. The legislation came into effect in July 2001, and it stipulated that any sales intermediary selling within the insurance environment would have to be accredited to sell insurance products.

At the time, this new requirement was a challenge for Liberty because a large percentage of Liberty's sales force was not accredited. There was an immediate need to create training for a large number of agents in the field.

The training had to be delivered within a six-month period to a geographically dispersed audience. Therefore, it was necessary to get the assistance of all the regional training staff and help from the regional managers to schedule and support the training.

This business goal was also in alignment with Liberty's overall business drivers—to increase sales and productivity. Within the insurance industry time-to-market is a critical success factor, as well as controlling associated costs, including those for training a large sales force.

Key Business Drivers

- ✓ Assess the sales force competency levels
- ✓ Educate sales force about products and market position
- ✓ Bring learning to large numbers of new employees
- ✓ Ensure accreditation of agents
- ✓ Comply with new industry legislation

How Was the Program Designed?

The Phase One Accreditation program (see Figure 16-4) is a combination of a self-paced e-learning, instructor-led and live e-learning workshops, and online assessments. It includes both product knowledge and marketing content.

Although Liberty markets a broad range of products, they selected eight key products to be included in the Phase One accreditation process. Liberty strongly believes in using a blended learning approach and included both online and classroom elements in the design of this program.

The basic structure of the program includes:

- ✓ One introduction module
- ✓ Eight product modules
- ✓ Eight workshops
- ✓ Eight accreditation exams

The **introduction** module provides an understanding of the insurance industry with particular reference to the way in which Liberty structures its services and products. It also covers terminology and legislation. This self-paced, e-learning module is approximately two hours in duration and consists of mostly text screens.

The eight **product modules** provide a theoretical understanding of Liberty's main products. Information is conveyed in both a text and video format with links to pre-recorded Web conferencing sessions. The product modules contain a number of self-assessments and enrichment questions. Each of the product modules focus on:

✓ Overview of the product

✓ Product specifications

✓ Business rules

✓ Marketing opportunities

These modules can be completed in smaller segments whenever the agent has available time, and it takes approximately two hours per module to complete.

The **workshops** are a combination of instructor-led classroom sessions and live e-learning sessions using Centra. They focus on understanding the market and the opportunities in each product line. The workshops further enhance the learner's understanding of the various products as covered in the online self-paced sessions. Learning methodologies used in the workshops include application-based role plays that are interactive and based on real experiences. In some instances, the workshops include process and technical exercises.

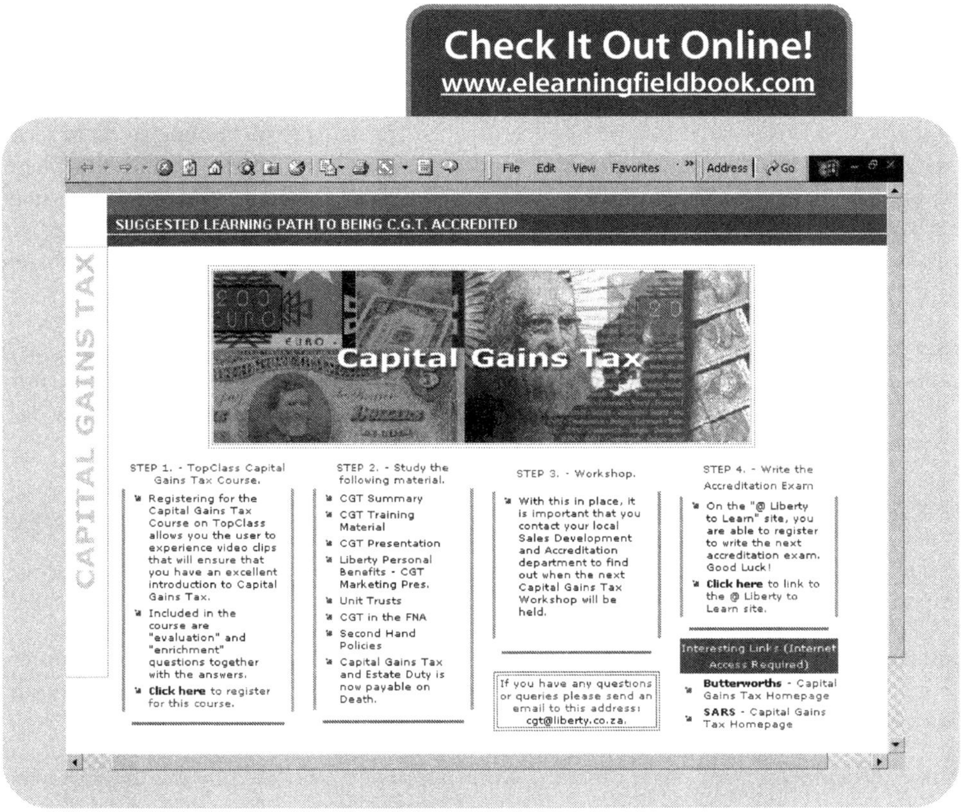

Figure 16-4: Liberty's Phase One Accreditation Program

Initially, Liberty chose not to record the live e-learning sessions, but they do use recorded Centra sessions now in the interest of speeding up time-to-market and also to add another dimension of learning for a diverse target audience.

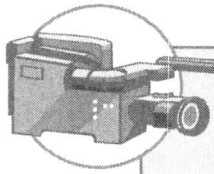

Media and Tools

✓ Macromedia Dreamweaver

✓ Centra live-learning and recorded sessions

✓ HTML and JavaScript

✓ Adobe PDF files, Microsoft PowerPoint, and Microsoft Word

The eight **accreditation exams** consist of a bank of randomized multiple choice questions and open-ended questions based on various case studies and scenarios. The questions were designed to test application of knowledge. The learners could select whether they wanted to complete the assessments online or as a paper-based assessment.

The design team for the Phase One Accreditation program was grouped according to specific product sets. At any one time there were at least three teams developing the content required for this program. A typical design team for this project included:

✓ 1.0 Project lead

✓ 1.0 Subject matter expert / Instructional designer

✓ 1.0 Developer

✓ 0.5 Technical support

When Liberty first investigated the use of e-learning for the delivery of training to their sales force, they had very little of the required skills and experience internally to develop this blended learning program. They made a decision to update the skill set for their existing training staff so that they could act as the instructional designers and developers for the Phase One Accreditation program. It is important to note that the trainers are subject matter experts, and it was therefore possible for them to fill that role and the instructional designer role.

It is estimated that the project team was able to develop a single two-hour online module as well as the associated workshop and assessment in a period of approximately six weeks. These numbers varied depending on the availability of content, level of interaction, complexity of media elements, existing workshop material, and the skill level of the design team.

How Was the Program Deployed?

Liberty deployed the learning program to the Liberty agents, as well as to the brokers, through the company's existing intranet portal and the TopClass learning management system.

The various online modules were scheduled for specific periods of time as Liberty only purchased 1,500 concurrent TopClass licenses. This meant that learners had to register to access a module for a particular time period (see Figure 16-5).

At the time of deployment of Phase One, the workshops were scheduled by the branch managers and invitations were sent to the appropriate learners. The program was mandatory for the Liberty agents but voluntary for the brokers who form part of the extended sales force.

The sales force is a mobile one, and as such all brokers use laptops to capture information from clients and complete the required documents so Liberty wanted the program to be as easily accessible as possible. Both the overview and product courses were made available over the Internet, and the sales force was able to access the content from their office desk or from home. They could also access the modules directly, or they could download them to their PC. In some instances, it was necessary to make the program available on a CD-ROM due to server problems, bandwidth issues, and other technical difficulties.

Click the events below to view further details.				
Mon	Tues	Wed	Thur	Fri
		1	2	3
6	7	8 January Launch AM Session * January Launch PM Session	9	10
13 Module Six - Annuities	14 Module Six - Annuities	15 Module Six - Annuities	16 Module Six - Annuities	17 Module Six - Annuities
20 Module Seven - Investment Selection	21 Module Seven - Investment Selection	22 Module Seven - Investment Selection	23 Module Seven - Investment Selection	24 Module Seven - Investment Selection
27 Module Eight - Delta/Multiple Choice	28 * FIC (Financial Intelligence Centre Act) * Module Eight - Delta/Multiple Choice	29 Module Eight - Delta/Multiple Choice	30 Module Eight - Delta/Multiple Choice	31 Module Eight - Delta/Multiple Choice

Figure 16-5: Learner's Project Training Schedule for Phase One

The workshops were scheduled within the various regions and the sales force was required to attend them. Sometimes the marketing workshops were combined or integrated with existing courses. The workshops were facilitated by the existing field trainers and occurred mostly in the regions, thereby avoiding additional missed work time for travel days.

Accreditation exams were scheduled once a month at specific times. Due to the diverse target group, some people were already competent enough in some areas to take the exam without completing a particular online module or workshop.

For management reporting and certification, the assessment results were sent to a database. Managers were able to access the database to generate reports for a particular branch or an entire region. These reports primarily tracked completion percentages and scores. Once the learner passed the assessment with at least an 80 percent, they were sent a system-generated certificate via e-mail.

The program was launched three months after the new accreditation rules came into effect, thereby placing enormous pressure on both the training team and the sales consultants themselves.

Leading up to the launch, the training team conducted a number of road shows in the various regions with the purpose of exposing the sales team and management to the program. As part of the overall communication plan, the sales team received various marketing items such as mouse pads.

The main strategy however was to use the field managers and field trainers to promote the program to both the Liberty agents as well as the brokers.

Marketing Approach

✓ Presented road shows in all main regions

✓ Established champions in the regions to encourage and monitor participation

✓ Gave out marketing items

✓ Placed notices on the internal Web site

What Was the Business Impact of the Program?

The Phase One Accreditation program was deployed to 6,000 learners in September 2001. Within a six-month period, almost all of the 2,500 Liberty agents had completed the eight accreditation exams. The brokers' completion rate was much lower, as they had not been mandated to complete the program during this time frame. At present approximately 250 consultants are completing the program each month.

As a result of the program Liberty has managed to certify its sales consultants and is also providing the brokers with an opportunity to become accredited to sell Liberty products.

As part of the overall strategy to use e-learning as a delivery medium for training the sales force, it was important to gather feedback from the learners who had completed the program as well as from the regional managers and the program sponsor.

Learner Perspectives

✓ "I was not restricted to a particular study method."

✓ "Learning is available 24 hours per day."

✓ "The online environment allowed me to study in my own time."

✓ "I improved my sales potential."

The learners were required to complete an online questionnaire. For many of them this was their first online learning experience, and it took some time to get comfortable and see the benefit. Once the learners started working through the modules, they were able to provide valuable feedback

Some constructive conclusions drawn from the feedback are that the program needs to:

✓ Consider a more blended learning approach

✓ Adjust for different learning styles

✓ Take into account the specific requirements of the different audiences, such as agents versus brokers, and well-experienced versus new hires

✓ Have more interactions

✓ Focus on essential content versus nice-to-have

The training team has also reported a positive impact. Before the implementation of an e-learning infrastructure they were not able to cope with the number of new staff joining the company each month or the regular launching of new products and product updates. Other impacts include being able to:

✓ Deliver training to the sales force as and when they need it

✓ Use the reports to draw a correlation between training and performance

✓ Gain high profile for training and support from executives

Liberty's management team has fully supported this initiative and has identified a number of business impacts, including:

✓ Stakeholder satisfaction: A large percentage of their sales force meet the regulatory compliance requirements

✓ Efficient deployment: 2,500 people accredited in six months, with additional accreditations monthly

✓ Increased market share and new business, although these achievements cannot be directly attributed to the impact of the program they have undoubtedly influenced the results

✓ Recognition in the market as being focused on the development of the Liberty staff

✓ Credibility in the market place due to accredited sales consultants

Summary

Purpose: To provide product education for the extended sales force to meet legal requirements, improve sales and productivity, and reduce training costs

Program Structure: The program consisted of:

✓ Eight self-paced, e-learning modules

✓ Eight marketing workshops, with a combination of instructor-led classroom sessions and live e-learning sessions

✓ Online assessments

Number of Learning Hours per Learner: A total of approximately 41 hours, as listed below:

✓ Overview: 1 hour

✓ Product modules: 16 hours

✓ Workshops: 16 hours

✓ Assessments: 8 hours

Number of Learners: 6,000

Completion Requirements:

✓ Mandatory for Liberty agents and voluntary for brokers

✓ 80 percent proficiency on assessment

Media and Tools:

✓ Macromedia Dreamweaver

✓ HTML and JavaScript

✓ Adobe PDF files, Microsoft PowerPoint and Word

✓ Centra live-learning sessions

Deployment Mechanism: The program was deployed over the Internet, on CD-ROMs, and in a classroom environment. Marketing approaches included:

✓ Road shows in all main regions

✓ Established champions in the regions to encourage and monitor participation

✓ Marketing items

Lessons Learned

✓ Understand the target audience.

✓ Get the right blend for the different target groups.

✓ Pitch the content at the correct level.

✓ Train the training team.

✓ It is extremely important to identify potential change management issues and then address these before, during, and after the learning intervention.

✓ Don't forget about the training team–address their fears and concerns too.

✓ Understand your requirements for a learning management system and check that it can integrate with existing systems and infrastructure.

✓ Work closely with IT.

✓ Get senior management buy-in early in the process so that they will champion the program.

✓ Marketing, communication, and feedback mechanisms must be in place.

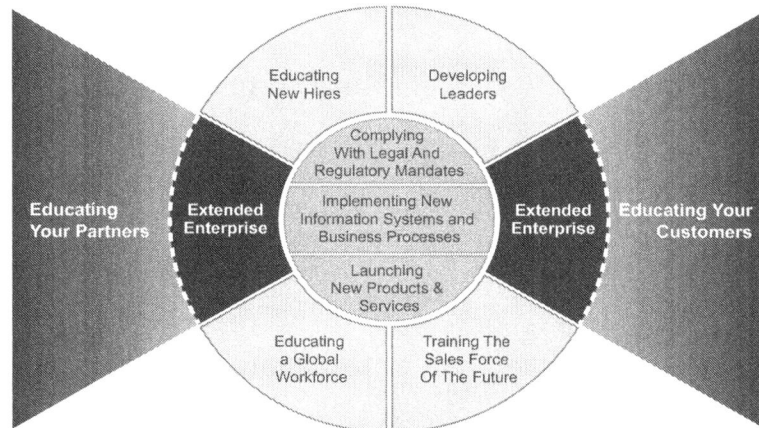

Educating Your Customers and Partners

The cases for this chapter are:

- *Invensys/Foxboro*
- *Oracle Corporation*
- *3Com*

Introduction

Why Did They Choose an e-Learning Solution?

The extended enterprise goes well beyond the direct employee-base to include business customers and partners. A definition of the term extended enterprise is that a company is made up not just of its employees, but includes a web of relationships that embraces not only its board members and executives, but also its business partners, its suppliers, and even its customers. This extended enterprise is successful only if the delivery, integration, and sharing of information is accessible to all component groups and individuals, providing synergistically the critical information they need to do business effectively.

The value of the extended enterprise spans company boundaries and is grounded in an intricate web of information and knowledge. Customers and partners need to know about the latest products or services as soon as they are available. Resellers and agents need access to training on new and existing products and services, especially if certification in these products is a requirement for their profession. Organizations that have extended their enterprise are now looking at learning as a key component of this network.

Many organizations have selected e-learning initiatives to extend the learning beyond company boundaries to external business customers and partners, and have found that this enables them to:

- Meet the changing requirements of customers and business partners

- Maintain and improve competitiveness by educating customers and partners in their products and services

- Provide partners with increased levels of service

- Boost sales and revenues by incorporating the benefits of learning into contractual agreements with customers and partners

Three companies from vastly different industries in this chapter extended their learning outreach beyond internal employees to reach business partners and customers with extraordinary results. These include: Invensys Foxboro, a provider of process controls, devices, software, and consulting services to the manufacturers in the cement, chemicals, oil, and gas industries; Oracle Corporation, a major, global database software management company; and 3Com, a producer of wireline and wireless networking products.

e-Learning Enables the Extended Enterprise to Serve Customers and Partners

Company learning organizations already serve as aggregators and integrators of knowledge for internal learning customers and can easily repurpose this content and make it available to key external customers and partners in a manner that fosters continued sales and customer loyalty through product knowledge, familiarity, and ease of use. This was the experience of all three case companies featured here.

Beginning in 2000, Invensys Foxboro experienced an erosion of customers attending its traditional classroom-based training events. This was due to cost-cutting measures in the customer companies, and a related need for the plant operators to be on-the-job. However, it was also noted that customers were continuing to purchase new and existing Foxboro products, thus building a need for further training and skills development in the uses of its software applications. Foxboro determined that they would bring learning to the customers, and selected its Intelligent Automation I/A series of devices training for its initial venture. They chose a blended model of learning for this extended learning audience. The existing I/A classroom-based training was divided into discrete e-learning objects, providing the customer with the ability to customize selected learning into what they really needed, when they needed it, a feature that was impossible in the classroom version. The business impact of this outreach has led Foxboro to realize that learning can be a profit center, with e-learning a standard component of the sales pitch to new and existing customers. They have added two full-time sales people just to sell e-learning!

Oracle Corporation had an audience of learning customers who needed to acquire the Oracle Database Administrator (DBA) certification to solidify their professional standing and gain promotions and related salary increases. Again, the need to compress 20 days of classroom training involved in gaining this certification was surfaced by Oracle's customers. Wanting to retain the reputation that the best place to learn about Oracle products was at Oracle, the learning organization determined to convert the classroom materials into a blended format. During 10 weeks of self-paced e-learning, supported by faculty access and live e-learning sessions, learners engaged in group interaction, direct coaching, lecture, lab support, feedback and reinforcement, leading to four examinations and certification. Some participants achieved DBA certification in as little as 15 weeks instead of 18 months. Almost 600 learners have completed the program since its inception, and the goal is now to extend the learning to multiple nationalities in their own languages.

Finally, a similar experience in serving the extended enterprise with e-learning solutions is found at 3Com. Selling its products through a two-tiered sales channel of distributors and resellers, 3Com needed to train both its partners and the end users who purchase the products. 3Com created a Partner Learning Center section on the 3Com Web site, giving access to their Bronze, Silver, and Gold Partners to 150 courses, certifications, and ultimately the ability to provide customized learning Web sites at no additional cost. Because this site is a part of 3Com University, it utilizes the same learning materials and functionality. 3Com has had eight customer learning Web sites go live in 2003, and anticipates that this number will double in the near future. 3Com executives realize that this service places them in an unparalleled competitive position with their partners.

Customer and partner relationships definitely improve when e-learning opportunities are provided.

Case 1: Invensys Foxboro

Company Facts and Figures

✔ **Industry:** Technology, Manufacturing, Professional Services

✔ **Scope of Services and Products:** Foxboro provides process control devices, software, and consulting services

✔ **Estimated Number of Employees:** 76,000 (globally)

✔ **Year e-Learning Introduced:** 2002

✔ **Offices and Locations:** Offices worldwide, headquarters in Foxboro, Massachusetts

✔ **Web Site:** www.foxboro.com

✔ **Number of e-Learning Programs in Entire Curriculum:** Nine current courses, plus an ongoing series of online seminars and access to the complete SkillSoft (formerly SmartForce) library of Web-based training titles

Introduction

Invensys Foxboro is part of the Invensys Production Management Division and provides world-class Foxboro information technology, automation, and process solutions to a wide range of manufacturing applications for the cement, chemical, metals and mining, oil and gas, pulp and paper, power, pharmaceutical, and specialty chemicals industries.

Foxboro is one of several companies within this division and targets its products at maximizing a client's return on investment and optimizing performance across their supply chain.

Why e-Learning?

Invensys Foxboro selected an e-learning approach to:

✔ Meet the changing training requirements of customers

✔ Maintain competitiveness by giving customers the information needed to use their products and services

✔ Increase the value of learning by providing customers with the learning they need, when it is needed

Foxboro products have both software and hardware components, both of which require thorough training for all plant operators, process engineers, and maintenance personnel involved with their use.

How Was the Program Aligned with the Business?

Knowing Their Audience

The great majority of Foxboro customers are involved in traditional manufacturing. Until recently, the training Foxboro provided to their clients was also traditional with classes offered either at Foxboro facilities or the customer's site. Occasionally there was a side venture into something such as selling videotape-based training. There were also one or two failed experiments with e-learning.

According to Michael Bleyhl, now Invensys' Director of e-learning and then leader of Foxboro's learning efforts, the economic slowdown that started in 2000 began to slow customer participation in training.

Initially, some customers tried to accommodate their changing economic circumstances by sending fewer plant operators (the primary audience) to classes, intending for them to train their colleagues upon their return to the workplace. However, the returning operators did not necessarily have the training skills necessary to transfer their knowledge. There was also a hesitation on the part of some to do so, as this knowledge was seen as a layer of job security in a now uncertain economy.

This situation forced a re-examination of the training function within Foxboro. Operating as a profit and loss center with US$6 million in annual revenue, all from classroom-based courses, the department's revenue stream started to dry up as Foxboro customers began to see a slow down in their own businesses and an increasing need to keep operators on duty to maintain productivity. Foxboro was faced with a decision on whether to exit the training business entirely or rethink their approach to stay relevant to customer needs and financially viable.

It was immediately apparent that training needs were not going away. Customers were still buying new Foxboro products and using existing ones. Plant personnel still needed to know how to prepare, operate, and maintain these devices and their associated software. What had changed was that the delivery model for the training no longer matched the learners' needs.

In addition to the loss of revenue for the training department, there was also a longer-term risk that a lack of product knowledge among customers would lead to decreased sales of Foxboro products. If customers do not understand a product, they are less likely to use it, particularly for business critical needs such as manufacturing process control.

Because learners were having difficulty coming to the training, Foxboro decided to take the training to them. A decision was made to convert some of the business product training to e-learning. This would enable plant personnel to take at least some training while remaining on site at their plants. Some clients still preferred classroom courses, so these were kept active.

Key Business Drivers

✔ Loss of revenue caused by a drop-off in enrollment in classroom-based learning

✔ Loss of product knowledge, which would ultimately lead to lower product use among customers and lower sales

How Was the Program Designed?

Once the decision to move to e-learning offerings was made, the learning strategy needed to be assembled. One of the first decisions made by Bleyhl was to outsource e-learning design and development to a subcontractor. Foxboro's own instructional design resources were limited, as their primary experience was in developing classroom materials, and they were already committed to supporting the existing 20 course curriculum. Earlier efforts to design e-learning in-house had been unsuccessful and Bleyhl decided to continue to support his department's core competencies. His group would serve as primary contact point, subject matter experts, and reviewers of the materials, but design and development would be outsourced.

Additionally, since Foxboro products are sold and used worldwide, and are used by shift workers around the clock, an extensive technical infrastructure would be needed to support 24 hour a day, seven day a week training delivery so that workers could learn on breaks, or before or after their shift. To avoid the high costs, complexity and ramp-up time needed to develop such a platform in house, Foxboro partnered with SkillSoft (then known as SmartForce) to provide the delivery platform and user support for the learning program. Again, it was a question of deciding what Foxboro did well and finding partners to assist with the rest.

Foxboro decided to convert several classroom courses as part of the initial launch. It was their feeling that an e-learning Web site that featured only one course would have little value. As their starting point, they chose an overview course of the Foxboro control system software.

Among Foxboro's products are the Intelligent Automation (I/A) series of process automation devices. When interfaced with plant machinery, these devices are used by plant operators to monitor and manage the steps of industrial processes such as grinding, mixing, and refining. A group of these devices can be controlled through a central PC workstation using Foxboro-developed software, enabling one operator to centrally monitor and control their piece of a process.

It took three days to complete classroom training for this software. However, it was only available as part of a larger two-week training program for plant operators.

Because of its broad appeal and because it had already been reworked for a video-based course in the past, this three-day segment, Introduction to the I/A Series System for the Process Operator (see Figure 17-1), was selected as the first to be converted to e-learning. This course consisted almost entirely of knowledge transfer, rather than skills transfer, so it could have a simpler design, lending itself well to a first effort.

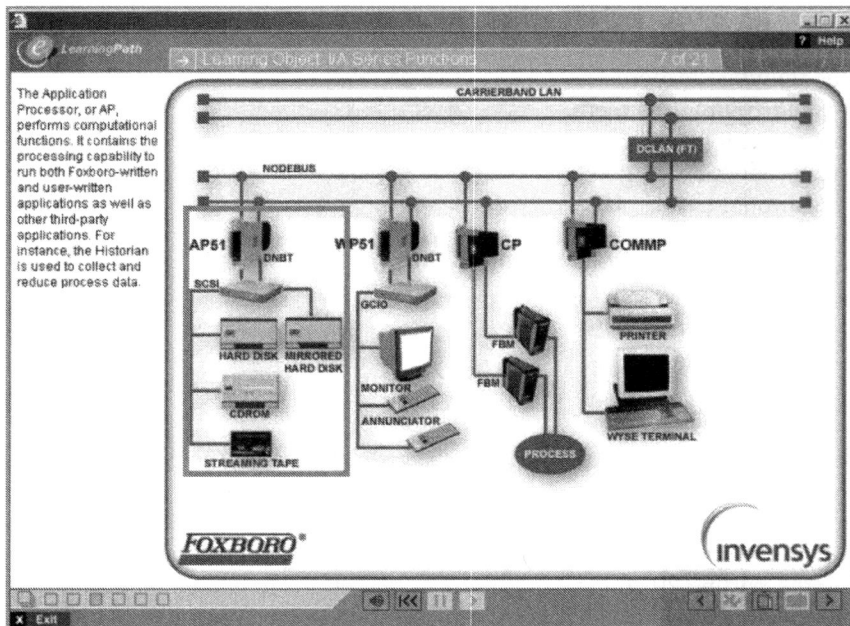

Figure 17-1: Sample Invensys Foxboro Course

The e-learning version was modeled on the set of video tapes referenced earlier, as well as on the content of the three-day classroom course. The objectives of the course included enabling learners to:

✓ Navigate around the Foxboro software control system

✓ Define Foxboro-specific terminology and system architecture

✓ Acknowledge alarms

✓ Identify trends using the software

Supporting each of these were a set of subsidiary objectives and learning content, resulting in the student gaining a solid overview of the Foxboro software, the terms and concepts associated with the company's products, and an operational knowledge of the control system. The course has graphics and animation, as well as spoken narration that mirrors the on-screen text. This enables learners to see, hear, and read content elements, which provides reinforcement of the course's message.

Other classroom courses entered the conversion process shortly thereafter. With Foxboro's learning department serving as primary contact point and working with multiple developers through the subcontractor, several courses could be involved in design and development simultaneously, enabling Foxboro's Lifetime Learning site to have multiple courses available when it went live.

All learning components used industry-standard development tools, such as Macromedia Flash. Each course is AICC and SCORM compliant so the learning environment and components can grow. This also eases capture of usage statistics and individual usage information that can be passed to a client's learning management system when requested.

Because neither the Foxboro technology infrastructure, nor that of most of their clients, was set up to handle e-commerce, a decision was made to handle course registration through conventional means. Learners would go to the Lifetime Learning Web site, select what they wanted to take, and then telephone in to register.

As the material was developed, classroom content was generally divided into small pieces. Only the Introduction to the I/A Series System course was a duplicate of the classroom material, and even it moved from requiring three days of class time to six hours of online time.

Moving to e-learning, with its multiple learning components, provided the learner with a level of customization not available in the classroom-based learning. Customers could now sign-up for exactly what they needed—perhaps selecting a few days of e-learning rather than attending a week or two of training. It also made it easier for shift workers to fit in learning on breaks, lunch, or before or after work.

A modular design also enabled the courses to be positioned as supplements and reinforcement to training. "Many of our customers do certain things twice a year," says Bleyhl.

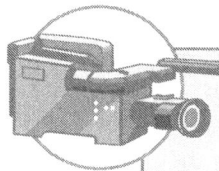

Media and Tools

✓ Self-paced, self-guided Web-based training

✓ Extensive graphics of the Foxboro software's interface with animations of onscreen tasks

✓ Text combined with spoken narration

✓ Developed with Macromedia Flash

✓ Hosted by SkillSoft on an Invensys-specific site

"We wanted to empower customers to say I can use this learning tool from Invensys Foxboro to go and get the knowledge when I need it and I can make the choice of what knowledge I want to keep in my head and what I can get just in time." Using a modular design, the courses also served as an electronic performance support system for those who had already been through a course, but might need a refresher.

How Was the Program Deployed?

The primary marketing effort consisted of contacting existing Foxboro clients. Because 95 percent of these clients have service level agreements with the company, there was a ready base of prospects for whom to market the program. There is also an ongoing effort by Foxboro's service sales group, who sell the agreements, to mesh the offerings with their sales message. The e-learning program came at an opportune time. With the economy in a downturn, clients were questioning the money they spent on such agreements, so factoring in learning to the contracts added value.

Selling the learning through service contracts also had a beneficial budget impact for clients. When dealing with classroom training, clients would usually arrange events once or twice a year, resulting in one or two big hits to the training budget all at once. However, as part of the service contract, the training dollars are built into the overall billing cycle for the contract, allowing for a steadier, predictable commitment of funds. And all funds apply to learning, as opposed to some being required for travel and expenses. This enables companies to expand the amount of training they receive. Clients also get an increased choice, because those who purchase e-learning from Invensys have access to SkillSoft's complete library of training as well.

Pricing for the online subscription is competitive with that for classroom offerings. The Introduction to the I/A Series System course takes only six hours to complete as an e-learning course. Classroom offerings of the course are three days in length, plus travel and living expenses would be incurred.

As mentioned, these selections can be made from either the Foxboro or SkillSoft learning catalogs. Tiered subscription pricing is available for those clients who have multiple users, and almost all do, so the price goes down even more.

Attendance in e-learning courses is tracked through SkillSoft's integrated learning management system. However, only general usage statistics are usually communicated to clients, as there are often labor issues around tracking and reporting individual performance on tests and assessments. Skill checks and assessments are provided within the materials too, but for self-check purposes only. In the classroom, aggregated assessment statistics are provided to show knowledge transfer, but again, there are usually no individually identifiable test results communicated to customers.

Finally, with the division of most courses into discrete pieces, clients can buy exactly the training they need, when they need it, rather than purchasing entire courses that they may not need.

Marketing Approach

✓ Contacted existing clients with service level agreements

✓ Gained commitment by positioning training as "just what you need, just-in-time"

✓ Blended training payment factored into the service level agreement.

✓ Added value through access to the Skillsoft library.

What Was the Business Impact of the Program?

Given the resistance you might expect from a market as traditional as industrial controls, user acceptance has been high. About 200 people have completed the Introduction to I/A Series System for Process Operators Course in the first year. Operators can now take basic training from their work site and have access to the course as a refresher or support system whenever they need it.

An unexpected benefit has been high acceptance of the training courses by systems integrators and other third-party consultants who assist companies in implementing Foxboro controls. These firms subscribe to the training to keep their practitioners skilled with the latest Foxboro knowledge, while reducing training and opportunity costs from having practitioners away on training.

Having skilled practitioners at hand means these firms are more likely to work with and sell Foxboro solutions, giving Foxboro a competitive edge.

Customer acceptance has grown to the point that Foxboro is adding two full time sales people, just to sell e-learning. It has become a standard part of the service sales pitch. In the first three months of the program, Bleyhl, acting as the single part-time sales person generated $200,000 worth of revenue. As start-up costs for the program were about $650,000, it can be seen that it is well on its way to generating a return on investment. A business plan completed by Bleyhl before his move to the directorship estimated that if the program were expanded to just the Invensys division of which Foxboro was a part, there was a multi-million dollar revenue opportunity.

Based on the success of the work within Foxboro, Invensys is now in the process of building its own Corporate University for internal training. With an expected user base within Invensys of about 55,000, the company expects to have significant economies of scale when dealing with e-learning vendors. They plan to negotiate content, delivery, and pricing models that enable them to sell more advanced learning solutions to their customers, who may not have the financial, human, or technology resources to build or buy their own. Invensys is also creating customer facing e-learning for its other various divisions.

Summary

Purpose: Provide just-in-time training for plant operators, engineers, and maintenance personnel who use Foxboro products and reduce need for classroom-based training

Program Structure: The overall learning program is:

- ✔ Foxboro-specific self-paced e-learning
- ✔ Live Web-based seminars offered through SkillSoft's infrastructure
- ✔ A complete library of Skillsoft training materials comprising hundreds of business- and technology-related titles

Number of Learning Hours per Learner: 25 hours of Foxboro-specific content

Total Number of Hours of Learning in the Program: 25

Number of Learners: Approximately 200 in the first year

Completion Requirements:

- ✔ Aggregate completion statistics are tracked and passed to customers who desire them.

Media and Tools Used:

- ✔ Macromedia Flash
- ✔ Text, combined with spoken narration
- ✔ Animations of on-screen tasks

Deployment Mechanism:

- ✔ Initially marketed to existing Foxboro clients who hold Service Level Agreements
- ✔ Now a standard part of the service sales message
- ✔ Deployed through a Web site hosted and managed by SkillSoft

Lessons Learned

- ✔ Stay with the organization's core competencies. If you do not have the expertise to develop or deliver e-learning, partner with those who do.
- ✔ Start small, but keep the program growing and evolving.
- ✔ Leverage your existing customer base for sales efforts.

Case 2: Oracle Corporation

Company Facts and Figures

✔ **Industry:** Enterprise Software Developer

✔ **Scope of Services and Products:** Provides database software, development tools, and enterprise business applications; also provides consulting, education and support services

✔ **Estimated Number of Employees:** 42,000

✔ **Year e-Learning Introduced:** 1999

✔ **Offices and Locations:** Offices globally with headquarters in Redwood Shores, California

✔ **Estimated 2002 Revenues:** US$9.4 billion

✔ **Web Site:** www.oracle.com

✔ **Number of e-Learning Programs in Entire Curriculum:** Oracle offers hundreds of courses and learning objects through Oracle University, including the ability to obtain certifications online.

Introduction

Oracle Corporation is the leading provider of enterprise-scale relational database management systems and tools, as well as one of the top providers of enterprise application software. As such it has a global customer base requiring extensive initial and ongoing training.

Oracle University now hosts a broad range of classroom, live and self-paced e-learning, and blended learning programs. The approach to many of these programs grew from one of Oracle's first experiments in blended learning, the e-Learning Fast Track Program.

Why e-Learning?

Oracle selected an e-learning approach to:

✔ Reduce the classroom time commitment required for customers seeking to achieve Database Administrator certification

✔ Reduce the overall time required to achieve certification

✔ Maximize the efficiency and profitability of its training services and infrastructure

✔ Scale the ability of Oracle instructors to reach and teach more learners

✔ Blend the benefits of self-paced e-learning and classroom models

How Was the Program Aligned with the Business?

As one of Oracle's first e-learning ventures, the Fast Track Program arose in response to growing customer demand for shortening the classroom time required to achieve an Oracle Database Administrator (DBA) certification. A substantial portion of Oracle's learner population stood to benefit because about 60 percent were seeking DBA Certification.

The classroom version of the certification comprised four courses of five days each for twenty total days of instruction. These four courses were typically completed over an 18-month period. After coursework completion, candidates completed four certification tests. These were offered through third-party testing centers that supplied proctoring services.

Oracle's customer personnel increasingly had difficulty getting away for 20 days of classroom training, both due to the direct expenses incurred for travel and related costs and concerns about time away from the job.

Because holding an Oracle DBA certification usually had a positive impact on a person's earnings and position in the workforce, these individuals increasingly also wanted to shorten the average 18 months required to complete the program.

In the meantime, Oracle was looking for a way to maximize the efficiency and profitability of its training operations. Given that its classrooms, instructors, and the associated infrastructure are fixed costs, one way to both increase the efficiency and profitability would be to increase the number of learners who cycle through a program in a given time period.

Oracle had also set, as a goal of their e-learning program, that Oracle be recognized as the best place to learn about Oracle products.

Says Chris Pirie, Vice President of Oracle's Learning Network, "The goal we set ourselves was that anybody in the world could learn Oracle from Oracle. That meant offering cost-effective programs in India and Pakistan as well as in the United States. It meant we could scale the assets and resources we have and make sure that there was really as little distinction as possible between an e-learning approach and a traditional learning approach."

Key Business Drivers

✓ Customer demand for less time in a classroom

✓ Customer demand for shorter overall program duration

✓ Maximize efficiency and profitability of its existing training infrastructure

✓ Maintain Oracle's position as the best place to acquire Oracle knowledge and skills

✓ Grow the Certification Program

✓ Increase instructor utilization

How Was the Program Designed?

The vision for the new program, which went into design in 2000, was a result of balancing the various business drivers with the needs of the learners. The result was a blended program that combined reduced class time embracing a period of self-paced e-learning and seminar offerings.

General Structure

The original plan called for participants in the e-Learning Fast Track Program to attend an initial week of classroom training and orientation, followed by a ten-week period of self-paced e-learning punctuated with a weekly live e-learning seminar. There would then be a concluding week of class time. After this week, learners could then sit for the certification exams as before.

Out-of-the-Box Program Design

According to Pirie, the original design process for converting the classroom materials to a blended format consisted of sitting down with a virtual cardboard box of content from the classroom and reworking the materials.

It was an abbreviated effort, taking three people three months. The first focus was on restructuring the opening five-day session. This would stay in the classroom, but could not be the same as the original opening five- day course. The team needed to decide what information, concepts, and skills must be covered in this limited face-to-face time because people would not be coming back to the classroom for some time. The final design is that during this week, participants meet with instructors and their peers, learn basic concepts, and get started with basic skills, such as installing the software.

Oracle's blended approach enables learners to get the best mix of learning experiences. The instructors provide group interaction, direct coaching, lecture, lab support, motivation, and feedback and reinforcement. The self-paced e-learning includes reading material, hand-on labs and exercises, quizzes, and communication with instructors and peers.

The next task was to build a self-study guide that made sense for someone spending 10 hours a week working on their own from a remote location. A substitute was also needed for the exercises students would complete using Oracle software in the classroom. Oracle now hosts an online lab where students can carry out these exercises in a computing environment that they can access remotely to practice various skills hands-on.

The final week of the program was then designed. It is again classroom-based and serves as the capstone and wrap-up experience, enabling participants to consolidate their learnings and address any remaining questions or issues.

At this point, learners are eligible to sit for the four certification exams to become an Oracle-certified database analyst.

The design team for the program was made up of one instructional designer and two instructors. Oracle wanted to capture instructor experience because the instructional components were of more interest to them than the content. Says Pirie, "Clearly from our experience, learners perceive a tremendous amount of value in those traditional instructional techniques of mentorship and guidance, and even discipline to some extent."

Pirie continues, "The content needs to be good, it needs to be engaging, it needs to be accurate, it needs to be up-to-date, but really it is just a small piece of the instructional process."

The structure continues to evolve. For example, the initial sessions featured periodic live e-learning sessions during the self-study period. These sessions brought the participants together virtually for live e-learning via the Internet. These have now been replaced by virtual office hours—times when the instructor is available online to the remotely located learners. This change was a result of participant feedback that indicated they could learn well on their own, but they wanted access to instructors for other purposes, such as mentoring or individual instruction and feedback.

Additionally, the self-study material in the original program consisted primarily of standard computer-based training (CBT) titles created by e-learning vendors and hosted on Oracle's site. Over time these have been replaced by more focused learning objects developed by Oracle and hosted through its learning management system, iLearning.

Yet even in its original form, the program resulted in a substantial level of customer satisfaction, as well as a drop in the total time required to complete the program. Some participants achieved DBA certification in as little as 15 weeks instead of 18 months.

Design Issues

One key design factor from Oracle's perspective was that they wanted the technology platform managing the effort to be compatible with the other business systems used by Oracle University. This would enable those registering for the online version of the program to receive the classroom components as well. It is also Oracle's experience that for most companies, e-learning infrastructure is discreet and separate from their traditional learning management systems. It was important to have an infrastructure that worked across both delivery approaches.

"A lot of the challenges very early on were around integration," says Pirie. "When somebody signs up for a class can we really give them a choice for that class of how they take it? And can we sell it to them in a way that we sell the class first and the delivery mode second? And then there is just pure integration work with e-commerce systems and various other systems that we use to run our business."

At the start of the design process for the e-Learning Fast Track Program, the vision was that each of Oracle's programs would become a vertically blended effort, with some pieces of each program being classroom-based and others online, either using live or self-paced, e-learning methods. It was believed that this would become the predominant way to do things, with each program becoming a predetermined blend of components available in a particular format.

However, Oracle ended up with much more of a horizontal blend. That is, where each learning component is available in different modes of delivery, like a menu selection. Says Pirie, "I can decide in what mode I am going to take [each] class, rather than buying the whole track already preconfigured for me."

Things have evolved this way because many in Oracle's audience now just want to take one or two classes and do not want to complete the certification. Having alternative formats for components gives each participant the ability to choose the best mix for themselves. In other words, Oracle now finds itself dealing more with learners wanting learning objects than with learners wanting programs.

One design issue that did not arise as part of the program was the target audience's readiness for e-learning. Those learning Oracle's database and application software spend their days around computers and the Internet and are accustomed to using the network to locate information and answers. The audience was, in fact, asking for online alternatives to classroom work.

Supporting Infrastructure

Oracle developed the e-Learning Fast Track Program around their own learning management system, using standards such as SCORM and a reusable content object model structure. The same framework is used for both Oracle internal and customer-facing programs, such as the e-Learning Fast Track. This enables learning objects to be easily interchanged. Content developed for internal use can quickly be made available to customers, and vice versa. Oracle now has about 2000 hours worth of content, much of it, according to Pirie, built in a very disposable manner because of its short shelf life.

The Importance of Assessment

Finally, from a design standpoint, Oracle's learning management system also includes another piece of functionality that Pirie considers very important—an assessment engine for creating and scoring tests.

Assessment and certification tests are critical to the program because learners can now take the DBA Certification Program in a classroom environment with some online pieces, as entirely online self-study, or as entirely online, live e-learning sessions. Regardless of the format, the learning objectives and the certification are always the same.

Pirie believes assessment is a key factor when working with e-learning. "I think certification and accreditation in general are much, much more important for online learning than they are for classroom," Pirie says. According to Pirie, the classroom experience provides more real-time valida-

Media and Tools

✔ Oracle has used various live e-learning tools or environments in its courses, including Rain Dance Communications and Centra's online learning products. Oracle will be moving to a product of their own that is almost ready to launch and will become part of the learning management system.

✔ Macromedia Dreamweaver and Flash

✔ Microsoft PowerPoint

✔ RealNetworks' RealPlayer, as well as other streaming media products

✔ XStream Software's RapidBuilder for simulations and RapidExam

tion that you are on the right track as a learner because you answer questions, interact with the instructor and see others do the same. Observing all of this gives you a better sense of your own level of understanding. "There is some sort of perception that because I have physically been locked in a room for five days that I have been trained. People learning in a self-paced way or even in a kind of instructor-led way through the Internet, need even more validation."

Also assessment provides a provisional baseline for measuring the success of program components offered in different formats. Testing of people who have used the different modes of learning has indicated very favorable results. Particularly for the live e-learning courses, participants perform as well as in the classroom version.

How Was the Program Deployed?

Once the e-Learning Fast Track Program was complete, Oracle established its value proposition based on time-to-certification. This path took less time overall and disrupted peoples' work schedules less. The rich multimedia approach also appealed to many learners.

Pirie says that the learners who chose this path did not, in fact, need convincing. As mentioned earlier, people in the Oracle space use networks and computers to learn all the time. They are constantly on the Internet, searching and learning.

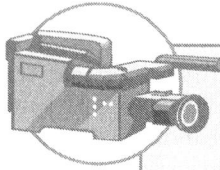

Marketing Approach

✔ Minimal marketing required, as audience was "e-learning ready"

✔ Marketed as an offering of Oracle University

✔ Value proposition- based on reduced time-to-certification

What Was the Business Impact of the Program?

One primary impact of implementing the e-learning Fast Track Program was a marked increase in the efficiency of classroom and instructor utilization. Through the use of staggered launch dates for program offerings, one instructor can handle several classes of participants at time. Taking them into the classroom for a week and then sending them off on their own and moving on to the next. Each program then progresses at its own rate.

The instructors like the approach of the blended learning as well because they build up long-term, closer relationships with the learners through the ongoing virtual office hours. To the instructors, it is almost as if they are working in a university setting. They also see it as a validation of their skill set, as they are still very much involved in a program throughout its lifecycle.

Because Oracle University is organized as a global business unit, with all parties involved constantly looking for ways to increase profitability, there was no tension between a learning group and a different group that would be in charge of, and responsible for, the utilization of classrooms or training centers.

Despite the early success, the program proved not to be as scalable as originally thought. There are segments of the program that still need to be offered in a classroom, so learners still need to go to a location, and they still need materials in their language and instructors who speak their language.

The program is run on a country basis, rather than consolidating it into a global program, which would bring maximum efficiency. "One thing we would like to do is run these across national borders and to consolidate and essentially run these programs by language," says Pirie. "It has proved impossible to do because you still need people to go to physical locations, and it is just kind of tough to do that."

Learner Perspectives

"I was in the original e-learning DBA class that was taught in San Mateo last year. I am now an Oracle Certified Professional DBA. I want to thank you for your work in developing the e-learning curriculum. Due to family obligations, it would have taken several years to complete this had it not been for your program."

Looking back, what would Oracle do differently, if anything? Pirie believes Oracle may have been too ambitious in tackling a 20-day program first. "I would have started on a five-day class and apply similar principles to smaller kinds of learning," says Pirie. "I also think we were far too anxious about the live e-learning aspect of this than we needed to be. We really wanted to create a virtual classroom that was like a classroom. It took us a while to realize that that is not what learners wanted."

The future looks bright for Oracle University. They project teaching about one million people in 2003.

Summary

Purpose: The e-Learning Fast Track Program was designed to:

- ✔ Reduce the classroom time and costs required for people seeking Oracle DBA certification
- ✔ Reduce the time required to achieve the certification
- ✔ Maximize use of Oracle's learning infrastructure and instructors

Program Structure: The e-Learning Fast Track Program comprised:

- ✔ An initial week of classroom learning, covering basic software skills and knowledge
- ✔ An extended period of self-paced Web-based training
- ✔ Several live e-learning sessions scheduled through the self-paced e-learning period of the original program were later replaced with scheduled virtual office hours for each instructor
- ✔ A final week of classroom learning serving as a program capstone and wrap-up
- ✔ Four certification exams to measure achievement

Total Number of Hours of Learning in the Program: 332 hours available

Number of Learners:

- ✔ 564 learners have completed the program in the United States since its inception.

Completion Requirements:

- ✔ Learners must attend beginning and ending classroom sessions, complete the self-paced e-learning portion, and pass certification exams.

Media and Tools:

- ✔ Pre-packaged content from SkillSoft and Netg
- ✔ Custom designed learning objects from Oracle, created using Macromedia products
- ✔ Live e-learning sessions using Centra and Rain Dance

Deployment Mechanism: The program was deployed through Oracle University using Oracle's iLearning platform, which integrated with Oracle's other business systems. This provided:

- ✔ Learner access to all of Oracle University, not just the e-learning components
- ✔ Integration with other Oracle business systems

Lessons Learned

✓ When converting a classroom course to a virtual or blended model, do not worry about mimicking the classroom experience exactly. Rather, create a structure that best communicates the concepts, skills, and interactions of the original classroom course.

✓ Test assumptions. Once a program is launched, monitor learning use and reaction to it. Oracle initially implemented live e-learning sessions only to find them unnecessary. Replacing them with virtual offices hours increased the utility of the course for learners.

✓ Start small and then keep the program growing.

✓ A blended learning model often enables you to make maximum use of all resources while providing the most benefit to learners.

Case 3: 3Com

Company Facts and Figures

✔ **Industry:** Technology

✔ **Scope of Services and Products:**
Provides wireline and wireless
networking products

✔ **Estimated Number of Employees:**
4,615

✔ **Year e-Learning Introduced:**
1997

✔ **Offices and Locations:** Offices
worldwide, with headquarters in
Santa Clara, CA

✔ **Estimated 2002 Revenues:**
US$1.48 billion

✔ **Web Site:** www.3com.com

✔ **Number of e-Learning Programs
in Entire Curriculum:**
Approximately 100

Introduction

3Com Corporation produces wireline and
wireless networking products. Their approach
is to focus on ease of use and integration to
lower the cost of buying and owning 3Com
products.

3Com sells its products through a two-tiered sales
channel of distributors and resellers. The resellers
ultimately sell to various business end-users.

Given the rapidly changing nature of technology,
3Com regularly develops training materials to enable
its employees to sell and support its products, as well
as to help end users who purchase the products.

Why e-Learning?

**3Com selected an e-learning
approach to:**

✔ Increase product knowledge in their
reseller channel

✔ Provide sales partners with a higher level
of customer service

✔ Boost revenues by easing the sales
process for partners

3Com has also been successful in making its learning materials available to its sales partners,
thereby increasing customer service and product knowledge in its sales channel.

How Was the Program Aligned with the Business?

3Com operates in the increasingly competitive market for PC and telephony networking products. As such, a key factor in its success has been providing its sales and support personnel with
timely training on a sometimes quickly changing product line.

The company began providing its own employees with e-learning in 1997. e-Learning was adopted
slowly by the 3Com staff, which does not surprise Wendy O'Brien, 3Com's Director of Education.
"It was slow getting going because it is a cultural change to ask people to be more self-directed
with their learning," says O'Brien. "We started by offering small amounts of training online."

Starting with a selection of purchased off-the-shelf courses and a small selection of custom course-ware developed for the company by outside vendors, the offerings for employees have grown to include 700 purchased courses and approximately 150 custom-developed courses.

Some of these courses were mandatory learning in areas such as ethics, various legal concerns and corporate security. As a result, 100 percent of 3Com's workforce has taken one or more e-learning courses and O'Brien estimates that 25 percent of the population could be described as active e-learners—those who seek out new learning online.

As 3Com University grew, the company realized that at least some of the material could be used to aid in educating their sales partners as well. Similar to 3Com employees, these channel partners needed both general product knowledge, as well as information on how to position, sell and support particular products.

Key Business Drivers

✓ Costs are low because content developed for internal employees is leveraged for the Partner Learning Center. Once the site is established, the maintenance cost is low.

✓ Benefits are high, in both improved customer relationships and potential for increased sales.

The result was development of a Partner Learning Center Web site and, ultimately, individual learning centers tailored to 3Com's largest sales partners. These centers have boosted 3Com's customer service and increased the potential revenue sales partners, and ultimately improved what 3Com can earn by increasing product knowledge and familiarity in the sales channel.

How Was the Program Designed?

Original Design

3Com has three levels of Focus Partners within its sales channel: Bronze, Silver, and Gold. Partners at each level commit to a particular sales volume, as well as a particular level of employee certification on 3Com products.

3Com designed a Partner Learning Center section of 3Com University, called Partner Access, and made it available to the distributors, service providers, and resellers through the 3Com Web site. 3Com is able to develop customized visibility to content on the Partner Learning Center site utilizing CRM system profiling technology.

When employees of authorized partners log on to the Partner Access site and click on 3Com University, they are automatically associated with that particular partner. As a result, they see training that is appropriate for a channel partner of their level, Bronze, Silver, or Gold. Because the site is part of 3Com University and utilizes the same learning materials, it uses all the same functionality, including access to the Saba learning management system. The Saba system tracks the enrollment and completion status of partners, employees, and delivers content and records scores. This enables 3Com to provide sales partners with reports concerning employee use of the materials and the partner's ongoing certification status.

In another move to make access more convenient for their partners and their own employees, 3Com also eliminated the need to have certification tests offered in physical classrooms through third-party proctoring services. 3Com offers various certification tests and makes examinations available to partners online. Upon completion of a course or program requiring certification, the system issues a test ticket to the learner, which enables them to access the final examination. These results can also be tracked through 3Com's education management system (EMS), which is built around Saba and a customer relationship management system. The original partner learning center received a warm reception from the sales channel partners. O'Brien says 3Com's channel partners welcome vendor-sponsored training and particularly liked the fact that the online option kept their costs low.

Continuous Improvement Leads to Mass Customization

Given that up to 150 courses could be made available on the generic Partner Learning Center, it was not long before one of 3Com's largest resellers was asking if they could get content sorted by their particular needs. This led to the development the first partner-specific learning Web site at 3Com University.

Working with 3Com, the reseller assembled a preferred curriculum from the set of available courses. 3Com then created a Web site that featured this curriculum and branded it with the reseller's logo, look, and feel. A link was placed on the reseller's intranet portal that connected its employees directly to the customized learning Web site.

The reseller could now direct its employees to exactly those courses it deemed appropriate and necessary. Employees saved time because they did not need to sift through all the available courses, and 3Com gained a more satisfied customer who was better prepared to sell its products. All parties knew how things were going, because 3Com's EMS generated reports that were regularly available to 3Com and the reseller's management. What's more, the site could quickly be modified by 3Com to focus on different topics. For example, if the reseller decided to promote wireless networking products during a particular month, the curriculum could quickly be refocused to highlight wireless courses.

It did not take long for word of the success to spread. Between showing an example of a customized site at a reseller attended Solution Fair and news of the site spreading among 3Com account executives, there were soon several other Gold level resellers requesting their own customized learning site. Eight sites went live during 2002, with at least four more planned for activation in January of 2003. According to O'Brien, it is an ideal solution for both 3Com and their resellers.

"They love it and it's free," says O'Brien. "We've made it very easy for them. They ask for it, and we build it. We're able to turn a site for them around within as little as a week depending on the partner's training requests."

Best practices for implementing a customized partner site in this short time rely on a close relationship between 3Com's sales representative, the partner, and the partner's training manager. This relationship affords the opportunity to quickly identify the partner's training needs. "Partners really like this program," says O'Brien. "The feedback about the courseware is good, but more importantly, our partners appreciate our more personal touch."

What's Inside the Box?

The current set of learning materials made available to partners, both on the general site and on the partner-specific sites, consists of a mix of learning products, all of them 3Com specific. 3Com does not currently provide partners with the off-the-shelf courseware they have purchased for internal use.

The material that is available is provided in a variety of formats. The company offers classroom training and conducts live e-learning events using WebEx software. They also create blended programs that combine self-paced e-learning with live e-learning events or classroom learning.

As mentioned, the 3Com University EMS environment is supported by the Saba learning management system, which tracks enrollment, completion and scoring, as well as handling registration for classroom or live e-Learning events. In the future, this functionality may move into one of 3Com's core business systems. O'Brien feels that organizations considering purchase of a learning management system should also consider using their existing business applications, such as the various enterprise resource planning (ERP) software packages. Often, the latest versions of these packages offer learning management functionality that is sufficient for most purposes while maintaining integration with a company's primary business systems.

Design Considerations

When designing new content, one step in 3Com's process involves determining the content's shelf life. In the area of e-learning, basic product training courses, and other courses that might have a short shelf-life, are scripted PowerPoint presentations that can be downloaded.

Courses that would benefit from basic interactivity are created in-house by 3Com's staff using Vuepoint Learning System tools. These courses can also have assessments attached to them, as this is an integral feature of the Vuepoint Learning System.

Courses which would benefit from more sophisticated interactivity or presentation are outsourced to a variety of third-party vendors for development. 3Com is now working with a third-party company to offer learners remote access to a virtual lab that they can connect to over the Internet. Once online, they can practice configuring 3Com network products, gaining valuable hands-on familiarity with the equipment.

Most importantly the vendors or software applications that 3Com leverages to deliver their blended learning materials integrate well with 3Com's education management system.

Development Considerations

When new material is developed, 3Com employees are viewed as the primary audience. Once the course is complete, it is provided to the reseller channel either as is, or with slight modifications to make it appropriate for each audience.

A needs analysis is conducted by 3Com's staff of learning professionals. Basic learning modules, such as the scripted PowerPoint decks or VuePoint courses are developed in-house. More sophisticated learning programs are outsourced.

When outsourcing work, 3Com prefers to work with specialized vendors, who provide a particular service. Their experience is that a vendor that claims to do everything, often is more expensive and does not necessarily have the expertise where needed.

This approach has delivered a low-cost, low-maintenance learning program for 3Com partners, which provides better customer service, resulting in more knowledgeable resellers, distributors, and service providers.

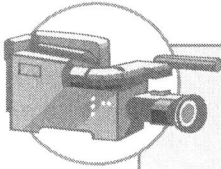

Media and Tools

✔ Saba's learning management system pro-vides the repository, delivery, and tracking capabilities for both 3Com and the sales partner learning centers.

✔ WebEx software is used for live e-learning events.

✔ Microsoft PowerPoint is used to produce scripted slide shows.

✔ The Vuepoint Learning System is used for basic learning courses.

✔ Macromedia products, as well as other tools, if they can be proven to be compati-ble with Saba, are used by external vendors to produce the more sophisticated learning programs.

✔ Online exams are hosted by RWD Technologies.

✔ A virtual laboratory environment is hosted by e-Source.

How Was the Program Deployed?

Overall, the program has required very little marketing "push" on the part of 3Com and has been quickly adopted by the sales channel.

Word of mouth recommendations and demonstrations at a 3Com Reseller event began to gener-ate requests from 3Com sales and resellers for more customized learning centers

The 3Com account representatives also use the generally available partner learning center as a sell-ing tool when they call on resellers and potential resellers. However, there is as yet no formal recognition in Gold Partner contracts that the partner is entitled to custom learning center. These are developed on an as-requested basis. There are currently eight partner-specific learning centers in place, with at least twice that many to go live by the end of 2003. Marketing of 3Com learning by the partner to their employees is a shared responsibility of the partner and 3Com University. Often, the announcement will be made as part of a 3Com Day at the reseller or through internal e-mail.

Marketing Approach

✔ Partner-specific centers presented to Gold level partners one-on-one or created as requested by the partner

✔ Marketing of the learning by the partner to its employees is the shared responsibility of the partner and 3Com University

✔ Ongoing course participation tracked and reported to partner

All partner centers tie into the same materials and EMS that is used by 3Com itself. Partners can select from a menu of reports used by 3Com, or receive modified reports if they are uncomplicated to produce.

What Was the Business Impact of the Program?

Between the general partner learning center and the partner-specific learning centers that are in place, O'Brien finds that thousands of reseller employees have accessed 3Com learning programs. However, given the early stages of the customized learning center program, there are no hard metrics or trends available yet. 3Com senior management supports the program, and O'Brien expects it to become a more formalized part of the Gold Partner agreement.

"There's nothing bad about it," says O'Brien. "It's fairly simple to build. It's a lot of bang for the buck." She also feels that the program provides many benefits, including increased sales of 3Com products. Says O'Brien, "I think there is the revenue impact, and then I also think there is just the basic customer relationship impact. We're going one step above what a competitor might be doing for them."

Summary

Purpose: 3Com launched the Partner Learning Centers to provide its distributors and resellers with product and marketing information. The goal of this program is to:

- ✔ Increase sales channel knowledge and skill with 3Com products and assist partners with achieving and maintaining certification status
- ✔ Provide better customer service to sales channel partners
- ✔ Boost sales of 3Com products

Program Structure: 3Com offers a generic learning center for all of its sales partners. This site contains all 3Com developed training that is provided to its own employees. Gold level sales partners can request a custom designed site. This site can:

- ✔ Contain those programs of particular interest to the reseller
- ✔ Be used to focus learning efforts of the partner's employees
- ✔ Be updated frequently to present new or different sets of courses as the partner's learning needs change

Number of Learning Hours per Learner: Varies by partner

Total Number of Hours of Learning in the Program: Varies by partner

Number of Learners:

- ✔ Thousands of 3Com partner employees have completed courses through the various learning centers.

Completion Requirements:

- ✔ Determined by partner

Media and Tools:

- ✔ Microsoft PowerPoint
- ✔ Vuepoint Learning System courses
- ✔ Macromedia and other development tools

Deployment Mechanism: Generic and partner learning centers are available to 3Com resellers, distributors, and service providers through a secure section of the 3Com partner Web site. This Web site can be accessed directly from the partner's internal intranet site if so desired.

Lessons Learned

✓ Consider your business culture when implementing e-learning. It can be tough to move learners to e-learning, particularly among sales and marketing personnel who are people-oriented.

✓ Start small and provide many chances for people to get exposure to the system.

✓ When considering a learning management system, review what functionality might already be available through your core business software. Some enterprise resource management packages include, or are introducing, functionality to track skills, user learning, and learning events. You might be able to avoid buying a separate system to do this.

✓ Do not hesitate to work with multiple vendors to complete a program. Vendors who say they do everything are often more expensive and less experienced where you need the expertise.

References

Active Education Learning Solutions Group. 2003. *Unlocking the Secrets of ROI*. Active Education. January 2003. www.activeeducation.com.

Aldrich, Clark. 2002. *Measuring Success*. Online Learning Magazine. http://www.onlinelearningmag.com/onlinelearning/magazine/article_display.jsp?vnu_content_id=1278801.

Anderson, C. 2002. *The Future of Live eLearning: Vendor Challenges and Recommendations*. IDC. Framingham, MA.

ASTD/The Masie Center. 2001. *E-learning: If we build it will they come?* 15, 22.

ASTD. 2002. *State of the Industry 2002*. www.astd.org.

Athey, R. 2001. *From e-Learning to Enterprise Learning*. Deloitte Research.

Beach, Barbara K. 2002. *The e-Learning Industry: Retrospect and Prospect*. Learning Circuits. ASTD. January. www.learningcircuits.org/2002/sep2002/beach.html.

Brennan, M. 2003. *Begin Act II: Worldwide and US Corporate eLearning Forecast, 2002 – 2006*. IDC. Framingham, MA.

Brown, Mark Graham. 1996. *Keeping Score: Using the Right Metrics to Drive World-Class Performance*. New York: Quality Resources.

Butcher, D. 2002. *The Future of e-Learning*. Human Resources. September, 17.

Cassarino, Connie, Brandon Hall, and Richard Nantel. 2003. *DigitalThink, NETg, and SmartForce, An In-Depth Comparison Of The Three Largest Providers Of Online IT Training*. Brandon-Hall.com. January. http://www.brandon-hall.com/itvendor.html.

Chief Learning Officers Link Training and Business Goals. 2003. Workforce: HR Trends & Tools for Business Results. February.

Clark, Carol. 2002. *Using Standardized Content Architectures to Improve eLearning's Impact Within Your Organization*. SkillSoft. October.

Cross, Jay. 2001. *A Fresh Look at ROI*.

Docent, Inc. 2003. *Calculating the Return on Your eLearning Investment*. Docent, Inc. January. http://www.docent.com/elearning/ROI_01.html.

Evaluating the Effectiveness and the Return on Investment of E-learning. 2003. ASTD. February. http://www.astd.org/virtual_community/research/What_Works/e-learning/top_10.html.

Goldwasser, Donna. 2002. *Beyond ROI*. Training Magazine Training. December. http://www.trainingsupersite.com/publications/magazines/training/101cv.htm

Hofstede, Geert. 1997. *Cultures and Organizations: Software of the Mind*. New York: McGraw-Hill.

International Society for Performance Improvement. 2003. ISPI. January. http://www.ispi.org/.

Kirkpatrick, D.L. 1996. *Evaluating Training Programs: The Four Levels*. San Francisco: Berrett-Koehler.

Let employees learn their own way: A lesson from Barclays University. 2002 Corporate Universities International. September/October, 8 (5):2.

Levy, Jonathon D. 2001. *Measuring and Maximizing Results through eLearning*. Harvard Business Online. October.

Mantyla, Karen. 2001. *Blending e-Learning*. Alexandria, VA: ASTD.

The Masie Center E-learning Consortium. 2002. *Virtual classroom technology scan*. The Masie Center E-learning Consortium. February, 7:31.

McGarvey, R. 2002. *On Site from Afar: Distance Training is Changing the Way IT Managers Keep Employee Skills Fresh*. Computer User. December. www.computeruser.com/articles/2107,1,1,1,0701,02.html.

Neuhauser, P.C., R. Bender, and K.L. Stromberg. 2000. *Culture.com: Building Corporate Culture in the Connected Workplace*. New York: John Wiley & Sons.

Norton, David P. 2000. *Measuring Value Creation with the Balanced Scorecard*. Harvard Business School Publishing.

Obstfeld, Mark. 2002. *E-learning is where the money is at- new reports*. Europemedia.net. December. http://www.europemedia.net/shownews.asp?ArticleID=13031&Print=true.

Online Learning News. June 26, 2001, 4 (14) OLNews@vnulearning.com.

Oubenaissa, Laila, Max Giardina, and Madhumita Bhattacharya. 2002. *Designing a framework for the implementation of situated online, collaborative, problem-based activity: Operating within a local and multi-cultural learning context*. International Journal on E-Learning (IJEL). 1 (3): 41-46.

Philips, Jack J. 1997. *Return on Investment and Performance Improvement Programs*. Butterworth-Heinemann.

Philips, Jack J. and Ron D. Stone. 2002. *How To Measure Training Results*. New York: Mc-Graw-Hill.

Philips, P.P. 2002. *The Bottomline on ROI*. Atlanta: CEP Press.

Prensky, M. 2001. *Digital Natives, Digital Immigrants*. On the Horizon. NCB University Press, 9 (5).

Resources: Preparing for e-Learning Costs, Benefits and ROI of e-Learning. 2003. E-Learning Centre. January. http://www.e-learningcentre.co.uk/eclipse/Resources/costs.htm.

Robinson, Dana Gaines and James C. Robinson. 1998. *Moving from Training to Performance: A Practical Guidebook*. Berrett-Koehler Publishers.

Saba. 2002. *The Business of Learning: The Economic Value of Investing in Saba*. December. http://64.211.240.12/english/solutions/white_papers/index.htm.

Schooley, Claire. 2003. *Measurement and Evaluation Key to E-Learning ROI*. Giga Information Group. January.

Setaro, John. 2001. *E-Learning 1.0, Many Happy Returns: Calculating E-Learning ROI*. Learning Circuits. ASTD: June. http://www.learningcircuits.org/2001/jun2001/elearn.html.

SkillSoft e-Learning Leaders To Merge. 2002. SkillSoft. 2002 Press Releases, December. http://www.skillsoft.com/about_sf/news_events/press.room/2002/merger.asp.

Sullivan, Christine. 2003. *Getting the Organization to Adopt e-Learning: From Challenge to Action*. Hawthorne Associates. January. www.hawthorneassociates.com.

Symonds, W.C. 2002. *Giving It the Old Online Try*. Business Week Online. December. http://www.businessweek.com/magazine/content/01_49/b3760072.htm.

Taylor, Craig R. 2002. *E-Learning: The Second Wave.* Learning Circuits. ASTD. www.learningcircuits.org.

The Internet Goes to College: How Students are Living in the Future with Today's Technology. 2002. Pew Internet and American Life. October. http://www.pewinternet.org/reports/toc.asp?Report=71.

Trompenaars, Fons and Charles Hampden-Turner. 1998. *Riding the Waves of Culture: Understanding Diversity in Global Business.* New York: McGraw-Hill.

van Dam, Nick. 2002. *E-Learning by Design. e-learning Enterprise Learning and Knowledge Management Strategies.* E-learning. December. http://www.elearningmag.com/elearning/article/articleDetail.jsp?id=6705.

Wilson, Eric. 2002. *E-learning Will be Par for the Course.* The Sydney Morning Herald. November. www.smh.com.au/articles/2002/10/20/1034561357515.html.

Index

About the Author

Nick H. M. van Dam, born The Netherlands (1961)

Author, Consultant, Program Designer, and Lecturer.

He is Deloitte Consulting's Chief Learning Officer. Mr. van Dam has held a variety of leadership roles throughout his career in various countries. He led the transformation of Deloitte Consulting's classroom-based Global Education function to a just-in-time and highly e-enabled learning environment. This effort was awarded the London Financial Times/Corporate University Exchange (CUX) 2001 Award of Excellence for *Using Technology to Create a Continuous Learning Environment*, and the 2002 Financial Times/CUX Award for *Innovative and Best Practices in Learning*. Prior to joining Deloitte Touche Tohmatsu, one of the world's leading professional services organizations with more than 119,000 people in over 140 countries, he was employed by Siemens in Europe.

Since 1987, Nick has been involved in the design of technology-based learning solutions including simulations and business games. As an internationally recognized consultant and thought leader in Learning and Human Resource Development (HRD), he has written articles and/or has been quoted by: Financial Times, Forbes, Fortune, Business Week, Management Consulting, Learning & Training Innovations, T+D Magazine, Chief Learning Officer Magazine, Bizz, IK, and others.

He has lectured on globalization, cross-cultural competence, and Human Resource Development (HRD) at Business Schools in the U.S. and Europe. Nick van Dam is a visiting lecturer at the International Consortium for Executive Development and Research (ICEDR) HRD Leadership Forum. ICEDR is a global learning alliance of approximately 40 of the world's leading companies and 25 outstanding business schools (see www.icedr.org).

Furthermore, he has authored and co-authored a number of books in Dutch and English including: *Ondernemerschap* (1994), *Integrale Bedrijfsvoering* (1994), *Marketing & Sales* (1995), *Een praktijkbenadering van Organisatie & Management* (4th edition 2002), and *Change Compass* www.changecompass.com (2001).

Nick is the Founder of *e-Learning for Kids* a non-profit foundation for children (www.e-learningforkids.org), which provides schools in need with Internet-based learning solutions. All royalties of this book will be donated to this organization.

Nick van Dam is a graduate of Vrije Leergangen - *Vrije Universiteit van Amsterdam* (Economics, Education) and *Universiteit van Amsterdam* (Organization and Management). Nick lives in Chadds Ford, Pennsylvania with his wife, photographer Judith Grimbergen, and their son Yannick (1997). He can be reached at: nickvandam@elearningfieldbook.com.

www.ingramcontent.com/pod-product-compliance
Lightning Source LLC
Chambersburg PA
CBHW080903220326
41598CB00034B/5457